WITHDRAWN

film

film
A REFERENCE GUIDE

Robert A. Armour

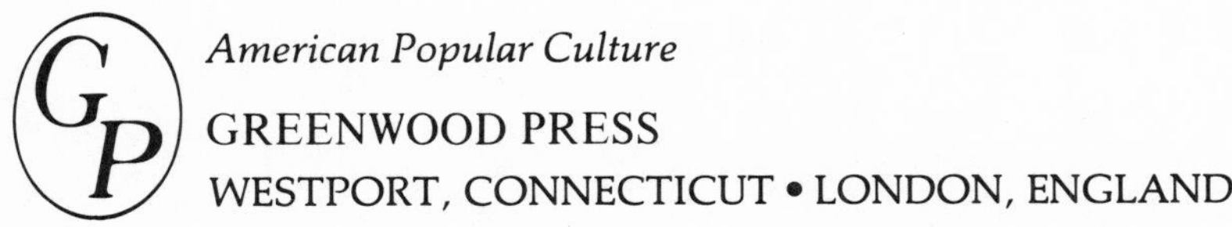
American Popular Culture
GREENWOOD PRESS
WESTPORT, CONNECTICUT • LONDON, ENGLAND

Library of Congress Cataloging in Publication Data

Armour, Robert A
Film, a reference guide.

(American popular culture ISSN 0193-6859)
Includes bibliographies and indexes.
1. Moving-pictures—Dictionaries. 2. Moving-Pictures—Bibliography. I. Title. II. Series.
PN1993.45.A75 791.43'029 79-6566
ISBN 0-313-22241-X

Copyright © 1980 by Robert A. Armour

All rights reserved. No portion of this book may be reproduced, by any process or technique, without the express written consent of the publisher.

Library of Congress Catalog Card Number: 79-6566
ISBN: 0-313-22241-X
ISSN: 0193-6859

First published in 1980

Greenwood Press
A division of Congressional Information Service, Inc.
88 Post Road West, Westport, Connecticut 06881

Printed in the United States of America

10 9 8 7 6 5 4 3 2 1

This book is
dedicated
to my parents
Ruth and Alex Armour

Contents

	PREFACE	xi
	ACKNOWLEDGMENTS	xv
	Introduction	**xvii**
	Historic Outline	*xvii*
	The Impact of Film	*xxii*
Chapter 1	**History of Film**	**3**
	General Histories	3
	Histories of the Silent Era	8
	Histories of the Sound Era	10
	The Industry and the Studios	13
	Hollywood	16
	Bibliography	18
Chapter 2	**Film Production**	**22**
	Technique	22
	Special Types of Production	25
	The Production Team	26
	Bibliography	31
Chapter 3	**Film Criticism**	**34**
	Film Theorists	36
	Film Critics and Analysts	38
	Reviewers	43
	Books of Introduction	45
	Bibliography	50
Chapter 4	**Film Criticism by Genre**	**55**
	Adventure	55
	Animation	56

	Comedy	56
	Crime, Gangsters, and Villains	57
	Detectives	58
	Suspense and Film Noir	59
	Fantasy and Horror	59
	Musicals	62
	Newsreels	62
	Sex and Violence	63
	War Movies	64
	Westerns	65
	Shorts and Serials	67
	Documentaries	68
	Experimental Films	69
	Bibliography	71
Chapter 5	**Film and Related Arts**	**77**
	Film and Literature	78
	Film and the Visual Arts	82
	Film and Music	83
	Film and the Popular Arts	83
	Bibliography	84
Chapter 6	**Film and Society**	**87**
	Film and History	87
	Film and Politics	88
	Film and Propaganda	88
	Film and Censorship	89
	Film and Sociology	90
	Film and Anthropology	92
	Film and Minorities	92
	Film and Psychology	95
	Film and Religion	96
	Film and Education	97
	Bibliography	99
Chapter 7	**Major Actors**	**104**
	Books on Individual Actors	105
	Books on More Than One Actor	130
	Bibliography	133
Chapter 8	**Major Directors and Other Production Personnel**	**143**
	Books on Individual Directors	143

	Books on More Than One Director	157
	Books on Producers	160
	Other Production Personnel	163
	Bibliography	166
	A Checklist of Filmmakers Interviewed in the American Film Institute's *Dialogue on Film*	173
Chapter 9	**Major Films**	**174**
	Screenplays	174
	Collections of Screenplays	176
	General Books on Films	177
	Books on Specific Films	178
	Bibliography	181
Chapter 10	**International Influence on American Film**	**185**
	International Overviews	185
	Specific National Film Industries	186
	Bibliography	190
Chapter 11	**Reference Works and Periodicals**	**193**
	General References	193
	Bibliographic Works	194
	Reference Books on Films	196
	Reference Books for and about Screen Personalities	199
	Periodicals	200
	Bibliography	207
	Checklist of Periodicals	210
Appendix 1	**Selected Chronology of American Films and Events**	**213**
Appendix 2	**Research Collections**	**217**
	Major Research Centers and Archives	218
	College and University Collections	221
	Public Libraries	222
	Studio and Corporate Collections	222
	Miscellaneous Holdings	223
	Canada	223
	A Final Note	224
	Bibliography	224
	SUBJECT INDEX	225
	INDEX OF AUTHORS, EDITORS, AND INTERVIEWEES	239

Preface

The scenario is a familiar one: a student appears at the doorway of my office to discuss a problem. He is taking a film course from me, has to write a research paper, and does not know where to begin. He has a topic for research—probably something too broad, such as Faulkner as screenwriter or D. W. Griffith's place in movie history—but at least he has a topic; his problem, however, is that he does not know where to find the library material he needs. It is for such a student that this reference guide has been written. My primary purpose is to provide a reference guide to film for the person beginning the serious study of the medium or for the viewer wanting to pursue in depth what has been a casual interest.

Compared with the study of philosophy, mathematics, or even literature, the study of film is a new enterprise. The public has been viewing films for only eighty-five years, and college courses have been widely accepted only in the past two decades. It is not surprising that the student does not have much experience with film research. Most students have, until they take a course in film, viewed movies as places to go on dates, as objects of entertainment. When they are suddenly required to treat film as seriously as chemistry or the history of Italian painting, they are both pleased and perplexed: pleased that they can study an art form they enjoy and perplexed as to how to apply the academic rigor of more traditional subjects to the study of this relatively new subject. This book will help them resolve their perplexity without, it is hoped, diminishing their pleasure.

The scope of this reference guide is not, however, limited to students. Anyone who wishes to pursue an interest in movies will find stimulation in the books discussed here. Viewers may wish to enrich their experiences at the movies by a deeper understanding of film history, of the lives of the filmmakers, of analysis and reviews of the films, or of the nature of film criticism. These viewers, like the student, will find that the books discussed here provide enrichment.

A secondary—but crucial—purpose is to provide librarians with an evaluation of some of the important books on film, an evaluation made by a teacher who has himself used these books. With the growth of film courses in the schools and the growing interest in film scholarship, scholastic, collegiate, and public libraries have the need for a basic film collection based on informed purchases. This guide should offer the librarians the information they need to build a quality film study collection. Larger libraries and those intended for graduate students may be able to go beyond the limitations of this book, but it will still serve as a check to insure that they have not overlooked important books.

The method of this reference guide is unlike that of most bibliographies on film. This is not a checklist of every source that might be located or even a briefly annotated bibliography. Such books already exist, and chapter 9 of this book will lead the reader to them. Instead, this guide is in the form of a bibliographic essay. Most of the books listed are described, evaluated, and placed in relation to other books on the same subject. The essay format allows for a discussion and comparison of the important books on a particular topic, such as Western films or the history of the silent era. A bibliography is provided at the end of each chapter so that the reader will have full bibliographical information on all books cited.

This format, however, has a limitation; essays are lengthier than lists. Therefore, not every book published on film can be listed here and discussed. Some of the checklist bibliographies contain five or six thousand entries; this reference guide has almost fifteen hundred. My goal has been to provide detailed information about the books discussed rather than to list every available publication.

In order to keep the number of books manageable, I have decided not to list every published screenplay (there are two reference books, mentioned in chapter 7, that provide reasonably complete lists). I have also not discussed every dissertation written about film, although I have included reference to many of those that have been reprinted as part of the Arno Press film book series. Moreover, I have not included books written in languages other than English, unless they have been translated, been made readily available in the United States, and become well-known. In addition, I have not discussed many highly technical books, such as technical production manuals. Regretfully, since my emphasis has been on books, I have not had space for discussion of all of the many fine periodical articles on film.

One limitation has been imposed by the fact that this book is part of a series of research guides to American popular culture, and therefore its focus has had to be on American films and their creators. I have not tried to draw too fine a distinction about what is American, and I have discussed a few filmmakers who spent only part of their careers in the United States. Additionally, my overriding emphasis has been on popular film since the series deals with popular culture. This may help to explain why there is discussion of a book on the Three Stooges, and mention of the impact of fan magazines.

The reader, especially the student, should remember that I have not attempted to establish complete bibliographies on any subject. Instead, my goal has been to identify rewarding books on different aspects of film study with the hope that these books will provide basic information and then lead the reader to additional sources. The reader should view the references here as the first clues in a treasure hunt; subsequent clues will be found in the material suggested by this guide.

Dunnsville, Va.
August 1979

Acknowledgments

My heartfelt thanks go to

M. Thomas Inge for his friendship and his editorial guidance;

Leo Braudy and the fellows of the 1978 NEH seminar at Johns Hopkins, especially Judy Riggins and Judy Weiner;

Elizabeth Brewer, Janet R. Howell, Eileen Pearson, and Jane W. Westenberger, interlibrary loan librarians and staff at Virginia Commonwealth University;

Abigail Nelson, Chris Spillsburg, and Debbie Davidson, staff members of the library of the American Film Institute at Kennedy Center, and especially to Chris for her work on film periodicals;

William McIlwaine for sharing his personal library with me;

Anastasia Cossitt and Susan Woolford for typing the manuscript;

Elizabeth and Leandra Armour for helping prepare the indexes.

Part of the research for this book was done while I was a fellow in the summer seminar at Johns Hopkins. Special thanks, therefore, must go to the National Endowment for the Humanities.

Introduction

HISTORIC OUTLINE*

The date was December 28, 1895. The place was the basement of a cafe in Paris. The audience was the first public one to pay its way to watch movies, paying to be fascinated by moving images of a baby eating his meal, workers leaving a factory, and a train rushing into a station. The scenes were taken from ordinary life, but the experience was far from ordinary. This event was produced by the Lumière brothers, but the technology that led to this moment had been the result of the imagination and persistence of many inventors, both in Europe and America.

Eadweard Muybridge in 1877 had discovered that sequential still photographs of a horse running could be placed in a series and "projected" in such a manner as to make the photographic image of the horse appear to be running. In New Jersey in the late 1880s Thomas Edison and his crew led by William Dickson developed the idea of putting photographs on a single piece of continuous film, and George Eastman supplied the film. For projection Edison decided on the Kinetoscope, a peephole machine through which the film could be shown to one person at a time. Several creative inventors worked on the idea of a projector, but it was finally the Lumière brothers who were able to adapt Edison's ideas and develop the first practical means of allowing many people to view a movie simultaneously. The history of this new art form was then to be written in light.

Once the photographic technology had been developed, the next stage was to decide what to do with it. Obviously audiences could not long be enthralled by shots of a baby eating and would demand more. Both the Lumières and Edison attempted to expand the cinematic subject matter; but it was another Frenchman, Georges Méliès, who first achieved any

*Reprinted from "Film" by Robert A. Armour in M. Thomas Inge, ed., *Handbook of American Popular Culture,* vol. 1 (Westport, Conn.: Greenwood Press, 1978).

success at telling a story with film. He was a magician who used the medium as part of his act, but in the process he began to depict plot as well as action. His most famous film was *A Trip to the Moon* (1902) which described a fanciful space voyage.

In order to develop a narrative process for film, the filmmaker had to learn to manipulate both space and time, to change them, and to move characters and action within them much as a novelist does. What Méliès had begun, Edison and his new director of production continued. Edwin S. Porter learned how to use dissolves and cuts between shots to indicate changes in time or space, or both; the result was *The Great Train Robbery* (1903). This Western, shot in the wilds of New Jersey, told the complete story of a train robbery, the chase of the bandits, and their eventual defeat in a gunfight with the posse. Cross-cutting allowed Porter to show in sequence activities of both the posse and the bandits that were supposed to take place at the same time.

Businessmen began to realize the financial potential for movies. While movies were first shown as part of other forms of entertainment, they soon became the featured attraction themselves. By 1905 the first nickelodeon had opened in Pittsburgh, where customers each paid a nickel to see a full program of a half dozen short films. The opening of theaters completed the elements necessary for an industry: product, technology, producer, purchaser, and distributor.

In 1907, a would-be playwright came to Edison with a filmscript for sale. Edison did not like the script, but he hired its author, David Wark Griffith, as an actor. Griffith refused to use his real name, which he wanted to save for his true profession of the stage, but he needed money and accepted the job. Thus began the career of the man who would turn this entertainment into an art. He began making films himself shortly. His tastes in plots were melodramatic, but his interests in technique were both innovative and scientific. Guided by his cameraman, Billy Bitzer, he began to experiment with editing and shots, finding many ideas for cinematic technique in the sentimental novels and poems of nineteenth-century literature. Gradually he persuaded both audiences and company bosses to accept the idea of a more complicated plot told in a lengthy movie. The result was the first major, long film. In 1915, after unheard-of amounts of time in production, Griffith released *The Birth of a Nation,* a story of the South during the Civil War and Reconstruction. The racial overtones of the film caused considerable controversy, but the power of the images and the timing of the editing created a work of art whose aesthetic excellence is not questioned. In response to the criticism of his racial views, the next year Griffith directed *Intolerance,* which interwove four stories of intolerance into a single film. Griffith was to continue as one of America's leading directors until audiences began to lose their taste for melodrama, and other directors had learned his methods. He had been responsible for launching the careers of several directors, such as Raoul Walsh, and numerous actors, such as Lillian and Dorothy Gish, Mary Pickford, and H. B. Walthall.

While Griffith was learning how to get the most from screen actors, Thomas Ince was polishing the art of telling a story efficiently. In the early 1900s, he directed a few films (*Civilization,* 1916, is the best known), but he quickly turned his attention to production, leaving the details of directing to others under his close supervision. His talent was for organization, and today he is credited with perfecting the studio system. Film is actually a collaborative art, and Ince learned how to bring the talents of many different people into a system that produced polished films, without the individualizing touches found in those films of Griffith or others who work outside the strict studio system.

One man who learned his trade from Griffith was Mack Sennett. Sennett worked for Griffith for a few years as a director and writer, but his interests were more in comedy than in melodrama. In 1912 he broke away and began to work for an independent company, Keystone. Here he learned to merge the methods of stage slapstick comedy with the techniques of film; the results were the Keystone Kops, Ben Turpin, and Charles Chaplin. Sennett's films used only the barest plot outline as a frame for comic gags that were improvised and shot quickly. From the Sennett method, Charles Chaplin developed his own technique and character. He began making shorts under the direction of Sennett, but in 1915 he left and joined with another company, Essenay, which agreed to let him write and direct his own films at an unprecedented salary. Here he fleshed out his tramp character; one of his first films for Essenay was *The Tramp* (1915). He continued making films that combined his own comic sense and acrobatic movements with social commentary and along with Mary Pickford became one of the first "stars." Later he made features, such as *The Gold Rush* (1925) and *Modern Times* (1936). Sennett and Chaplin began a period of great film comedy. Buster Keaton combined a deadpan look with remarkable physical ability and timing. He too began making shorts, but soon was directing and starring in features, such as *The General* (1926). Harold Lloyd (*The Freshman,* 1925) and Harry Langdon (*The Strong Man*, 1926) also created comic characters that demonstrated their individuality and imagination.

From these ingredients came the studio system and the star system. The demands of the moviegoing audiences created a need for a great number of films, and small companies were unable to meet the demands. Adolph Zukor at Paramount and Marcus Loew, Louis B. Mayer, and Irvin Thalberg at Metro-Goldwyn-Mayer quickly learned the means of applying American business methods to this new industry. They bought out their competition and eventually controlled film production, distribution, and exhibition. Even the actors and directors got into the act as Chaplin, Griffith, Pickford, and Douglas Fairbanks joined together to create United Artists, intended at first to distribute the various productions of its founders. Later it too became a studio force, along with Columbia, Fox, Warner Brothers, and others.

With the studios came the stars. The public hungered for new heroes and new sex objects, and the studios were quick to give the public what it wanted. Along with the stars who had been established in the early 1900s came the new generation of the 1920s: Rudolph Valentino, Gloria Swanson, Clara Bow. The stars soon became the nucleus of American myth, and the public followed the stars' affairs, marriages, and extravagant lives with keen interest. This was the stuff Hollywood was made of. Fortunately there were behind these stars creative directors, such as Cecil B. DeMille, Erich Von Stroheim, and Henry King, who were able to mold the talents of the stars into movies.

During the 1920s American films dominated the worldwide industry, but they were greatly influenced and enhanced by developments and personalities from Europe. The Russians Sergei Eisenstein (*Potemkin,* 1925) and V. I. Pudovkin (*Mother*, 1926) were especially influential in their understanding of montage (the relationship of the images to each other and the meaning that results). American interest in fantasy was influenced both directly and indirectly by *The Cabinet of Dr. Caligari* (1919), directed by the German Robert Wiene, and *Destiny* (1921), directed by an Austrian working in Germany, Fritz Lang.

Some Europeans came to America to make films: Ernst Lubitsch, Victor Seastrom, and F. W. Murnau, for examples. The influence on American film of these films and filmmakers was profound; they left their strong impression on what came to be known as the Hollywood movie.

The story surrounding the coming of sound to movies is a complex and complicated one. The idea of connecting sound to the visuals was an old one; Edison had in fact entered the movie business because he was searching for visuals to go with the phonograph he was already marketing. To convert the movie technology to sound was expensive. Despite development of the necessary technology (most notably in this country by Lee de Forest), the industry was reluctant to invest in the change. In the mid-1920s Western Electric developed a method for putting the sound on a disk that could be roughly synchronized with the film. None of the big studios could be convinced to try it, but Warner Brothers was about to be forced out of business by the other, larger companies. It had little to lose and decided to take the risk. For a year Warner distributed a program with short sound films of slight interest, but on October 6, 1927, it premiered *The Jazz Singer* with Al Jolson. Sound was used to help tell the story, and the public loved it. Quickly, Warner established its financial base, and other studios rushed to emulate it; but problems developed. Studios had to reequip themselves. The camera, which had been struggling to free itself and discover new methods of expression, found itself confined to a large box and immobile. Actors had to learn to speak to their audiences, and exhibitors had to invest in sound projectors and speakers. Once the problems were overcome, however, the marriage of sound to the visuals became a natural extension of the art.

The period between the coming of sound and World War II was dominated by the studios. They controlled the production—including story, the role of the directors, and the selection of actors—distribution, and exhibition (they owned their own theaters). In the 1930s America went to the movies; by the end of the decade some eighty million people saw a movie every week. The studios provided them with the means to live out their fantasies, find heroes, and escape from the Depression.

One factor directly affecting the films of the 1930s was censorship. Hollywood movies in the late 1920s and early 1930s had become rather open in their use of sex, and the scandals in the private lives of the stars shocked the public even as it hungered for vicarious living. Fear of government intervention and of the Depression forced the studios to censor themselves. They established the Hays Office under the directorship of Will Hays, former postmaster-general, and this office published a strict moral code for on-screen activities and language. The results stifled creativity, but the new moral tastes of the public were satisfied.

The stars captured the public's imagination as in no other time in American popular culture: Fred Astaire and Ginger Rogers, Jean Harlow, Clark Gable and Vivien Leigh, Edward G. Robinson, and Marlene Dietrich. The comics maintained the traditions of the silent comedians: Charlie Chaplin continued to make movies and was joined by the Marx brothers, Mae West, and W. C. Fields.

At the same time, the directors had to find a path through the maze created by the studios, the Hays Office, and the stars. They had to bring all these divergent elements together and make movies. Men such as John Ford and Howard Hawks created their own visions of America and discovered methods of capturing the American myth on film. Many of the directors of the period were immigrants: Josef von Sternberg, Alfred Hitchcock, Fritz Lang, Otto Preminger, and Frank Capra. Each discovered for himself the essence of this country and its people. Perhaps that essence was most fittingly expressed in a film that came at the end of the prewar period, *Citizen Kane* (1941), the first film Orson Welles directed.

The war changed the industry. Many residents of Hollywood took time off to participate in the war effort. Some like John Ford and Frank Capra made films for the government. Others like Fritz Lang continued to make commercial films, but they were propaganda-oriented and helped build morale. The stars went to the battle areas to entertain the troops. Even studio space was commandeered to produce war documentaries, and war films became a dominant fictional genre.

After the war the rate of change accelerated. Anti-trust suits broke up the large companies and forced them to sell their theaters. And television began to keep the public at home. The movie industry responded with attempts at expanding the medium to attract new interests: 3-D, CinemaScope, Technicolor; and it continues to experiment: quadraphonic sound, sensurround, holographic images, and giant leaps in special effects have been tried.

However, in responding to competition from television, the use and type of subject matter has taken precedence over the development of technology. The movie makers have thought it necessary to give the public something that cannot be beamed into private living rooms. The results have been increased depiction of explicitness in sex and violence. Both sex and violence have been staples of the movies since the beginning, but the contemporary cinema has found new methods of enticing the public with them.

As the major Hollywood studios began to lose their domination of the American movie industry and turn their attention to television production, the leadership was taken up by independent producers and directors, making their own films and then distributing them through the networks originally established by the Hollywood companies. Stanley Kubrick, Robert Altman, Arthur Penn, Peter Bogdanovich, and Francis Ford Coppola have provided America with a new group of filmmakers, men who have demonstrated a certain independence of subject and method. Part of the void left by the diminishing importance of Hollywood has been filled by foreign filmmakers whose films have been greeted with enthusiasm by American audiences. Ingmar Bergman, François Truffaut, and Federico Fellini have dominated, but for the first time countries outside of Europe have begun to leave their mark. Japan has been especially productive.

Perhaps, however, the most important change in movies in recent years has been in the audience. By no means the number of people who went to the movies in the late 1930s still do, but those who do go are younger and more knowledgeable about film. They read the books, subscribe to film journals, watch filmed interviews with movie people on television, and read daily reviews. Many in today's audience are college-educated and have taken film courses while in school; they can talk intelligently about montage, jump cuts, and fade outs. It is for this audience that *Scenes from a Marriage* is imported from Europe and *Star Wars* is made.

THE IMPACT OF FILM

Until the coming of television, no cultural force had a more profound impact on American society than the movies. At the peak during the 1930s, some 80,000,000 people a week passed the turnstiles into America's movie theatres. Hollywood became the central myth in America's consciousness, the symbol of the American dream. The people there were beautiful and godlike, but their origins were ordinary; therefore, everyone had the potential for being discovered by an important director. Success in love, in finances, and in career were all possible in Hollywood and in the movies produced there. The American people longed to identify with this myth, to be part of the glamour and success. They named their babies after movie stars, and adopted stars' clothing styles. When Clark Gable appeared in a movie without an undershirt, the undershirt business was almost ruined by men imitating The King. When the producers' censorship board decreed that no couple could share a double bed on screen, twin beds became both the movie solution to the censorship problem and the next craze among people who longed to emulate the stars. In other words, the American public would imitate almost anything in the hopes of having some of the attributes of the celluloid gods rub off. The movie palaces even became the architectural equivalents of medieval cathedrals.

More recently, movies—themselves a form of entertainment—have spawned other forms of entertainment. When the movie *Animal House* depicted the riotous fun of a toga party in which fraternity men and their dates imitated the orgies of ancient Rome, the country was swept by toga parties on college campuses. What Mickey Mouse did for children in the 1930s, *Star Wars* has done in the 1970s. Every street has its seven-year-old Princess Leias and Han Solos. The fictionalized games of the movies have become the fantasies of people—both adults and children—seeking entertainment.

Even our politics have been influenced by movies. During World War II, for example, the movies became the prime motivator of nationalism on both sides of the Atlantic. Here in the United States, Hollywood became a primary spokesman for the American way of life, and both documentaries and fiction films reinforced the view that America must defend her way of life against the Nazis and Japanese. Movie stars took to the road to sell war bonds, went into the battle zones to entertain the troops, or even went to war.

Perhaps, however, the most important influence of the movies has been on our mores. Clearly, the sexual revolution of the 1960s and 1970s has been closely connected to the depiction of sex in the movies. Whether the use of explicit sex in the movies led the growing permissiveness or followed it is a debatable issue, but surely the portrayal of sex on the screen has been closely intertwined with changing American sexual mores. At the very least, movies have been the most influential and visible advertisement for the new sexuality. Similar conclusions may be drawn on the movies' influence on attitudes toward violence.

In the early days, movies borrowed heavily from other art forms. Early cinematic acting techniques came from the legitimate stage, as did the concept for the location of the camera as though it occupied a seat in the third row of the audience. Even many of the actors themselves were borrowed from the theater. Movie plots were borrowed from novels, plays, and even poems. Set designs came from trends in painting, such as Expressionism and Surrealism. But now the influence often seems to be going the other way, as other arts are beginning to borrow from the movies. Playwrights now try to re-create in the theatre some of the devices of the cinema. Novels now take their plots from movies; a whole new subgenre of the novel—the novelization—is based on screenplays. Since some of the best musicians and composers devote their energies to the creation of film music, some of the most memorable recent popular music has been written for the screen. Even some innovative sculptors have sought ways of combining traditional sculpture with moving images.

Movies have clearly had an impact on our social and artistic lives. Except for television, there has been no more pervasive medium in our century, or any medium that has done more to shape the way we live. It has influenced our view of men and women, of blacks, and of our enemy in war. It has created customs and added new words to our vocabulary. It has influenced us as sexual and social beings. It has reinforced those things about ourselves that we most like, and it has drawn us toward new dreams. The influence of the medium has perhaps diminished in the last decade, but nonetheless it remains one of the important forces shaping our society.

film

CHAPTER I

History of Film

The study of the history of film is one of the more rewarding and productive pursuits of twentieth-century American studies. To study the history of American film is to study American social history, because for the past seventy years film and society have been indistinguishably mixed. Additionally, film is one of the few art forms for which we have preserved almost an entire history. Many films from the early period have been lost; however, most important films have survived, the people who made them have recorded their memories, and a large amount of printed material dealing with them has been saved. In this latter group are such materials as scripts, early reviews, letters, memoranda from the members of the production crew, and newspaper advertisements—material that will be called "the archeology of film," after the title of a book by C. W. Ceram.

The purpose of this chapter is to discuss and describe the important books that have recorded the history of film. General histories will be discussed first, to be followed by those dealing primarily with the silent era, then those covering the 1930s, then the 1940s, and so on. At the end of the chapter, books dealing with the industry, the studios, and those depicting Hollywood will be discussed.

GENERAL HISTORIES

The first important history of the movies was *A Million and One Nights* by Terry Ramsaye, which came out in 1926. Written in close consultation with Thomas Edison, this book supports the idea that Edison was the major developer of American motion picture technology and virtually ignores the early contributions of people such as W. K. L. Dickson. The book includes chapters on Mary Pickford, D. W. Griffith, Charles Chaplin, the Gishes, and many more movie people. It is informative and highly readable although some of its facts might be questioned. Following Ramsaye was *A History of the Movies* by Benjamin B. Hampton, which came out in 1931. This history is written from the perspective of a corporate officer fascinated by the economic aspects of the movie industry, and therefore concentrates on the movie companies and the financial empires they represented.

Another important early history of American film was *The Rise of American Film* by Lewis Jacobs. First published in 1939, this book has become a classic and has also been reprinted. Jacobs places his emphasis on the industry (he is especially interested in the artistic freedom of the industry) and the way that film has been influential in our society, but he covers many films in great detail.

From England came *The Film Till Now* by Paul Rotha, which has since been revised and expanded by Richard Griffith. Originally published in 1930, this book was written by a man who well knew the theoretical, critical, and historical aspects of film study, and was the first comprehensive history of world cinema. It is still considered standard because of its thoroughness and completeness. At about the same time, Iris Barry translated into English a history by two Frenchmen, Maurice Bardèche and Robert Brasillach. *The History of Motion Pictures* has a fairly unimaginative chronological format, but the book does include much information on the development of the art form in Europe.

The first of the histories in the modern period was Arthur Knight's *The Liveliest Art: A Panoramic History of the Movies,* published in 1957. This study is now a bit dated but remains one of the standards. It is both readable and reliable but somewhat scant in detail. Knight discusses the birth of the art form, its growth in the 1920s, the coming of Hollywood, the development of sound and its impact, international influences on American film, and recent changes.

Less well known than Knight's book but from the same period is a history by A. R. Fulton, *Motion Pictures: The Development of an Art from Silent Films to the Age of Television.* In a sense this study is more than a history because it introduces the art form as well. Fulton has chapters on editing, Expressionism, naturalism, montage, sound, documentary films, drama and film, novels and film, short stories and film, and finally television.

Reel Plastic Magic by Laurence Kardish is a solid history of films and filmmaking in America. The author begins with the work of Thomas Edison and covers the history through the underground films of the 1970s. Along the way he discusses topics such as the czars of the industry, the House Un-American Activities Committee and its investigation of Hollywood, innovations in the medium, and the impact of television.

Peter Cowie edited *A Concise History of the Cinema,* a book which gives an English view of world cinema. The emphasis of this useful book is on providing plot summaries of major films.

Development of the Film is a fairly ordinary history of world film by Alan Casty. Casty has chapters on D. W. Griffith, the Russians and the concept of montage, the Germans and Expressionism, realism, comedy, genre, sound, new directions, as well as an analysis of new European directors.

Basil Wright's *The Long View* is a filmmaker's loving view of his art form. Basil Wright gives his history a different look from most histories. He has chapters on the musicals of the 1930s, patriotism of the 1930s, the war films of the 1940s, neo-realism in the 1950s, and the new wave of the 1960s; he also has one innovation. He has singled out particular years as signposts, years which were watersheds for the history of film: 1895, 1915, 1927, 1939, 1945, 1956, 1960, 1970 (the first public showing of movies, the premiere of *Birth of a Nation*, the coming of sound, and so on). Wright has indicated the special importance of each of these years and surveyed film production around the world for each.

Light and Shadows by Thomas W. Bohn and Richard L. Stromgren is a study that covers the history from the early days of prehistory of the art to the cinema of today. The authors concentrate on the development of the industry, technology, and the cinematic style and form of both narrative and non-narrative genres. The latter part of the book is devoted to movies in the age of television and the changes taking place in American cinema.

From its Origins to 1970 is the way Eric Rhode has described his *A History of the Cinema.* Rhode follows the history decade by decade but highlights D. W. Griffith, the Soviets, Hollywood, the coming of sound and the Depression, World War II, neorealism, and the internationalism that followed the Cold War. This is a more extensive history than most books of this sort.

A continuing favorite among the shorter and readily available histories is Gerald Mast's *A Short History of the Movies.* The second edition is no longer short, but the book has retained the title of the first edition. His format is not unlike those of the other histories, but the style is readable and the information reliable. The author highlights film narrative, Griffith, the comics, the international influences, sound, the studios, and the important American films that followed the development of new social mores in the 1960s.

Film: The Democratic Art by Garth Jowett was sponsored by the American Film Institute. It is a detailed history with an emphasis on Hollywood and the social impact of film. This first-rate book has much to say about the controversies that surround the movies and about censorship.

A recent history is *A History of Films* by John Fell. This book is a concise and interesting history of world cinema. Fell's format is to cover the history chronologically but to set off his discussion graphically and to provide a filmography of each important filmmaker. He also includes a full bibliography at the end of each chapter. This book will make a good textbook.

Another recent book in the history textbook mode is *A History of Film* by Jack C. Ellis. His approach is international, and his discussions of Asian films in the 1950s and the cinema of the Third World are unusual for such histories. Each unit is followed by a brief filmography and bibliography. This, like Fell's, is a book that could be used as a college textbook.

For a number of years, the American Film Institute has been interested in fostering a rediscovery of the history of American film. It has run several rediscovery courses, and it has, in connection with this, published *The American Film Heritage,* edited by Tom Shales. This is actually less of a history and more of an eclectic gathering of impressions from the AFI archives, a collection of materials on film history that often are forgotten or neglected. The book includes chapters on little remembered films such as *Miss Lulu Bett* and *Here Comes Mr. Jordan* and on narrowly defined genres such as musicals made at Warner Brothers. Also included are ethnic studies of blacks and Indians on film and overviews of actors such as Mary Pickford and W. C. Fields.

The independent filmmaker is the artist working outside the studio system and often outside Hollywood. *Film Is* by Stephen Dwoskin is a history of film from the point of view of the independent filmmakers. Dwoskin begins with the early history of independent filmmaking and works his way through the contemporary scene. His concluding chapter is on the expanded cinema, the experimental movie making of the 1960s and 1970s that takes advantage of expanding technology.

One special aspect of the history of American film has been the contributions by Europeans who immigrated here and two books have concentrated on these contributions. *The Hollywood Exiles* by John Baxter is a study of the impact Europeans have had on Hollywood. Baxter discusses the studio bosses, the directors, and the actors who were attracted to this country by the fame, money, and political freedom it offered. A more complex study of these directors has been edited by Don Whittemore and Philip Alan Cecchettini. *Passport to Hollywood* is an excellent, but at times uneven, combination of history and critical analysis of the films of the men who came here to direct. The editors begin with the pioneers: Charles Chaplin and Erich von Stroheim. Their second chapter covers the directors Hollywood was able to hire when it set out to stop its European competition: Ernst Lubitsch, Michael Curtiz, Victor Seastrom, James Wale, and Alfred Hitchcock. Their third chapter discusses Hollywood as it went highbrow—a charge not often made against the American movie industry—as it attracted F. W. Murnau, Paul Fejos, and Slavko Vorkapich. The fourth chapter of this book deals with the directors who left Europe because of Nazism and sought work here: Otto Preminger, Fritz Lang, and others. The last chapter presents the new Hollywood and directors who have come to work in it such as Milos Forman. The editors have written a thorough and scholarly introduction to the work of each director and have included reviews and articles on specific important films made by the Europeans in Hollywood.

Some of the histories have more of a pictorial value, in that they preserve stills from movies many readers have not had a chance to view, but the reader looking for helpful critical or historical commentary will be disappointed. The most valuable of these books is *The Movies* by Richard Griffith and Arthur Mayer. This excellent book covers the history of the American motion picture industry from the beginning to the 1970s and combines many pictures with brief but informative commentary. Richard Lawton's *A World of Movies: Seventy Years of Film History* has a similar format, a full introduction, and quality photographs. *Cinema* by Kenneth W. Leish is a photographic history with more commentary than these two books, but it still treats its subjects briefly. Leish covers important films and directors, with an emphasis on the rise and fall of Hollywood. His appendixes include such useful lists as the Academy Awards and the top grossing films.

Deems Taylor and many others have put together *A Pictorial History of the Movies,* which also has little commentary but many photographs. Some of their chapter topics include *Birth of a Nation* and D. W. Griffith, the coming of sound, and talkies 1929-1949. The emphasis is on the stars, *Gone with the Wind, Mrs. Miniver,* and *All the King's Men.* Alan G. Barbour's *The Thrill of It All* is less analytical and more laudatory than most of these books. He provides many pictures and a brief essay for each chapter.

Some books rely less on photographs but still try to cover so much material they cannot give much depth on any topic. These books are useful because they do provide an overview of the history of film. John Baxter in *Sixty Years of Hollywood* presents the history year by year. For each year he summarizes the productions of the industry and then covers the two or three best films of the year, giving the credits and a brief paragraph of commentary on each. Very similar is *Eighty Years of Cinema* by Peter Cowie, another English critic/historian. Cowie, too, proceeds year by year, for each year listing the major films, citing brief credits, and giving a short analytic essay. His book also includes a listing of many of the lesser films for each year.

Two final histories warrant discussion. What marks *Hollywood: The Golden Era* by Jack Spears are the unusual topics Spears chose to cover: Max Linder, Norma Talmadge, comic strips on film, Mary Pickford's directors, Colleen Moore, Charles Chaplin's collaborators, baseball on the screen, Marshal Neilan, Robert Flaherty, and both doctors and Indians on the screen. Many of these interesting topics are ignored by other critics. *Photoplay Treasury,* edited by Barbara Gelman, is a collection of articles and photographs reprinted from *Photoplay Magazine.* Arranged by decades, the book recaptures the glamour of Hollywood from 1917 to 1949: the productions, the stars, the scandals. Gelman's introduction on the importance of screen magazines to the movie industry is a useful piece of history itself. Unfortunately, the lack of an index limits the use of this book by the serious student.

HISTORIES OF THE SILENT ERA

The history of the development of motion picture technology in the period before the first public showing of a movie in 1895 is important to anyone wanting a complete knowledge of the art form. The most useful book for this purpose is *Magic Shadows* by Martin Quigley, Jr. This is a detailed and scholarly history of the development of the motion picture camera before Thomas Edison. An informative and readable book, it begins with the early theorizing of Leonardo di Vinci and Roger Bacon and proceeds to the experimentations of the late nineteenth century. *The Magic Lantern* by Judith Thurman and Jonathan David is more elementary than Quigley's book, but still interesting. Its subtitle is *How the Movies Got to Move*, and it is basically a study of the development of the technology. Joseph H. North's dissertation, *The Early Development of the Motion Picture (1887-1909),* has been reprinted and includes much little known material on the early years. A rather specialized addition to this list of books is *The Movies Begin* by Paul C. Spehr. Sponsored by the Newark Museum, it deals with the making of movies in New Jersey from 1887-1920. The focus is on Edison, William Dickson, and Edwin Porter and their work in the Black Maria at Edison's studios. Since this is where much of the technology and early technique of motion pictures was developed, this book is significant. The quality photographs add to its charm.

The history of the silent era has been documented since the publication in 1914 of *The Theatre of Science* by Robert Grau. This early history of motion pictures is full of illustrations and has now been reprinted as a curiosity piece. In 1926 Terry Ramsaye published *A Million and One Nights,* a book discussed above. In 1929 Will H. Hays published *See and Hear,* a brief history, including a chapter on sound, of interest only because Hays was the director of the censorship office. The histories by Hampton and Jacobs, along with Ramsaye's, established the basis for more recent histories of the silent screen.

Of all the recent histories of the silent period, the one by William K. Everson stands out. *American Silent Film* is an important and scholarly book that will probably become one of the standard works in film bibliography. Everson covers the history of film from its beginning to the coming of sound. His emphasis is on the directors, especially D. W. Griffith, and on genre, especially Westerns and comedies.

D. J. Wenden's *The Birth of the Movies* is briefer and less formidable than Everson's book, but it is readable and complete enough for most. Wenden also takes the history up to the coming of sound. He describes the way movies became an art form and then comments on the movies as big business, movies and society, and movies and politics; he concludes with observations on the growth of Hollywood.

A personal history of the silent era is *The Movies in the Age of Innocence* by Edward Wagenknecht, a well-known literary scholar. Wagenknecht knew and admired Lillian Gish and loved the movies. His history pays tribute to the silent stars—especially Miss Gish—and the directors of the period.

One of the most knowledgeable of the younger scholars of the silent film is Anthony Slide, who for a time worked at the American Film Institute and edited a now defunct journal that dealt exclusively with the silents. His book, *Early American Cinema,* starts with the beginning of the medium, and continues to discuss Edison; the Vitagraph, Kalem, Essanay, and Biograph companies; D. W. Griffith; comedy and Keystone; and Pearl White and the serials. In *Aspects of American Film History Prior to 1920,* Slide shares more of his eclectic knowledge. His topics include the evolution of movie stars, child stars, forgotten directors, the Thanhouser and Paralta companies, the O'Kalems, early film magazines, and Katherine Anne Porter and the movies. Also included is a bibliography of material dealing with early movie companies.

The Silent Voice by Arthur Lennig is intended to guide students to an appreciation of early cinema. Lennig discusses the early American films such as *Tol'able David, Dancing Mothers, Seventh Heaven,* and *Queen Kelly.* He also includes chapters on the German and Russian silent era. *The Silent Cinema* by Liam O'Leary is a short introduction of limited value to an understanding of the period, its chief virtue being its collection of stills. Daniel Blum's *A Pictorial History of the Silent Screen* is similarly a history whose prime value is pictorial.

David Robinson's *Hollywood in the Twenties* is more valuable for the reader seeking to analyze and understand the period. Robinson focuses on the master directors of the decade (Charles Chaplin, Buster Keaton, Erich von Stroheim, Josef von Sternberg, John Ford, and Robert Flaherty) and on the star/idols (Mary Pickford, Douglas Fairbanks, Sr., Charles Chaplin, Rudolph Valentino, and Greta Garbo).

One of the most important contributions to the history of the silents is a collection of interviews conducted by Kevin Brownlow and published as *The Parade's Gone By.* Brownlow interviewed almost every important contributor to the development of the art form still alive in the 1960s, and from their comments compiled a first-hand account of the making of movie magic. His own intelligent comments intermingle with the answers to his questions, and the result is one of the few indispensable tools to the study of the period.

Archaeology of the Cinema suggests that the materials related to the development of the movies have become artifacts of importance not only to an understanding of the medium but also to an understanding of the society that produced the medium. C. W. Ceram's book makes available materials dealing with the prehistory and early history of cinema; it ends with 1897. His attention to the descriptions and photographs of early equipment and experiments set the book apart from other early histories.

A further exploration into the archaeology of cinema is George Pratt's *Spellbound in Darkness.* This is a history of the silent film told both through Pratt's commentary and the reprinting of movie reviews of that period. This is an important book because of the many hard to locate reviews Pratt has included, but the book is a little difficult to follow because of an unorthodox graphic format.

Kemp R. Niver in *The First Twenty Years* describes over one hundred little known films from the paper print collection at the Library of Congress. In the early years a copyright was secured by sending a paper print of the film to the Library of Congress; these prints, unlike nitrate film, have not disintegrated. Niver has presented some of the more important of these films through plot summaries and frame enlargements in a book that is both enjoyable and useful.

Eileen Bowser is the knowledgeable and helpful curator of films at the Museum of Modern Art in New York, one of the chief archives of film in this country. Her *Film Notes* is a collection of comments she prepared for screenings at the Museum. This book contains good source materials for a study of well-known early short films. Her later publication *Biograph Bulletins, 1908-1912,* is a collection of the advertising brochures sent out by the Biograph Company at the time D. W. Griffith was in residence. These bulletins provide a rich source of information about the plots and other characteristics of the Griffith films.

HISTORIES OF THE SOUND ERA

In the late 1920s, the coming of sound was imminent and expected. The story of the sound experiments from the time that Thomas Edison had the idea that he could produce moving pictures to go with his record player is told by Harry M. Geduld in *The Birth of the Talkies.* He follows the development of sound technology from its early days through Vitaphone and *The Jazz Singer.* The book is both an obituary of the silent era and an introduction to the coming of sound.

An Hour with the Movies and the Talkies by Gilbert Seldes is a 1939 book dealing with the impact of sound on film in which the author makes interesting speculations about the future of the medium. Frank Manchel's *When Movies Began to Speak* is a brief but profusely illustrated history of the early days of sound movies suitable for readers of secondary school age.

The first decade of sound films is well depicted in John Baxter's *Hollywood in the Thirties.* One of a series covering each decade, this book highlights MGM, Paramount, Warner Brothers, and Universal, as well as important directors and producers. *We're in the Money* by Andrew Bergman takes its title from a popular song of the Depression taken from *Golddiggers of 1933.* The title illustrates an attitude toward the Depression depicted in many of the movies of the 1930s; movies were one of the few diversions from the economic horrors of the time, and many of the films presented characters seeking to compensate for the lack of money. Bergman's book documents the Depression as seen in films.

The importance of stars of the 1930s has been the subject of numerous books, many of which are about specific artists. Anthony Curtis has edited a volume of essays entitled *The Rise and Fall of the Matinee Idol* in which he begins with the idols of the stage, but quickly moves on to Rudolph Valentino, Douglas Fairbanks, Sr., Greta Garbo, and Marlene Dietrich. The stars are also featured in *The Talkies,* edited by Richard Griffith. Like Barbara Gelman's *Photoplay Treasury* mentioned above, *The Talkies* is a collection of articles and illustrations from *Photoplay Magazine,* from through 1928-1940. This interesting and entertaining book includes articles on the stars, Hollywood, the fans, recent movie releases, and trends in the industry.

From one perspective, the best book on the 1930s is *Those Fabulous Movie Years: The 30s* by Paul Trent. While intended to be a popular remembrance of the films of the decade, the commentary and quality pictures of the book make it even more valuable. Trent's book covers individual films, stars, partnerships, and directors and is useful for the student trying to obtain an overview of the decade or the scholar trying to find out, for example, the name of the author of the screenplay for John Ford's *The Informer.*

The films of the 1940s are analyzed in *Hollywood in the Forties* by Charles Higham and Joel Greenberg. This solid if brief book, also part of a series, is a popular study of the decade's films including *film noir,* melodrama, fantasy and horror films, problem and war films, biographies, action films, women's films, comedies, and musicals. *The Films of the Forties* by Tony Thomas is a large format book intended to give an overview with stills, brief commentary, and credits. The author discusses and illustrates over one hundred films from the decade.

The 1950s brought change to Hollywood movies. At the beginning of the decade the House Un-American Activities Committee and other agencies of the government determined to ferret out the Communists suspected of dominating the movie industry. Some movie personalities went to jail and many others were unable to obtain jobs because of the blacklist, and the fears generated brought chaos to the movie community. In addition, by the end of the decade, television had become a major influence in our society and was clearly affecting movie revenues. But the decade was nevertheless to produce some important films: *Sunset Boulevard, Rebel without a Cause,* and *On the Waterfront.*

Hollywood in the Fifties by Gordon Gow, part of the series mentioned above, presents a good overview of the films of the decade. Gow starts with *Sunset Boulevard* and discusses the changes that occurred in movies during the decade, finishing with the coming of television and the development of the wide screen. Naturally he discusses Joseph McCarthy and social and political commentary in the movies. A valuable chapter is one in which he discusses acting in the 1950s. A good pictorial overview is presented by Douglas Brode in *The Films of the Fifties.* He covers the decade from *Sunset Boulevard* to *On the Beach* film by film, describing more than one hundred films, citing credits, and giving a few photographs and brief commentary for each.

One of the better-respected books of the postwar era is *The Contemporary Cinema, 1945-1963* by Penelope Houston. The author comments on the work of the Italian and French during the contemporary period and on the efforts of the movie industry to adjust to the new audience of the postwar period. The new cinema and new directors that have emerged are the focus of her study. *Hanging On In Paradise* by Fred Lawrence Guiles is another history of making movies in Hollywood with emphasis on the production code and the House Un-American Activities Committee. In *The Films of the Fifties,* Andrew Dowdy explores the relationship between the era and its movies. Combining criticism with history, he analyzes the cinematic influences of the Communist witch hunt, television, and pornography and includes chapters on stars, sex, and rebellious youth.

That social issues forced Hollywood to change is the theme of *Hollywood in Transition* by Richard Dyer MacCann, a scholar who has devoted much of his thinking to the interrelation between the movies and society. One unit of the book concerns itself with images of Hollywood: technology, world competition, and the coming of television. The latter part of the book presents Hollywood at work: producers David O. Selznick, Sam Spiegel, Ross Hunter, and Samuel Goldwyn; directors Delmer Davis, Elia Kazan, George Stevens, and William Wyler; writers Dudley Nichols and Frank Gruber; and stars Janet Leigh, William Holden, Marlon Brando, James Dean, Joanne Woodward, Judy Holliday, and Sir Alec Guinness.

Some viewers point to the late 1950s as the period of decline for the movie industry. Economist John Spraos in *The Decline of the Cinema* analyzes the impact on the industry of television, the closing of the movie palaces, and the shortage of films. His financial analysis leads him to roughly the same conclusions reached by Charles Higham in *Hollywood at Sunset.* Higham begins his study in 1946 and continues through the decline of the movie industry. Focusing on governmental interference in the industry, Higham discusses the problems the industry had in the 1950s with anti-trust suits and the House Un-American Activities Committee.

The films of the 1960s and 1970s as a group have yet to receive the same attention as those of earlier decades. Several books, of course, have recognized these periods, but the number is slight when compared with the other decades. John Baxter wrote *Hollywood in the Sixties* as part of the series mentioned for the other decades. It is a useful survey and can serve as an introduction to the new times for films that emerged from the turmoil of the 1950s. *Hollywood Today* by Pat Billings and Allen Eyles is a less useful guide to Hollywood and an analysis of the work of some three hundred seventy artists working there in the late 1960s. The brief comments on each of the artists will appeal more to the movie fan than to the student. Finally, Marie Brenner's *Going Hollywood,* describing itself as "an insider's look at power and pretense in the movie business," tries to tell the reader who is on top of the movie business (Barbra Streisand, among others), who is going up (Robert DeNiro and others), and who is on the way down (Tom Laughlin, Cher, and Ali MacGraw).

THE INDUSTRY AND THE STUDIOS

The history of the American film industry would not be complete without consideration of the financial empires that were responsible for making movies. At the core of the industry during Hollywood's glory were the studios—the companies that selected the material to be filmed, owned and controlled the stars, dictated which directors would make which films, owned the theatres, and decided which films would play where and when.

The entire industry has been the subject of a volume edited by Tino Balio, *The American Film Industry.* Some of his essays are by modern scholars; others are by the people who were creating the history. The units cover the early industry to 1908, the struggles for control from 1908 through 1930; the oligopoly of the 1930s and 1940s, and the reorganization of the industry in the modern period. *Motion Picture Empire* by Gertrude Jobes is a history of the development of the movie industry from the early days through the creation of the studios. She includes material on the entrance of Wall Street into the movie business, on the Hays office (the movie industry's own censorship board) and its code, and on the impact of the stock market crash on the industry. The author finishes with a brief discussion of the period from the mid-1930s to the mid-1960s. Philip French's *The Movie Moguls* is "an informal history of the Hollywood tycoons" in which French gives the backgrounds, careers, and lives of the men who controlled the studios: Louis B. Mayer, Samuel Goldwyn, Adolph Zukor, William Fox, and the Warner brothers. He also includes the production code and testimony before the House Un-American Activities Committee.

The history of the early studios has been recaptured in several volumes. Biograph, the company of D. W. Griffith, has not been accorded a history unto itself; but Robert Henderson's *D. W. Griffith: The Years at Biograph* is a study of the films Griffith made there and serves as an excellent study of the studio even though the primary focus of the book is the director himself. *Beginnings of the Biograph* is a history by Gordon Hendricks of the first year of the studio. Hendricks concentrates on the technological innovations that permitted Biograph to rival Thomas Edison's studio. Several studios sprang up and began to compete with Biograph and Edison, among them Vitagraph, controlled by Albert Smith and J. Stuart Blackton and boasting such stars as Norma Talmadge. The story of the studio is told by Anthony Slide in *The Big V*. This scholarly history includes a filmography of films made at the studio.

An almost forgotten company has been resurrected for the historical audience in *Motion Picture Pioneer: The Selig Polyscope Company* by Kalton C. Lahue. Lahue uses contemporary source material to help tell the story of the company, most of whose films have disappeared. The company made an impact in its day, and this book documents both the company and the era of which it was a part. Lahue has also written *Dreams for Sale: The Rise and Fall of the Triangle Film Corporation.* Triangle rose to great heights when Griffith, Mack Sennett, and Thomas Ince were associated with it; however, it folded when it was taken over by Harry Aitken. Lahue has been interested in why this company failed while so many other small companies followed the films to financial success.

The major studios—treated here alphabetically—are well recorded in history. Rochelle Larkin's *Hail Columbia* is a recent telling of the story of Columbia Studios, with an emphasis on Harry Cohn, the studio boss, and on Frank Capra, the director who won several Academy Awards while working at Columbia.

"More stars than there are in heaven" was the motto of Metro-Goldwyn-Mayer during its heyday. No studio had more important stars under contract or made more hit movies than did MGM in the 1930s and 1940s. *The MGM Story* by John Douglas Eames claims to recall "the complete history of fifty roaring years." Eames covers the work of MGM year by year, giving a brief paragraph description of every film made under the logo of the lion. Naturally he could not include much detail when covering so many films; not even *Gone With the Wind* warrants more than a paragraph, but the book presents a fine overview of the studio's activity. Bosley Crowther's *The Lion's Share* is more of a narrative history of the entertainment empire that was MGM. Now somewhat dated, *The Lion's Share* remains a tribute to the men and women who made this studio one of the important institutions in American culture. The actors of the studio get their recognition in *The MGM Stock Company: The Golden Era* by James Robert Parish and Ronald L. Bowers. MGM placed its emphasis on its actors, rather than on its directors; it is therefore fitting that Parish and Bowers should capture the essence of the stars. They describe the work of about one hundred fifty actors and actresses; for each they include a four- to seven-page critical essay, photographs, and filmography. They feature the great ones—the Barrymores and Greta Garbo—but one significant contribution they make is to include surveys of the careers of many lesser known actors and actresses who do not have books devoted to their lives and films.

James Robert Parish has also written *The Paramount Pretties*, a survey of the actresses working at Paramount: Gloria Swanson, Clara Bow, Carole Lombard, Marlene Dietrich, Sylvia Sidney, Mae West, Dorothy Lamour, and others. He includes an essay on the life and career of each. In *The RKO Girls* he does the same for the women of RKO: Ann Harding, Ginger Rogers, Katharine Hepburn, Lucille Ball, Jane Russell, and others. These essays include biography, a discussion of the star's critical reception, and a filmography. Using the same format in *The Fox Girls*, Parish recalls the careers of the women who worked for the Fox Studio: Theda Bara, Janet Gaynor, Shirley Temple, Alice Faye, Loretta Young, Linda Darnell, Betty Grable, Marilyn Monroe, Raquel Welch, and seven more.

The history of Twentieth Century-Fox in the 1960s under the control of Darryl Zanuck is told by John Gregory Dunne, a novelist who began as a screenwriter. Dunne was working at Fox at the time, and *The Studio* is perhaps more a memoir than a history. He includes material on the making of such films as *Hello, Dolly!* and *Dr. Dolittle.*

Tino Balio's *United Artists* recalls the history of "the company built by the stars." In the 1920s D. W. Griffith, Mary Pickford, Douglas Fairbanks, Sr., and Charles Chaplin banded together to form their own company so as to maintain control over their own productions and profits. *United Artists* is the story of their company and the films they made.

The story of Universal is told in two books. I. G. Edmonds tells the first part of the history in *Big U,* which deals with the silent days, 1912 through the late 1920s. The emphasis is on Carl Laemmle, who ran the studio, and on Lon Chaney, its chief star. Edmonds also highlights Hoot Gibson and John Ford, who got their start at Universal during this period, and the original *Hunchback of Notre Dame,* made there in 1923. Michael G. Fitzgerald's *Universal Pictures* completes the story. This is a history of the studio, its awards, stars, and films, from 1930 to 1976.

Charles Higham sees Warner Brothers as a studio that sought to instruct as well as entertain. His *Warner Brothers* suggests that the brothers who ran the studio were heartless men who made important films. This is a history of the studio from 1918, when it was founded, until the 1950s, when it began to decline. Highlights are on the coming of sound and *The Jazz Singer*, and on films of social realism and war. *Here's Looking at You, Kid* by James Silke claims to be the story of "fifty years of fighting, working and dreaming at Warner Brothers." He includes chapters on the early period, writers, musicians, producers, directors, actors and actresses, character performers, and on the recent era.

HOLLYWOOD

Hollywood: a city, a collection of studios, an institution, the residence of stars, a dream factory, a state of mind. It is these and more, and without a doubt no history of American film is complete without a survey of the importance of Hollywood. There are many approaches to the study of the Hollywood phenomenon, some of which will be discussed in the chapter dealing with movies and society, but Parker Tyler in *The Hollywood Hallucination* tries to analyze the Hollywood experience. This imaginative writer considers the impact on Hollywood—and on society in general—of surrealism, the love themes of the movies, and Mickey Mouse, among other influences. He asks the question: is Hollywood a dream, a hallucination? In *Hollywood and After* European critic Jerzy Toeplitz asks what has happened to the movie industry now that Hollywood and the czars are finished. This book becomes a study of the new filmmakers, such as Haskell Wexler, Francis Ford Coppola, and George Lucas.

The story of Hollywood can never be told better than by the people who were part of it, many of whose stories will be discussed in the chapter on film personalities. Some of the books on and by movie people highlight the town and the industry. *It Was Fun While it Lasted* by Arthur H. Lewis, for example, is a series of interviews with Mae West, Glenn Ford, Zsa Zsa Gabor, Lewis Milestone, Dore Schary, and John Wayne. Anita Loos's autobiography *Kiss Hollywood Good-by* recites the craziness of Hollywood in its golden years. Loos was a screenwriter (*San Francisco*) known as one of those who most enjoyed the social life of Hollywood. Robert Parrish was an Academy Award-winning editor and director (of minor films), and his reminiscences in *Growing Up in Hollywood* include interesting views of John Ford, as well as of the Communist witch hunt.

Hollywood Speaks! by Mike Steen is an oral history of Hollywood. The author has interviewed people from each movie craft: actors (Henry Fonda, Jane Russell, Agnes Moorehead), a director (William Wellman), producers (such as Hal Roach, Sr.), a director of photography (James Wong Howe), and a designer (Edith Head).

In the popular mind the history of Hollywood is told by the gossip columnists. The writers who made everyone's business their business clearly contributed to the creation of the myth of Hollywood, and without them the impact of the industry and the stars on society would no doubt have been different. The better-known columnists were as influential as the stars they wrote about. Hedda Hopper was among the most widely recognized names in America at one time. *The Whole Truth and Nothing But* is her personal account of the Hollywood she covered. Portraits of Elizabeth Taylor, Judy Garland, and many others are the main feature of the book.

Rex Reed made his early reputation by asking personal questions during interviews with stars. *Do You Sleep in the Nude?* is a collection of his interviews with Barbra Streisand, Marlene Dietrich, Leslie Uggams, Buster

Keaton, and other stars. His personal bias is evident in his characterizations: some people he likes; others he shows in the worst light. In *Conversations in the Raw,* Reed includes interviews with some "oldies but goodies" such as Bette Davis, Ruth Gordon, and Ingrid Bergman, as well as newcomers such as Jon Voight. In *People are Crazy Here* Reed tries to capture the spirit of Hollywood through essays on Hollywood people. Part one focuses on those who live "the crazy life"—Tennessee Williams, Bette Midler, and Sylvia Miles; part two those who ignore "the crazy life"—George C. Scott, Elia Kazan, and Joanne Woodward; and part three those who are "digging the crazy life"—Jacqueline Susann, Ann-Margret, Jack Lemmon, and Jack Nicholson.

Earl Wilson's *The Show Business Nobody Knows* includes gossipy stories about Lauren Bacall and Humphrey Bogart, Robert Mitchum, Marilyn Monroe, and Dean Martin; Wilson also talks about the rise of black stars and about sex in the movies. In *Show Business Laid Bare,* Wilson continues to live up to his reputation as a gossip columnist and even includes a lengthy study of the relationship between President John Kennedy and Marilyn Monroe. He also has stories about Marlon Brando, Burt Reynolds, Woody Allen, and Elliott Gould.

The lesser-known columnists have had their say as well. Sidney Skolsky covered Hollywood for forty years. *Don't Get Me Wrong* is his memoir, which, as he says, is "profusely illustrated." Similarly, *Radie's World* describes the life and friends of Radie Harris, gossip columnist for the *Hollywood Reporter.* Another chronicler of Hollywood, Joseph Hyams, was the Hollywood correspondent for the *New York Herald Tribune,* and he describes his life among the stars in *Mislaid in Hollywood.*

No story of Hollywood would be complete without the contribution of a private eye. In his *Investigation Hollywood* Fred Otash opens his files to reveal the inside stories of Judy Garland, Frank Sinatra, Vic Damone, Jeff Hunter, Mickey Cohen, and Anita Ekberg. What the stars' detective does not know, their secretaries do. Alice Marchak and Linda Hunter have been secretaries to the stars, and in *The Super Secs* they describe the private lives of their bosses and give a realistic picture of what stardom is like on a daily basis.

If the reader wants the dirty gossip—some based on fact, much based on wishful thinking—the book to go to is *Hollywood Babylon* by Kenneth Anger. This infamous book contains lurid stories on stars from Mary Astor to Lana Turner. Another in a similar vein is William H. A. Carr's *Hollywood Tragedy,* which claims to be "a book of scandals about Hollywood's greatest stars." While less shocking than Anger, Carr does tell lurid tales of Fatty Arbuckle, Mary Astor, Errol Flynn, Charles Chaplin, Ingrid Bergman, Lana Turner, Marilyn Monroe, Bruce Lee, James Dean, Sharon Tate, Elizabeth Taylor, Jayne Mansfield, and Judy Garland.

Another approach to the history of Hollywood is through the movies that

Hollywood has made about itself. Two recent books have studied the countless movies about life in Hollywood. In *Hollywood According to Hollywood* Alex Barris surveys moves about movies. He gives history, critical commentary, and photographs of movies from *Merton of the Movies* to *W. C. Fields and Me. Movies on Movies* by Richard Meyers is another account of "how Hollywood sees itself." Meyers presents a review by decade of the biographies, mysteries and horror films, comedies, musicals, and Westerns that have all reflected life in Hollywood.

BIBLIOGRAPHY

Anger, Kenneth. *Hollywood Babylon.* New York: Dell, 1975.

Balio, Tino, ed. *The American Film Industry.* Madison: University of Wisconsin Press, 1976.

______. *United Artists: The Company Built by the Stars.* Madison: University of Wisconsin Press, 1976.

Barbour, Alan G. *The Thrill of It All.* New York: Macmillan, 1971.

Bardèche, Maurice and Robert Brasillach. *The History of Motion Pictures.* Translated by Iris Barry. New York: Norton and The Museum of Modern Art, 1938.

Barris, Alex. *Hollywood According to Hollywood.* New York: A. S. Barnes, 1978.

Baxter, John. *The Hollywood Exiles.* New York: Taplinger, 1976.

______. *Hollywood in the Sixties.* New York: A. S. Barnes, 1972.

______. *Hollywood in the Thirties.* New York: A. S. Barnes, 1968.

______. *Sixty Years of Hollywood.* New York: A. S. Barnes, 1973.

Bergman, Andrew. *We're in the Money: Depression America and Its Films.* New York: New York University Press, 1971.

Billings, Pat and Allen Eyles. *Hollywood Today.* New York: A. S. Barnes, 1971.

Blum, Daniel. *A Pictorial History of the Silent Screen.* New York: Grosset and Dunlap, 1953.

Bohn, Thomas W. and Richard L. Stromgren. *Light and Shadows: A History of Motion Pictures.* Port Washington, N.Y.: Alfred Publishing Co., 1975.

Bowser, Eileen, ed. *Biograph Bulletins, 1908-1912.* New York: Farrar, Straus and Giroux, 1973.

______, ed. *Film Notes.* New York: Museum of Modern Art, 1969.

Brenner, Marie. *Going Hollywood: An Insider's Look at Power and Pretense in the Movie Industry.* New York: Delacorte, 1978.

Brode, Douglas. *The Films of the Fifties.* Secaucus, N.J.: Citadel, 1976.

Brownlow, Kevin. *The Parade's Gone By.* New York: Ballantine Books, 1968.

Carr, William H. A. *Hollywood Tragedy.* Greenwich, Conn.: Fawcett, 1972.

Casty, Alan. *Development of the Film: An Interpretive History.* New York: Harcourt, Brace, Jovanovich, 1973.

Ceram, C. W. *Archaeology of the Cinema.* New York: Harcourt, Brace, and World, 1965.

Cowie, Peter, ed. *A Concise History of the Cinema.* New York: A. S. Barnes, 1971.

______. *Eighty Years of Cinema.* New York: A. S. Barnes, 1977.

Crowther, Bosley. *The Lion's Share: The Story of an Entertainment Empire.* New York: E. P. Dutton, 1957.

Curtis, Anthony, ed. *The Rise and Fall of the Matinee Idol: Past Deities of Stage and Screen, Their Roles, Their Magic, Their Worshipers.* New York: St. Martin's Press, 1974.

Dowdy, Andrew. *The Films of the Fifties.* New York: William Morrow, 1973. Original Title: *Movies Are Better than Ever.*

Dunne, John Gregory. *The Studio.* New York: Farrar, Straus, and Giroux, 1969.

Dwoskin, Stephen. *Film Is: The International Free Cinema.* Woodstock, N.Y.: The Overlook Press, 1975.

Eames, John Douglas. *The MGM Story: The Complete History of Fifty Roaring Years.* New York: Crown, 1975.

Edmonds, I. G. *Big U: Universal in the Silent Days.* New York: A. S. Barnes, 1977.

Ellis, Jack C. *A History of Film.* Englewood Cliffs, N.J.: Prentice-Hall, 1979.

Everson, William K. *American Silent Film.* New York: Oxford University Press, 1978.

Fell, John. *A History of Films.* New York: Holt, Rinehart and Winston, 1979.

Fitzgerald, Michael G. *Universal Pictures.* New Rochelle, N.Y.: Arlington House, 1977.

French, Philip. *The Movie Moguls: An Informal History of the Hollywood Tycoons.* Chicago: Henry Regnery, 1969.

Fulton, A. R. *Motion Pictures: The Development of an Art from Silent Films to the Age of Television.* Norman: University of Oklahoma Press, 1960.

Geduld, Harry M. *The Birth of the Talkies: From Edison to Jolson.* Bloomington: Indiana University Press, 1975.

Gelman, Barbara. *Photoplay Treasury.* New York: Bonanza Books, 1972.

Gow, Gordon. *Hollywood in the Fifties.* New York: A. S. Barnes, 1971.

Grau, Robert. *The Theatre of Science.* New York: Benjamin Blom, 1914, 1969.

Griffith, Richard and Arthur Mayer. *The Movies.* New York: Simon and Schuster, 1970.

Griffith, Richard, ed. *The Talkies: Articles and Illustrations from Photoplay Magazine, 1928-1940.* New York: Dover, 1971.

Guiles, Fred Lawrence. *Hanging On In Paradise.* New York: McGraw-Hill, 1975.

Hampton, Benjamin B. *History of the American Film Industry From Its Beginnings to 1951.* New York: Dover, 1970. Original title of the 1931 edition was *A History of the Movies.*

Harris, Radie. *Radie's World.* New York: G. P. Putnam's Sons, 1975.

Hays, Will H. *See and Hear.* N.P.: Motion Picture Producers and Distributors of America, 1929.

Henderson, Robert M. *D. W. Griffith: The Years at Biograph.* New York: Farrar, Straus and Giroux, 1970.

Hendricks, Gordon. *Beginnings of the Biograph: The Story of the Invention of the Mutoscope and the Biograph and their Supplying Camera.* New York: The Beginning of the American Film, 1964.

Higham, Charles. *Hollywood at Sunset.* New York: Saturday Review Press, 1972.

______. *The Warner Brothers,* New York: Charles Scribner's Sons, 1975.

______ and Joel Greenberg. *Hollywood in the Forties.* New York: A. S. Barnes, 1968.

Hopper, Hedda and James Brough. *The Whole Truth and Nothing But.* Garden City, N.Y. Doubleday, 1963.

Houston, Penelope. *The Contemporary Cinema, 1945-1963.* Baltimore: Penguin, 1963.

Hyams, Joseph. *Mislaid in Hollywood.* New York: Peter W. Wyden, 1973.

Jacobs, Lewis. *The Rise of the American Film: A Critical History.* New York: Teachers College Press, 1968.

Jobes, Gertrude. *Motion Picture Empire.* Hamden, Conn.: Archon, 1966.

Jowett, Garth. *Film: The Democratic Art.* Boston: Little, Brown, 1976.

Kardish, Laurence. *Reel Plastic Magic: A History of Films and Filmmaking in America.* Boston: Little, Brown, 1972.

Knight, Arthur. *The Liveliest Art: A Panoramic History of the Movies.* New York: New American Library, 1957.

Lahue, Kalton C. *Dreams for Sale: The Rise and Fall of the Triangle Film Corporation.* New York: A. S. Barnes, 1971.

______, ed. *Motion Picture Pioneer: The Selig Polyscope Company.* New York: A. S. Barnes, 1973.

Larkin, Rochelle. *Hail Columbia.* New Rochelle, N.Y.: Arlington House, 1975.

Lawton, Richard. *A World of Movies: Seventy Years of Film History.* New York: Delacorte, 1974.

Leish, Kenneth W. *Cinema.* New York: Newsweek Books, 1974.

Lennig, Arthur. *The Silent Voice.* Albany: Faculty-Student Association of the State University of New York at Albany, 1966.

Lewis, Arthur H. *It Was Fun While It Lasted.* New York: Trident, 1973.

Loos, Anita. *Kiss Hollywood Good-By.* New York: Viking, 1974.

MacCann, Richard Dyer. *Hollywood in Transition.* Boston: Houghton Mifflin, 1962.

Manchel, Frank. *When Movies Began to Speak.* Englewood Cliffs, N.J.: Prentice-Hall, 1969.

Marchak, Alice and Linda Hunter. *The Supersecs: Behind the Scenes with the Secretaries of the Superstars.* Los Angeles: Charles, 1975.

Mast, Gerald. *A Short History of the Movies.* New York: Pegasus, 1976.

Meyers, Richard. *Movies on Movies: How Hollywood Sees Itself.* New York: Drake, 1978.

Niver, Kemp R. *The First Twenty Years: A Segment of Film History.* Los Angeles: Locare Research Group, 1968.

North, Joseph H. *The Early Development of the Motion Picture (1887-1909).* New York: Arno, 1973.

O'Leary, Liam. *The Silent Cinema.* New York: E. P. Dutton, 1965.

Otash, Fred. *Investigation Hollywood.* Chicago: Henry Regnery, 1976.

Parish, James Robert. *The Fox Girls.* New Rochelle, N.Y.: Arlington House, 1971.

______. *The Paramount Pretties.* New Rochelle, N.Y.: Arlington House, 1972.

______. *The RKO Girls.* New Rochelle, N.Y.: Arlington House, 1974.

______ and Ronald L. Bowers. *The MGM Stock Company: The Golden Era.* New Rochelle, N.Y.: Arlington House, 1973.

Parrish, Robert. *Growing Up in Hollywood.* New York: Harcourt, Brace, Jovanovich, 1976.

Pratt, George C. *Spellbound in Darkness: A History of the Silent Film.* Greenwich, Conn.: New York Graphic Society, 1973.

Quigley, Martin, Jr. *Magic Shadows: The Story of The Origin of Motion Pictures.* New York: Biblo and Tannen, 1969.

Ramsaye, Terry. *A Million and One Nights: A History of the Motion Picture.* New York: Simon and Schuster, 1926.

Reed, Rex. *Conversations in the Raw: Dialogues, Monologues, and Selected Short Subjects.* New York: World, 1969.

______. *Do You Sleep in the Nude?* New York: New American Library, 1968.

______. *People Are Crazy Here.* New York: Delacorte, 1974.

Rhode, Eric. *A History of the Cinema From Its Origins to 1970.* New York: Hill and Wang, 1976.

Robinson, David. *Hollywood in the Twenties.* New York: A. S. Barnes, 1968.

Rotha, Paul with Richard Griffith. *The Film Till Now: A Survey of World Cinema.* London: Spring Books, 1967.

Seldes, Gilbert. *An Hour with the Movies and the Talkies.* New York: Arno, 1973.

Shales, Tom and others. *The American Film Heritage: Impressions from the American Film Institute Archives.* Washington, D.C.: Acropolis Books, 1972.

Silke, James R. *Here's Looking at You, Kid: Fifty Years of Fighting, Working and Dreaming at Warner Bros.* Boston: Little, Brown, 1976.

Skolsky, Sidney. *Don't Get Me Wrong—I Love Hollywood.* New York: G. P. Putnam's Sons, 1975.

Slide, Anthony. *Aspects of American Film History Prior to 1920.* Metuchen, N.J.: Scarecrow, 1978.

______. *Early American Cinema.* New York: A. S. Barnes, 1970.

______. *The Big V.* Metuchen, N.J.: Scarecrow, 1976.

Spears, Jack. *Hollywood: The Golden Era.* New York: A. S. Barnes, 1971.

Spehr, Paul C. *The Movies Begin: Making Movies in New Jersey, 1887-1920.* Newark, N.J.: The Newark Museum, 1977.

Spraos, John. *The Decline of the Cinema: An Economist's Report.* London: George Allen and Unwin, 1962.

Steen, Mike. *Hollywood Speaks!* New York: G. P. Putnam's Sons, 1974.

Taylor, Deems and others. *A Pictorial History of the Movies.* New York: Simon and Schuster, 1950.

Thomas, Tony. *The Films of the Forties.* Secaucus, N.J.: Citadel, 1975.

Thurman, Judith and Jonathan David. *The Magic Lantern: How the Movies Got to Move.* New York: Atheneum, 1978.

Toeplitz, Jerzy. *Hollywood and After: The Changing Face of Movies in America.* Translated by Boleslaw Sulik. Chicago: Henry Regnery, 1974.

Trent, Paul. *Those Fabulous Movie Years: The 30s.* Barre, Mass.: Barre Publishing, 1975.

Tyler, Parker. *The Hollywood Hallucination.* New York: Simon and Schuster, 1970.

Wagenknecht, Edward. *The Movies in the Age of Innocence.* New York: Ballantine Books, 1962.

Wenden, D. J. *The Birth of the Movies.* New York: E. P. Dutton, 1974.

Whittemore, Don and Philip Alan Cecchettini, eds. *Passport to Hollywood: Film Immigrants Anthology.* New York: McGraw-Hill, 1976.

Wilson, Earl. *Show Business Laid Bare.* New York: G. P. Putnam's Sons, 1974.

______. *The Show Business Nobody Knows.* Chicago: Henry Regnery, 1971.

Wright, Basil. *The Long View.* London: Secker and Warburg, 1974.

CHAPTER 2

Film Production

As with many arts, film is a marriage of the ideas of the filmmakers with the techniques of their medium. In order to appreciate the final product, the serious viewer and the critic must be generally familiar with the basic techniques of film production. In fact, were the critic to make one or two short films—even on super 8mm film—it would greatly enhance his understanding of what the professionals do. The books mentioned in this chapter will provide the basic information needed by the serious viewer, the critic, and the prospective filmmaker.

TECHNIQUE

The language of film is as special as the jargon and slang of any profession. The words used to describe the particular activities are often unique to the art form. Therefore, a good glossary of film terms is essential to both the beginning filmmaker and the critic. Many introductions to film study include a glossary as an appendix, but there are several glossaries that are independently available. Perhaps the most useful is by Harry M. Geduld and Ronald Gottesman, *An Illustrated Glossary of Film Terms.* This brief book lists the important items in alphabetical order and illustrates words that lend themselves to visual interpretation. The entries are usually only a sentence or two in length, and the prose is generally free of jargon.

More complex, and threfore more important for the advanced filmmaker, is *A Grammar of the Film* by Raymond Spottiswood. The aim of the book is "to make as precise as possible the language and grammar" of film. Toward this goal, the author begins with definitions of the critical terms and then places these terms in the context of the history of film in outline form. He next discusses categories of film, with an emphasis on the relation between film and drama and goes on to show that film has developed its own techniques, distinct form drama, and that these techniques have become the focal point for film criticism. Finally, Spottiswood discusses various types of films, especially the documentary. This is a complicated book, but the rewards justify its reading.

Daniel Arijon's *Grammar of the Film Language* is also a guide to the language of film narrative and visual communication techniques. A practical book designed for the professional or the near-professional, it discusses advanced techniques such as parallel film editing or multiple person dialogues in addition to defining the basic tools of the filmmaker.

Before consulting the detailed analyses of production, the beginner might want to start with an introduction to the entire process of film production. Such a book is *Handbook of Film Production* by John Quick and Tom La Bare, which gives an overview of the task before the prospective filmmaker. A similar, but still more basic book, is by Emil E. Brodbeck, *Handbook of Basic Motion Picture Techniques.* This book is clearly for the beginner. More useful for the critic will be Carl Linder's *Filmmaking: A Practical Guide.* Its discussion is easy to follow and goes on from the tools of film-making to analyze several types of film, such as the documentary, the fictional narrative film, and the expressionist film. Perhaps the most useful of the handbooks for the serious beginning filmmaker is the *Handbook of Motion Picture Production* by William B. Adams. Adams begins by presenting definitions of film terms and goes on to cover the nature of the production unit, the writing of a script, the devices of narration, shooting, adding sound, and editing.

Many of the books on production are designed for the amateur. Kirk Smallman's *Creative Film-Making* claims that it is "a concise introduction to the fundamentals of film-making and how they can be employed for personal cinematic expression at little expense." Paul Petzold's *All-in-One Movie Book* also tells the amateur what he needs to know to make films. He discusses the use of the camera, aiming a film at a special audience, time in film, and the methods of using a lens.

Many amateurs are using super 8mm equipment because it is both less expensive and more available than the larger formats; in fact, now that the equipment has become versatile, some professionals have begun to use it as well. In general the elementary and basic production techniques are the same regardless of the format, but there are books written exclusively for the filmmaker working in super 8mm. *Super 8 Filmmaking from Scratch* is an excellent introduction to the format. Bebe Ferrell McClain begins with a theoretical justification for making films and then discusses format, equipment, steps in production, planning, shooting, editing, and adding sound. Lenny Lipton's *The Super 8 Book* is more sophisticated but not overly technical. This author also discusses format and then continues with instruction on the camera, sound, processing and striping, editing, making prints, and projection.

Needless to say, many of the production books are aimed at the student filmmaker. *Making Movies: Student Films to Features* by Hila Colman has a general audience. Colman tires to be helpful to all filmmakers, but there is an emphasis on student movies. The book discusses the director and assistant director, the editor and script supervisor, the producer, the director of photography, the sound technician, and other production personnel. There are chapters on the documentary, television commercials, and hobby filmmaking. William Bayer's *Breaking Through, Selling Out, Dropping Dead* is an idiosyncratic collection of notes addressed to the young filmmaker who wants to get into the business. Bayer covers topics from raising money to exhibiting films.

A book clearly directed at filmmakers of secondary school age is *Movie Making* by David Coynik. Coynik discusses the basic equipment, planning the film, shooting, lighting, editing, sound, and using special effects. *Filmmaking for Beginners* by Joan Horvath is another book geared to the same level; the author covers the camera, scripts, shooting, special effects, editing, sound, and animation. A book for the teachers of these students is *Introduction to Film Making* by Robert E. Davis. This short book provides teachers with enough background to guide students into filmmaking. Davis gives a brief film history and discusses film types, the mechanics of film, and film production; he goes on to present projects for the classroom and ends with a bibliography.

Once past the handbook stage, readers will want more detailed books about film production. A basic introduction to production is another of Raymond Spottiswood's books, *Film and Its Techniques.* The author starts with the beginning of film as an idea in the head of the artist, then proceeds to discuss the camera, editing, the use of space and time, laboratory work (where some of the complex steps in production are performed on the film long after it has been exposed in the camers), and the use of color, sound, and lighting. Another book designed for the serious prospective filmmaker is *Basic Motion Picture Technology* by Bernard L. Happé. Happé gives the principles and history of the medium and then discusses techniques of basic photography. He covers the photographic image and camera work. Also included are units on sound recording, studio production, film processing (laboratory work), and presentation, as well as many more elements of production.

One of the best books on production for the classroom, as preparation for either production or criticism, is *Making Movies: From Script to Screen* by Lee R. Bobker and Louise Marinis. This fine book is divided into three units. The first discusses what is done before the filming begins—creating the storyboard and preparing to shoot; the second treats the filming itself—directing, photographing, and recording sound; the last deals with what happens after the filming—editing, adding sound, laboratory work, and distribution. There is a final chapter on careers in filmmaking.

A book for the more experienced filmmaker is *A Primer for Film-Making* by Kenneth Roberts and Win Sharples, Jr. Claiming to be "a complete guide to 16mm and 35mm film production," it is a thorough study of the process from planning the budget to making the final prints. Less serious in style but equally serious in intention is a book on production by Jerry Lewis. *The Total Film-Maker* describes the fun and craziness of the world of this actor/director. The units of the book are on production, post production, and the making of comedy.

For the person considering a career in filmmaking, *All About Cinema* by Derek Bowskill serves as good introduction to the profession. Bowskill discusses how a film is made and exhibted, but he also gives a personal description of what it feels like to work in film and make movies. He concludes with thoughts on how to find a career in film. A book with a similar purpose is Mel London's *Getting into Film.* London begins by describing the film industry and what specific jobs in the industry entail, then covers production in general and the problems of writing for films. His basic unit deals with cinematography, editing, adding music and sound, animation, acting, and directing.

Four Aspects of the Film by James L. Limbacher is an unusual study of production because it limits its scope to color, width, depth, and sound. For each of these techniques, Limbacher discusses the early development, recent innovations, and creative use. This book is useful for the filmmaker, the critic, and the historian.

SPECIAL TYPES OF PRODUCTION

Two books that deal with special types of filmmaking are *Independent Filmmaking* by Lenny Lipton and *The Technique of Documentary Film Production* by W. Hugh Baddeley. Lipton's book can be considered a general guide to production, but the emphasis is on the filmmaker working outside the industry. While Lipton covers the same topics as the books for students of secondary school age (format, the camera, lens, shooting, editing, sound, and the laboratory) he does so in much more depth and with more of a technical emphasis. Baddeley's book is a how-to study of the production of documentary films.

Another special type production is animation, and there are many books dealing specifically with animation techniques. *Film Animation as Hobby* by Andrew and Mark Hobson is a brief and simple book for the general audience. A more sophisticated guide to animation is *Making it Move* by John Trojanski and Louis Rockwood. This book gives a history of animation and a description of its tools. After discussing how animation works, the authors describe types of animation—object, cutout, cel, and puppet-doll—as well as animation done without a camera, kinestasis, and pixillation. Anthony Kinsey's *How to Make Animated Movies* is a basic book for the more advanced filmmaker that begins with an overview of the process of animation and a description of the equipment. Kinsey then covers the general techniques of animation, from the simple to the more complex. His final chapter is on planning the film, including a section on creating the storyboard. In *Making Your Own Animated Movies* Yvonne Anderson has described her pioneering work with young children and animation at the Yellow Ball Workshop. The teacher will find a wealth of materials here on the camera, editing, sound, using flip cards, modeling and shooting clay figures, drawing on film, and pixillation.

Scriptwriting for Animation by Stan Hayward deals with a specific aspect of animation production: the development of a narrative structure for animated films. This book is intended to give the serious animator the background to plan both fiction and scientific films.

Finally, John Halas has written a more general book on animation. *Art in Movement: New Directions in Animation* begins with a long essay on the theory of animation and then discusses new developments in the technique of animation. Halas describes what is happening internationally with animation and concludes with some speculation about the future of the process.

THE PRODUCTION TEAM

The person who wants to know more about what each member of the production team does has a wide array of books from which to choose. Several of the books cover the entire team; others deal with a specific member of the team. Of the general books the most authoritative is *Filmmaking: The Collaborative Art.* Written by Donald Chase and sponsored by the American Film Institute, the book is designed to demonstrate that all of the members of the production team are important and that the director is dependent on them all for the final product. Chase includes essays on the producer, screenwriter, actor, editor, director of photography, production designer, costume designer, script supervisor, composer, and director of special effects. This book is a superior overview of the act of production. Ivan Butler has accomplished much the same effect in *The Making of Feature Films—A Guide.* His method has been to interview people involved in making films and to ask each to describe what he does. Specifically, he interviewed two of each of the following: producers, scriptwriters, directors, actors, cameramen, art directors, costume designers, special effects creators, continuity girls, editors, composers, sound men, distributors, and even censors. Less serious, but still useful, is William Fadiman's *Hollywood Now,* a survey of the industry in which Fadiman analyzes the work of the agent, director, star, writer, and producer.

The Director

Naturally many books deal with the work of the director, the single most important member of the production team. The work of many directors will be discussed in chapter 6, but a few books dealing with the nature of the director's responsibilities will be mentioned here.

One way to gain an understanding of the work of directors is to allow them to describe this work in their own words, and several books are collections of interviews with directors who talk about their craft. Harry M. Geduld edited a collection of conversations with directors who describe their work. In *Film Makers on Film Making* he includes directors from the early period, such as Louis Lumière, to contemporary directors, such as Kenneth Anger. Many of the people included are Americans or have worked extensively here: Edwin S. Porter, Mack Sennett, D. W. Griffith, Charles Chaplin, Erich von Stroheim, Alfred Hitchcock, Fritz Lang, Josef von Sternberg, and Orson Welles. A similar book is *The Director's Event* by Eric Sherman and Martin Rubin, which includes interviews with Budd Boetticher, Peter Bogdanovich, Samuel Fuller, Arthur Penn, and Roman Polanski.

Sherman followed this book with another in which the directors describe their profession: *Directing the Film.* A companion volume to Chase's *Filmmaking: The Collaborative Art* mentioned above, this book was also sponsored by the American Film Institute. For a number of years the AFI has been conducting interviews with filmmakers as part of the educational process at the AFI West Coast research center. Sherman has edited the comments of visiting directors and arranged them by topic. This book is a collection of their comments on the different aspects of their job: the use of the script, putting together a team, rehearsals, shooting, directing actors, editing, and viewing the film. The most important American directors are represented, among them Howard Hawks, George Cukor, and King Vidor, as well as important European directors.

A. J. Reynertson has analyzed the work of the director in *The Work of the Film Director.* Because of its detailed description of the director's role in making a film, this book is a good reference for the critic who wants to analyze the contributions of the director. Terence Marner's *Directing Motion Pictures* is designed more for the prospective filmmaker than for the critic. It is a how-to book on making a film which follows the duties of the director step by step. *Film and the Director* by Don Livingston is a general book which is older but still useful. This too is a production book that covers screen technique, the cut, movement, art and visual technique, the camera, directing actors and actions. adding sound, the entire production process, and budgeting.

This last aspect of the director's work, and one of the most important, is the subject of an entire study by Sylvia Allen Costa: *How to Prepare a Production Budget for Film and Video Tape.* This is a specialized book for the advanced filmmaker. Costa's chapters include advice on studio expenses; purchasing, exposing, and processing raw stock; laboratory charges, sound costs, and other technical matters.

The Screenwriter

One member of the production team often overlooked in the past is the screenwriter. It is difficult in many cases to give any one person credit for a screenplay because many have contributed to the shape of the script, and actually it is the film that counts rather than the screenplay. But recently critics have come to believe that the success of a film may well depend on the ability of the writer. Again, it is helpful to understand the artist through his comments on his own work. William Froug interviewed twelve writers and asked them to describe their work and frustrations in *The Screenwriter Looks at the Screenwriter.* Represented are Jonathan Axelrod, Ring Lardner, Jr., I. A. L. Diamond, Buck Henry, and Nunnally Johnson.

A companion to this book is *Talking Pictures* by Richard Corliss. Subtitled *Screenwriters in American Cinema,* this book attempts to understand the role of the screenwriter by analyzing the scripts of important authors. The first group of writers Corliss analyzes is the "author-auteur" group, men such as Ben Hecht, Preston Sturges, and Billy Wilder, men who have a recognized impact on the films for which they write. A second group is "the stylists," such as Nunnally Johnson, Garson Kanin, and Ruth Gordon. A third group is the "themes in search of a style" group, represented by such writers as Dudley Nichols, Joseph and Herman Mankiewicz. The fourth group is "the chameleons," such as Frank Nugent and Ring Lardner, Jr. Finally Corliss deals with writers he calls "a new wind from the East": Terry Southern, Erich Segal, and Buck Henry.

Wolf Rilla describes the methods of the screenwriter in film and television in *The Writer and the Screen.* This book covers the role of the screenwriter, the nature of the screenplay, and the importance of the documentary and is designed for the person who thinks he has an idea that could be sold if only it could be written up properly. A more complex study is *The Technique of Screenplay Writing* by Eugene Vale, "an analysis of the dramatic structure of motion pictures," which focuses on the form (language of film), the dramatic construction (characterization), and the story. John Halas's book, *Visual Scripting,* is designed primarily for the person interested in writing scripts for animation. Halas takes a storyteller's approach to writing both feature films and commercials.

The Actor

While there are many books on acting in general, there are surprisingly few dealing with acting on the screen. As far back as 1922 Inez and Helen Klumph described the actor's job in *Screen Acting.* They discussed working with the director, makeup men, and costume designers. The book was prefaced by Lillian Gish and was intended to help aspiring actors break into the business. More recently Michael Pate has written *The Film Actor* for aspiring actors. A major part of his book presents the terminology of the actor's craft. The aspiring critic could also learn much from this study.

A special type of actor is the stuntman. He or she performs the dangerous stunts calling for special skill and knowledge but rarely achieves star status and recognition. In *Stunting in the Cinema* Arthur Wise and Dereck Ware give a history of stunting including famous stuntmen such as Douglas Fairbanks, Sr. The authors also describe the different types of stunts used in movies: with horses and animals, with vehicles, in the air, and in combat. In *Stunt* John Baxter presents a fascinating behind-the-scenes look at the craft. He discusses the actual technique used in famous stunt scenes, such as the one in which Yakima Canutt jumped from the stagecoach to the horses in *Stagecoach.* Baxter also concentrates on actors who did their own stunts, such as Tom Mix and Douglas Fairbanks, Sr. The feminine stunt artist's work is described by Audrey Scott in *I Was A Hollywood Stunt Girl.*

Others on the Production Team

No movie can be made without the services of the cameramen, or cinematographers as they are now being called. Charles Higham edited a collection of personal statements on the craft by Leon Shamroy, Lee Garmes, William Daniels, James Wong Howe, Stanley Cortez, Karl Strauss, and Arthur Miller (the cameraman). *Hollywood Cameramen: Sources of Light* gives them credit for their contribution to the art, while at the same time allowing them to describe their work in their own words. In *The Work of the Motion Picture Camerman* Freddie Young and Paul Petzold have written a more technical study of the craft. Their how-to book describes the camera and lens, discusses lighting and camera techniques, compares studio work with shooting on location, and analyzes the use of artificial backgrounds and marine sequences.

The public is more conscious of the work of the costume designer than that of the cinematographer but probably no more aware of the intricacies of the craft. In *Hollywood Costume* Dale McConathy and Diana Vreeland have provided a beautiful decade by decade survey and analysis of designing costumes for the movies. Theirs is a large book containing many lush color pictures. A factual guide to costume designing is *Costume Design in the Movies* by Elizabeth Leese. Beginning with an essay on "couture on the screen," the author gives an alphabetical listing of designers and a one-sentence description of their work, a list of awards won, and a filmography. The result is a short on analysis but long on information.

Set design is the craft of conceiving the sets on which the movie is made. *Caligari's Cabinet and Other Grand Illusions* is the major work on the craftsmen who create the background and scenery for movies. Léon Barsacq devotes the first unit of the book to the history of design, beginning with the concept of painted sets and progressing to constructed sets. He describes the Russians' use of natural scenery, the coming and triumph of realism, and postwar trends. In the second unit, Barsacq, a designer himself, discusses the technique of set design—the need to research the set, the use of color, the actual creation of the set, and the use of special effects. *Film Design* by Terence St. John Marner and Michael Stringer is a book for the serious amateur or beginning professional on how the designer works and fits into the production team. One unusual book dealing with design is *Fit for the Chase* by Raymond Lee. This is a book of photographs on the cars used in the silent films and early sound movies with a brief introduction by Lee and a wealth of stills and publicity photographs. This unusual approach to the study of movies gives the book its own integrity.

The story of the use of special effects is told in John Brosnan's *Movie Magic.* Brosnan covers the techniques of using special effects historically, beginning with the pioneers and continuing through the work of the early 1970s. Along the way he discusses the work of the Disney Studio, the particular special effects called for in war films, the work of the model animators, and the importance of special effects in science fiction films. Jeff Rovin's *Movie Special Effects* is an introduction to the subject intended for a more popular audience. Rovin's is a well-illustrated historical survey decade by decade of the use of special effects.

Once all the other members of the production team have done their jobs, it is the duty of the film editor to put the pieces of film into an order that will convey the story or aesthetic quality to the audience. The work of the editor has saved many a film and deserves the attention given to it by Karel Reisz and Gavin Millar in *The Technique of Film Editing*. This is basically a how-to book that begins with a history of editing and discusses the practices and principles of the craft, with an emphasis on innovations in the business during the 1950s and 1960s.

No commercial movie can succeed without distribution, the final step in production and perhaps the most chancy of all the steps. Several of the books mentioned above have suggestions for distributing a film, but *Those Great Movie Ads* by Joe Morella, Edward Z. Epstein, and Eleanor Clark is an interesting look at the advertising aspect of distribution. The book opens with a long introduction on the importance of movie advertisements by critic Judith Crist; then the authors have reproduced the ads, grouping by type: great ad lines, the director as star, selling technical changes, and so on.

The books discussed in this chapter will not make a professional filmmaker out of a person who has never held a camera, but they will guide the beginner to the basic primers on filmmaking. They will also provide the student or the critic with the technical knowledge necessary for a full appreciation of the art of the film. Film is a union of technology and content, and these books will assist the viewer in understanding the impact that technology has on the content.

BIBLIOGRAPHY

Adams, William B. *Handbook of Motion Picture Production.* New York: John Wiley, 1977.

Anderson, Yvonne. *Making Your Own Animated Movies.* Boston: Little, Brown, 1970.

Arijon, Daniel. *Grammar of the Film Language.* New York: Hastings House, 1976.

Baddeley, W. Hugh. *The Technique of Documentary Film Production.* New York: Hastings House, 1963.

Barsacq, Léon. *Caligari's Cabinet and Other Grand Illusions: A History of Film Design.* Boston: New York Graphic Society, 1976.

Baxter, John. *Stunt: The Story of the Great Movie Stunt Men.* Garden City, N.Y.: Doubleday, 1974.

Bayer, William. *Breaking Through, Selling Out, Dropping Dead.* New York: Macmillan, 1971.

Bobker, Lee R. and Louise Marinis. *Making Movies: From Script to Screen.* New York: Harcourt, Brace, Jovanovich, 1973.

Bowskill, Derek. *All About Cinema.* New York: W. H. Allen, 1976.

Brodbeck, Emil E. *Handbook of Basic Motion Picture Techniques.* Englewood Cliffs, N.J.: Prentice-Hall, 1975.

Brosnan, John. *Movie Magic: The Story of Special Effects in the Cinema.* New York: St. Martin's Press, 1974.

Butler, Ivan. *The Making of Feature Films—A Guide.* Baltimore: Penguin, 1971.

Chase, Donald. *Filmmaking: The Collaborative Art.* Boston: Little, Brown, 1975.

Colman, Hila. *Making Movies: Student Films to Features.* New York: World, 1969.

Corliss, Richard. *Talking Pictures: Screenwriters in the American Cinema.* Woodstock, N.Y.: Overlook Press, 1974.

Costa, Sylvia Allen. *How to Prepare a Production Budget for Film and Video Tape.* Blue Ridge Summit, Penn.: Tab Books, 1975.

Coynik, David. *Movie Making.* Chicago: Loyola University Press, 1974.

Davis, Robert E. *Introduction to Film Making.* Urbana, Ill.: Eric Clearinghouse on Reading and Communication Skills, 1975.

Fadiman, William. *Hollywood Now.* New York: Liveright, 1972.

Froug, William. *The Screenwriter Looks at the Screenwriter.* New York: Macmillan, 1972.

Geduld, Harry M., ed. *Film Makers on Film Making: Statements on Their Art by Thirty Directors.* Bloomington: Indiana University Press, 1969.

______ and Ronald Gottesman. *An Illustrated Glossary of Film Terms.* New York: Holt, Rinehart and Winston, 1973.

Halas, John. *Art in Movement: New Directions in Animation.* New York: Hastings House, 1970.

______. *Visual Scripting.* New York: Hastings House, 1976.

Happé, L. Bernard. *Basic Motion Picture Technology.* New York: Hastings House, 1975.

Hayward, Stan. *Scriptwriting for Animation.* New York: Hastings House, 1977.

Higham, Charles, ed. *Hollywood Cameramen: Sources of Light.* Bloomington: Indiana University Press, 1970.

Hobson, Andrew and Mark Hobson. *Film Animation as Hobby.* New York: Sterling Publishing, 1975.

Horvath, Joan. *Filmmaking for Beginners.* New York: Thomas Nelson, 1974.

Kinsey, Anthony. *How to Make Animated Movies.* New York: Viking, 1970.

Klumph, Inez and Helen Klumph. *Screen Acting.* New York: Falk, 1922.

Lee, Raymond. *Fit for the Chase: Cars and the Movies.* New York: Castle, 1969.

Leese, Elizabeth. *Costume Design in the Movies.* New York: Frederick Ungar, 1977.

Lewis, Jerry. *The Total Film-Maker.* New York: Random House, 1971.

Limbacher, James L. *Four Aspects of the Film.* New York: Brussel and Brussel, 1969.

Linder, Carl. *Filmmaking: A Practical Guide.* Englewood Cliffs, N.J.: Prentice-Hall, 1976.

Lipton, Lenny. *Independent Filmmaking.* San Francisco: Straight Arrow Books, 1972.

______. *The Super 8 Book.* San Francisco: Straight Arrow Books, 1975.

Livingston, Don. *Film and the Director: A Handbook and Guide to Film Making.* New York: Capricorn Books, 1953.

London, Mel. *Getting into Film.* New York: Ballantine Books, 1977.

McClain, Bebe Ferrell. *Super 8 Filmmaking from Scratch.* Englewood Cliffs, N.J.: Prentice-Hall, 1978.

McConathy, Dale and Diana Vreeland. *Hollywood Costume.* New York: Harry N. Abrams, 1976.

Marner, Terence St. John. *Directing Motion Pictures.* New York: A. S. Barnes, 1972.

______ and Michael Stringer. *Film Design.* New York: A. S. Barnes, 1974.

Morella, Joe, Edward Z. Epstein, and Eleanor Clark. *Those Great Movie Ads.* New Rochelle, N.Y.: Arlington House, 1972.

Pate, Michael. *The Film Actor: Acting for Motion Pictures and Television.* New York: A. S. Barnes, 1970.

Petzold, Paul. *All-in-One Movie Book.* New York: Amphoto, 1972.

Quick, John and Tom La Bare. *Handbook of Film Production.* New York: Macmillan, 1972.

Reisz, Karel and Gavin Millar. *The Technique of Film Editing.* New York: Hastings House, 1968.

Reynertson, A. J. *The Work of the Film Director.* New York: Hastings House, 1970.

Rilla, Wolf. *The Writer and the Screen: On Writing for Film and Television.* New York: William Morrow, 1974.

Roberts, Kenneth H. and Winn Sharples, Jr. *A Primer for Film-Making: A Complete Guide to 16mm and 35mm Film Production.* Indianapolis: Bobbs-Merrill, 1971.

Rovin, Jeff. *Movie Special Effects.* New York: A. S. Barnes, 1977.

Scott, Audrey. *I Was a Hollywood Stunt Girl.* Philadelphia: Dorrance, 1969.

Sherman, Eric. *Directing the Film: Film Directors on Their Art.* Boston: Little, Brown, 1976.

______ and Martin Rubin. *The Director's Event: Interviews with Five American Film-Makers.* New York: Atheneum, 1970.

Smallman, Kirk. *Creative Film-Making.* New York: Macmillan, 1969.

Spottiswood, Raymond. *A Grammar of the Film: An Analysis of Film Technique.* Berkeley: University of California Press, 1951.

———. *Film and Its Techniques.* Berkeley: University of California Press, 1966.

Trojanski, John and Louis Rockwood. *Making It Move.* Dayton, Ohio: Pflaum, 1973.

Vale, Eugene. *The Technique of Screenplay Writing: A Book About the Dramatic Structure of Motion Pictures.* New York: Grosset and Dunlap, 1972.

Wise, Arthur and Dereck Ware. *Stunting in the Cinema.* New York: St. Martin's Press, 1973.

Young, Freddie and Paul Petzold. *The Work of the Motion Picture Cameraman.* New York: Hastings House, 1972.

CHAPTER 3
Film Criticism

In the relatively short period—only sixty-odd years—that critics have been writing about movies, a surprisingly large number of different critical approaches have been developed. Some critics approach the appreciation of film from a historical perspective (see chapter 1); others study film's relationship with and impact on society (see chapter 6). Others gain insights by comparing film to other arts, such as painting or music (see chapter 5). But the heart of film criticism lies in the theories of the way the medium works and the way it affects the people watching it. Ever since Vachel Lindsay in 1915 discussed the poetic and architectural qualities of the photoplay, and Hugo Münsterberg, the following year, discussed its psychology and aesthetics, critics have been speculating on film theory. The major critics are clearly international: Siegfried Kracauer is German, Hugo Münsterberg and Rudolf Arnheim are Germans with connections to Harvard, Sergei Eisenstein is Russian, Béla Balázs Hungarian, and André Bazin, Jean Mitry, and Christian Metz are all French.

Genre criticism, a concept borrowed from literary criticism, is another useful approach to organizing our cinematic experiences. Many important critics have discussed movie genres, and clearly the differences between a Western and a gangster film contribute both to our appreciation of the two films and to the ways we respond to them. Therefore, the next chapter is devoted to genre criticism. Since documentaries and experimental films are most often departures from the narrative form common to other genres (it also can be argued that they are individual genres) and both have been influential on all other types of filmmaking, the books on these two film types are discussed in separate parts of chapter 4.

Trying to place the theorists and other critics into schools is a difficult task, for film critics have almost as much independence of mind as do filmmakers, but the reader first coming to film theory may profit from some categorization of the theorists. The categories of J. Dudley Andrew's

The Major Film Theories reduce the major theorists to three excessively general groups, but they do provide a framework for following the development of film theory. Andrew begins with those critics in the formative tradition—Eisenstein, Balázs, and others—who were concerned with the form of the medium and the way that form differed from the forms of other arts and human experiences. He then discusses the realist critics who followed—such as Kracauer and Bazin—who were interested in the way film realistically reflected the society of which it was a part. These critics were influenced by the development of the documentary, and all believed in the political and social power of the medium. Finally, Andrew considers the more recent critics who have striven to develop a theory of film that is not so dependent on other art ideologies. From France has come the impetus for structuralism and semiology. Critics such as Christian Metz have tried to encourage their audience to consider the structure of film. They have demonstrated that film communicates like a language and therefore should be studied like a language, using the techniques of linguistics and the science of signs. Surely not all critics fall into these three traditions, but Andrew's groups do suggest several dominant areas of film thought. The first section of this chapter will discuss the theorists and their books, but the reader should remember that film theory is a difficult subject and should not be approached without a considerable background in films.

Readers who are just beginning to study film may wish to begin with one of the introductions to film discussed later in this chapter. Many of these books are intended as introductions to college courses in film. Some of them contain some film theory, but for the most part this theory is mixed with film analysis and with suggestions on film evaluation.

One of the major forms of film criticism in this country is the review, the essay in a magazine or newspaper intended to help a reader decide whether a particular movie would appeal to him or her. Much of the best writing about movies in America is done by reviewers such as Pauline Kael, Andrew Sarris, and John Simon. Reviewers have been very influential in developing the ways that Americans look at films. In particular, the "auteur" theory, popularized by Sarris, has led to a new way of analyzing the work of the director. Since the purpose of a review is somewhat different form that of film commentary, collections of reviews have been treated in a separate part of this chapter.

Film criticism dates from the end of the first decade of this century when people began to take the medium seriously. The first important American book on film criticism was *The Art of the Moving Picture* by Vachel Lindsay, mentioned above. Lindsay was a well-known poet who, in 1915, published his theory of the function of the photoplay. Working in what would become the formulist tradition, Lindsay defined the movie in terms of both poetry and architecture and held great hope for its future. Hugo Münsterberg, chairman of the philosophy department at Harvard, was interested in the ways that cinema influenced the mind of man, both psychologically and aesthetically. In *The Film: A Psychological Study*, published in 1916, he discussed depth and movement, memory and imagination, the purpose of art, and the method of the photoplay. Another interesting early stage in the development of movie criticism is found in *Let's Go to the Movies* written in 1926 by Iris Barry, who later became director of the film library at the Museum of Modern Art. Her book proposed that movies were an art form and that "going to the pictures is nothing to be ashamed of."

FILM THEORISTS

The three books discussed below lead the reader into the difficulties of film theory. *Film: A Montage of Theories,* edited by Richard Dyer MacCann, is widely regarded as one of the best. Its first unit deals with film as a plastic material and includes essays on the nature of the medium by Sergei Eisenstein and Alfred Hitchcock. Its second unit treats film and the other arts, including poetry, novels, and theatre. The third unit is on the essence of cinema, the fourth on the psychology of the art, and the last on film as an evolving art. Theorists discussed include Vachel Lindsay, Ingmar Bergman, Béla Balázs, and Hugo Mauerhofer.

The second book is *Theories of Film* by Andrew Tudor, sponsored by the British Film Institute. Tudor defines film theory through the major ways of looking at film criticism and of thinking about the medium: realism, auteur, genre, and so forth. He also considers the language of film, and the social context of film. *The Major Film Theories* by J. Dudley Andrew, mentioned earlier in this chapter, is another good introduction to theory in which the author covers the major theorists from Eisenstein to André Bazin to Christian Metz in three broad categories: "the formative tradition," "realist film theory," and "contemporary French film theory."

These three books present overviews of film theory, but the reader who wishes further study of film theory should consult the book-length studies by individual theorists, presented below alphabetically by last name of the author.

Film and Reality by Roy Armes is "an historical survey." Armes begins with film reality: the Lumière brothers, Georges Méliès, Robert Flaherty, the documentaries, Italian neorealism, and *cinéma vérité.* He then considers film illusition with a discussion of D. W. Griffith, the great comedians, the Western, and Alfred Hitchcock. In his last section on film modernism, he considers Expressionism and surrealism.

Film as Art by Rudolf Arnheim is a collection of Arnheim's essays from 1933 to 1957 and combines film theory with a practical study of filmmaking. Arnheim is concerned with defining the difference between the experiences of reality and the experiences of film.

Béla Balázs was a filmmaker—as were many of the better theorists—who wrote as well. *Theory of the Film,* his final work and a summary of his thought, discusses theory and history, the use of the camera, actors' physiognomy (their faces and voices), editing, avant-garde film, sound, color, and comedy.

The man largely responsible for the resurgence of French filmmaking and thoughts about filmmaking following World War II was André Bazin, founding editor of *Cahier du Cinema,* the leading French film journal. *What is Cinema?* is a theory of film that attempts to define the myth of the total cinema. The first volume of this work deals with montage, theater and film, Robert Bresson, Charles Chaplin, painting and cinema; the second volume discusses realism, the Western, and European directors and films.

René Clair, director of *Entr'acte* and *A Nous La Liberté,* was a French filmmaker whose books were a personal theory of film. *Cinema, Yesterday and Today* contains his views of filmmakers such as Eisenstein, D. W. Griffith, Mack Sennett, and Charles Chaplin and on topics such as surrealism, film and theater, comedy, and film and poetry. *Reflections on the Cinema* is Clair's view of the history of film, with chapters on the American film and his thoughts on Hollywood.

Few filmmakers have written more than the Russian Sergei Eisenstein, and few theorists have been more important. *The Film Sense* places an emphasis on the word and the image and includes a bibliography of his writings. *Film Form* discusses the relation between film and the theater, montage, and D. W. Griffith's dependence on the novels of Charles Dickens, with emphasis throughout on the structure of film. In *Film Essays and a Lecture,* he is concerned with the new language of cinema and the lessons film has learned from literature.

In *Theory of Film* Siegfried Kracauer discusses his general theory and his concepts of acting, sound, and music. He includes chapters on different types of films—experimental, documentary, and dramatic—and a chapter on the film and the novel.

Lev Kuleshov was a pioneer Soviet theoretician, director, and teacher who helped Eisenstein develop the theory of montage. In *Kuleshov on Film* his essays range from montage and the Soviet film to D. W. Griffith and Charles Chaplin.

Semiotics is contemporary film criticism that attempts to differentiate itself from literary criticism. Semiologists have attempted to apply to film criticism the objective methods of linguistics and the science of signs. The foremost practitioner of semiotics is Christian Metz. His *Language and Cinema* is a difficult book but one impossible to dismiss, for in it he establishes his theory of semiology. *Film Language* by Metz is on the same theme but easier to read. Other semiologists provide the reader with additional samples of this type of criticism. In *Semiotics of Cinema* Jurij Lotman outlines the Russian thinking on semiology. He discusses the illusion of reality, the shot, filmic narration, montage, time and space, and the problems of the actor. In *The Language and Technique of Film,* Gianfranco Bettetini tries to show that visuals are signs between the sender (the filmmaker and actors) and the viewer. In *Signs and Meaning in the Cinema* Peter Wollen presents a retrospective look at the theories of Eisenstein and the auteur theory and an in depth study of semiology.

In returning to the alphabetical listing of the non-semilogists, the reader will find Ivor Montagu, a film personality associated with Eisenstein. His theory is solid and useful, but compared to the semiologists he is a lightweight. His *Film World* discusses film as science (sound and color), film as art (shot and rhythm), film as commodity (scale and costs), and film as vehicle (realism and range).

Vladimir Nilsen is a Russian cameraman who analyzes the process of making films visual in *The Cinema as a Graphic Art.* He claims that the book is "a theory of representation in the cinema," but his work is not as important as that of the other Russians.

V. I. Pudovkin developed the theory of montage along with Eisenstein and Kuleshov, and editing remained the central emphasis of his theory. His two volume *Film Technique and Film Acting* was first published in 1927 and 1937 and is now available in a single volume translated by Ivor Montague. The focus of the book is the scenario, the director, and the actor.

In *The Shadow of an Airplane Climbs the Empire State Building,* Parker Tyler creates what he calls "a world theory of film." He deals with the relation between art and life as well as with time and space in film and in reality and includes a unit on film as a self-conscious art.

FILM CRITICS AND ANALYSTS

Many fine books on film cannot properly be considered theory since their goal is to foster intelligent viewing rather than to speculate on the nature of the medium. Surely it would be difficult to analyze a film or to lead a reader into a more educated viewing of the film without a theoretical base, but these books have not placed an emphasis on that base. The books of this type comment upon and analyze films, and many of them have become valuable guides to watching movies. Of course, many other books accomplish the same goal and are discussed in other chapters in this guide. This section, like that on film theorists, is arranged alphabetically by author's last name. Books by one or two authors are discussed first and anthologies are considered last.

With *The World in a Frame* Leo Braudy has emerged as one of the important contemporary film critics. This book is addressed to "what we see in films," to "what films are like in the experience of the audience and how they achieve those effects." In this connection Braudy discusses the varieties of visual coherence, genre, and acting and characterization.

Theory of Film Practice is a difficult, theoretical book by Noël Burch, but it is of considerable value for those who wish to delve into the depths of theory. It deals with the basic elements of space, time, and editing as well as with dialectics and structure.

The World Viewed by Stanley Cavell claims to be "reflections on the ontology of film." Cavell includes several chapters on the medium—color, sound, and photography—and others on audience, actors, and stars. Most of the book, however, is devoted to the study of the myths of films.

Charles Champlin is a renowned critic and host of television movie specials. His book *The Flicks: Or Whatever Happened to Andy Hardy* covers thirty years of films from the sweetness and simplicity of Andy Hardy to the violence and complexity of *Who's Afraid of Virginia Woolf?* and *Midnight Cowboy.*

Bosley Crowther has been a critic for the New York *Times,* but *Vintage Films* is his own survey of important films from *Broadway Melody* (1929) to *The Godfather* (1972). He has sought to identify "breakthroughs"—films that "opened new ground" in technique, dramatic subjects or the social aspects of their subjects.

Anatomy of Film by Bernard F. Dick "examines the exterior and interior of the narrative film—its outer form and its inner structure." Dick covers film language, editing, literary devices, filmic subtexts, and film authorship.

Two books by Raymond Durgnat warrant mention. *Films and Feelings* contains excellent essays on topics such as Expressionism in film and poetry in film. *Durgnat on Film* reproduces some parts of his earlier books and includes essays on auteurs, *The Cabinet of Dr. Caligari,* and poetry and film.

Negative Space by Manny Farber is a collection of Farber's essays on directors Howard Hawks, John Huston, Val Lewton, Frank Capra, Don Siegel, Samuel Fuller, and Preston Sturges; on films including *The Third Man, Detective Story,* and *In the Street;* and on general topics such as the underground film and the decline of the actor. The book explores the importance of negative space, "the command of experience which an artist can set resonating within a film . . . [a] sense of terrain created partly by the audience's imagination and partly by camera-actors-director."

In *Godard and Others,* Louis D. Giannetti concentrates on Jean-Luc Godard, but the theory that underlies this book makes it valuable to readers interested in directors in general. Giannetti discusses the aesthetics of the mobile cameras, cinematic metaphors, and the narrative devices of the plotless film.

The Art of the American Film, 1900-1971 by Charles Higham is a combination of history and aesthetics. Arranged chronologically, the book covers the silent era, the talkies, the 1940s and after, and the new techniques and new directors of contemporary film. Higham uses history to demonstrate his thesis that a film is the result of the collaboration of many artists, a business that results in art.

Scrutiny of the Cinema is a reprint of a 1932 book by William Hunter. It gives period reviews of Fritz Lang, Sergei Eisenstein, the avant-garde, René Clair, G. W. Pabst, Charles Chaplin, and V. I. Pudovkin.

One of the more interesting recent critical studies is *Mindscreen* by Bruce F. Kawin. Kawin is one of the few critics to attempt to write about the way films try to become the mind's eye, to enter the characters' inner space. Kawin concentrates on the first person films of Bergman and Godard.

The Origins of American Film Criticism, 1909-1939 is a reprint of a dissertation by Myron Osborn Lounsbury. It outlines the development of film criticism from Frank Wood and Vachel Lindsay to Lewis Jacobs.

Two separate but related critical problems are considered in *Authorship and Narrative in the Cinema* by William Luhr and Peter Lehman. Lehman's concern is authorship and Luhr's is narrative; each discusses his problem in depth and with intelligence. They illustrate their points with case studies of *The Man Who Shot Liberty Valance, The Searchers,* and *Dr. Jekyll and Mr. Hyde.* Lehman considers the questions of what a film is and who is responsible for it and seeks his answers in the career of John Ford. Luhr considers the question of how narrative works in fiction film and illustrates his points by discussing cinematic adaptations of the literature of Robert Louis Stevenson.

The Film and the Public by Roger Manvell contains commentary on the silent film, sound, the industry, cinema and society, and television and film. One chapter includes analysis of films, such as *Siegfried, Greed, Mother, Citizen Kane* and *The Informer.*

The Impact of Film by Roy Paul Madsen has a similar focus. Madsen includes chapters on filmic concepts: the viewer, language, grammar, syntax, sound, video, animation, and special effects; on the dramatic structrue of film, and the problems of translating novels and plays into film; and on the documentary (including television commercials) and the use of film in education. He is especially interested in "how ideas are communicated through cinema and television."

Film/Cinema/Movie by Gerald Mast is one of the more important critical books to come out recently. Mast is concerned with the relation of the arts to "natural and human experience" and with "the particular pleasures and effects of the cinematic art."

The Spoken Seen: Film and the Romantic Imagination by Frank D. McConnell is made up of interesting personal essays on aesthetics and theory of film. He covers the early development of the medium and the relation of the aesthetics of the medium to other art forms. He then goes on to discuss the reality of film, its language, its politics, its genres, and its use of personality.

William S. Pechter's *Twenty-four Times a Second* is a collection of his essays on films and filmmakers. He includes a piece on Hollywood in 1960, discussions of violence in the films and the anti-Western, analysis of the work of Frank Capra and Sergei Eisenstein, and comments on the criticism by James Agee. His final chapter is entitled "Toward Film Appreciation."

"Understanding and judging the movies" is the goal of *Film as Film* by V. F. Perkins. Perkins discusses early criticism, the importance of technical knowledge and the importance of directors in attempting to develop criteria which will aid in evaluating movies.

The Compound Cinema is a collection of essays by the remarkable Marxist critic, Harry Alan Potamkin, who died in 1933 while still in his thirties. The book deals with film as art and with film and society.

Paul Rotha is one of the few indispensable critics of film, and his *Rotha on the Film* has now been reprinted. He begins with general essays on the art form, with a special emphasis on Douglas Fairbanks, Sr., Sergei Eisenstein, and Charles Chaplin. He includes samples of his reviews, an essay on the documentary, and another on the problems and future of British films.

Another collection of essays is *Mastering the Film and Other Essays* by Charles Thomas Samuels. This collection, put together after Samuels' early death, includes his comments on directors (Carol Reed, Jean Renoir, Alfred Hitchcock, and Federico Fellini) and on films (*Blow-up, Bonnie and Clyde,* and *Clockwork Orange*).

The Primal Screen is a collection of essays from another important critic, Andrew Sarris. Part one contains several of his critical credos on topics such as the auteur theory, the American Film Institute, and film education. Part two deals with the personal styles of directors and actors (John Ford and James Stewart especially). Part three is on genres (musical, spectacular, comedy, science fiction, and Western). Part four deals with political films, such as *Z* and *Catch 22.* The last part consists of obituaries for Josef von Sternberg, Judy Garland, and Harold Lloyd.

Richard Schickel's *The History of an Art and an Institution* is a scholarly analysis of the various forces trying to influence the types of movies made. The publicity for the book claims that its "focus is on the constant interplay among the technical, entrepreneurial, and aesthetic forces that have created the movies as they are."

Film: The Medium and the Maker by James F. Scott explains the differences between the auteur theory and the cooperative art theory. Then he explores the basic analytical devices of film: composition, lighting, sound, story and script, acting, staging, and editing.

Ralph Stephenson and Jean R. Debrix have collaborated on *The Cinema as Art.* Trying to analyze the art of film, they discuss film's depiction of space, its use of time, and its use of time and space. They then discuss film's surface reality (soft focus, double exposures, and related subjects) and the role of sound in film. They are especially interested in the way that film relates, or does not relate, to reality and to other art forms.

Movie Man by David Thomson presents a theory of a visual society and the role of film in it; he is especially interested in the way humans are shaped by the movies they watch. He comments on many directors, including Joseph Losey, Fritz Lang, Howard Hawks, and Otto Preminger, and on many films.

Many of the best critical studies are anthologies of essays on different aspects of film study. *Film as Film: Critical Responses to Film Art* by Joy Gould Boyum and Adrienne Scott is such a book. Part one deals with film theory: film as art and film criticism; part two deals with the theory in practice. In this part are journal reviews of twenty-five films including *Accident, The Birds, Bonnie and Clyde, Citizen Kane, Dr. Strangelove, The Graduate, High Noon, A Night at the Opera, On the Waterfront, Stagecoach*, and *The Treasure of the Sierra Madre*.

Celluloid and Symbols, edited by John C. Cooper and Carl Skrade, is an interesting collection of essays on the general topic of theology in film. The focus in the essays is on the search for old symbols for God and man in a contemporary medium. The essays are by theologians, such as Harvey Cox, and film people, such as Anthony Schillaci.

Lewis Jacobs has edited two important anthologies. The first, *The Emergence of Film Art*, deals primarily with film history from the beginning through the late 1960s. Jacobs' emphasis here is on the development of the art form, with most of his essays by film scholars, and a few by film practitioners. *The Movies as Medium* deals more with the aesthetics of film. In the beginning of the book Jacobs quotes thirty-six directors as they discuss their aims and attitudes, and he himself discusses the raw materials of film. He then presents selected essays from others who discuss movement, time and space, color, and sound.

Movies and Methods, edited by Bill Nichols, is one of the more useful recent anthologies. Part one contains essays of contextual criticism (political, generic, and feminist) and part two articles on film theory and structuralism—semiology. Some of his essays are by Susan Sontag, André Bazin, François Truffaut, and Andrew Sarris.

The Movies on Trial, edited by William J. Perlman, is a 1936 collection of essays expressing "the views and opinions of outstanding personalities about screen entertainment past and present." Authors include E. G. Robinson, William Lyon Phelps, and Upton Sinclair.

W. R. Robinson's book *Man and the Movies* is unique in that it presents film from the point of view of the humanities. The articles in the collection are written by people not normally considered to be film scholars: Martin C. Battestin (literary scholar), Larry McMurtry (novelist), R. H. W. Dillard (literary scholar), O. B. Hardison (scholar and director of the Folger Shakespeare Library), Walter Korte (literary scholar), Richard Wilbur (poet), and

George Garrett (novelist). The articles are first-rate film criticism and cover general topics such as the art, the artist, and personal encounters with the medium.

Film: An Anthology, edited by Daniel Talbot, is an eclectic collection of essays on the aesthetics and history of film. Part one deals with the aesthetics of film, social commentary, and analysis; part two with theory and technique; and part three with history and personal observations on the medium. Authors range from Allardyce Nicoll, Parker Tyler, and Jean Cocteau to Lewis Jacobs.

REVIEWERS

A special type of film critic is the reviewer. Reviews serve a different purpose from the close critical analysis found in scholarly journals and books, but several reviewers have become the best known writers on film in America, and their reviews published in book form sometimes become best sellers.

Several books will lead the reader to groups of critics: *Nine American Film Critics* by Edward Murray is an analysis of the writing of some of the best-known reviewers, including Andrew Sarris, Pauline Kael, and John Simon.

A reference book that will aid the reader in locating reviews in the anthologies of criticism discussed in this reference guide is *Film Criticism: An Index to Critics' Anthologies* by Richard Heinzkill. Heinzkill has indexed the collections of twenty-seven reviewer/critics so that the reader can quickly locate all the reviews on a particular film by these critics.

Garbo and the Night Watchmen is an anthology of criticism edited by Alistair Cooke, who was himself a writer about films before he began introducing them on television. This book first came out in 1937 and is a collection of reviews by both British and American reviewers from both newspapers and magazines. Included in the book is a special section on *Modern Times.*

An annual collection of film reviews is *Film Review,* edited by F. Maurice Speed. Published yearly since 1944, it contains essays on the important events and developments during the past year, reviews of film books, and an overview of the films released during the year.

Many reviews have collected their reviews into single volumes: *A Year in the Dark* is a "year in the life of a film writer, 1968-69," which author-critic Renata Adler spent as a reviewer for *The New York Times.* Although this was a rather weak year for American films, the volume does include reviews of *Planet of the Apes, 2001, Rosemary's Baby,* and *Petulia.*

James Agee was perhaps best known for his creative fiction and drama, but he was most comfortable writing movie reviews. *Agee on Film* is a two-volume collection of reviews and scripts. Volume one contains the reviews he wrote for *The Nation* and *Time,* an important essay on comedy, and another on John Huston. Volume two contains the scripts he wrote for *Noa-Noa, The African Queen, The Night of the Hunter, The Bride Comes to Yellow Sky*, and *The Blue Hotel*.

Hollis Alpert, now the editor of *American Film,* earned that post in part by writing reviews. *The Dreams and the Dreamers* is a collection of essays on diverse subjects. Some essays are on directors, such as Alfred Hitchcock and Ingmar Bergman; some are on actors, such as Marlon Brando and Marilyn Monroe; others are on film and theater, the Italian filmmakers, and other topics.

Marilyn Beck has been a popular Hollywood gossip columnist for many years. In *Marilyn Beck's Hollywood* she gives her impressions of Hollywood and Hollywood people. While she does not write reviews, her columns on sex, drugs, violence, television, and the new morality offer another view of movies.

Now a widely respected director, Peter Bogdanovich began as a movie critic. *Pieces of Time* reprints his essays on actors (such as Humphrey Bogart, Cary Grant, James Cagney, John Wayne), and on directors (such as John Ford and Frank Capra). Also included are essays on his favorite films, sex and violence, and other topics. His ideas are challenging and often fascinating.

The Private Eye, The Cowboy, and The Very Naked Girl is a collection of reviews by Judith Crist from 1963 to 1967. Films from *Cleopatra* to *Bonnie and Clyde* are covered.

The Film Criticism of Otis Ferguson contains his collected essays from 1934 to 1941. His reviews cover the films released during this period, and he also includes a general essay on Hollywood as the "promissory" land.

Penelope Gilliatt has collected her reviews in *Unholy Fools.* The book contains essays on directors from Jacques Tati to Ingmar Bergman.

Like James Agee, Graham Greene achieved his primary reputation as a creative writer, but he also left film reviews that continue to interest readers and movie fans. *The Pleasure-Dome* is a collection of his reviews and criticism from 1935 to 1940.

Pauline Kael is perhaps the best-known reviewer in America today. Her widely respected opinions have appeared primarily in the *New Yorker.* She has published four collections of reviews: *I Lost It at the Movies, Kiss Kiss Bang Bang, Going Steady,* and *Deeper into Movies.* Each collection contains her reviews and an essay or two on special topics, such as fantasy and art movies and "Trash, Art, and the Movies."

Stanley Kauffmann has reviewed film for the *New York Times,* the *New American Review,* and the *New Republic.* His reviews have been collected into three books: *A World on Film, Figures of Light,* and *Living Images.*

Pare Lorentz is a director who writes. Known primarily for his documentary films, Lorentz also had a career as a movie reviewer, and *Lorentz on Film* is a collection of ninety-nine of his best reviews from 1927 to 1941. Many of his reviews include discussion of actors and production as well as of the films themselves.

Dwight Macdonald became respected as the curmudgeon of the reviewers for his attacks on popular films and his defense of serious cinema. *On Movies* is a collection of his essays on such widely disparate topics as D. W. Griffith and Doris Day.

The chief spokesman for independent filmmakers and experimental films has been Jonas Mekas. *Movie Journal* is a collection of his writing for *The Village Voice* at a time when the *Voice* was one of the few national publications taking note of experimental films. This book then became a history of the rise of the new American cinema.

Rex Reed is perhaps best known for his interviews with stars, but his *Big Screen, Little Screen* contains his reviews from *Women's Wear Daily*. The reviews cover the year 1968-1969 and, as the title suggests, both television and the movies are included.

Confessions of a Cultist: On the Cinema, 1955-1969 is a selection of the reviews of Andrew Sarris. There is an interesting introduction about Sarris' early writings for *Film Culture* and his development as a critic. Most of the articles are reviews of films, with a concentration on the mid-1960s, but some of them deal with specific topics such as the spaghetti Westerns.

Second Sight contains the reviews Richard Schickel wrote for *Life* from 1965 until 1970. This was an important period for films and the films reviewed include *Bonnie and Clyde*, *The Graduate*, and *Midnight Cowboy*.

Dwight Macdonald has been succeeded as curmudgeon by John Simon, and *Private Screenings* is a collection of Simon's reviews from 1963 through 1966. The introduction is his critical credo, a statement of his view of his craft.

BOOKS OF INTRODUCTION

For the most part, introductions to film are designed as textbooks. They are intended as the first books on film to be read by students and become, therefore, guides to a basic appreciation of the medium. The fact, however, that a book is an introduction to film does not mean that it is itself elementary; in fact, some of the introductions contain important film criticism. Most of the introductions are written for a college audience; but a few secondary-level textbooks have been included in this section, with an indication that the general reader may find their style rather simplistic.

These introductions discussed below are arranged alphabetically by last name of the author or editor. They have been divided into books by a single writer and anthologies by several writers.

In the Dark by Richard Meran Barsam claims to be "a primer for the movies." His focus is on history, production, and criticism of movies and his goal to guide the reader "to a deeper appreciation of the technical and esthetic aspects of the film." He includes detailed criticism of *The Grapes of Wrath* and *Louisiana Story.*

Critical Focus: An Introduction to Film is written by Richard Blumenberg, a scholar, teacher, and part-time filmmaker. This book gives detailed analysis of the process of making and watching movies. Part one is an introduction to film, part two deals with the narrative film, part three with the documentary, and part four with the experimental film.

Elements of Film by Lee R. Bobker has become one of the most highly respected of the introductions. Bobker's units are on the story, the image, sound, editing, the director, the actor, and film criticism.

Joseph M.Boggs' *The Art of Watching Films* is a handbook for the "analytical study of film." Boggs discusses the dramatic elements of the film (plot, action, and so on), the visual elements (editing and lighting), and the role of sound, music, acting, and direction. This is a good recent addition to the field of introductions.

Film Art: An Introduction by David Bordwell and Kristin Thompson treats film production and film history, and focuses on film form, style, and criticism. The authors deal with narrative and non-narrative film forms and provide close analysis of films such as *Citizen Kane* and *His Girl Friday.*

Film Appreciation by Allan Casebier opens with a discussion of the medium: its visual elements, sound effects, and audience and goes on to discuss cinema's power to portray life, with an emphasis on the old question of the relation between reality and art. Casebier also considers different types of film criticism.

Film: Real to Reel by David Coynik is a teaching text. It is undistinguished but satisfactory and includes chapters on the shot, motion, editing, rhythm, lights, color, sound, the director, genre, documentaries, animation, "now films," and filmmaking.

In *Film: Encounter* we have a different sort of introduction. Hector Currie and Donald Staples ask us to encounter films in a book that portrays films visually rather than in words. Through stills, frame enlargements, and brief quotations the reader is invited to experience film.

Film and the Critical Eye introduces the reader to film through analysis of important films. Dennis DeNitto and William Hermon begin with an introduction to film language and then analyze fourteen films, including *The Gold Rush* and *The Last Laugh.*

A Discovery of Cinema is a British entry into the field of introductions. By Thorold Dickinson, the book begins with a brief introduction for teachers and then proceeds to discuss three historical phases of cinema: the silent film, the early sound film, and the modern sound film. This is a solid book that is historically oriented.

Film: An Introduction by John Fell opens with a discussion of film theory and language, then presents the technical side of filmmaking in simplified fashion, and finally goes on to discuss the nature of film criticism and the future of film.

The Moving Image is a fine book by Robert Gessner that begins with the concept of literary criticism and then shows how this is adapted to film criticism. It is a guide to cinematic literacy through its discussion of conflict, character, editing and shots, manipulation of time and space, and sound.

One of the most highly regarded introductions is *Understanding Movies* by Louis D. Giannetti. This well-illustrated book provides a working knowledge of the picture, movement, editing, sound, the relation between film and drama and literature, and film theory.

Despite its trendy title, *Into Film* by Laurence Goldstein and Jay Kaufman is a solid introduction that describes the experience of directors, writers, cameramen, sound men, and editors; in other words, it concentrates on the process of making a movie. In one sense this is a guide to film production, but it does provide the critic with the technical tools needed for the art of criticism. The emphasis is on frame-by-frame analysis of the films.

The Rhetoric of Film is a book designed to apply some of the techniques of freshman English courses to film criticism. John Harrington discusses recording visual reality, point of view, theme and unity, structure and organization, rhythm and continuity, and extended rhetoric such as metaphors.

After a decade of use *The Film Experience* remains one of the more highly regarded introductions. Authors Roy Huss and Norman Silverstein discuss continuity, rhythm, structure, image, and point of view.

The Celluloid Literature is another book intended to appeal to English teachers. William Jinks discusses film as language, point of view, structure, sound, and film criticism, as well as the relation between film and literature.

The title of Lincoln Johnson's book, *Film: Space, Time, Light and Sound* clearly indicates the focus of the content. In addition, Johnson covers movement, modes, genre, and filmmakers.

Understanding the Film by Ron Johnson and Jan Bone is a high school introduction (many of the books in this section would be well-suited to use in high school classes, but some are specifically aimed at that level). Johnson and Bone discuss viewing the film, perceiving the film, the language of film, script to film (including a close analysis of *The Sting*), evaluating the film, and great directors and their films. Overall, this book presents an intelligent approach to the beginning of film study.

Close-Up by Marsha Kinder and Beverley Houston is *A Critical Perspective on Film* with close analysis of individual films. Units include the silent cinema, technology and illusion, documentaries, realism, filmmaking in the 1960s, myth in the movies, and politics in films.

Movies in America is another of the highly respected high school introductions. By William Kuhns, this book is intended to increase the students' understanding of the medium and the relation between the films and their historical context. The book is historically oriented, but special chapters on the people in films, genres, and other topics interrupt the chronological pattern.

Film: The Creative Process claims to be "The search for an audio-visual language and structure." John Howard Lawson's book is part history, part analysis of films, and part theory. He includes chapters on the silent film, sound, language, theory, and structure.

Reflections on the Screen by George W. Linden is an introduction for people serious about film. Linden discusses film and drama, film and novels and narration, film and reality, film and society, and film form.

Another basic introduction is *The Art of the Film* by Ernest Lindgren. Lindgren discusses the mechanics and techniques of film (including fiction films, editing, sound, cameramen, music, and acting) and the purpose and form of criticism.

Kenneth Macgowan's *Behind the Screen* presents the history and techniques of the movies. He discusses the mass art for a mass audience, beginning with the innovation and inventions of the early silent period, the influence of D. W. Griffith, foreign directors, and the coming of sound. In the modern period he covers the studios, censorship, the director's role, and new directions.

The Living Screen by Roger Manvell provides "background to the film and television." Manvell has designed the book to answer the questions of what a film is, how it gets made or shown, and whether it was good. He had chapters on genre and film as art.

How to Read a Film by James Monaco has in the past two years become an important introduction. He discusses film as art, technology, the language of film, the shape of film history, film theory, and film and other electronic media.

A rather unusual introduction to film is *Moviemaking Illustrated: The Comicbook Filmbook* by James Morrow and Murray Suid. The authors approach film through its similarities with comic books. By demonstrating the use of motion, shots, and subject selection in comic books, they intend to show readers how a film works. They discuss stories, shots, cuts, sounds, and actors.

Film: The Creative Eye by David A. Sohn is one of the few books to introduce film through the study of short films. He looks carefully at some of the shorts distributed by Pyramid Films and introduces the reader to cinematic concepts through these films.

The Film Idea by Stanley J. Solomon begins with a discussion of the nature of the narrative film. It next discusses the development of film form from a historical perspective, and closes with an analysis of film theory and aesthetics: shots, movement, editing, and structure.

Cecile Starr characterizes her book, *Discovering the Movies,* as "an illustrated introduction to the motion pictures." She discusses three types of film: story films, reality films, and fantasy films.

Cinematics by Paul Weiss is an introduction with a difference. He treats film as an art form and compares it with other arts. He opens with a discussion of the art of film in which he presents general theory and analyzes the contributions of the script, actors, directors, and others. In a philosophical interlude in the middle of the book, he discusses appearance and reality in film, and concludes with a section on films with a purpose, such as documentaries and experimental films.

Cinema by Thomas Wiseman is a popular introduction without too much depth, but it is of value to a reader who wants his or her introduction in small doses.

A number of anthologies also serve as introductions to film. The purpose of *The Art of Cinema,* edited by George Amberg, is to define the art of the medium. Amberg has included six essays: two by Myra Deren on the use of cinema to shape reality, one by Hugo Mauerhofer on the psychology of the film experience, and others by Herbert Reed, Vernon Young, and Amberg himself on film aesthetics.

Crossroads to the Cinema, edited by Douglas Brode, is a collection of essays on topics that might be of interest to the teacher. He covers the movie medium, the makeup of the movies, film and other arts, genre (Western, gangster, monster, musical, comedy and spectacular), and themes, trends, and transitions.

Awake in the Dark, edited by David Denby, begins with essays by older critics (such as Vachel Lindsay and James Agee) in defense of a popular new art form. Denby also includes essays on film as a high form of art, critical methods, genres (comedy, Western, film noir), directors, performers, and entertainment.

Sharon Feyen and Donald Wigal have edited a volume of essays designed for teachers, *Screen Experience: An Approach to Film.* This anthology provides an introduction to film and essays on literary adaptations, forms of film (shorts, Westerns, comedies, and others), the art of film, film programming, and practical information needed in the classroom.

One of the standard books on film is Lewis Jacobs' anthology, *Introduction to the Art of the Movies.* Described as "an anthology of ideas on the nature of movie art," the book is a collection of important essays on the art of the medium that demonstrate the development of cinematic thinking decade by decade.

Film by Allen and Linda Kirschner is a series of "readings in mass media." The essays discuss form and technique of film, its audience and its effect, and critics and criticism. A highlight is the critics' discussion of their craft and of the nature and function of the art form.

One of the finest of the anthologies is *Film Theory and Criticism,* edited by Gerald Mast and Marshall Cohen. The editors have included essays on reality, language, theory, literature and film, genre, artists, and audience. No anthology can be complete, but the interesting selection of material in this anthology constitutes one of the best introductions to the medium.

Cecile Starr has edited a volume for teachers and librarians called *Ideas on Film.* The book is a little dated now, but it contains essays on the general ideas of film, production, audience, children as audience, classroom films, and reviews of films for the classroom.

David Manning White and Richard Averson have edited a book focusing on the role of film and television in society. *Sight, Sound, and Society* discusses audiences of the screen, the aesthetics of the media, and the movies as a business and controller of people.

BIBLIOGRAPHY

Adler, Renata. *A Year in the Dark: Journal of a Film Critic, 1968-1969.* New York: Berkley Medallion Books, 1969.

Agee, James. *Agee on Film.* 2 vols. New York: Grosset and Dunlap, 1969.

Alpert, Hollis. *The Dreams and the Dreamers.* New York: Macmillan, 1962.

Amberg, George, ed. *The Art of Cinema: Selected Essays.* New York: Arno, 1972.

Andrew, J. Dudley. *The Major Film Theories.* New York: Oxford University Press, 1976.

Armes, Roy. *Film and Reality: An Historical Survey.* Baltimore: Penguin, 1974.

Arnheim, Rudolf. *Film as Art.* Berkeley: University of California Press, 1967.

Balázs, Béla. *Theory of the Film: Character and Growth of a New Art.* Translated by Edith Bone. New York: Dover, 1970.

Barry, Iris. *Let's Go to the Movies.* New York: Payson and Clarke, 1926.

Barsam, Richard Meran. *In the Dark.* New York: Viking, 1977.

Bazin, André. *What is Cinema?* 2 vols. Translated by Hugh Gray. Berkeley: University of California Press, 1967.

Beck, Marilyn. *Marilyn Beck's Hollywood.* New York: Hawthorn, 1973.

Bettetini, Gianfranco. *The Language and Technique of Film.* Paris: Mouton, 1973.

Blumenberg, Richard. *Critical Focus: An Introduction to Film.* Belmont, Calif.: Wadsworth Publishing, 1975.

Bobker, Lee R. *Elements of Film.* New York: Harcourt, Brace, and World, 1974.

Bogdanovich, Peter. *Pieces of Time: Peter Bogdanovich on the Movies.* New York: Arbor House, 1973.

Boggs, Joseph M. *The Art of Watching Films.* Menlo Park, Calif.: The Benjamin/Cummings Publishing Co., 1978.

Bordwell, David and Kristin Thompson. *Film Art: An Introduction.* Reading, Mass.: Addison-Wesley Publishing, 1979.

Boyum, Joy Gould, and Adrienne Scott. *Film as Film: Critical Responses to Film Art.* Boston: Allyn and Bacon, 1971.

Braudy, Leo. *The World in a Frame: What We See in Films.* Garden City, N.Y.: Doubleday, 1976.

Brode, Douglas, ed. *Crossroads to the Cinema.* Boston: Holbrook Press, 1975.

Burch, Noël. *Theory of Film Practice.* Translated by Helen R. Lane. New York: Praeger, 1973.

Casebier, Allan. *Film Appreciation.* New York: Harcourt Brace Jovanovich, 1976.

Cavell, Stanley. *The World Viewed: Reflections on the Ontology of Film.* New York: Viking, 1971.

Champlin, Charles. *The Flicks: Or Whatever Happened to Andy Hardy.* Pasadena, Calif.: Ward Richie, 1977.

Clair, René. *Cinema, Yesterday and Today.* Translated by Stanley Appelbaum. New York: Dover, 1972.

______. *Reflections on the Cinema.* Translated by Vera Traill. London: William Kimber, 1953.

Cooke, Alistair, ed. *Garbo and the Night Watchmen: A Selection Made in 1937 from the Writings of British and American Film Critics.* London: Secker and Warburg, 1971.

Cooper, John C. and Carl Skrade, eds. *Celluloid and Symbols.* Philadelphia: Fortress Press, 1970.

Coynik, David. *Film: Real to Reel.* Evanston, Ill.: McDougal, Littell, 1976.

Crist, Judith. *The Private Eye, The Cowboy, and The Very Naked Girl: Movies from Cleo to Clyde.* New York: Holt, Rinehart and Winston, 1967, 1968.

Crowther, Bosley. *Vintage Films.* New York: G. P. Putnam's Sons, 1977.

Currie, Hector and Donald Staples. *Film: Encounter.* Dayton, Ohio: Pflaum, 1973.

Denby, David, ed. *Awake in the Dark.* New York: Vintage Books, 1977.

DeNitto, Dennis, and William Hermon. *Film and the Critical Eye.* New York: Macmillan, 1975.

Dick, Bernard F. *Anatomy of Film.* New York: St. Martin's Press, 1978.

Dickinson, Thorold. *A Discovery of Cinema.* London: Oxford University Press, 1971.

Durgnat, Raymond. *Durgnat on Film.* London: Faber and Faber, 1976.

______. *Films and Feelings.* Cambridge, Mass.: MIT Press, 1967.

Eisenstein, Sergei. *Film Essays and a Lecture.* New York: Praeger, 1970.

______. *Film Form: Essays in Film Theory.* Translated by Jay Leyda. London: Dennis Dobson, 1963.

______. *The Film Sense.* Translated and edited by Jay Leyda. New York: Harcourt, Brace, and World, 1947.

Farber, Manny. *Negative Space: Manny Farber on the Movies.* New York: Praeger, 1971.

Fell, John L. *Film: An Introduction.* New York: Praeger, 1975.

Ferguson, Otis. *The Film Criticism of Otis Ferguson.* Philadelphia: Temple University Press, 1971.

Feyen, Sharon, and Donald Wigal, eds. *Screen Experience: An Approach to Film.* Dayton, Ohio: Pflaum, 1969.

Gessner, Robert. *The Moving Image: A Guide to Cinematic Literacy.* New York: E. P. Dutton, 1968.

Giannetti, Louis D. *Godard and Others: Essays in Film Form.* Rutherford, N.J.: Fairleigh Dickinson University Press, 1975.

______. *Understanding Movies.* Englewood Cliffs, N.J.: Prentice-Hall, 1976.

Gilliatt, Penelope. *Unholy Fools, Wits, Comics, Disturbers of the Peace.* New York: Viking Press, 1960-1973.

Goldstein, Laurence, and Jay Kaufman. *Into Film.* New York: E. P. Dutton, 1976.

Greene, Graham. *The Pleasure-Dome: The Collected Film Criticism of Graham Greene.* London: Secker and Warburg, 1972.

Harrington, John. *The Rhetoric of Film.* New York: Holt, Rinehart and Winston, 1973.

Heinzkill, Richard. *Film Criticism: An Index to Critics' Anthologies.* Metuchen, N.J.: Scarecrow, 1975.

Higham, Charles. *The Art of the American Film, 1900-1971.* Garden City, N.Y.: Doubleday, 1973.

Hunter, William. *Scrutiny of the Cinema.* New York: Arno, 1972.

Huss, Roy, and Norman Silverstein. *The Film Experience.* New York: Harper and Row, 1968.

Jacobs, Lewis, ed. *The Emergence of Film Art: The Evolution and Development of the Motion Picture as an Art from 1900 to the Present.* New York: Hopkins and Blake, 1969.

______, ed. *Introduction to the Art of the Movies: An Anthology of Ideas on the Nature of Movie Art.* New York: Noonday Press, 1960.

______, ed. *The Movies as Medium.* New York: Farrar, Straus and Giroux, 1970.

Jinks, William. *The Celluloid Literature: Film in the Humanities.* Beverly Hills, Calif.: Glencoe, 1974.

Johnson, Lincoln. *Film: Space, Time, Light and Sound.* New York: Holt, Rinehart and Winston, 1974.

Johnson, Ron, and Jan Bone. *Understanding the Film.* Skokie, Ill.: National Textbook Co., 1976.

Kael, Pauline. *Deeper into Movies.* Boston: Little, Brown, 1973.

______. *Going Steady.* New York: Bantam, 1970.

______. *I Lost It at the Movies.* New York: Bantam, 1965.

______. *Kiss Kiss Bang Bang.* New York: Bantam, 1968.

Kauffmann, Stanley. *Figures of Light: Film Criticism and Comment.* New York: Harper and Row, 1971.

______. *Living Images: Film Comment and Criticism.* New York: Harper and Row, 1970-75.

______. *A World on Film: Criticism and Comment.* New York: Dell, 1966.

Kawin, Bruce F. *Mindscreen.* Princeton: Princeton University Press, 1978.

Kinder, Marsha, and Beverley Houston. *Close-Up: A Critical Perspective on Film.* New York: Harcourt Brace Jovanovich, 1972.

Kirschner, Allen, and Linda Kirschner, eds. *Film: Readings in the Mass Media.* New York: Odyssey Press, 1971.

Kracauer, Siegfried. *Theory of Film: The Redemption of Physical Reality.* New York: Oxford University Press, 1960.

Kuhns, William. *Movies in America.* Dayton, Ohio: Pflaum, 1972.

Kuleshov, Lev. *Kuleshov on Film.* Translated by Ronald Leuaco. Berkeley: University of California Press, 1974.

Lawson, John Howard. *Film: The Creative Process.* New York: Hill and Wang, 1967.

Linden, George W. *Reflections on the Screen.* Belmont, Calif.: Wadsworth, 1970.

Lindgren, Ernest. *The Art of the Film: An Introduction to Film Appreciation.* New York: Macmillan, 1963.

Lindsay, Vachel. *The Art of the Moving Picture.* New York: Liveright, 1970.

Lorentz, Pare. *Lorentz on Film: Movies 1927 to 1941.* New York: Hopkins and Blake, 1975.

Lotman, Jurij. *Semiotics of Cinema.* Translated by Mark E. Suino. Ann Arbor: Michigan Slavic Contributions, 1976.

Lounsbury, Myron Osborn. *The Origins of American Film Criticism, 1909-1939.* New York: Arno, 1973.

Luhr, William, and Peter Lehman. *Authorship and Narrative in the Cinema.* New York: G. P. Putnam's Sons, 1977.

MacCann, Richard Dyer, ed. *Film: A Montage of Theories.* New York: E. P. Dutton, 1966.

McConnell, Frank D. *The Spoken Seen: Film and the Romantic Imagination.* Baltimore: Johns Hopkins University Press, 1975.

Macdonald, Dwight. *On Movies.* New York: Berkley Publishing, 1971.

Macgowan, Kenneth. *Behind the Screen: The History and Techniques of the Motion Picture.* New York: Delacorte, 1965.

Madsen, Roy Paul. *The Impact of Film: How Ideas Are Communicated Through Cinema and Television.* New York: Macmillan, 1973.

Manvell, Roger. *The Film and the Public.* Baltimore: Penguin, 1955.

______. *The Living Screen: Background to Film and Television.* London: Geroge G. Harrap, 1961.

Mast, Gerald. *Film/Cinema/Movie.* New York: Harper and Row, 1977.

______ and Marshall Cohen, eds. *Film Theory and Criticism: Introductory Readings.* New York: Oxford University Press, 1974.

Mekas, Jonas. *Movie Journal: The Rise of the New American Cinema.* New York: Macmillan, 1972.

Metz, Christian. *Film Language: A Semiotics of Cinema.* Translated by Michael Taylor. New York: Oxford University Press, 1974.

______. *Language and Cinema.* Translated by Donna Jean Umiker-Sebeok. Paris: Mouton, 1974.

Monaco, James. *How to Read a Film.* New York: Oxford University Press, 1977.

Montagu, Ivor. *Film World: A Guide to Cinema.* Baltimore: Penguin, 1964.

Morrow, James and Murray Suid. *Moviemaking Illustrated: The Comicbook Filmbook.* Rochelle Park, N.J.: Hayden, 1973.

Münsterberg, Hugo. *The Film: A Psychological Study.* New York: Dover, 1970. Original 1916 title was *The Photoplay: A Psychological Study.*

Murray, Edward. *Nine American Film Critics: A Study of Theory and Practice.* New York: Frederick Ungar, 1975.

Nichols, Bill, ed. *Movies and Methods.* Berkeley: University of California Press, 1976.

Nilsen, Vladimir. *The Cinema as a Graphic Art: (On a Theory of Representation in the Cinema).* Translated by Stephen Garry. New York: Hill and Wang, [1959].

Pechter, William S. *Twenty-four Times a Second: Films and Filmmakers.* New York: Harper and Row, 1971.

Perkins, V. F. *Film as Film: Understanding and Judging Movies.* Baltimore: Penguin, 1972.

Perlman, William J., ed. *The Movies on Trial: The Views and Opinions of Out-*

standing Personalities Anent Screen Entertainment Past and Present. New York: Macmillan, 1936.

Potamkin, Harry Alan. *The Compound Cinema.* New York: Teachers College, Columbia University, 1977.

Pudovkin, V. I. *Film Technique and Film Acting.* Translated by Ivor Montagu. New York: Grove, 1970.

Reed, Rex. *Big Screen, Little Screen.* New York: Macmillan, 1971.

Robinson, W. R., ed. *Man and the Movies.* Baltimore: Penguin, 1967.

Rotha, Paul. *Rotha on the Film.* New York: Garland, 1978.

Samuels, Charles Thomas. *Mastering the Film and Other Essays.* Knoxville: University of Tennessee Press, 1977.

Sarris, Andrew. *Confessions of a Cultist: On the Cinema, 1955-1969.* New York: Simon and Schuster, 1970.

______. *The Primal Screen: Essays on Film and Related Subjects.* New York: Simon and Schuster, 1973.

Schickel, Richard. *The History of Art and an Institution.* New York: Basic Books, 1964.

______. *Second Sight: Notes on Some Movies.* New York: Simon and Schuster, 1972.

Scott, James F. *Film: The Medium and the Maker.* New York: Holt, Rinehart and Winston, 1975.

Simon, John. *Private Screenings.* New York: Macmillan, 1967.

Sohn, David A. *Film: The Creative Eye.* Dayton, Ohio: Pflaum, 1970.

Solomon, Stanley J. *The Film Idea.* New York: Harcourt Brace Jovanovich, 1972.

Speed, F. Maurice, ed. *Film Review, 1975-76.* London: W. H. Allen, 1975. Annual volumes published since 1944.

Starr, Cecile. *Discovering the Movies: An Illustrated Introduction to the Motion Picture.* New York: Van Nostrand Reinhold, 1972.

______, ed. *Ideas on Film: A Handbook for the 16mm Film User.* Freeport, N.Y.: Books for Libraries Press, 1971.

Stephenson, Ralph and Jean R. Debrix. *The Cinema as Art.* Baltimore: Penguin, 1969.

Talbot, Daniel, ed. *Film: An Anthology.* Berkeley: University of California Press, 1966.

Thomson, David. *Movie Man.* New York: Stein and Day, 1967.

Tudor, Andrew. *Theories of Film.* London: Secker and Warburg, 1974.

Tyler, Parker. *The Shadow of an Airplane Climbs the Empire State Building: A World Theory of Film.* Garden City, N.Y.: Doubleday, 1973.

Weiss, Paul, *Cinematics.* Carbondale: University of Southern Illinois Press, 1975.

White, David Manning and Richard Averson, eds. *Sight, Sound, and Society: Motion Pictures and Television in America.* Boston: Beacon, 1968.

Wiseman, Thomas. *Cinema.* New York: A. S. Barnes, 1964.

Wollen, Peter. *Signs and Meaning in the Cinema.* Bloomington: Indiana University Press, 1969.

CHAPTER 4

Film Criticism by Genre

One of the major forms of film criticism concerns genre, or film type, a concept borrowed from literary criticism. It is not the purpose of this book to debate the issues of what constitutes a genre; suffice it to say that there are few areas of total agreement about genre. For the purpose of covering as many films as possible, this chapter will include any type of film that can remotely be considered a genre. It is clear that fantasy may well overlap with Western and that comedy may not be a genre at all, but to resolve that controversy is not the purpose of this book.

There are several books that deal with the general concept of genre. *Beyond Formula* by Stanley J. Solomon devotes a chapter to each of the important genres: Western, musical, horror, crime, detective, and war. Each chapter begins with a general discussion of the genre and its characteristics. It then discusses in depth seven or eight feature-length films of the genre.

American Film Genres by Stuart M. Kaminsky begins with an intelligent essay on film genre, then moves to a discussion of comparative genre (samurai and Western), literary adaptation of genre, horror and science fiction, musicals, comedy, and genre directors (such as Donald Siegel and John Ford).

Film Genre: Theory and Criticism opens with six essays on the theory of genre. The editor, Barry K. Grant, has selected essays on several major genres: screwball comedy, disaster, epics, gangster, horror, musicals, sports, Western, and science fiction.

ADVENTURE

One genre that is especially difficult to define is adventure, but Ian Cameron has put together a book called *Adventure in the Movies.* This is a picture book with an emphasis on adventure and action. *Swordsmen of the Screen* by Jeffrey Richards captures the essence of one of the leading types of adventures, the swashbuckler. This is a good book that discusses the men from Douglas Fairbanks, Sr. to Michael York and sets the films in a historical perspective. In *The Great Romantic Films,* Lawrence J. Quirk covers fifty of the world's most beloved films from *Smilin' Through* in 1931 to *Love and Pain and the Whole Damn Thing* in 1973. One adventurer who has contributed much to the genre is celebrated in *Tarzan of the Movies* by Gabe Essoe, subtitled *A Pictorial History of More Than Fifty Years of Edgar Rice Burroughs' Legendary Hero.* Some critics would consider the epic a genre unto itself, but since it also deals with adventure, this is a good place to include *The Hollywood Epic* by Foster Hirsch. He discusses the style and history of the genre with useful essays covering foreign epics, moral and religious epics, national epics, historical epics, and the epic hero.

ANIMATION

Animation may be a method rather than a genre, but there is a book that differentiates animated feature films from other types of movies. *Full Length Animated Feature Films* by Bruno Edera serves as an introduction to the genre. Edera discusses animation's aesthetics, production, and history both in America and the rest of the world. He also discusses new directions in feature length animation, including animation for adults.

COMEDY

Genre or mode, comedy is one of the most popular cinematic types. *The Comic Mind* by Gerald Mast is an excellent place to begin the study of cinematic comedy. This book is a major study which places an emphasis on the silent comedians. As with all of Mast's books, this one combines theory with history. Mast's study of the great comic films leads him to the conclusion that comedy reminds us of our humanity and reveals "the paradoxes, ironies, and ambiguities of existence." In *Movie Comedy* the National Society of Film Critics presents its best essays on film comedy. Edited by Stuart Byron and Elisabeth Weis, the book contains reviews of great comic films and essays on several directors and stars (Charles Chaplin and Frank Capra, for example). The editors have divided their material into three major sections: classical traditions, contemporary trends, and European comedy. Another study of comedy is *The Crazy Mirror* by Raymond Durgnat, which delineates the images of American life portrayed in the crazy mirror of over five hundred films.

Funny Men of the Movies by Edward Edelson is more descriptive than analytic, but the book does cover the careers of many comedians, beginning with Keystone and then progressing chronologically through Charles Chaplin, Buster Keaton, Harold Lloyd, Harry Langdon, Laurel and Hardy, the Marx brothers, screwball comedians, and others through the present day. *The Great Funnies* by David Robinson begins with a discussion of the early

French development of screen comedy and its influence on American comedy. Robinson discusses comedians through the postwar period, including detailed commentary on Mack Sennett, Charles Chaplin, Buster Keaton, Harold Lloyd, Harry Langdon, Laurel and Hardy, and W. C. Fields.

Walter Kerr covers the great ones in *The Silent Clowns.* This is a serious historical study of a funny subject. He opens with an introduction to silent film art and then covers the important actors/directors of the period: Mack Sennett, Charles Chaplin, Harold Lloyd, Hal Roach, and Buster Keaton, as well as others. *Comedy Films, 1894-1954* is another history and analysis of comedy films. John Montgomery begins with a discussion of early comedy work in Britain and then concentrates on American comedy. He covers the usual silent comedians and includes an essay on the end of visual comedy with the coming of sound. His coverage of the 1930s and 1940s devotes special attention to Bing Crosby and Walt Disney. *The Golden Age of Sound Comedy* by Donald W. McCaffrey is about comic films and comedians in the 1930s. He covers his subject from the birth of the talkies to the end of the great comedy era in about 1940. The book contains many pictures but limited commentary. *Lunatics and Lovers* is a study of the screwball and romantic comedies of the 1930s and 1940s in which Ted Sennett discusses themes, characters, actors, directors, and methods. An especially interesting chapter deals with the adaptation of stage comedy to the screen.

Kalton C. Lahue has written three books on film comedy. *World of Laughter* covers the motion picture short from 1910 to 1930. His emphasis here is on the studios producing comedies: Mutual, Keystone, Roach, and others. In *Kops and Custards* he and Terry Brewer describe life at Keystone; they also analyze the nature of a Keystone comedy and discuss the formation of new companies based on the Keystone model. *Clown Princes and Court Jesters* is a description of the careers of fifty silent comedians or comic groups. Lahue's essays here include both description and analysis of the styles of these actors.

CRIME, GANGSTERS, AND VILLAINS

Crime films make up one of the major film genres, and many of them deal with the gangster. *Born to Lose* by Eugene Rosow is the major work on gangster films. Rosow discusses the origins of the movie gangster stereotype, including its roots in the myths of Robin Hood. He also traces the rise to prominence of the genre during the Roaring Twenties and the peak of the gangster films during the 1930s, and follows the genre into the modern period. *Underworld U.S.A.* is a study of the genre by Colin McArthur in which McArthur first defines the genre and then analyzes the work of Fritz Lang, John Huston, Robert Siodmak, Elia Kazan, Nicholas Ray, Samuel Fuller, Don Siegel, and Samuel Melville. *Dreams and Dead Ends* by Jack Shadoian seeks to discover what the genre of gangster films does that cannot be done in other genres. To answer this question he provides close analysis of specific films: classics (*Little Caesar* and *Public Enemy*), *film noir* (*High Sierra* and *The Killers*), the enlightenment (*Kiss of Death*), change at mid-century (*White Heat*), focus on feeling (*Kiss Me Deadly*), and the modernist perspective (*Bonnie and Clyde* and *The Godfather*). A useful reference book to the genre is *The Great Gangster Pictures* by James Robert Parish and Michael R. Pitts. The authors include an essay by Edward Conner on "Gangsters of the Screen" that treats the history of the gangster in the movies and then list the films in the genre, citing credits, distributors, and a plot summary for each. Some critical commentary is provided.

Some of the books on gangsters are intended for a popular audience. *The Gangster Film* by John Baxter provides a cursory view of the players and films. The primary value of Baxter's book is to jog memories of films seen years ago. *A Pictorial History of Crime Films* is a popular picture book by Ian Cameron, as is *Gangsters and Hoodlums* by Raymond Lee and B. C. Van Hecke.

Not all villains are gangsters, but many are. *The Great Villains* by Janet Pate seeks out the villans wherever they may be—literature, stage, or screen. From the Sheriff of Nottingham and Uriah Heep to Brer Fox, the book describes the villains, tells their stories and lists their appearances in literature, on the stage, and in films.

DETECTIVES

On the other side of the law, most of the time, is the detective. Perhaps the most penetrating of the studies of the detective is *The Detective in Hollywood* by Jon Tuska. This book is basically a study of what happens to the detective novel when it is made into a film, but the thoroughness of Tuska's research makes this a valuable study of both novels and films. Almost all of the important detectives are covered. *The Detective in Film* by William K. Everson is a popular history with much description of the plots of detective films. Everson covers a wide range of topics: Sherlock Holmes, silent film sleuths, private eyes, the FBI, British detectives, and detectives in comedy. Of special interest is Everson's discussion of three classic films: *The Maltese Falcon*, *Green for Danger*, and *The Kennel Murder Case*.

Sherlock Holmes is probably the most famous fictional detective in the world, and his cinematic career is well documented in three books. *Sherlock Holmes on the Screen* by Robert W. Pohle, Jr. and Douglas C. Hart discusses how actors around the world played the role of the super sleuth. *The Films of Sherlock Holmes* by Chris Steinbrunner and Norman Michaels considers both the actors (John Barrymore, Clives Brooks, Raymond Massey, and Basil Rathbone) and many of the films. *Deerstalker!* by Ron Haydock is a historical and critical survey of "Holmes and Watson on the screen" with attention to the critical receptions of the various films.

SUSPENSE AND FILM NOIR

Suspense is closely allied to crime films. *Suspense in the Cinema* by Gordon Gow is a solid study of the means of bringing us to the edge of our seats. He covers isolation, irony, phobia, identity with the character in trouble, the loner among thieves, accident, the supernatural, and the twilight zone between reality and fantasy. Altan Löker's *Film and Suspense* is a study of the audience's response to film. Löker is especially interested in the role our instincts and our daydreaming play in our response to film, and he analyzes their roles in terms of our reactions to the suspense film. *The Dangerous Edge* by Gavin Lambert is "an inquiry into the lives of nine masters of suspense." Lambert begins with the fiction of Arthur Conan Doyle, Graham Greene, Raymond Chandler, and Alfred Hitchcock; since many of the works of these writers became films, this, is a study of film as well.

One particular type of film that combines crime and suspense is the *film noir. Toward a Definition of the American Film Noir* (1941-1949) is a dissertation by Amir Massoud Karimi that has now been reprinted. Karimi discusses the definition and origins of the genre and then looks closely at numerous films.

FANTASY AND HORROR

Another genre difficult to define is fantasy, but few genres have more fans. *Cinema of the Fantastic,* another book by Chris Steinbrunner and Burt Goldblatt, gives photographs and plot summaries for the most important fantasy films. Included are *King Kong, The Black Cat, Bride of Frankenstein, The Thief of Baghdad*, *The Thing*, *20,000 Leagues Under the Sea*, *Invasion of the Body Snatchers*, and *Forbidden Planet*. *The Fabulous Fantasy Films* by Jeff Rovin works with a loose definition of fantasy that excludes hardcore science fiction. He has chapters on fantasy creatures, mythology, fantastic science, and incredible lands. *Movie Fantastic* by David Annan is basically a picture book, but it has an interesting discussion of myths, machines, visions, and nightmares in fantasy. Walt Lee's *Reference Guide to Fantastic Films: Science Fiction, Fantasy, and Horror* is a standard reference book for all types of fantasy films. Lee provides extensive information on many films, including the film's date, running time, director, source, and an outline of its fantasy element.

The horror film is a special type of fantasy film. Carlos Clarens' *An Illustrated History of the Horror Film* is a fine introduction to the genre. Clarens has not overburdened his excellent text with too many photographs, yet the book is truly an illustrated history. *The Rise and Fall of the Horror Film: An Art Historical Approach to Fantasy Cinema* by David Soren focuses on highlights in the history of the horror film. Soren begins with the horror films made in Paris, moves on to those of Germany, and finally those of the United States. He covers Jean Vigo and Jean Cocteau, Carl

Dryer, America in the 1940s, nuclear horrors, television horrors, and violence. In *Terrors of the Screen* Frank Manchel presents a history of horror films from *A Trip to the Moon* to *Rosemary's Baby.* The book is brief but to the point.

A good introduction to the horror film is *Focus on the Horror Film,* an anthology edited by Roy Huss and T. J. Ross. The introduction is by Ross, followed by a unit on the domain of horror, which consist of three essays of definition. The editors have included units on gothic horror, which focuses on *Frankenstein* and the vampire; monster terror, which deals especially with *King Kong;* and the psychological thriller, which covers Val Lewton, the terror of the surreal, and *Rosemary's Baby. Dark Dreams* by Charles Derry deals with *The Horror Film From Psycho to Jaws.* His three units are horror of personality, horror of Armageddon, and horror of the demonic.

Another book, *Horror Films,* contains an intelligent essay on the genre by editor R. H. W. Dillard and then discusses *Frankenstein, The Wolf Man, Night of the Living Dead,* and *Satyricon.* Bruce Dettman and Michael Bedford have written the history of the horror films made at Universal Studio from 1931 to 1955. *The Horror Factory* contains chapters on Universal's classic horror films and their important actors.

The best reference book, in addition to Lee's mentioned above, is *Horror and Science Fiction Films: A Checklist* by Donald C. Willis. Willis includes references to some forty-four hundred films, giving each film's date, running time, director, writer, producer, major actors, and a one-sentence annotation.

The key element in many horror films is the monster, and several books have focused on these characters. *Monsters from the Movies* by Thomas Aylesworth classifies the types of monsters: man-made (Frankenstein), self-made (Dr. Jekyll and Mr. Hyde), the human friend (Dr. Moreau), back from the dead (Dracula), and things from another workd (*War of the Worlds*). *Great Monsters of the Movies* by Edward Edelson is a readable, although short and superficial, survey of the genre. Edelson includes comments on the legends, the pioneers (such as *Dr. Caligari* and *Nosferatu*), the stars (Bela Lugosi, Boris Karloff, and Lon Chaney, Jr.) and the big beasts (King Kong). *Movie Monsters* by Denis Gifford has a different orientation from most of the other books on the genre. "The creation" deals with the golem; "resuscitation" discusses mummies and zombies; and "metamorphosis" covers vampires, werewolves, and other such creatures. This book is brief and composed largely of photographs.

Classic Movie Monsters by Donald F. Glut is a more substantial book. Its chapters discuss the major monster films, their myths and spinoffs. Covered are the wolfman, Dr. Jekyll, the invisible man, the mummy, the hunchback of Notre Dame, the phantom of the opera, the creature from the black lagoon, King Kong, and Godzilla.

Of all the monsters, the vampire has received the most critical attention. *The Vampire Film* by Alain Silver and James Ursini is a popular and useful book, amply illustrated. It gives background and analysis of the vampire in film and litrature and includes a full filmography and bibliography. *The Vampire Cinema* by David Pirie deals with more recent films. Pirie includes an introductin to the history of the vampire films in Britain, America, and Latin America. He includes a fascinating chapter on the sex vampire.

The most scholarly of the vampire books is *In Search of Dracula* by Raymond McNally and Radu Florescu. This book traces the legends of the vampire back to central Europe and Vlad the Impaler and is largely historical, but its filmography makes it valuable to anyone researching cinematic vampires.

One of the most popular fantasy areas is science fiction. *Science Fiction Movies* by Philip Strict tries to redefine science fiction and to expand its boundaries. This book deals with what H. G. Wells called "fantasies of possibility" and includes topics such as "men like gods" and time warps. Denis Gifford's book, *Science Fiction Film,* offers a different approach. Gifford begins with a consideration of invention in science fiction: the machine, airplane, vehicle, submarine, tunnel, robot, and ray; he then discusses explorations by both aliens and astronauts; and his final section is on predictions of the future: the time machine, the bomb, and the end. The thesis of *Visions of Tomorrow* by Edward Edelson is that a science fiction film is itself a time machine that takes us into the future. He discusses films made from the novels of Jules Verne and H. G. Wells, serials in the genre, invaders from space, the images of the end of the world, space travel, monsters, and science fiction on television.

An anthology edited by Thomas Atkins, *Science Fiction Films,* provides an interesting but limited view of selected science fiction films and topics. Following his general introduction on the genre, Atkins has included essays on *Metropolis, 2001*, science fiction in the 1950s, *Invasion of the Body Snatchers,* and *Solaris.*

Hal in the Classroom: Science Fiction Films, edited by Ralph J. Amelio, is an anthology of essays on science fiction films that are especially well suited for classroom use. Amelio includes general essays on the genre, as well as essays on specific films: *THX 1138, Metropolis, Invasion of the Body Snatchers,* and *Solaris.* Another book, *Focus on the Science Fiction Film,* edited by William Johnson, contains essays by scholars on the beginnings of the genre (with an emphasis on *Things to Come*), the heyday for science fiction in the 1950s (the period of *When Worlds Collide* and *Invasion of the Body Snatchers,* among others), and issues and answers, which deals with the more modern films such as *2001.*

A number of books deal with science fiction films in less detail than those mentioned so far. *Things to Come* by Douglas Menville and R. Reginald is an illustrated history which includes many plot descriptions but little analysis. The authors cover travel films from Méliès to George Lucas. *Science Fiction in the Cinema* presents a popular overview of the history of the genre by John Baxter. Baxter deals with the aesthetics of the genre and includes chapters on specific films.

In addition to the reference books mentioned above that treat science fiction films, the reader should consult *The Great Science Fiction Pictures* by James Robert Parish and Michael R. Pitts. This useful book lists many films, citing their casts and credits and giving brief commentary on each.

MUSICALS

For whatever reason, musicals have not received the same critical attention as other major film genres. *The World of Entertainment* by Hugh Fordin focuses on Arthur Freed and "Hollywood's greatest musicals." This book documents Freed's films and provides background on their production, including production drawings for the sets and costumes. *Gotta Sing, Gotta Dance!* by John Kobal is a popular history of musicals with a broader scope than Fordin's book. A third book, *The Movie Musical from Vitaphone to 42nd Street* by Miles Kreuger, recites the history of the early musicals through essays from *Photoplay* which illustrate the popularity of the musicals during their heyday.

NEWSREELS

The newsreel that preceded the feature film at the theatre is now a thing of the past, killed off by the coming of television and its omnipresent news coverage. However, the memory of the news shorts of the past has been preserved in *The American Newsreel, 1911-1967.* Raymond Fielding's book is the definitive history of movie news. In a second book, *The March of Time, 1935-1951,* Fielding deals specifically with the company that produced the "March of Time" newsreel. Fielding views the films as a valuable pictorial record of the social issues important during the sixteen years they were made; he interviewed many of the people responsible for the newsreels in writing his book. *Movietone Presents the 20th Century* covers the films of another of the newsreel companies. Lawrence Cohn introduces Movietone and discusses its importance; he uses frame enlargements from the films to document their period. A rather unusual approach to the news in films is Alex Barris' *Stop the Presses!* This book is not at all about newsreels, but instead is a study of "the newspaper in American films." Barris seeks out the images of newspaper people in the films and finds the reporter as crime buster, as scandalmonger, as crusader, as sob sister, and in a variety of other roles.

SEX AND VIOLENCE

Sex has been one of the more enduring features of the movies, and some of the most astute critics have tried to determine what that means about us and our movies. Alexander Walker and Parker Tyler have both devoted much of their energies to studying sex in the cinema. Walker's book, *The Celluloid Sacrifice,* is subtitled *Aspects of Sex in the Movies.* He deals with the screen goddesses: Theda Bara, Clara Bow, Mary Pickford, Mae West, Marlene Dietrich, Greta Garbo, Jean Harlow, Marilyn Monroe, and Elizabeth Taylor; he then focuses on the guardians, the censors who protect us from ourselves; finally, he discusses the victims, the men who succumb to the goddesses. Of particular interest is his analysis of the nature of the actresses' appeal. In *A Pictorial History of Sex in Films,* Tyler covers topics from romance to hard-core pornography. He has chapters on different approaches to sex: the kiss, bosoms and bottoms, bedroom and bath, gays, and others. In *Sex, Psyche, Etcetera in the Film,* Tyler discusses different ways to arrive at an understanding of film. First he discusses films that deal with sexual rituals, then proceeds to discuss the modern psyche and the films of Michaelangelo Antonioni and Ingmar Bergman. The book closes with a discussion of the pros and cons of film aesthetics. In *Screening the Sexes* Tyler deals with homosexuality in the movies. This is the standard study of gay films and the image of gays in films.

Thomas R. Atkins has edited an anthology on *Sexuality in the Movies.* In the opening unit the essays, some dealing with censorship, establish a social and cultural perspective on the topic. The second unit covers sexual genres, including monsters and homosexuality. The last unit consists of analysis of specific films: *I Am Curious Yellow, Midnight Cowboy, Carnal Knowledge, Deep Throat,* and *Last Tango in Paris.*

Male sexuality in the movies has been the subject of two books. *Big Bad Wolves* by Joan Mellen is about "masculinity in the American film." She covers the images projected by actors from W. S. Hart to Robert Redford. Also included are Rudolph Valentino, Douglas Fairbanks, Sr., John Barrymore, Clark Gable, Gary Cooper, John Wayne, Humphrey Bogart, Clint Eastwood, and Warren Beatty. Another recent analysis of male sexuality in movies is *Heroes of Eros* by Michael Malone. He divides his study into three units: "lovers," "pinups and pectorals," and "heroes and rebels." He discusses such actors as Robert Redford, Humphrey Bogart, James Dean, Clark Gable, and Elvis Presley. *The Sexy Cinema* by Marv Strick and Robert I. Lethe is a decade by decade history of sex in the movies.

Some films, of course, pass over the line into pornography, and some books become guides to this extreme version of the sex genre. *I Know It When I See It* is a study of pornography by Michael Leach. He observes the paradox that society has accepted violence in cinema but rejected sex and hopes that we will know ourselves better when we understand what pornography does for us. *Erotic Movies* by Richard Wortley covers his topic from soft-core to hard-core, and from simple nudity to serious pornography with many photographs. The process of making a pornographic movie is analyzed in *The Film Maker's Guide to Pornography*. Steven Ziplow discusses the script, sets, props, sound, mix, distribution and the law; and how to shoot a sex scene.

Sex is linked with violence in the minds of many people. *Savage Cinema* by Rick Trader Witcombe includes an essay on violence and photographs from movies to illustrate the tie between sex and violence. He covers many films, including *Straw Dogs, Bonnie and Clyde,* and *Chinatown.* Another anthology by Thomas R. Atkins is *Graphic Violence on the Screen.* The essays in this book cover *film noir,* Terrence Fischer, Italian Westerns and Kung Fu, the *Texas Chain Saw Massacre*, and violent deaths in cinema.

Films involving Oriental violence have had a special appeal in this country, and three books have discussed this particular brand of the genre. *The Samurai Film* by Alain Silver provides background on the Samurai tradition in history and fiction. His discussion of Akira Kurosawa is useful to anyone who appreciates Japanese films. *The Martial Arts Film* by Marilyn Mintz is history, criticism, and analysis together. This serious and professional study covers the films and directors from Kurosawa to Bruce Lee and proposes that these films constitute a genre. *Kung Fu* by Verina Glaessner is about the "cinema of violence" and deals with Angelo Mao, Bruce Lee, Wong Yu, David Chiang, and Ti Lung.

WAR MOVIES

Violence probably finds its most horrible expression in war. *Guts and Glory* by Lawrence H. Suid is a serious study of war films. Suid is concerned especially with the impact of Hollywood on war. Beginning with an overview of Hollywood and the military image, he discusses World War II as both fantasy and reality, followed by analysis of the image of the Marines and John Wayne, the military as enemy, and film biography as reality. He concludes with a look at Hollywood's view of Vietnam. *The War Film* by Norman Kagan is an illustrated history of America at war. Kagan covers the major American wars chapter by chapter; additional chapters are organized thematically: comedy and war, anti-war films, and other topics. His text is brief and somewhat superficial.

Jack Spears has devoted one of the essays in his book to films of the Civil War. *The Civil War on the Screen and Other Essays* covers Civil War films from *Birth of a Nation* to *Gone with the Wind*. His filmography mentions over one hundred more films. Other essays in the book deal with director E. S. Porter, actress Alla Nazimova, and actor Louis Wolheim.

Hollywood at War: The American Motion Picture and World War II is a popular study by Ken D. Jones and Arthur F. McClure. They cite the important films of this war and give credits, casts, dates, and plots for each film. *The Films of World War II* by Joe Morella, Edward Z. Epstein, and John Griggs, is a brief treatment of the films of the war. Following a short introduction by Judith Crist, these men give the usual data for an expanded filmography, including a short commentary and excerpts from reviews.

There are several books on more recent wars in film. The thesis of Julian Smith's *Looking Away: Hollywood and Vietnam* is that Hollywood ignored the most recent war. Another book on modern wars is *Nuclear War Films*, a volume of essays edited by Jack Shaheen. This book describes feature films dealing with nuclear holocaust such as *Hiroshima, Mon Amour*, *Dr. Strangelove*, and *Fail Safe*. It also presents essays on documentaries (such as *The War Game*) and on shorts (such as *Hiroshima-Nagasaki*). In all, the essays cover twenty-one films.

WESTERNS

No genre is more typically American than the Western. An important and standard study of the genre is *The Western* by George N. Fenin and William K. Everson. The book covers Westerns "from the silents to cinerama," and opens with an introduction on Hollywood, the history of Westerns, and the moral influence of the Western. The book surveys the important Westerns decade by decade, with interludes on such topics as costuming and the Western serial. *The Filming of the West* by Jon Tuska is another important study of the genre. This mammoth work covers Westerns from *The Great Train Robbery* to the films of Sam Peckinpah and John Wayne in the 1960s. *Sixguns and Society: A Structural History of the Western* by Will Wright, is a study of the myth of the West in films. He discusses films in the classical mode, those with a vengeance variation, those with a transition theme, and those with a professional plot. In *Westerns: Aspects of a Movie Genre* Philip French studies several characteristics of the genre. He discusses the politics of the Western, heroes and villains, and women and children as portrayed in the Westerns. He goes on to consider the image of Indians and blacks, the use of landscape, and the role that violence plays in the genre. He ends with a look at the post-Western, especially *The Shootist*.

There Must Be a Lone Ranger is a general study of the genre by Jenni Calder. The purpose of the book is "to describe and explain the essential ingredients of the Western in terms of the contributions to the myth and their appeal." She includes chapters on the frontier, the post-Civil War period, Indians, the law of the gun, gold, women, and saddle tramps. *A Pictorial History of the Western Film* is another book by William K. Everson. It is a useful, but secondary, book that proceeds decade by decade and presents its subject through photographs and brief commentary. The book is intended for a popular audience, but like most of Everson's books it is a solid work.

Horizons West is a study by Jim Kitses of the Westerns of three "auteur" directors: Anthony Mann, Budd Boetticher, and Sam Peckinpah. *The American West on Film: Myth and Reality* is a utilitarian book by Richard Maynard intended primarily as a teaching guide to the classroom study of the genre. Maynard has included a historical unit that presents the West as fact, then a literary unit that presents it as fiction. Finally, he discusses the West in film myth and the rise of the cowboy anti-hero. Another book on Westerns is *Focus on the Western,* edited by John G. Nachtbar. The essays, by Jon Tuska, John Cawelti, T. J. Ross, and others, discuss the origins, development, and definition of the genre, the Western as cultural artifact, and contemporary Westerns.

They Went Thataway is by James Horwitz, a writer who as a boy sat at the Saturday matinées and revered the cowboy heroes. In his book he tries to bring back the good guys—Gene Autry, Tim McCoy, Joel McCrea, the Cisco Kid, the Durango Kid, and the Lone Ranger. Diana Serra Cary grew up on the Hollywood sets where her father was an extra in many Western posses. Now she is a historian whose personal remembrance of the Westerns and her understanding of their place in our society make for a readable book, *The Hollywood Posse.*

Who Was That Masked Man: The Story of the Lone Ranger by David Rothel contains the history of the Lone Ranger, along with some limited criticism and analysis of the Lone Ranger films. Rothel includes information on the production of the films and interviews with key personnel. Rothel has also written *The Singing Cowboys,* a book about the singing Western heroes of the 1930s, 1940s, and 1950s. His commentary and photographs cover Gene Autry, Roy Rogers, Tex Ritter, Eddie Dean, Jimmy Walker, Monte Hale, and Rex Allen.

Kalton C. Lahue has written a pair of books that serve as reference books to the Westerns. *Winners of the West: The Sagebrush Heroes of the Silent Screen* is an alphabetical listing of the movie men (and one woman—Helen Holmes) who made the West. He has included essays of several pages and a few photographs on each of the heroes. Covered are Bronco Billy Anderson, W. S. Hart, Ken Maynard, Tom Mix, and others. *Riders of the Range* is a companion volume dealing with the "B Western" from the coming of sound until its death in the early 1950s. Heroes included here are Gene Autry, William Boyd, Tim Holt, Tex Ritter, and Roy Rogers.

Other reference books include *The Western* by Allen Eyles, a list of Western actors and their films. Another book, *Western Films: An Annotated Critical Bibliography,* is one of the important scholarly books on the genre. John G. Nachbar's annotated bibliography lists both books and articles on topics such as the films, their makers, and their themes; the brief annotations are in themselves worthwhile. *The Great Western Pictures* by James Robert Parish and Michael Pitts lists the important (and many less important) Westerns, giving both the credits and several paragraphs of commentary on each film; also included is information on Westerns on radio and television. The introduction by Edward Connor is an interesting discussion of the genre.

SHORTS AND SERIALS

One difficult type of film to find material on is the short film. Shorts of all sorts are generally overlooked by the critics, but some useful material does exist. *The Great Movie Shorts* by Leonard Maltin deals with the shorts from the period 1930 to 1950. Maltin discusses the studios (Hal Roach, RKO, and others), the series, and the actors (including Harry Langdon, W. C. Fields, and Buster Keaton). George Rehrauer's *The Short Film; An Evaluation Selection of 500 Recommended Films,* is aimed at librarians and contains the sort of data they will need: date, running time, annotation, audience level, and subject category. William Kuhns has written two books on short films aimed at teachers. *Themes: Short Films for Discussion* covers approximately seventy-five films. In addition to technical data about each film, Kuhns includes a three or four paragraph summary, a statement about its use in the classroom, and some questions that might stimulate classroom discussion. *Themes Two: One Hundred Short Films for Discussion* is similar to Kuhns' first book, but his discussions of the films are longer. Another book for teachers is Jeffrey Schrank's *Guide to Short Films.* Schrank presents 228 short films that are especially suited for classroom use and discusses each in about a page. Teachers will find ideas that stimulate here as well as a good guide to selecting films and preparing for a classroom discussion. Of specialized intrest is *A Long Look at Short Films* by Derrick Knight and Vincent Porter. In this book, sponsored by the British movie industry, the authors look at short films, with an emphasis on their marketability. The technical and statistical slant of the book will appeal to those interested in the production aspect of the shorts.

The serial is, of course, a particular type of short, and several books have documented this form of film no longer produced. *The Great Movie Serials,* by Jim Harmon and Donald F. Glut captures "their sound and fury." Based on scripts. anecdotes, interviews, and old photographs, this book covers the serials from Pearl White to Rin Tin Tin. *The Serials* by Raymond William Stedman, subtitled *Suspense and Drama by Installment,* claims to be "the true life story of the serials." It is a historical analysis which also covers serials on radio and television.

Kalton C. Lahue also has written two books on the serials. *Bound and Gagged: The Story of the Silent Serials*, contains full commentary on the men who put the serial empire together, their studios, and their actors and actresses. *Continued Next Week: A History of the Moving Picture Serial* is a more general history that follows the serials up to their demise. The extensive appendix gives the credits and other data for all the important serials. *To Be Continued . . .* is another excellent reference book on the serials. Ken Weiss and Ed Goodgold have listed the casts, number of episodes, dates, studios, and directors for serials from 1929 until 1956. They have also outlined the story lines.

Sequels bring forth some of the same audience responses as did the serials. Michael B. Druxman has written two books on sequels. *One Good Film Deserves Another* deals with twenty-five movies and how their sequels came to be made, how the original characters and story lines were expanded in the sequel, and the critical reception of the sequel. He considers older films such as *Boy's Town, Brother Rat,* and *Here Comes Mr. Jordan* as well as newer ones such as *Planet of the Apes, French Connection,* and *The Godfather.* In his second book on sequels, *Make It Again, Sam,* Druxman provides *A Survey of Movie Remakes,* analyzing each film and its remakes and comparing the original with its successors. He covers *Dr. Jekyll and Mr. Hyde, Stagecoach, Mutiny on the Bounty,* and thirty more.

DOCUMENTARIES

The history of documentary films is told by Richard Meran Barsam in *Nonfiction Film: A Critical History.* Barsam begins with a chapter of definition and another on the beginnings of the documentary, then moves on to discuss John Grierson and the British tradition, Robert Flaherty, and World War II on film. Finally, he devotes several chapters to what has happened with documentaries since the war. Another study of the genre is Erik Barnouw's *Documentary,* "a history of the non-fiction film." This is a fine book which seeks out the themes and images of the documentaries rather than the personalities behind them. Barnouw looks at Louis Lumière as the prophet of the documentary, Flaherty as its explorer, Grierson and Leni Riefenstahl as its advocates, Frederick Wiseman as its observer, and so on.

Cinéma Vérité by M. Ali Issari is a history of the documentary—especially in its particular form, *cinéma vérité*—from Flaherty to television. Issari describes both the major trends and the technical developments of the form. Stephen Mamber has studied the same films in *Cinéma Vérité in America: Studies in Uncontrolled Documentary.* This book is a history of the development and theory of the form, with chapters on the Drew Associates, the Maysles Brothers, Richard Leacock, and Frederick Wiseman.

In *The People's Films: A Political History of U.S. Government Motion Picture,* Richard Dyer MacCann demonstrates how the documentary has worked for Uncle Sam, covering Pare Lorentz, the U.S. Film Service,

World War II, the work for the government by Frank Capra, the USIA, and television. *Documentary Diary: An Informal History of the British Documentary Film, 1928-1939* by Paul Rotha, who is renowned for both his filmmaking and his knowledge of the history of film.

A good place to begin reading documentary criticism is *The Documentary Tradition,* edited by Lewis Jacobs. Jacobs defines the tradition, traces its growth, analyzes its achievements and trends, and offers insights into the present films. The essays in his collection are arranged by decades, but they provide far more than a history of the form. *Nonfiction Film: Theory and Criticism,* edited by Richard Meran Barsam, is another excellent anthology of critical essays on the documentary. His units deal with the concept of the form, the documentary and history, the documentary artists, and documentary production. Essays are by Leni Riefenstahl, Willard Van Dyke, Lindsay Anderson, John Grierson, Paul Rotha, and others. *Studies in Documentary,* by Alan Lovell and Jim Hillier, focuses on Grierson's work and tradition and includes a chapter on his associates.

The documentary filmmakers often speak for themselves. In *Documentary Explorations,* G. Roy Levin begins by outlining the history of the documentary film, but the bulk of the book consists of interviews with fifteen major documentary filmmakers. A few of the directors are Europeans, but most are Americans: Willard Van Dyke, Richard Leacock, D. A. Pennabaker, Albert and David Maysles, Arthur Barron, Frederick Wiseman, Ed Pincecs, Michael Shamberg, and David Cort. *Grierson on Documentary* contains the theories of the British filmmaker John Grierson, a key figure in the development of the form. Grierson speaks about the background of the documentaries, their early history, achievements, and future.

Films Beget Films is a book by Jay Leyda on a special type of movie. This book discusses the compilation film, films that are made from clips of other movies. This is a documentary of sorts, and Leyda concentrates on the compilation films that were propaganda for World War II.

EXPERIMENTAL FILMS

It is not easy to decide what to call the films dealt with in this section: underground, avant-garde, independent, or experimental. Whatever the term, these are the films that have been made outside the studio system, for an audience interested in innovative techniques and in non-narrative styles. There are some who believe that the experimental film is where much of the creative energy of today's filmmakers is being channeled.

The basic introduction to experimental films in this country is *An Introduction to the American Underground Film* by Sheldon Renan. This is an important book containing definition, history, and theory, as well as studies of the important filmmakers and films. Renan's appendix includes an excellent list of significant experimental films and a brief bibliography.

The history of the experimental movies is told in a number of good books. *The Underground Film: A Critical History* by Parker Tyler is both readable and popular. Tyler wants to explain "the personality of the underground films," and to do so he defines them and puts their traits into a historical context. *Experimental Cinema* by David Curtis emphasizes the economic aspect of the experimental films, an important consideration since these films are rarely shown in big money markets.

Abstract Film and Beyond by Malcolm Le Grice begins with an introduction that deals with the art of cinematography. The body of the book is a well-illustrated historical survey that follows the experimental movement up to the present. *A History of the American Avant-Garde Cinema* is a catalogue made up by the American Federation of the Arts for a traveling exhibition. The major periods of experiments in films from 1943 to 1972 are discussed and specific, important films analyzed.

One of the leading historians and critics of the experimental movement is P. Adams Sitney, who has been working at the Anthology Films Archives in New York. His *Visionary Film* is an excellent guide to this type of film. It gives an overview of the avant-garde tradition in America and analyzes the work of twenty-four filmmakers, including Maya Deren, Kenneth Anger, Jonas Mekas, and Stan Brackage. In addition to history and analysis, Sitney deals with influences on the movement, such as surrealism and Dada, and with the theoretical and mythical aspects of the films. In *The Essential Cinema,* Sitney and his group have selected films important to them and invited critics and filmmakers to write essays on them. Their choices are for the most part underground films.

Living Cinema by Louis Marcorelles deals with new directions in filmmaking with a special emphasis on what the author calls "the direct cinema." He is concerned with the work and politics of filmmakers such as Richard Leacock, Pierre Perrault, and Jean Rouch. In *Experiment in the Film,* Roger Manvell presents nine essays on experimental film around the world. His essays cover experimental work in America, France, Russia, Germany, Austria, and Britain. One essay deals with the scientific film. This book was written in 1949 and was one of the first books to pay attention to cinematic experimentation.

The best study of the technology of the experimental film is *Expanded Cinema.* This outstanding book by Gene Youngblood begins with a complex but sound discussion of the nature of the experimental film and its effect on audiences. The first chapter deals with the sociology and the criticism of this type of film, the second and third chpaters with its theory and cosmic consciousness, and the latter part of the book with the major attempts at expanding the technological limits of the medium.

Four useful anthologies of essays on the experimental film have been published. Gregory Battcock edited *The New American Cinema,* which includes essays by critics, such as Andrew Sarris, and by filmmakers, such as Stan VanDerBeck and Stan Brakhage. P. Adams Sitney's *Film Culture Reader* is a collection of the most important essays from the journal that calls itself "America's Independent Motion Picture Magazine." The essays include history and criticism, but the emphasis is on theory.

Structural Film Anthology, edited by Peter Gidal and sponsored by the British Film Institute, deals with structural/materialist films, a type of avant-garde film that attempts to "be non-illusionist." The book begins with an introduction to definition and theory and then includes essays on the major filmmakers in the movement such as Hollis Frampton and Peter Kubelka. *Art in Cinema*, edited by Frank Stauffacher, is a reissue of essays taken from a 1947 symposium on the avant-garde film. Man Ray, Luis Buñuel, and John and James Whitney discuss their work, and Eric Pommer discusses *The Cabinet of Dr. Caligari.* The essays are brief and somewhat superficial, but interesting, and are complemented by notes on surrealism and on poetry and film.

BIBLIOGRAPHY

Amelio, Ralph J., ed. *Hal in the Classroom: Science Fiction Films.* Dayton, Ohio: Pflaum, 1974.

Annan, David. *Movie Fantastic: Beyond the Dream Machine.* New York: Bounty Books, 1974.

Atkins, Thomas R., ed. *Graphic Violence on the Screen.* New York: Simon and Schuster, 1976.

______. *Science Fiction Films.* New York: Simon and Schuster, 1976.

______. *Sexuality in the Movies.* Bloomington: Indiana University Press, 1975.

Aylesworth, Thomas G. *Monsters from the Movies.* Philadelphia: J. B. Lippincott, 1972.

Barnouw, Erik. *Documentary: A History of the Non-Fiction Film.* New York: Oxford University Press, 1974.

Barris, Alex. *Stop the Presses!* New York: A. S. Barnes, 1976.

Barsam, Richard Meran. *Nonfiction Film: A Critical History.* New York: E. P. Dutton, 1973.

______, ed. *Nonfiction Film: Theory and Criticism.* New York: E. P. Dutton, 1976.

Battcock, Gregory, ed. *The New American Cinema: A Critical Anthology.* New York: E. P. Dutton, 1967.

Baxter, John. *The Gangster Film.* New York: A. S. Barnes, 1970.

______. *Science Fiction in the Cinema.* New York: A. S. Barnes, 1970.

Byron, Stuart and Elisabeth Weis, eds. *Movie Comedy.* New York: Grossman Publishers, 1977.

Calder, Jenni. *There Must be a Lone Ranger: The American West in Film and in Reality.* London: Hamish Hamilton, 1974.

Cameron, Ian. *Adventure in the Movies.* New York: Crescent, 1973.

______. *A Pictorial History of Crime Films.* New York: Hamlyn, 1975.

Cary, Diana Serra. *The Hollywood Posse: The Story of a Gallant Band of Horsemen Who Make Movie History.* Boston: Houghton Mifflin, 1975.
Clarens, Carlos. *An Illustrated History of the Horror Film.* New York: Capricorn Books, 1967.
Cohn, Lawrence. *Movietone Presents the 20th Century.* New York: St. Martin's Press, 1976.
Curtis, David. *Experimental Cinema.* New York: Dell, 1971.
Derry, Charles. *Dark Dreams: The Horror Film from Psycho to Jaws.* New York: A. S. Barnes, 1977.
Dettman, Bruce and Michael Bedford. *The Horror Factory.* New York: Gordon Press, 1976.
Dillard, R. H. W. *Horror Films.* New York: Simon and Schuster, 1976.
Druxman, Michael B. *Make It Again, Sam: A Survey of Movie Remakes.* New York: A. S. Barnes, 1975.
______. *One Good Film Deserves Another.* New York: A. S. Barnes, 1977.
Durgnat, Raymond. *The Crazy Mirror: Hollywood Comedy and the American Image.* New York: Delta, 1969.
Edelson, Edward. *Funny Men of the Movies.* Garden City, N.Y.: Doubleday, 1976.
______. *Great Monsters of the Movies.* Garden City, N.Y.: Doubleday, 1973.
______. *Visions of Tomorrow: Great Science Fiction from the Movies.* Garden City, N.Y.: Doubleday, 1975.
Edera, Bruno. *Full Length Animated Feature Films.* New York: Hastings House, 1977.
Essoe, Gabe. *Tarzan of the Movies: A Pictorial History of More than Fifty Years of Edgar Rice Burroughs' Legendary Hero.* New York: Cadillac Publishing, 1968.
Everson, William K. *The Detective in Film.* Secaucus, N.J.: Citadel, 1972.
______. *A Pictorial History of The Western Film.* New York: Citadel, 1969.
Eyles, Allen. *The Western: An Illustrated Guide.* New York: A. S. Barnes, 1975.
Fenin, George N. and William K. Everson. *The Western; From Silents to Cinerama.* New York: Bonanza, 1962.
Fielding, Raymond. *The American Newsreel, 1911-1967.* Norman: University of Oklahoma Press, 1972.
______. *The March of Time, 1935-1951.* New York: Oxford University Press, 1978.
Fordin, Hugh. *The World of Entertainment: Hollywood's Greatest Musicals.* Garden City, N.Y.: Doubleday, 1975.
French, Philip. *Westerns: Aspects of a Movie Genre.* London: Secker and Warburg, 1977.
Gidal, Peter, ed. *Structural Film Anthology.* London: British Film Institute, 1976.
Gifford, Denis. *Movie Monsters.* New York: E. P. Dutton, 1969.
______. *Science Fiction Film.* New York: E. P. Dutton, 1971.
Glaessner, Verina. *Kung Fu: Cinema of Vengeance.* New York: Bounty Books, 1974.
Glut, Donald F. *Classic Movie Monsters.* Metuchen, N.J.: Scarecrow, 1978.
Gow, Gordon. *Suspense in the Cinema.* New York: Paperback Library, 1968.
Grant, Barry K., ed. *Film Genre: Theory and Criticism.* Metuchen, N.J.: Scarecrow, 1977.
Grierson, John. *Grierson on Documentary.* London: Collins, 1946.
Harmon, Jim and Donald F. Glut. *The Great Movie Serials: Their Sound and Fury.* Garden City, N.Y.: Doubleday, 1972.

Haydock, Ron. *Deerstalker!* Metuchen, N.J.: Scarecrow, 1978.

Hirsch, Foster. *The Hollywood Epic.* New York: A. S. Barnes, 1978.

A History of the American Avant-Garde Cinema. New York: American Federation of Arts, 1976.

Horwitz, James. *They Went Thataway.* New York: E. P. Dutton, 1976.

Huss, Roy and T. J. Ross. *Focus on the Horror Film.* Englewood Cliffs, N.J.: Prentice-Hall, 1972.

Issari, M. Ali. *Cinéma Vérité.* East Lansing: Michigan State University Press, 1971.

Jacobs, Lewis, ed. *The Documentary Tradition: From Nanook to Woodstock.* New York: Hopkins and Blake, 1971.

Johnson, William, ed. *Focus on the Science Fiction Film.* Englewood Cliffs, N.J.: Prentice-Hall, 1972.

Jones, Ken D., and Arthur F. McClure. *Hollywood at War: The American Motion Picture and World War II.* New York: A. S. Barnes, 1973.

Kagan, Norman. *The War Film.* New York: Pyramid, 1974.

Kaminsky, Stuart M. *American Film Genres: Approaches to a Critical Theory of Popular Film.* New York: Dell, 1974.

Karimi, Amir Massoud. *Toward a Definition of the American Film Noir (1941-1949).* New York: Arno, 1976.

Kerr, Walter. *The Silent Clowns.* New York: Alfred A. Knopf, 1975.

Kitses, Jim. *Horizons West: Anthony Mann, Budd Boetticher, Sam Peckinpah: Studies of Authorship Within the Western.* Bloomington: Indiana University Press, 1970.

Knight, Derrick and Vincent Porter. *A Long Look at Short Films: An A.C.T.T. Report on the Short Entertainment and Factual Film.* Oxford: Pergamon Press, 1967.

Kobal, John. *Gotta Sing, Gotta Dance!: A Pictorial History of Film Musicals.* New York: Hamlyn, 1971.

Kreuger, Miles, ed. *The Movie Musical From Vitaphone to 42nd Street: As Reported in a Great Fan Magazine.* New York: Dover, 1975.

Kuhns, William. *Themes: Short Films for Discussion.* Dayton, Ohio: Pflaum, 1968.

______. *Themes Two: One Hundred Short Films for Discussion.* Dayton, Ohio: Pflaum, 1974.

Lahue, Kalton. *Bound and Gagged: The Story of the Silent Serials:* New York: Castle, 1968.

______. *Clown Princes and Court Jesters: Some Great Comics of the Silent Screen.* New York: A. S. Barnes, 1970.

______. *Continued Next Week: A History of the Moving Picture Serial.* Norman: University of Oklahoma Press, 1964.

______. *Riders of the Range: The Sagebrush Heroes of the Sound Screen. The Legend of Keystone Films.* New York: Castle, 1973.

______. *Winners of the West: The Sagebrush Heroes of the Silent Screen.* New York: A. S. Barnes, 1970.

______. *World of Laughter: The Motion Picture Comedy Short.* Norman: University of Oklahoma Press, 1966.

Lambert, Gavin. *The Dangerous Edge.* New York: Grossman, 1976.

Leach, Michael. *I Know It When I See It: Pornography, Violence, and Public Sensitivity.* Philadelphia: Westminister, 1975.

Lee, Raymond and B. C. Van Hecke. *Gangsters and Hoodlums: The Underworld in the Cinema.* New York: Castle, 1971.

Lee, Walt. *Reference Guide to Fantastic Films: Science Fiction, Fantasy, and Horror.* Los Angeles; Chelsea-Lee Books, 1972.

Le Grice, Malcolm. *Abstract Film and Beyond.* Cambridge, Mass.: The MIT Press, 1977.

Levin, G. Roy. *Documentary Explorations: 15 Interviews with Filmmakers.* Garden City, N.Y.: Doubleday, 1971.

Leyda, Jay. *Films Beget Films.* London: George Allen, 1964.

Löker, Altan. *Film and Suspense.* Istanbul: Altan Löker, 1976.

Lovell, Alan and Jim Hillier. *Studies in Documentary.* New York: Viking, 1972.

McArthur, Colin. *Underworld U.S.A.* New York: Viking, 1972.

McCaffrey, Donald W. *The Golden Age of Sound Comedy: Comic Figures and Comedians of the Thirties.* New York: A. S. Barnes, 1973.

MacCann, Richard Dyer. *The People's Films: A Political History of U.S. Government Motion Pictures.* New York: Hastings House, 1973.

McNally, Raymond and Radu Florescu. *In Search of Dracula.* New York: Galahad Books, 1972.

Malone, Michael, *Heroes of Eros.* New York: E. P. Dutton, 1979.

Maltin, Leonard. *The Great Movie Shorts.* New York: Crown, 1972.

Mamber, Stephen. *Cinéma Vérité in America: Studies in Uncontrolled Documentary.* Cambridge, Mass.: MIT Press, 1974.

Manchel, Frank. *Terrors of the Screen.* Englewood Cliffs, N.J.: Prentice-Hall, 1970.

Manvell, Roger. *Experiment in the Film.* London: The Grey Walls Press, 1949.

Marcorelles, Louis. *Living Cinema: New Directions in Contemporary Film-Making.* New York: Praeger, 1973.

Mast, Gerald. *The Comic Mind: Comedy and the Movies.* Indianapolis: Bobbs-Merrill, 1973.

Maynard, Richard A. *The American West on Film: Myth and Reality.* Rochelle Park, N.J.: Hayden, 1974.

Mellen, Joan. *Big Bad Wolves.* New York: Pantheon, 1977.

Menville, Douglas and R. Reginald. *Things to Come.* New York: Times Books, 1977.

Mintz, Marilyn D. *The Martial Arts Film.* New York: A. S. Barnes, 1978.

Montgomery, John. *Comedy Films, 1894-1954.* London: George Allen and Unwin, 1954.

Morella, Joe, Edward Z. Epstein, and John Griggs. *The Films of World War II.* Secaucus, N.J.: Citadel, 1973.

Nachbar, John G., ed. *Focus on the Western.* Englewood Cliffs, N.J.: Prentice-Hall, 1974.

______. *Western Films: An Annotated Critical Bibliography.* New York: Garland, 1975.

Parish, James Robert and Michael R. Pitts. *The Great Gangster Pictures.* Metuchen, N.J.: Scarecrow, 1976.

______. *The Great Science Fiction Pictures.* Metuchen, N.J.: Scarecrow, 1977.

______. *The Great Western Pictures.* Metuchen, N.J.: Scarecrow, 1976.

Pate, Janet. *The Great Villains.* Indianapolis: Bobbs-Merrill, 1975.

Pirie, David. *The Vampire Cinema.* London: Hamlyn, 1977.

Pohle, Robert W., Jr. and Douglas C. Hart. *Sherlock Holmes on the Screen.* New York: A. S. Barnes, 1977.

Quirk, Lawrence J. *The Great Romantic Films.* Secaucus, N.J.: Citadel, 1974.

Rehrauer, George. *The Short Film: An Evaluative Selection of 500 Recommended Films.* New York: Macmillan, 1975.

Renan, Sheldon. *An Introduction to the American Underground Film.* New York: E. P. Dutton, 1967.

Richards, Jeffrey. *Swordsmen of the Screen.* London: Routledge and Kegan Paul, 1977.

Robinson, David. *The Great Funnies: A History of Film Comedy.* New York: E. P. Dutton, 1969.

Rosow, Eugene. *Born to Lose.* New York: Oxford University Press, 1978.

Rotha, Paul. *Documentary Diary: An Informal History of the British Documentary Film, 1928-1939.* New York: Hill and Wang, 1973.

Rothel, David. *The Singing Cowboys.* New York: A. S. Barnes, 1978.

______. *Who Was That Masked Man: The Story of the Lone Ranger.* New York: A. S. Barnes, 1976.

Rovin, Jeff. *The Fabulous Fantasy Films.* New York: A. S. Barnes, 1977.

Sennett, Ted. *Lunatics and Lovers: A Tribute to the Giddy and Glittering Era of the Screen's "Screwball" and Romantic Comedies.* New Rochelle, N.Y.: Arlington House, 1973.

Shadoian, Jack. *Dreams and Dead Ends.* Cambridge, Mass.: MIT Press, 1977.

Shaheen, Jack G., ed. *Nuclear War Films.* Carbondale: Southern Illinois University Press, 1978.

Silver, Alain. *The Samurai Film.* New York: A. S. Barnes, 1977.

______ and James Ursini. *The Vampire Film.* New York: A. S. Barnes, 1975.

Sitney, P. Adams. *The Essential Cinema: Essays on Films in the Collection of the Anthology Film Archives.* New York: Anthology Film Archives and New York University Press, 1975.

______, ed. *Film Culture Reader.* New York: Praeger, 1970.

______. *Visionary Film: The American Avant-Garde.* New York: Oxford University Press, 1974.

Smith, Julian. *Looking Away: Hollywood and Vietnam.* New York: Scribner's, 1975.

Solomon, Stanley J. *Beyond Formula: American Film Genres.* New York: Harcourt Brace Jovanovich, 1976.

Soren, David. *The Rise and Fall of the Horror Film: An Art Historical Approach to Fantasy Cinema.* Columbia, Mo.: Lucas Brothers Publishers, 1977.

Spears, Jack. *The Civil War on the Screen and Other Essays.* New York: A. S. Barnes, 1977.

Stauffacher, Frank. *Art in Cinema: Selected Essays.* New York: Arno, 1968.

Stedman, Raymond William. *The Serials: Suspense and Drama by Installments.* Norman: University of Oklahoma Press, 1971.

Steinbrunner, Chris and Burt Goldblatt. *Cinema of the Fantastic.* New York: Saturday Review Press, 1972.

______ and Norman Michaels. *The Films of Sherlock Holmes.* Secaucus, N.J.: Citadel, 1978.

Strick, Marv and Robert I. Lethe. *The Sexy Cinema.* Los Angeles: Sherbourne Press, 1975.
Strict, Philip. *Science Fiction Movies.* London: Octopus Books, 1976.
Suid, Lawrence H. *Guts and Glory.* Reading, Mass.: Addison-Wesley, 1978.
Tuska, Jon. *The Detective in Hollywood.* Garden City, N.Y.: Doubleday, 1978.
______. *The Filming of the West.* Garden City, N.Y.: Doubleday, 1976.
Tyler, Parker. *A Pictorial History of Sex in Films.* Secaucus, N.J.: Citadel, 1974.
______. *Sex, Psyche, Etcetera in the Film.* New York: Horizon, 1969.
______. *Screening the Sexes: Homosexuality in the Movies.* New York: Holt, Rinehart and Winston, 1972.
______. *The Underground Film: A Critical History.* New York: Grove, 1969.
Walker, Alexander. *The Celluloid Sacrifice: Aspects of Sex in the Movies.* New York: Hawthorne, 1966.
Weiss, Ken and Ed Goodgold. *To Be Continued. . . .* New York: Crown, 1972.
Willis, Donald C. *Horror and Science Fiction Films: A Checklist.* Metuchen, N.J.: Scarecrow, 1972.
Witcombe, Rick Trader. *Savage Cinema.* New York: Bounty Books, 1975.
Wortley, Richard. *Erotic Movies.* London: Studio Vista, 1975.
Wright, Will. *Sixguns and Society: A Structural Study of the Western.* Berkeley: University of California Press, 1975.
Youngblood, Gene. *Expanded Cinema.* New York: E. P. Dutton, 1970.
Ziplow, Steven. *The Film Maker's Guide to Pornography.* New York: Drake, 1977.

CHAPTER 5

Film and Related Arts

In a sense, film is a synthesis of all the arts that have preceded it. It has borrowed devices or techniques from the theater, photography, fiction, dance, music, architecture, painting, sculpture and even comics. Since these art forms have contributed to the development and aesthetics of film and are part of its heritage, an important approach to understanding and appreciating film study is the relationship between film and these other art forms.

Cineliteracy: Film Among the Arts is a recent introduction to film and its relationship to the other arts by Charles Eidsvik. Eidsvik begins by describing how films work, with an emphasis on their narrative devices. He then places cinema in a cultural perspective: film and the popular arts, film and literature, film and theater. He also analyzes films based on literary works, such as *Jules and Jim*, made from a novel, and *A Midsummer Night's Dream,* taken from Shakespeare's play. For anyone interested in learning more about film and its relationships with other arts, this book is a fine place to begin.

T. J. Ross has edited an excellent anthology of essays called *Film and the Liberal Arts* which provides an overview of the interrelationships between film and other arts. In particular, the essays consider film and literature, film and the visual arts, and film and music.

The Immediate Experience by Robert Warshow covers "movies, comics, theatre, and other aspects of popular culture." Warshow discusses the gangster as a tragic figure, the Westerns, the work of Charles Chaplin—especially *Monsieur Verdoux*—and the European film in America.

Authors on Film is an interesting anthology edited by Harry M. Geduld. Geduld has located and reproduced articles on film by well-known writers, among them Frank Norris' ideas on making *McTeague* into a film, Carl Sandburg's analysis of *The Cabinet of Dr. Caligari,* and H. G. Wells' famous attack on Fritz Lang's *Metropolis.* Other essays include screenwriting in the writer's view; impressions of working in Hollywood by William Faulkner, Theodore Dreiser, F. Scott Fitzgerald, and James Farrell; and critiques of Valentino by H. L. Mencken and John Dos Passos.

A good reference source for film and the other arts is *Filmed Books and Plays: A List of Books and Plays from Which Films Have Been Made, 1928-1974* by A. G. S. Enser. This book contains a film title index, an author index, and an index of titles which have been changed.

FILM AND LITERATURE

Ever since the early filmmakers made one-reel films from such literature as *Hamlet, Ramona,* and *Enoch Arden,* critics have devoted much of their analysis to the relationship between literature and film. A surprising number of films have literary sources, and the discussion of the relationship between the film and its source has been fruitful.

The basic resource for the study of film and literature is *Literature and Film* by Robert Richardson. Richardson's analysis of the relationships is thorough, and his emphasis is on the novel and drama. Moreover, he is one of few writers who has seriously considered the relationships between film and poetry. Many teachers of film have backgrounds in literature, and they will appreciate Richardson's preparation in the literary arts.

The Cinematic Imagination by Edward Murray deals with *Writers and the Motion Pictures.* Murray's first unit concerns drama and film in which he analyzes films based on the plays of Eugene O'Neill, Tennessee Williams, Gertrude Stein, Arthur Miller, and several European writers. Murray's second unit deals with the novel and film. Here his discussion ranges over many topics, from Theodore Dreiser in Hollywood to the stream of consciousness in novel and film (especially in the novels of James Joyce, Virginia Woolf, and William Faulkner). In addition, he covers John Dos Passos, F. Scott Fitzgerald, Nathanael West, Thomas Wolfe, Robert Penn Warren, Ernest Hemingway, Graham Greene, John Steinbeck, and Henry Miller.

Film and Literature: Contrasts in Media is an anthology edited by Fred Marcus. Marcus includes essays on the general theories of the relationships among the arts, as well as on specific films and literary works. Novels such as *Catch 22, The Grapes of Wrath,* and *Tom Jones* are analyzed, as are the plays *Romeo and Juliet* and *Pygmalion.*

Literature and/as Film is a fine anthology edited by John Harrington. The essays in this book cover adaptations (Martin Battestin on *Tom Jones,* for example), film and theater, film and the novel, and even film and poetry. Other essays deal with authorship and auteurship; the message, the medium, and the literary arts; and the literary sources of films.

The Screenplay as Literature by Douglass Garrett Winston is not as broad a study as its title suggests. Winston focuses on the relationships between film and the novel and on narrative technique; occasionally, however, he expands his horizons.

Film and the Novel

Among those books concentrating on the relationships between film and fiction, one would do well to start with those that deal broadly with the narrative devices of film. *Film and the Narrative Tradition* by John L. Fell compares the narrative forms of film to the narrative in both novels and the graphic arts. Morris Beja opens his *Film and Literature* by discussing the narrative visions of both media and proceeds to analyze the narrative devices in twenty-five films with strong narratives—some based on novels, others on plays, and still others on original screenplays. Included are *The Treasure of the Sierra Madre, Cat on a Hot Tin Roof,* and *Citizen Kane.*

The pioneering critical study of novels and film is George Bluestone's now classic *Novels into Film.* The theoretical introduction, widely reprinted in the anthologies discussed above, discusses "the limits of the novel and the limits of film," the different ways in which audiences of the two media respond, and how time, space, and myth work in the media. His extended analyses of films cover *The Grapes of Wrath, The Ox-Bow Incident, The Informer, Wuthering Heights, Pride and Prejudice,* and *Madame Bovary.*

The Novel and the Cinema by Geoffrey Wagner contains ideas that many will question but Wagner's wide experience with both literature and film makes the book worthwhile reading. Wagner opens with discussion of the roots of the two media. He also analyzes *Citizen Kane* as the synthesis of cinematic development up to that point. In addition, he discusses relationships between the technologies of the two media, and the "three principal manners by means of which novels to date have been adapted for the screen": transposition (*Wuthering Heights* and others), commentary (*Catch 22* and others), and analogy (*Cabaret* and others).

The Classic American Novel and the Movies is the first of a valuable series of books designed to provide thorough analysis of important novels that have been made into films. This volume, edited by Gerald Peary and Roger Shatzkin, deals with the filmed versions of American novels written before 1930 and is comprised of essays on twenty-seven novels/films, including *The Scarlet Letter, Moby Dick, The Great Gatsby, A Farewell to Arms,* and *The Sound and the Fury.*

A useful case study of a single novel made into a film is *Fiction into Film: A Walk in the Spring Rain.* This book includes the story by Rachel Maddux, the screenplay by Stirling Silliphant, and an analysis of the project by critic Neil Isaacs.

Film and the Short Story

Several critics have recently become interested in the short story and film. *Short Story/Short Film* by Fred Marcus presents films and stories especially suitable for classroom use. For each story/film, Marcus has included the story, a story board, and a film continuity (a shot analysis); stories/films included are "Young Goodman Brown," "The Lottery,"

"Bartleby," "The Upturned Face," and others. *The American Short Story* is a collection of tales that have been made into movies for the PBS television series, "The American Short Story." These films are now available in 16mm for classroom use and this anthology, edited by Calvin Skaggs, is a companion volume. Skaggs has introduced the entire series, then reprinted the short story for each film, an excerpt from the script, and a brief essay on the author. Included are nine short stories, including "The Blue Hotel" by Stephen Crane, "Bernice Bobs Her Hair" by F. Scott Fitzgerald, and "Almos' a Man" by Richard Wright.

Short Stories on Film is a valuable reference book by Carol A. Emmens. This book lists all the films made from short stories by the writers catalogued and provides technical data for each film; it is indexed by film title and by short story title.

Cinema of Mystery is Rose London's study of the influence of Edgar Allan Poe on film. Few writers have inspired so many films as Poe, and this book seeks out the major Poe images in film: the raven, the grave, the cat, the heart, the beast, and the haunted palace. London has sought out these images in other art forms as well as in film, and the result is an interesting pictorial study.

Film and Drama

The standard critical studies on film and theater are by Nicholas Vardac and Allardyce Nicoll, and both books are now classics which have recently been reprinted. *Stage to Screen* by Vardac is a good starting point because it deals with the roots of theater's influence on film. First published in 1949, this book is subtitled *Theatrical Methods from Garrick to Griffith* and is a study of nineteenth century drama and its influence on early cinema. Nicoll's *Film and Theatre* first appeared in 1936 and is based on the thesis that "stage characters are types and that in the cinema we demand individualization."

Focus on Film and Theatre is a good anthology edited by James Hurt which presents essays by critics, filmmakers, and playwrights who comment on the relationships between the two media. Hurt has included commentary by critics Vachel Lindsay, Allardyce Nicoll, Eric Bentley, Richard Gilman, and Stanley Kauffmann; by actors/directors Josef von Sternberg, Lillian Ross, Sergei Eisenstein, and Elia Kazan; and by playwrights George Bernard Shaw, Harold Pinter, and Clive Donner.

No study of film and theatre is complete without a survey of books on films of Shakespearean plays. *Focus on Shakespearean Films,* edited by Charles Eckert, provides a good overview. Eckert has included general essays on these films and essays dealing with the following specific films/plays: *A Midsummer Night's Dream*, *Henry V*, *Hamlet*, *Macbeth*, *Othello*, *Julius Caesar*, *Romeo and Juliet*, *Richard III*, *The Taming of the Shrew*, and *Chimes at Midnight* (parts taken from five plays to form Orson Welles' view of Falstaff). Another general study is *Shakespeare and the Film* by Roger Manvell. Manvell begins by considering the problems of adapting theater to the screen and then considers the adaptations of Shakespeare topically: the early sound films, Laurence Olivier, Orson Welles, the Russians, adaptations of *Julius Caesar,* the Italians, Akira Kurosawa, theater into film in the 1960s, and Peter Brook on *King Lear. Shakespeare on Film* is an important and scholarly book edited by Jack J. Jorgens. This anthology includes analysis of sixteen important films, including *A Midsummer Night's Dream, Romeo and Juliet, Julius Caesar, Othello, Henry V, Richard III, Hamlet, King Lear,* and *Macbeth.* The authors are Orson Welles, Laurence Olivier, Franco Zeffirelli, and others, who have been important in transforming Shakespeare into film. What Manvell and Jorgens have done for sound films, Robert Hamilton Ball has done for silent films. *Shakespeare on Silent Film* is rich with information and covers Shakespearean adaptations from Méliès and Griffith up to 1925. This valuable book describes Shakespearean film actors from Buster Keaton as Hamlet to Emil Jannings as Othello.

An Irishman whose plays have been popularized into films in the United States is George Bernard Shaw. *The Serpent's Eye* is a study of Shaw and the cinema by Donald P. Costello. After introductory essays describing Shaw's personal interest and involvement in the film, Costello provides detailed analysis of *Pygmalion, Major Barbara,* and *Caesar and Cleopatra.* This book deserves the highest praise as film criticism. Gabriel Pascal was the man who worked with Shaw to bring his three plays to the screen, and *The Disciple and His Devil* is by Valerie Pascal, Gabriel's wife. Using Shaw's correspondence as well as her own recollections, she has provided insight into the three films mentioned above and into *My Fair Lady* as well.

Another popular writer whose works have been made into film is Tennessee Williams. Maurice Yacowar has written about the films made from Williams' plays in *Tennessee Williams and Film.* This book contains solid analysis of *A Streetcar Named Desire*, *Cat on a Hot Tin Roof*, *Suddenly Last Summer*, and other films of Williams' plays, with a helpful discussion of the differences between the plays and the films.

Film and Poetry

There is no one book that analyzes the relationships between poetry and film. Several of the anthologies and other books described above contain sections dealing with poetry and film, but a book on the subject is yet to be written. Until that time one can begin a study of the two media with *The Poet as Filmmaker* by Alexander Dovzhenko, a Russian who has been both poet and filmmaker.

FILM AND THE VISUAL ARTS

Books that deal specifically with the relationships between film and other visual arts are difficult to find. One of the few available is Rudolf Arnheim's *Art and Visual Perception: A Psychology of the Creative Eye*. This book deals with the audience's response to the visual arts and establishes a kinship between film and other media. Another book dealing with film and other visual arts is *Modern Culture and the Arts,* an anthology edited by James B. Hall and Barry Ulanov. Music, painting and sculpture, novels, poetry, theater and dance, television and motion picture photography, and architecture and design are discussed by authors known as the best in their field. Taken as a whole, the book contributes to our understanding of the roles these arts play in our culture. The aesthetic side of these arts is considered in another anthology, *Aesthetics and the Arts* by Lee A. Jacobus. Jacobus considers dance, literature, music, painting and sculpture, architecture, and film in essays which explore the nature of the various media. Neither of these anthologies discusses the relationships between film and the visual media, but they do present essays on each in formats that invite the reader to draw his own conclusions as to their similarities and interrelationships. One book that does deal specifically with the relationship between film and one of the visual arts is *The Cubist Cinema* by Standish D. Lawder. Lawder "focuses on the interrelationships between film and modern art, predominantly painting from 1895 to 1925," and is interested in how artists have viewed and used cinema, among them Pablo Picasso and Wassily Kandinsky. *The Haunted Screen* by Lotte H. Eisner is a thorough study of the influence of Expressionism on film. Eisner concentrates on the German silent screen, but her principles apply to cinema in general. She is able to trace some film shots and techniques directly to Expressionistic paintings.

The relationship between surrealism and film have been covered in two books. The first, Michael Gould's *Surrealism and the Cinema,* opens with a chapter on the surrealist sensibility and includes chapters on specific topics: Luis Buñuel, Josef von Sternberg, Alfred Hitchcock, Samuel Fuller, animated films, and the artist-inventor such as Thomas Edison and Andy Warhol. The second, *Surrealism and Film* by J. H. Matthews, deals with surrealism and commercial films. Matthews is concerned with the genres of terror, comedy, and love films; he covers the filmmakers one would expect: in this regard Buñuel, René Clair, Man Ray, and Salvador Dali. He also includes topics one might not expect: Charles Chaplin and *King Kong.*

A reference book that might be helpful in the study of the relationships between film and the visual arts is *Films on Art,* prepared by the Canadian Centre for Films on Art. This book lists the critical information on over 2,000 films.

FILM AND MUSIC

There has always been music associated with film. Even in the silent era, movies were accompanied by some sort of music. In the large cities and for major films, orchestras as large as sixty players were sometimes used; in small towns there was at least a piano. Arno Press has now reprinted a 1920 guide to playing the accompaniment to the silent pictures, *Musical Accompaniment of Moving Pictures* by Edith Lang and George West. This is now a period piece, but is still of interest.

A more recent study of film music is *Music for the Movies* by Tony Thomas. Thomas begins with an overview of the topic and then focuses on the important composers for the screen: Alfred Newman, Elmer Bernstein, Bernard Herman, Ernest Gold, Max Steiner, and others. *Knowing the Score* is a more theoretical book by Irwin Bazelon in which the author delineates the role of the composer in film production, the role of music in the film, the technique for scoring a film, and discusses other technical matters. *Soundtrack: The Music of the Movies* by Mark Evans has chapters on the music of the silent era, the coming of sound, the golden age of film music, the function of the film score, and the aesthetics and ethics of film music. The most recent of the books on music and film is *Film Music: A Neglected Art* by Roy Prendergast. This is a scholarly book covering the aesthetics, history, and techniques of film music from silent films to the present day.

Musical films have been studied as much as musical scores for films. *The American Musical* by Tom Vallence is a brief alphabetical listing of films and personalities in American musicals. This is not an analytical book, but it does contain a wealth of information. A more analytical book is *The Hollywood Musical* by John Russell Taylor and Arthur Jackson. The authors discuss the role of music and dance in Hollywood musicals and include indexes to names, songs, and titles. Another reference guide is Allen L. Woll's *Songs from Hollywood Musical Comedies, 1927 to the Present: A Dictionary*. Woll has listed the titles of major films as well as the dates, stars, directors, song credits, and song titles.

Jazz in the Movies: A Guide to Jazz Musicians, 1917-1977 is by David Meeker. This is an alphabetical listing of jazz films and the musicians who performed in them.

Finally, David Parker and Esther Siegel have edited a reference book for dances in the movies, *Guide to Dance in Film: A Catalogue of U.S. Productions including Dance Sequences, with Names of Dancers, Choreographers, and Directors.*

FILM AND THE POPULAR ARTS

A few recent anthologies have invited the student to consider film as it relates to the other popular arts in our society. There have been a great number of these books through the years, but a few examples will illustrate the relationships. While few of these books actually include essays that specifically relate film to the other popular arts, all include essays on film in a context that allows the reader to make the comparisons. *The Popular Arts in America: A Reader,* edited by William M. Hammel, is one such book. It opens with essays that discuss the general role of the popular arts and includes units on movies, television and radio, popular music, and popular print with emphasis on the roles and aesthetics of each medium. A similar book is *American Mass Media* by Robert Atwan, Barry Orton, and William Vesterman. The authors discuss the industries related to the mass media and the forces in society which influence these industries and are influenced by them. After covering audiences, advertising, and government regulation, the authors consider books, newspapers, magazines, radio, recordings, films, television, and the personal media (public-access cable television and graffiti).

Mass Media and the Popular Arts, edited by Frederic Rissover and David C. Birch, includes essays on advertising, journalism, cartoons and comic strips, popular print, radio, television, photography, films, popular music, and media in education. The editors' goal is to promote understanding of how the media and art forms shape our lives and society. *Popular Culture: Mirror of American Life* is an anthology edited by David Manning White and John Pendleton. The thesis of the book is that the media of popular culture mirror our society. One unit deals with the way popular culture shapes our institutions and is shaped by them and includes essays on movies, television, music, sports, and the print media. Other units deal with the role of popular culture as an agent for change in our society and with the future of popular culture itself. The emphasis of the book is on the "hype" that energizes the popular media.

Mediamerica by Edward Jay Whetmore is not an anthology but rather, one man's view of the ways the popular media have shaped our society. Concerned with the "form, content and consequences of mass communication," Whetmore considers both the printed word and the electronic media, including film.

The New Languages: A Rhetorical Approach to the Mass Media and Popular Culture is by Thomas H. Ohlgren and Lynn M. Berk. This anthology is concerned primarily with the way the popular media have created new modes of communication. After a general discussion of the theories and practices of popular culture and mass media, the editors focus on propaganda, the language of print, the language of film, and the languages of television and radio.

BIBLIOGRAPHY

Arnheim, Rudolph. *Art and Visual Perception: A Psychology of the Creative Eye.* Berkeley: University of California Press, 1965.

Atwan, Robert, Barry Orton, and William Vesterman. *American Mass Media*. New York: Random House, 1978.

Ball, Robert Hamilton. *Shakespeare on Silent Film: A Strange Eventful History*. New York: Theatre Arts Books, 1968.

Bazelon, Irwin. *Knowing the Score: Notes on Film Music*. New York: Van Nostrand Reinhold, 1975.

Beja, Morris. *Film and Literature*. New York: Longmans, 1979.

Bluestone, George. *Novels into Film*. Berkeley: University of California Press, 1957.

Canadian Centre for Films on Art. *Films on Art: A Specialized Study*. New York: Watson-Guptill, 1977.

Costello, Donald P. *The Serpent's Eye: Shaw and the Cinema*. Notre Dame: University of Notre Dame Press, 1965.

Dovzhenko, Alexander. *The Poet as Filmmaker*. Translated and edited by Marco Carnnyk, Cambridge: The MIT Press, 1973.

Eckert, Charles, ed. *Focus on Shakespearean Films*. Englewood Cliffs, N.J.: Prentice-Hall, 1972.

Eidsvik, Charles. *Cineliteracy: Film Among the Arts*. New York: Random House, 1978.

Eisner, Lotte H. *The Haunted Screen: Expressionism in the German Cinema and the Influence of Max Reinhardt*. Translated by Roger Greaves. Berkeley: University of California Press, 1973.

Emmens, Carol A. *Short Stories on Film*. Littleton, Colo.: Libraries Unlimited, 1978.

Enser, A. G. S. *Filmed Books and Plays: A List of Books and Plays from Which Films Have Been Made, 1928-1974*. London: André Deutsch, 1975.

Evans, Mark. *Soundtrack: The Music of the Movies*. New York: Hopkins and Blake, 1975.

Fell, John L. *Film and the Narrative Tradition*. Norman: University of Oklahoma Press, 1974.

Geduld, Harry M., ed. *Authors on Film*. Bloomington: Indiana University Press, 1972.

Gould, Michael. *Surrealism and the Cinema*. New York: A. S. Barnes, 1976.

Hall, James B. and Barry Ulanov. *Modern Culture and the Arts*. New York: McGraw-Hill, 1967.

Hammel, William M. *The Popular Arts in America: A Reader*. New York: Harcourt Brace Jovanovich, 1972.

Harrington, John, ed. *Literature and/as Film*. Englewood Cliffs, N.J.: Prentice-Hall, 1977.

Hurt, James, ed. *Focus on Film and Theatre*. Englewood Cliffs, N.J.: Prentice-Hall, 1974.

Jacobus, Lee A. *Aesthetics and the Arts*. New York: McGraw-Hill, 1968.

Jorgens, Jack J., ed. *Shakespeare on Film*. Bloomington: Indiana University Press, 1977.

Lang, Edith, and George West. *Musical Accompaniment of Moving Pictures: A Practice Manual for Pianists and Organists*. New York: Arno, 1970.

Lawder, Standish D. *The Cubist Cinema*. New York: New York University Press, 1975.

London, Rose. *Cinema of Mystery*. New York: Bounty Books, 1975.

Maddux, Rachel, Stirling Silliphant, and Neil D. Isaacs. *Fiction into Film: A Walk in the Spring Rain.* New York: Dell, 1970.

Manvell, Roger. *Shakespeare and the Film.* New York: Praeger, 1971.

Marcus, Fred, ed. *Film and Literature: Contrasts in Media.* Scranton, Pa.: Chandler, 1971.

______. *Short Story/Short Film.* Englewood Cliffs, N.J.: Prentice-Hall, 1977.

Matthews, J. H. *Surrealism and Film.* Ann Arbor: University of Michigan Press, 1971.

Meeker, David., *Jazz in the Movies: A Tentative Index to the Work of Jazz Musicians for the Cinema.* New Rochelle, N.Y.: Arlington House, 1977.

Murray, Edward. *The Cinematic Imagination: Writers and the Motion Picture.* New York: Frederick Ungar, 1972.

Nicoll, Allardyce. *Film and Theatre.* New York: Arno, 1972.

Ohlgren, Thomas H. and Lynn M. Berk. *The New Languages: A Rhetorical Approach to the Mass Media and Popular Culture.* Englewood Cliffs, N.J.: Prentice-Hall, 1977.

Parker, David and Esther Siegel. *Guide to Dance in Film.* Detroit: Gale Research, 1978.

Pascal, Valerie. *The Disciple and His Devil: Gabriel Pascal* [and] *Bernard Shaw.* New York: McGraw-Hill, 1970.

Peary, Gerald and Roger Shatzkin, eds. *The Classic American Novel and the Movies.* New York: Frederick Ungar, 1977.

Prendergast, Roy M. *Film Music: A Neglected Art.* New York: W. W. Norton, 1977.

Richardson, Robert. *Literature and Film.* Bloomington: Indiana University Press, 1969.

Rissover, Frederic and David C. Birch. *Mass Media and the Popular Arts.* New York: McGraw-Hill, 1977.

Ross, T. J., ed. *Film and the Liberal Arts.* New York: Holt, Rinehart and Winston, 1970.

Skaggs, Calvin, ed. *The American Short Story.* New York: Dell, 1977.

Taylor, John Russell, and Arthur Jackson. *The Hollywood Musical.* New York: McGraw-Hill, 1971.

Thomas, Tony. *Music for the Movies.* New York: A. S. Barnes, 1973.

Vallance, Tom. *The American Musical.* New York: A. S. Barnes, 1970.

Vardac, Nicholas. *Stage to Screen: Theatrical Methods from Garrick to Griffith.* New York: Benjamin Blom, 1968.

Wagner, Geoffrey. *The Novel and the Cinema.* Rutherford, N.J.: Fairleigh Dickinson University Press, 1975.

Warshow, Robert. *The Immediate Experience: Movies, Comics, Theatre, and Other Aspects of Popular Culture.* New York: Atheneum, 1971.

Whetmore, Edward Jay. *Mediamerica: Form, Content, and Consequence of Mass Communication.* Belmont, Calif.: Wadsworth, 1979.

White, David Manning, and John Pendleton, eds. *Popular Culture: Mirror of American Life.* Del Mar, Calif.: Publisher's Inc., 1977.

Winston, Douglas Garrett. *The Screenplay as Literature.* Rutherford, N.J.: Fairleigh Dickinson University Press, 1973.

Woll, Allen L. *Songs from Hollywood Musical Comedies, 1927 to the Present: A Dictionary.* New York: Garland Publishing, 1976.

Yacowar, Maurice. *Tennessee Williams and Film.* New York: Frederick Ungar, 1977.

CHAPTER 6

Film and Society

Film is often a reflection of the society that produces it, and an especially fruitful approach to understanding film is to study the social comments of films or to consider society's impact on the films' content. Obviously this topic is large and difficult to define precisely, but the sections of this chapter provide guides to a few social trends and disciplines important to film study.

FILM AND HISTORY

Many films are about history, and an analysis of these films can provide insights into the historical period or events. Films may or may not reflect historical facts, but a study of what films say about a historical period or event may well demonstrate the way cultural myth works.

Historians are beginning to discover uses for film in studying history. *Visions of Yesterday* by Jeffrey Richards deals with the cinema of political right. Richards' thesis is that films, through their mythologies and ideologies, illustrate and dramatize "the basic elements of movements in recent history." Richards demonstrates his point with three case histories: British imperialism, American populism (directors John Ford, Frank Capra, and Leo McCarey), and German national socialism.

Paul Smith has edited an anthology of essays that discuss ways the historian uses film. *The Historian and Film* contains articles on the raw material, on film as historical evidence, on film as historical factor, and on film as interpreter and tracer of history.

Another anthology is *American History/American Film,* edited by John E. O'Connor and Martin A. Jackson. The editors have collected essays that attempt to analyze American life in the twentieth century through films representative of each decade. From silents such as *Way Down East* and early sound films such as *Drums Along the Mohawk* to the more recent *Rocky,* the movies are studied closely to determine what they reveal about our society.

Media-Made Dixie: The South in the American Imagination is by Jack

Temple Kirby. Kirby considers the image of the South in film, television, and popular music. His topics include D. W. Griffith and race, the old South, the new South, and the changing South.

Film and Revolution by James Roy MacBean is a Marxist approach to film criticism. MacBean focuses on Jean-Luc Godard and his co-workers, with side glances at others including Dusan Makavajev and Roberto Rossellini. MacBean's essays are on film criticism in the "post-Bazin aesthetics," film criticism in the era after the influence of French critic André Bazin.

FILM AND POLITICS

Politics are often important in films and many books make reference to the political aspects of the films they are analyzing. Two books in particular are specifically devoted to political criticism in films. *Double Feature: Movies and Politics* by Michael Goodwin and Greil Marens discusses Marxist politics and the cinema of the late 1960s and early 1970s. The book is basically an interview with Jean-Luc Godard and Jean-Pierre Gorin on the politics of their films.

Politics and Film by Leif Furhammar and Folke Isaksson is a collection of "essays on movies that have clear political purpose." The authors first consider a history of politics and film, from World War I to the recent political revolution in Brazil. They go on to discuss specific films, such as *Triumph of the Will, Mrs. Miniver, Torn Curtin, Green Berets,* and *Che!* Finally, they analyze the principles and aesthetics of propaganda, personality cults, the image of the enemy, myth, and psychological defense.

Andrew Sarris has been one of the foremost film reviewers in this country for many years. Unlike many who write about film, he considers himself to be apolitical; despite this, he has reviewed a large number of films dealing with politics. In *Politics and Cinema* he has brought together his reviews of these films. Because he is not espousing any particular political philosophy *Politics and Cinema* stands as one of the most objective analyses of political films available.

FILM AND PROPAGANDA

The Celluloid Weapon by David Manning White and Richard Averson is a large, richly illustrated book on film as propaganda; it combines a history of propaganda in film with commentary on propaganda films. The authors have included chapters on propaganda films related to the Depression, the 1930s, World War II, the atomic bomb, and the 1950s.

Richard A. Maynard's *Propaganda on Film: A Nation at War* is a social scientist's view of World War II film propaganda. Maynard first discusses the concept of propaganda and the impact of propaganda in film. He then examines both German and American propaganda during World War II and concludes with a consideration of the propaganda of the Cold War.

FILM AND CENSORSHIP

A historical perspective on movie censorship can be found in *Censored* by Morris Ernst and director Pare Lorentz. This book is a study of what the censorship boards were deleting in the late 1920s and early 1930s.

During the 1930s the movie industry set up its own watchdog agency, and *The Hays Office* by Raymond Moley is a study of censorship activity during this period. The book came out at about the time Hays retired in the mid 1940s and is clearly pro-Hays, maintaining that Hays improved public tastes. It contains a detailed analysis of what the code did and what it did not do. The appendixes include the code itself and its clarifications.

The Face on the Cutting Room Floor: The Story of Movie and Television Censorhip by Murray Schumach is the story of the scenes left on the floor of the editing room for censorship reasons. This history is not complete, but it does present a good overview of the role of censorship in our electronic media. *The Unkindest Cuts: The Scissors and the Cinema* by Doug McClelland describes the scenes that have been cut out and tells why.

The legal side of the censorship issue is the subject of two books. Ira H. Carmen's *Movies, Censorship and the Law* discusses the Supreme Court and its rulings affecting censorship as well as local control of movies exercised by the states and cities. In *Censorship of the Movies,* Richard S. Randall analyzes the movies and the law, with emphasis on the *Burstyn v. Wilson* decision concerning the film *The Miracle,* which placed film under the protection of the First Amendment. Randall's organization makes this book somewhat difficult to follow, but the subject is the social and political control of the mass media.

Another approach to censorship is the personal perspective. *See No Evil* by Jack Vizzard, a former censor, is a humorous and insightful collection of anecdotes. *The Movie Rating Game* by Stephen Farber is a view from inside the rating board, the successor to the censorship office. Farber's personal account of the workings of the board places the activities of this board in a historical perspective.

The problems of censorship are often more severe abroad, and a number of books present an international perspective on this issue. Enid Wistrich, formerly chairman of the Film Viewing Board of the Greater London Council, wrote *Film Censorship Explored*, an analysis of censorship from the perspective of one who feels that the British censors have been too strict in judging movies intended for adults. *Film Censors and the Law* by Neville March Hunnings deals with the problem on a worldwide basis. His concentration is on Britain, but he also discusses censorship in the United States, India, Canada, Australia, Denmark, France, and the USSR. *World-Wide Influence of the Cinema* is a view of censorship around the world by John Eugene Harley. Writing in 1940, Harley focused on films exported from America and the need for care in the presentation of the American way of life to those abroad; his book is now an interesting period piece.

Screen Violence and Film Censorship by Stephen Brody is a review of research on the problems of violence and censorship. The author is an Englishman who has reviewed scientific investigations into topics such as the effects of filmed violence on audiences, learning through imitation, the arousal and stimulation of aggressive tendencies, the emotional reaction to films, and the influence of films on attitudes.

A special type of censorship invaded the American movie industry during the 1950s with the House Un-American Activities Committee. This infamous period is documented in John Cogley's *Report on Blacklisting,* a complete and objective study of HUAC hearings and the supposed influence of Communists on the movies. On the other hand *Hollywood on Trial* by Gordon Kahn is a subjective account of the period; the author tells the story of the screenwriters persecuted by HUAC, the so-called Hollywood Ten, and is clearly biased in their favor. Larry Ceplair and Steven Englund have provided the most comprehensive study of political censorship in *The Inquisition in Hollywood: Politics in the Film Community, 1930-1960.* The authors describe the work of Communists and other leftists in Hollywood, the hearings in Congress, the blacklist, and the efforts of those affected to recover their careers. The bias of this fine book is suggested by its dedication "to those who resisted." A look at the effects of blacklisting by one man whose career clearly survived the blacklist is *Dalton Trumbo* by Bruce Cook. *The Powers That Be* by David Halberstam provides a view of the way the mass media responded to McCarthy within a general study of the power of the media.

FILM AND SOCIOLOGY

One area of concern among scholars has been the impact that movies have on society. I. C. Jarvie has written two books that consider this impact. In the first, *Movies and Society,* Jarvie presents a sociologist's view of the influence of movies on society and considers topics such as the sociology of the film industry (why people make movies) and the sociology of the audience (who goes to the movies and why). In his second book, *Movies as Social Criticism,* Jarvis looks at aspects of the movies' "social psychology" and considers the role movies play in creating our social psychology. He considers the ways movies and society interact (for example, the movies' influence on marriage), the movies as social criticism, movies and reality, and the diverse audience of film.

In *Cinema and Society* Paul Monaco begins with a look at the role that film played in the development of society in France and Germany in the 1920s. Even though the book does not deal with America, the methods used here suggest methods and theories for considering the relationship between the medium and society in the United States as well. Monaco considers such topics as films as big business in France and Germany, film and government policy, film and the national folklore, the popular cinema in France, and obsession in the German film.

The Sociology of Film Art by George A. Huaco is a study of the importance and impact on American film of three schools of filmmaking: German Expressionism, Soviet expressive realism, and Italian neorealism; Huaco also considers the social, economic, and political contexts of these movements. The influence of film on American society is addressed in *The Movies: An American Idiom*, edited by Arthur F. McClure. McClure included essays by Lewis Jacobs, Hollis Alpert, Olivia de Havilland, and others to describe the historical relationship between American movies and the society in which they were made. The essays cover topics such as blacks in film, Hollywood, the blacklist, Disney, and *The Graduate.*

In *Image and Influence,* Andrew Tudor writes about the impact of film on society from a sociologist's point of view. His basic concerns are how people communicate and how movies communicate. He analyzes movie audiences and language, and discusses patterns of culture and how a film movement can affect society (he uses German Expressionism as a case study); he also discusses the popular genres (Westerns, gangster movies, and horror films) to demonstrate how the audience receives patterns of meaning.

Michael Wood has attempted to discover what the movies of the 1940s and 1950s were saying about America in *America in the Movies.* His thesis is that major actors and directors of that period reflected dominant trends in society. Humphrey Bogart represents the loneliness of our society, Gene Kelly the self-confidence, Alfred Hitchcock the sinister quality, and Marilyn Monroe the innocence.

America in the Dark: Hollywood and the Gift of Unreality is a study by David Thompson of the aesthetics and effects of film where he has analyzed the system, the artists, and the audience. His eclectic collection includes an analysis of *Citizen Kane* and a study of the images of the city in American films. This is an interesting book but one difficult to categorize.

Many of the books discussed in this section note the effect of movies on their audience, but several books deal specifically with the audience of movies. *Film and Society,* an anthology edited by Richard Dyer MacCann, addresses the extent and ways in which the audience is affected by the movies—if at all—with special attention to the roles of propaganda and censorship. In *Hollywood Looks at its Audience* Leo A. Handel presents a sociological analysis—complete with tests and data—of the audience of movies. The book includes an interesting consideration of the way filmmakers use audience's responses to working prints of a film to alter the finished product. *Clozentropy: A Technique for Studying Audience Response to Film* is a technical thesis by Dennis F. Lynch which presents an interesting "new test instrument with which we can explore the interaction among different types of film . . . , different types of audiences, and expectations about what is going to happen next in films.''

FILM AND ANTHROPOLOGY

An anthropologist's view of the movies is presented in *Hollywood: The Dream Factory* by Hortense Powdermaker. This classic study is now a bit dated (it came out in 1950), but is still of value in understanding how Hollywood has been important to the American imagination.

Two more recent books on anthropology in film deserve mention here. *About Documentary: Anthropology on Film* by Robert Edmonds presents ''a philosophy of people and art.'' It includes essays by Edmonds and other writers on various anthropological aspects of the documentary, such as the relation between the documentary and its culture, the way the films use culture, and the way films report on the culture. The second book, *Through Navajo Eyes,* is a report on the work of anthropologists Sol Worth and John Adair with the Navajo Indians. The authors worked with the Navajos, teaching them the use of the camera so that they might be able to record their own culture and capture the essence of their life style for themselves and posterity.

FILM AND MINORITIES

Ethnic Images in American Film and Television is a study supported by the Balch Institute and consists of papers read at one session held by the institute. The anthology, edited by Randall M. Miller, contains images in film and television of blacks, Jews, German-Americans, Irish, Italian-Americans, Polish-Americans, Puerto Ricans, and Asian-Americans.

Blacks

Most scholarly attention in the area of ethnic studies has been devoted to images of blacks. Black studies have received much attention in the past ten years, but the black image in films has been recognized for some time. *The Negro in Films* is a reissue of a book by Peter Noble that came out in the late 1940s. Noble's book is a historical survey that begins with a view of the black on the stage and then moves to the black in film; Noble also looks at the black in European films and the careers of major black actors.

Thomas Cripps has become one of the important critics of the roles of blacks in the movies. In *Slow Fade to Black* Cripps considers the black in American films from 1900 to 1942. This excellent scholarly book is not only a history of the black accomplishment in film, but is also social commentary on American racial attitudes during the early part of the century. In a second book, *Black Film as Genre,* Cripps begins with a definition and evolution of the black film and proceeds to analyze six important black films: *The Scar of Shame*, *The St. Louis Blues*, *The Blood of Jesus*, *The*

Negro Soldier, Nothing but a Man, and *Sweet Sweetback's Baadassss Song.*

In *From Sambo to Superspade,* Daniel J. Leab shows the progress—or the lack thereof—of the image of the black in films from *Birth of a Nation* to *Shaft.* Leab maintains that in some ways the image of *Shaft* is just as detrimental to the black as was the racism of the silent period.

Blacks in American Films: Today and Yesterday by Edward Mapp is a study of the images of blacks from a historical perspective. Mapp briefly covers the period from World War I to the early 1960s, and then each year since 1961 in detail. His focus is on the portrayal of the black in American films, especially the films of the 1960s. His lengthy bibliography is worthy of special note.

Toms, Coons, Mulattoes, Mammies and Blacks: An Interpretative History of Blacks in American Film is by Donald Bogle. Bogle's thesis is that even in stereotyped roles the black actor has asserted himself and his black identity.

Lindsay Patterson has edited an anthology of essays that contain both history and criticism of the roles that blacks have played in cinema. *Black Films and Film-Makers* is an excellent collection of essays which begins by establishing an overview of black roles in American films and goes on to analyze specific films and discuss the black actor.

James P. Murray claims that *To Find an Image: Black Films from Uncle Tom to Superfly* covers the history of black films. The book, however, is not so much a history as a valuable collection of interviews with important blacks in the movie industry, including Gordon Parks and Ossie Davis.

Richard Maynard has compiled two books for teachers on the images of blacks in films. *The Black Man on Film: Racial Stereotyping* is a useful guide containing both essays of interpretation and a filmography. *Africa on Film: Myth and Reality* is obviously more specialized. In this book, Maynard has chosen essays that cover a variety of topics including Tarzan, Stanley and Livingstone as seen in the movies, and the images of the black man on his home continent.

Several books have been written for a more popular audience than those discussed above. *Black Hollywood* by Gary Null is one such book; it is largely pictorial and covers (as the subtitle indicates) *The Negro in Motion Pictures* decade by decade with limited commentary. *Blacks in Films* by Jim Pines is a short book which focuses on the images of blacks in film from the silent period to the 1970s, with emphasis on the "blaxploitation" of the 1970s. Eileen Landay's *Black Film Stars* is another book whose main value is pictorial; it contains a brief overview of films and actors from *Uncle Tom's Cabin* to Cicely Tyson and Richard Roundtree.

There are also two reference sources for the study of blacks in films. Henry T. Sampson's *Blacks in Black and White: A Source Book on Black Films* begins with an overview of black cast production from 1910 to 1950, then discusses the major black production companies, and provides synopses of some black films of the period. *Blacks in American Movies: A Selected Bibliography* by Anne Powers is another useful reference. Unfortunately, only a few of the bibliographical entries are annotated, but her author and subject indexes are helpful. She also includes a filmography of feature films by and about blacks from 1904 to 1930.

Ethnic Groups

While much has been written on the black image in film, little has been written on other ethnic minorities in film. Allen L. Woll has discussed the image of Latin Americans in *The Latin Image in American Film.* This book is a historical survey of the image, from the "greaser" characters of the silent era to the realistic characters in *Viva Zapata* and *Salt of the Earth.*

The American Indian has been virtually ignored in books on film. One, *The Only Good Indian . . . The Hollywood Gospel* by Ralph E. and Natasha A. Friar provides a historical and critical survey of the roles native Americans have played in films and of the images those films have portrayed of the Indians.

Women

With the women's movement has come a new awareness of the way women have been portrayed in motion pictures, an awareness that is reflected in some of the more interesting books on film to have been written recently. *On the Verge of Revolt* by Brandon French develops the thesis that the women's movement had its roots in the guilt of the 1950s. French has studied the films of that decade to substantiate this thesis and concludes that attitudes in the 1950s toward sex, motherhood, alcoholism, and ambition led to the desire among women in the 1960s for new status. She covers *Sunset Boulevard, Shane, The Tender Trap, Picnic, Some Like It Hot,* and other films to demonstrate her points.

Two books stand out for their best overall analyses of the images of women in films. *From Reverence to Rape* by Molly Haskell contains both a history of the images and criticism of what these images have meant to our society and women in our society. *Popcorn Venus* by Marjorie Rosen also provides an overview through a panoramic look at the roles women have been assigned in films from the silent period through the early 1970s.

An anthology that provides an overview of women in film is *Women and the Cinema,* edited by Karyn Kay and Gerald Peary. The book includes essays on feminist perspectives (in *Klute* and other films), as well as essays on actresses, women in American productions, experimentalists, women in political films, and polemics. The concluding chapter asks whether there is, indeed, a feminist film theory.

Women and Their Sexuality in the New Film by Joan Mellen is an eclectic group of fascinating essays. Mellen has included essays on Mae West; on bourgeois women; on female sexuality in the movies; on lesbianism in the movies; on Bergman and women; and on sexual politics in *Last Tango in Paris, Death in Venice,* and *The Fox.* Mellen's book is feminist to a fault.

Several books discuss female archetypes on the screen. *Film Archetypes: Sisters, Mistresses, Mothers, and Daughters* by Janice R. Welsch is a reprint of a dissertation that analyzes the roles played by actresses Doris Day, Debbie Reynolds, Marilyn Monroe, Kim Novak, Elizabeth Taylor, Audrey Hepburn, and Grace Kelly, and then analyzes the stereotypes of the title as they have been portrayed in film. Marsha McCreadie has edited *The American Movie Goddess,* an anthology of essays, news clippings, photographs, and magazine advertisements that illustrate the impact the movie goddess has had on American society. McCreadie concentrates on Greta Garbo in the 1930s, Rita Hayworth in the 1940s, and Marilyn Monroe in the 1950s. *Love Goddesses of the Movies* by Roger Manvell is another study of the women of the movies, among them Mary Pickford, Theda Bara, Clara Bow, Greta Garbo, Marlene Dietrich, Jean Harlow, Vivien Leigh, Betty Grable, Marilyn Monroe, Ingrid Bergman, Brigitte Bardot, and Elizabeth Taylor. *Venus in Hollywood: The Continental Enchantress from Garbo to Loren* is a study of European actresses in American films. Michael Bruno also covers Pola Negri, Marlene Dietrich, Luise Rainer, Hedy Lamarr, Ingrid Bergman, and Simone Signoret.

Two books have dealt with women as directors. *Early Women Directors* by Anthony Slide is a brief collection of essays on the important women who were the first to break into the ranks of the directors. Slide provides criticism and a historical overview of the directing careers of Alice Guy Blanche, Lois Webber, Margery Wilson, Mrs. Wallace Reid, Frances Marion, and Dorothy Arzna. A study of more recent women directors is by Sharon Smith in *Women Who Make Movies.* Smith has surveyed hundreds of women who are making movies, from those who have a national reputation—such as Elaine May—to those working in 16mm trying to establish a reputation. The entries are short, but the book is valuable for its scope and its recognition of many fine women directors who have received little notice for their work.

Several books serve as reference guides to women in films. *Women's Films in Print* by Bonnie Dawson is an annotated guide to 800 films by women. *Women and Film: A Bibliography* by Rosemary Ribich Kowalski lists articles on women and on women critics with brief annotations. *Women in Focus* by Jeanne Betancourt is concrned with the images of women in film and with women filmmakers and includes an annotated list of films relevant to the study of women in films.

FILM AND PSYCHOLOGY

It is often difficult to separate psychological analyses of film from other forms of criticism, but two books clearly focus on the psychological aspects of movies. *Movies: A Psychological Study* by Martha Wolfenstein and

Nathan Leites focuses on active and passive roles in films. The authors discuss lovers and loved ones, parents and children, killers and victims, performers and spectators. *The Movies on Your Mind* by psychoanalyst Harvey R. Greenberg presents a psychoanalytic interpretation of some favorite films: *The Wizard of Oz, The Treasure of the Sierra Madre, The Maltese Falcon, Casablanca, Frankenstein, King Kong, 2001,* as well as of the work of Alfred Hitchcock and of horror films in general. Greenberg's book is enjoyable and insightful although some of his ideas are bizarre and must not be taken seriously.

FILM AND RELIGION

In *Religion in the Cinema*, Ivan Butler discusses the movie images of the Bible, Christ, the church, priests, nuns, and other clerics. He gives special attention to religious allegories, and to comedic and satirical treatment of religion in film.

Theology Through Film by Neil Hurley examines the theological statements made in the movies about freedom, sex, evil, sacrificial love, and the future. Hurley's chapter on death on camera is especially interesting. The book has been published in paperback under the title *Toward a Film Humanism.*

Approaches to the Religious Dimension in the Cinema is the subtitle of *Beyond the Image* by Ronald Holloway. This book, published by the World Council of Churches, begins by discussing the role of theology in the cinema and moves on to discussion of topics such as "from the passion play to *Intolerance,*" the religious significance of Chaplin's films, and faith in the cinema of Carl Theador Dryer.

Since movies often reflect the philosophical and social traumas of the twentieth century, it is fitting that scholars should use them to discuss the search for meaning that has characterized much of religious thinking since World War I. Two books concentrate on films on man's search for meaning.

Images of Man by Donald J. Drew presents a Christian view of modern films with a focus on man's search for meaning. The book urges caution against the mind control that film can exercise and pleads for personal censorship in film selection. Man's search for meaning is also the subject of *Film Odyssey* by Ernest Ferlita and John R. May. Writing from a Roman Catholic perspective, the authors have described the ways movies have portrayed that search in personal lives, in society in general, and in religion; they discuss such films as *La Strada*, *Easy Rider*, *The Godfather*, *The Seventh Seal*, and *2001*.

A number of books are designed to help establish a Christian ministry through the use of movies. Such books assist ministers or priests in setting up programs that will attract those who are especially interested in the medium. *Sunday Night at the Movies* by G. William Jones discusses film as a medium for delivering a Christian message and guides the clergy in the use of this medium. *Church and Cinema* by James M. Wall, editor of the

Christian Advocate, is in part, a book on the use films might have in church programs; Wall deals with films that have a spiritual message, such as *Midnight Cowboy, Diary of a Country Priest,* and *Persona.* In *Marquee Ministry,* Robert G. Konzelman concentrates on "the movie theatre as church and community forum" and discusses the use of movies in fostering Christian values. *Short Films in Religious Education* by William Kuhns is a reference guide for clergy and others who want to incorporate films into religious education; approximately fifty short films are cited with information including date, distributor, director, summary of plot, and suggestions on use.

FILM AND EDUCATION

An excellent place to begin the consideration of the role of film in education is *Perspectives on the Study of Film,* an anthology edited by John Stuart Katz. Essays in this book deal with film study and education at the college level; the film as art and humanities; the film as communications, environment, and politics; and curriculum design and evaluation in film study.

David A. Sohn has selected the best of *Media and Methods* for a useful anthology of essays, *Good Looking: Film Studies, Short Films, and Filmmaking.* Sohn is concerned with students at the secondary level and discusses both the problems with and the hopes for film use in the classroom; he also discusses short films that might work well with students and looks at the pitfalls and promises of filmmaking in school.

The best known survey of film study in colleges is an anthology edited by David C. Stewart, *Film Study in Higher Education.* Stewart's book was published in 1966 and, of course, much has happened in film education since then, but it is still interesting and useful. Stewart is a proponent of film study and outlines film courses in one hundred large colleges. The most recent guide to the study of film is The American Film Institute's *Guide to College Courses in Film and Television,* which lists courses in more than one thousand colleges.

Once it is decided to use film in the classroom, the next step is to determine how to incorporate it into the curriculum. John Stuart Katz has written another book, *A Curriculum in Film,* which will assist a teacher in establishing a first curriculum. The first part of the book deals with the study of film, with an emphasis on the relationship between literature and film; the second part gives the materials for a unit on "man and machines"; the last helps develop an understanding of the film medium. Another resource for teachers is *Film Study: A Resource Guide* by Frank Manchel. Although a rather routine aid in establishing a film curriculum, Manchel does discuss a representative genre (war films), stereotyping in film, a thematic approach, a representative period as seen in film (1913-1919), the history of film, and other topics of interest to teachers.

The social science teacher will find *The Celluloid Curriculum* especially valuable. Written by Richard A. Maynard, film editor for *Scholastic Magazine,* this book covers a wide range of possibilities for using film in social studies. Maynard suggests studying revolution, race, crime, marriage, and ethics through film; considers film as a historical and social object of study; and suggests units on the West, war, Africa, blacks in the movies, the Depression, McCarthy, and violence.

Film studies seems to fit most naturally into English programs, and English teachers have several guides to the use of film in their curricula. *The Complete Guide to Film Study,* an anthology edited by Howard G. Poteet and sponsored by the National Council of Teachers of English, covers the rationale for using film in the English classroom, film history, film language, film and literature, film in composition, film in the curriculum, and film study in the 1970s. NCTE also sponsored *The Motion Picture and the Teaching of English*, edited by Marion Sheridan and others. This good—but dated—introduction to film provides background on film theory and a consideration of film in the English classroom. The editors present film analysis (*Citizen Kane*), film structure (*The Grapes of Wrath*), and film criticism. *Film Study and the English Teacher* is a pamphlet by David A. Sohn which also discusses the rationale for using film in the classroom, types of film used, and approaches to film study.

A number of books deal with the role of film production in education. *Doing the Media,* edited by Kit Laybourne with assistance from friends at the Center for Understanding Media in New York, covers not only film production in the classroom, but storyboarding, animation, and scratch and doodle films (films made without a camera). This is an excellent book notable for its suggestions for use of film with younger students.

Other books cited in the chapter on production provide guidance in filmmaking, but there are several books geared to the younger student. *Filmmaking in Schools* by Douglas Lowndes describes filmmaking equipment and suggests projects, some for the English teacher, others for teachers of theatre, art, music, and movement. *Young Filmmakers* by Rodger Larson and Ellen Meade tells the teacher what he needs to know about making 8mm and 16mm films; the authors cover the camera and moviemaking equipment, movies without a camera, editing, sound, and projection. Harry Helfman's *Making Your Own Movies* is another book for young children with large print, a simple approach, and many illustrations. Helfman begins with a brief history of film and then discusses the camera, shooting, editing, animation, and sound.

Many books on film for children deal with animation. Perhaps the best-known of these is *Teaching Film Animation to Children* by Yvonne Anderson, one of the leading experimenters with children and filmmaking. Anderson discusses supplies, class organization, the general idea of animation, projection, editing, the story, and sound. *Young Animators and their Discoveries* by Rodger Larson, Lynne Hofer, and Jaime Barrios interviews twelve young filmmakers to determine what they learn while they are making a film; it is thus of interest to those wanting to make animated films in the classroom and those interested in how and what children learn. The teacher with limited resources might consider teaching cinematic production devices through scratch and doodle films and other means of making movies without a camera. A useful guide to such techniques is *Animating Films Without a Camera* by Jacques Bourgeois.

Personal Filmmaking by James Piper is "for use in general education programs in high schools and colleges." Piper goes from 8mm equipment for the novice to sophisticated soundtracks and discusses selecting equipment, finding ideas for a film, scripts, directing and acting, shooting, editing, sound, and screening.

There are two books helpful to elementary teachers for finding short films for classroom use. *Films Kids Like* by Susan Rice is one book every school should own. Rice's introduction discusses how films can be used with children, especially in the classroom, and cites countless films that do work. She provides a short description of each film, its method (animation, puppets, live action, and so on), running time, and distributor. Maureen Gaffney has supplemented Rice's work with *More Films Kids Like,* which has a similar format.

Librarians who want to set up a film center might wish to consult *Film Library Techniques* by Helen P. Harrison. This book describes the function of the film librarian and the history and development of this work. Harrison also discusses the principles and techniques of film selection, as well as the devices for handling and storing films.

Film Study Collections by Nancy Allen is another book designed for librarians. This book is a guide to the development and use of the many materials available for film study. Allen discusses how to build a basic film reference collection, the role of unpublished scripts in research, and selecting periodicals for the collection. This is an important book which should become a standard reference tool for librarians, and a valuable guide to the holdings of major research centers for serious students of film.

BIBLIOGRAPHY

Allen, Nancy. *Film Study Collections.* New York: Frederick Ungar, 1979.

The American Film Institute. *Guide to College Courses in Film and Television.* Princeton, N.J.: Peterson's Guides, 1978.

Anderson, Yvonne. *Teaching Film Animation to Children.* New York: Van Nostrand Reinhold, 1970.

Betancourt, Jeanne. *Women in Focus.* Dayton, Ohio: Pflaum, 1974.

Bogle, Donald. *Toms, Coons, Mulattoes, Mammies and Blacks: An Interpretive History of Blacks in American Films.* New York: Viking, 1973.

Bourgeois, Jacques. *Animating Films Without a Camera.* New York: Sterling Publishing, 1974.

Brody, Stephen. *Screen Violence and Film Censorship.* London: Her Majesty's Stationery Office, 1977.

Bruno, Michael. *Venus in Hollywood: The Continental Enchantress from Garbo to Loren.* New York: Lyle Stuart, 1970.

Butler, Ivan. *Religion in the Cinema.* New York: A. S. Barnes, 1969.

Carmen, Ira H. *Movies, Censorship and the Law.* Ann Arbor: University of Michigan Press, 1966.

Ceplair, Larry and Steven Englund. *The Inquisition in Hollywood: Politics in the Film Community, 1930-1960.* Garden City, N.Y.: Anchor Press, Doubleday, 1980.

Cogley, John. *Report on Blacklisting, Vol. I Movies.* n.p.: Fund for the Republic, 1956.

Cook, Bruce. *Dalton Trumbo.* New York: Charles Scribner's Sons, 1977.

Cripps, Thomas. *Black Film as Genre.* Bloomington: Indiana University Press, 1978.

______. *Slow Fade to Black: The Negro in American Film, 1900-1942.* New York: Oxford University Press, 1977.

Dawson, Bonnie. *Women's Films in Print: An Annotated Guide to 800 16mm Films by Women.* San Francisco: Booklegger Press, 1975.

Drew, Donald J. *Images of Man: A Critique of the Contemporary Cinema.* Downers Grove, Ill.: Inter Varsity Press, 1974.

Edmonds, Robert. *About Documentary: Anthropology on Film.* Dayton, Ohio: Pflaum, 1974.

Ernest, Morris and Pare Lorentz. *Censored: The Private Life of the Movies.* New York: Jonathan Cape and Harrison Smith, 1930.

Farber, Stephen. *The Movie Rating Game.* Washington: Public Affairs Press, 1972.

Ferlita, Ernest and John R. May. *Film Odyssey.* New York: Paulist Press, 1976.

French, Brandon. *On the Verge of Revolt: Women in American Films of the Fifties.* New York: Frederick Ungar, 1978.

Friar, Ralph E. and Natasha A. Friar. *The Only Good Indian . . . The Hollywood Gospel.* New York: Drama Book Specialists, 1972.

Furhammar, Leif and Folke Isaksson. *Politics and Film.* Translated by Kersti French. New York: Praeger, 1971.

Gaffney, Maureen. *More Films Kids Like.* Chicago: American Library Association, 1977.

Goodwin, Michael and Greil Marcus. *Double Feature: Movies and Politics.* New York: Outerbridge and Lazard, 1972.

Greenberg, Harvey R. *The Movies on Your Mind.* New York: E. P. Dutton, 1975.

Halberstam, David. *The Powers That Be.* New York: Alfred A. Knopf, 1979.

Handel, Leo A. *Hollywood Looks at its Audience: A Report on Film Audience Research.* Urbana: University of Illinois Press, 1950.

Harley, John Eugene. *World-Wide Influence of the Cinema.* Los Angeles: The University of Southern California Press, 1940.

Harrison, Helen P. *Film Library Techniques: Principles of Administration.* New York: Hastings House, 1973.

Haskell, Molly. *From Reverence to Rape: The Treatment of Women in the Movies.* New York: Holt, Rinehart and Winston, 1974.

Helfman, Harry. *Making Your Own Movies.* New York: William Morrow, 1970.

Holloway, Ronald. *Beyond the Image: Approaches to the Religious Dimension in the Cinema.* Geneva: World Council of Churches, 1977.

Huaco, George A. *The Sociology of Film Art.* New York: Basic Books, 1965.

Hunnings, Neville March. *Film Censors and the Law.* London: George Allen and Unwin, 1967.

Hurley, Neil. *Theology Through Film.* New York: Harper and Row, 1970.

Jones, G. William. *Sunday Night at the Movies.* Richmond, Va.: John Knox Press, 1967.

Jarvie, I. C. *Movies and Society.* New York: Basic Books, 1970.

______. *Movies as Social Criticism.* Metuchen, N.J.: Scarecrow, 1978.

Kahn, Gordon. *Hollywood on Trial: The Story of the Ten Who Were Indicted.* New York: Boni and Gaer, 1948.

Katz, John Stuart. *A Curriculum in Film.* Ontario: The Ontario Institute for Studies in Education, 1972.

______, ed. *Perspectives on the Study of Film.* Boston: Little, Brown, 1971.

Kay, Karyn and Gerald Peary, eds. *Women and the Cinema: A Critical Anthology.* New York: E. P. Dutton, 1977.

Kirby, Jack Temple. *Media-Made Dixie: The South in American Imagination.* Baton Rouge: Louisiana State University Press, 1978.

Konzelman, Robert G. *Marquee Ministry: The Movie Theatre as Church and Community Forum.* New York: Harper and Row, 1972.

Kowalski, Rosemary Ribich. *Women and Film: A Bibliography.* Metuchen, N.J.: Scarecrow, 1976.

Kuhns, William. *Short Films in Religious Education.* Dayton, Ohio: Pflaum, 1967.

Landay, Eileen. *Black Film Stars.* New York: Drake, 1973.

Larson, Rodger and Ellen Meade. *Young Filmmakers.* New York: E. P. Dutton, 1969.

Larson, Rodger, Lynne Hofer, and Jaime Barrios. *Young Animators and Their Discoveries: A Report from Young Filmmakers Foundation.* New York: Praeger, 1973.

Laybourne, Kit, ed. *Doing the Media: A Portfolio of Activities and Resources.* New York: The Center for Understanding Media, 1972.

Leab, Daniel J. *From Sambo to Superspade: The Black Experience in Motion Pictures.* Boston: Houghton Mifflin, 1975.

Lowndes, Douglas. *Filmmaking in Schools.* New York: Watson-Guptill, 1968.

Lynch, F. Dennis. *Clozentropy: A Technique for Studying Audience Response to Films.* New York: Arno, 1978.

MacBean, James Roy. *Film and Revolution.* Bloomington: Indiana University Press, 1975.

MacCann, Richard Dyer, ed. *Film and Society.* New York: Charles Scribner's Sons, 1964.

McClelland, Doug. *The Unkindest Cuts: The Scissors and the Cinema.* New York: A. S. Barnes, 1972.

McClure, Arthur F., ed. *The Movies: An American Idiom.* Rutherford, N.J.: Fairleigh Dickinson University Press, 1971.

McCreadie, Marsha, ed. *The American Movie Goddess.* New York: John Wiley, 1973.

Manchel, Frank. *Film Study: A Resource Guide.* Rutherford, N.J.: Fairleigh Dickinson University Press, 1973.

Manvell, Roger. *Love Goddesses of the Movies.* New York: Crescent, 1975.

Mapp, Edward. *Blacks in American Films: Today and Yesterday.* Metuchen, N.J.: Scarecrow, 1972.

Maynard, Richard A., ed. *Africa on Film: Myth and Reality.* Rochelle Park, N.J.: Hayden, 1974.

______, ed. *The Black Man on Film: Racial Stereotyping.* Rochelle Park, N.J.: Hayden, 1974.

______. *The Celluloid Curriculum: How to Use Movies in the Classroom.* New York: Hayden, 1971.

______. *Propaganda on Film: A Nation at War.* Rochelle Park, N.J.: Hayden, 1975.

Mellen, Joan. *Women and Their Sexuality in the New Film.* New York: Horizon Press, 1973.

Miller, Randall M., ed. *Ethnic Images in American Film and Television.* Philadelphia: The Balch Institute, 1978.

Moley, Raymond. *The Hays Office.* Indianapolis: Bobbs-Merrill, 1945.

Monaco, Paul. *Cinema and Society.* New York: Elsevier, 1976.

Murray, James P. *To Find an Image: Black Films From Uncle Tom to Super Fly.* Indianapolis: Bobbs-Merrill, 1973.

Noble, Peter. *The Negro in Films.* New York: Arno, 1970.

Null, Gary. *Black Hollywood: The Negro in Motion Pictures.* Secaucus, N.J.: Citadel, 1975.

O'Connor, John E. and Martin A. Jackson, eds. *American History/American Film.* New York: Frederick Ungar, 1979.

Patterson, Lindsay, ed. *Black Films and Film-Makers: A Comprehensive Anthology from Stereotype to Superhero.* New York: Dodd, Mead and Co., 1975.

Pines, Jim. *Blacks in Films: A Survey of Racial Themes and Images in the American Film.* London: Studio Vista, 1975.

Piper, James. *Personal Filmmaking.* Reston, Va.: Reston Publishing Co., 1975.

Poteet, Howard G., ed. *The Complete Guide to Film Study.* Urbana, Ill.: National Council of Teachers of English, 1972.

Powdermaker, Hortense. *Hollywood: The Dream Factory.* Boston: Little, Brown, 1950.

Powers, Anne. *Blacks in American Movies: A Selected Bibliography.* Metuchen, N.J.: Scarecrow, 1974.

Randall, Richard S. *Censorship of the Movies: The Social and Political Control of a Mass Medium.* Madison: The University of Wisconsin Press, 1968.

Rice, Susan. *Films Kids Like: A Catalogue of Short Films for Children.* Chicago: American Library Association, 1973.

Richards, Jeffrey. *Visions of Yesterday.* London: Routledge and Kegan Paul, 1973.

Rosen, Marjorie. *Popcorn Venus: Women, Movies and the American Dream.* New York: Coward, McCann, Geoghegan, 1973.

Sampson, Henry T. *Blacks in Black and White: A Source Book on Black Films.* Metuchen, N.J.: Scarecrow, 1977.

Sarris, Andrew. *Politics and Cinema.* New York: Columbia University Press, 1978.

Schumach, Murray. *The Face on the Cutting Room Floor: The Story of Movie and Television Censorship.* New York: Da Capo Press, 1964.

Sheridan, Marion and others. *The Motion Picture and the Teaching of English.* New York: Appleton-Century Crofts, 1965.

Slide, Anthony. *Early Women Directors.* New York: A. S. Barnes, 1977.

Smith, Paul, ed. *The Historian and Film.* New York: Cambridge University Press, 1976.

Smith, Sharon. *Women Who Make Movies.* New York: Hopkins and Blake, 1975.

Sohn, David A., ed. *Good Looking: Film Studies, Short Films and Filmmaking.* Skokie, Ill.: National Textbook Co., 1978.

______. *Film Study and the English Teacher.* Bloomington: Indiana University Audio-Visual Center, 1968.

Stewart, David C., ed. *Film Study in Higher Education.* Washington: American Council on Education, 1966.

Thompson, David. *America in the Dark: Hollywood and the Gift of Unreality.* New York: William Morrow, 1977.

Tudor, Andrew. *Image and Influence: Studies in the Sociology of Film.* New York: St. Martin's Press, 1974.

Vizzard, Jack. *See No Evil: Life Inside a Hollywood Censor.* New York: Simon and Schuster, 1970.

Wall, James M. *Church and Cinema: A Way of Viewing Film.* Grand Rapids, Mich.: William B. Eerdmans, 1971.

Welsch, Janice R. *Film Archetypes: Sisters, Mistresses, Mothers, and Daughters.* New York: Arno, 1978.

White, David Manning and Richard Averson. *The Celluloid Weapon: Social Comment in the American Film.* Boston: Beacon Press, 1972.

Wistrich, Enid. *Film Censorship Explored.* London: Marion Boyars, 1978.

Wolfenstein, Martha and Nathan Leites. *Movies: A Psychological Study.* Glencoe, Ill.: The Free Press, 1950.

Woll, Allen L. *The Latin Image in American Film.* Los Angeles: UCLA Latin American Center Publications, 1977.

Wood, Michael. *America in the Movies: Or "Santa Maria, It Had Slipped My Mind."* New York: Basic Books, 1975.

Worth, Sol and John Adair. *Through Navajo Eyes: An Exploration in Film Communication and Anthropology.* Bloomington: Indiana University Press, 1972.

CHAPTER 7

Major Actors

One of the most interesting and useful methods of studying film is to analyze the careers and lives of the people who make them. The actors, directors, and other members of the production team are often interesting people; insights into their careers become a main avenue for studying the art form. The list of actors included here is by no means complete, and often a reader's favorite movie personality may be omitted because of the inaccessibility of a book on that person. The intention here, and throughout this book, is not to provide a complete bibliography but to lead the reader to those sources that will permit him or her to begin the study of a particular film artist. In the sources cited, the reader will find references to other relevant books and articles.

The artists will be listed alphabetically by last name; groups will be listed under the name of the group (for example, the Three Stooges are under "T"). Pairs will be listed under the name of that member whose name comes first (for example, Laurel and Hardy are under "H"). The reader interested in one member of the pair should look under the names of both members. Fans of Mary Pickford will find under her name those books about her and her career; under Douglas Fairbanks, Sr. they will find those books that describe the joint careers and lives of Pickford and Fairbanks.

The artists are listed only in the category for which they are best remembered, even though they may have worked in various aspects of the movie business. Orson Welles was both actor and director, but he is listed under the directors in the following chapter; Paul Newman has also been both a director and an actor, but he is listed as an actor. Finally, the reader should consult the index for references to the artist elsewhere in this book.

Of general interest to those readers wishing information about actors is a series, "The Illustrated History of the Movies," first published by the Pyramid Publishing Company in the early 1970s and then taken over by Jove Publications, a division of Harcourt Brace Jovanovich. The series is now out of publication, but its volumes on individual actors remain useful.

The series was intended for a popular audience, and each volume included a large number of photographs of the actor and plot summaries of his films. The books provide an overview of each actor's career, some insights into his techniques, and a general idea of the critical receptions to his films. Volumes will be mentioned in this chapter along with other books on specific actors; but since the format is constant for the entire series, there will be little discussion of the books other than identifying it as a member of this series.

BOOKS ON INDIVIDUAL ACTORS

Roscoe "Fatty" Arbuckle was a rotund comedian who worked with Charles Chaplin and Mack Sennett. His career was ruined by the scandal that arose when he was tried for the rape and murder of a young actress in 1921. The story of Arbuckle's career and trial is told by David A. Yallop in *The Day the Laughter Stopped.* Yallop maintains Arbuckle's innocence and credits him as an actor, an ability often overlooked in the sensational treatment given his trial.

George Arliss was a British actor who made a number of American films during the late 1920s and 1930s. He wrote two autobiographies. The first, *Up the Years from Bloomsbury: An Autobiography,* deals largely with his early career on the stage, but toward the end he has a chapter on his tentative involvement with what he calls "this new field of the actor's art." His second book deals directly with the new field of movies. *My Ten Years in the Studios* is a complete biography of his career and provides a careful description of his work in his major films and lists the cast and credits for each.

Linda Arvidson was married to D. W. Griffith during his early movie career. An actress with Griffith's company, she starred in many of his early short films. The story of the early days at Biograph, of the development of film as an art, and of Griffith's craft have all been told in Arvidson's *When the Movies Were Young,* an autobiography first published in 1925 but now reprinted.

Elizabeth Ashley is a contemporary actress whose autobiography, *Actress: Postcards from the Road,* is a rather unglamorous view of a supposedly glamorous career. While she speaks of her love for her work, she does not pretend that the long hours and constant demands of her profession are always pleasant.

No dancer/actor is better known than Fred Astaire. His biography has been told by Michael Freedland in *Fred Astaire.* Freedland depicts Astaire as a perfectionist and follows both the private man and the artistic genius from the vaudeville days to the making of *Towering Inferno. Starring Fred Astaire* by Stanley Green and Burt Goldblatt deals more with Astaire's career than with his life. The authors have included essays on his stage and screen careers and on his image, but most of the book is devoted to a film by film survey, with credits, casts, musical numbers, photographs, and lengthy analysis. His radio and television work and a discography are also included. Another survey of his career is *Fred Astaire* by Stephen Harvey, a brief analysis of Astaire's major films intended for a popular audience; it is one of the Illustrated Histories of the Movies series. The joint careers of Astaire and Ginger Rogers are the subject of *The Fred Astaire and Ginger Rogers Book* by Arlene Croce. Croce has included photographs, casts, credits, and a list of musical numbers from each of their films, but it is her close and detailed analysis of their dance routines, film by film, that gives the book its special flavor. Astaire's autobiography, *Steps in Time,* is a chatty and personal record of his life from its beginnings in Omaha, Nebraska to his successes in New York and Hollywood and provides background on the production of his movies.

Mary Astor could play either the heroine or the villain, but in either role she was beautiful. Her autobiography, *A Life on Film,* is a good account of her movie career and is especially useful for the insights it provides into the work of her fellow actors, such as Humphrey Bogart, with whom she worked in *The Maltese Falcon.*

Back in the Saddle Again is the autobiography of singing cowboy, Gene Autry. Autry's account of his experiences from Hollywood to baseball becomes a study of American life during his long career.

Bogey's Baby by Howard Greenberger is a biography of Lauren Bacall, covering her life from her marriage to Humphrey Bogart to her success on Broadway with *Applause.* Greenberger's emphasis is on Bacall's life with Bogart, although he does describe briefly her life after the actor's death. In *By Myself*, Bacall's autobiography, she also focuses on the decade she was married to one of Hollywood's most famous men; but, as the title reflects, her thesis is that it is since his death that she has been forced by circumstances to make her own way as an actress.

Tallulah Bankhead was, in her day, one of Hollywood's most colorful characters. In *Miss Tallulah Bankhead* Lee Israel writes a biography that tells all. Israel describes the actress's intimate life (affairs with both men and women) as well as her career on stage and screen. Kieran Tunney claims that *Tallulah: Darling of the Gods* is "an intimate portrait," but this book is less sensational or revealing than Israel's. More the recollections of a personal friend than a scholarly biography, the book discusses the characteristics of the actress that made her especially popular with the occupants of the cheaper seats ("The Gods," in the slang of the British Isles). *Tallulah* by Brendan Gill is a more popular biography, full of photographs, letters, clippings, and other memorabilia. Bankhead's own book, *Tallulah: My Autobiography* discusses her career on both stage and screen. Ironically she maintains that she does not really like acting and then devotes many pages to describing how hard she worked at the profession.

The Barrymores have been one of America's premier families of both stage and screen, and their personal lives and acting careers have attracted much attention. *The Barrymores* by Hollis Alpert is a scholarly and detailed study of the entire family, but the book is limited by the attempt to cover several great actors in a single volume; the Barrymore films are covered only briefly. The movie career of John Barrymore is covered in more depth in *John Barrymore: The Legend and the Man* by Alma Power-Waters. The author is quite knowledgeable about her subject, but the book is now dated. *Good Night, Sweet Prince: The Life and Times of John Barrymore* by Gene Fowler is also old but has become a classic example of the 1940s movie biography. The flavor of the book can be derived from the titles of the four "cantos" into which the book is divided: "Songs of the Morning, The Sun on the Meridian, Golden Siesta, and The Stag at Eve." The Barrymores themselves have been active writers. *Confessions of an Actor* is John Barrymore's sketchy and brief autobiography, which deals largely with his life on the stage. His sister, Ethel, described her social life in Hollywood and her career as an actress in *Memories: An Autobiography.* And John's daughter, Diana, described her life in the movie and theatrical communities in *Too Much, Too Soon,* a tktle that clearly establishes the thesis.

Joan Bennett made a reputation for herself in both serious and comedy roles. *The Bennett Playbill* is her story of her career and the careers of five generations of actors in her family. The mention of specific films is brief and mainly descriptive rather than analytical, but the scope of the book is wide.

Ingrid Bergman, of course, is a Swedish actress, but her long career and continuing popularity in America (despite a notorious scandal) are the inspiration for Curtis Brown's *Ingrid Bergman,* part of a picture treasury series on actors. Brown describes Bergman's youth, the Hollywood years, her life with Roberto Rossellini, and finally her international success. In *The Films of Ingrid Bergman* Lawrence J. Quirk gives a long overview of her career and life, then discusses her early Swedish films, her international fame from 1939 on, her life with Rossellini, and the renewal of her career in the years following their breakup. Quirk also includes information on Bergman's stage and television appearances and a portrait gallery.

Few figures have fascinated the American public more than Humphrey Bogart. Allen Eyles tells the story in *Bogart,* a brief book that presents overly long plot summaries of Bogart's films but a fine analysis of his life and career. The introduction includes an attempt to describe and analyze Bogart's acting style and ability, a task that has frustrated many a movie critic. *Humphrey Bogart,* written by Nathaniel Benchley, a longtime friend of the Bogarts and a well-known fiction writer, is a more personal and less systematic portrait than Eyles'. Alan G. Barbour's *Humphrey Bogart* is a popular, rather superficial overview of Bogart's life and career that briefly describes his major films. This is another of the illustrated biographies published by Pyramid Books. *Bogart's Face* is a collection of frame enlargements of his face and is, therefore, an interesting exploration of Bogart's many facets.

Clara Bow, the "It Girl," became a symbol for a generation and her nickname became the ultimate compliment for a young woman. Joe Morella and Edward Z. Epstein have written *The "It" Girl: The Incredible Story of Clara Bow.* Opening with Bow waking up in a sanitarium, this is a somewhat sensationalized, although highly readable, account of her life.

No actor is more enigmatic than Marlon Brando, and to write his biography is to venture into troubled waters. David Shipman has written *Brando,* a brief biography that includes some criticism of Brando's career. After describing Brando's early life and his work on Broadway, Shipman discusses his first work in film under Elia Kazan in *A Streetcar Named Desire,* his later work performing Shakespeare and in commercial films (winning an Oscar), and his later career. Shipman maintains that in his later years Brando has made only one good film, *Reflections in a Golden Eye. Brando* by Ron Offen presents Brando in a slightly more favorable light, but is not uncritical. Offen's book is longer than Shipman's and more detailed. *Marlon* by Bob Thomas is the most complimentary of the books on Brando. While it is a bit gossipy and treats Brando's films only superficially, it is interesting. Thomas claims that Brando made movie acting more naturalistic with his role in *A Streetcar Named Desire*. In *The Films of Marlon Brando* Tony Thomas presents a popular view of the films and includes a long critical review of Brando's career by Pauline Kael and a description and brief analysis of each film.

Honored by the American Film Institute as one of the most important actors of the American screen, James Cagney got his start in the 1930s as a dancer and gangster. *Cagney* by Ron Offen contrasts the private man with the screen image; Offen's book focuses on Cagney's role as George M. Cohan in *Yankee Doodle Dandy* and on his work for his own production companies. Andrew Bergman's *James Cagney* is a Pyramid illustrated history of Cagney's life and career, beginning with an essay of appreciation, followed by a chronological view of Cagney's career. Bergman's book is aimed at a popular audience but the description of the Cagney's career is worthwhile. *Cagney* by Patrick McGillian has as its subtitle *The Actor as Auteur.* McGillian's theme is that Cagney as an actor clearly shaped the films in which he appeared, as much as if he had been the director. McGillian begins with Cagney's youth and his early roles as dancer and gangster/tough guy and finishes with Cagney as symbol and auteur. Cagney tells his own story in *Cagney by Cagney,* a folksy memoir of the movie career he so loved and the people who made it possible; what this book lacks in insight, it makes up for in charm. Cagney's work in films is the subject of *The Films of James Cagney* by Homer Dickens. Dickens begins with an essay on the antihero and a gallery of photographs, then presents each film with information including cast, credits, plot summaries, extracts from reviews, stills, and general commentary.

Perhaps no actor has received as much critical attention as Charles Chaplin. The best biography of Chaplin is John McCabe's *Charlie Chaplin.* This definitive study combines the story of Chaplin's life with close analysis of his films and a survey of critical reaction to them. *Chaplin* by Roger Manvell presents Chaplin's life and offers some ordinary criticism of his career; the most interesting part of the book is Manvell's attempt to describe Chaplin's transformation from the little tramp to the more complex character of the talkies. Denis Gifford's *Chaplin* is a popular book that emphasizes Chaplin's career during the silent period; as such, it presents an incomplete picture of Chaplin and should be read in conjunction with one of the other biographies. In *Chaplin, The Movies, and Charlie,* David Jacobs claims to have written more than a biography, but actually includes little film description and analysis. *The Little Fellow: The Life and Work of Charles Spencer Chaplin* is by Peter Cotes and Thelma Niklaus. These authors devote part one of their book to Chaplin's life and part two to analysis of his work. The book also contains an interesting introduction to the Chaplin phenomenon by W. Somerset Maugham, a filmography, and some of Chaplin's own writings.

Other members of his family have described their lives with him. His first wife Lita Grey Chaplin discussed her teenage marriage to Chaplin in *My Life with Chaplin: An Intimate Memoir,* which depicts the combination of brutality and passion that scandalized the world and that Chaplin refused to discuss in detail. *My Father: Charlie Chaplin* is by Charles Chaplin, Jr., the son of the comedian and Lita Grey Chaplin. The author, an actor in his own right, provides a detailed description of Chaplin's life and career, including background on the films and a summary of their critical receptions.

Chaplin's own writings have afforded insights into his life and career. In *My Life in Pictures* Chaplin tells his life's story through photographs and stills, linked together with his own captions. In *My Autobiography* Chaplin recalls his life in one of the most delightful books on the movies. He describes his early life, his immigration to America, early movie career, and the creation of the Tramp; the narrative continues through his screen success and his four marriages. His memoirs of the things he did and the people he knew make this an important book.

There have also been many excellent books dealing with the roles Chaplin played on the screen. *Chaplin: Genesis of a Clown* is Raoul Sobel's analysis of the way the films reflect the man; this scholarly book concentrates on the early films and almost ignores the later films such as *Modern Times.* Parker Tyler's *Chaplin: The Last of the Clowns* analyzes Chaplin's career by studying the roles he played; Tyler offers excellent criticism of the films without much discussion of Chaplin's life, although the chapters are arranged chronologically. In *Charlie Chaplin: His Life and Art*, a 1931 book, now reprinted, by William Dodgson Bowman, Chaplin's life and art are presented in detail; the book also contains a collection of essays on different aspects of the man and his career: Chaplin in Hollywood, Chaplin and women, Chaplin and his friends, Chaplin and his film roles.

Focus on Chaplin, edited by Donald W. McCaffrey, is a collection of writings by and about Chaplin that go far toward helping the student understand Chaplin's career. The book begins with an overview of his career and Chaplin's own view of his movies and methods; the main part of the book consists of scholarly essays on Chaplin's art and reviews of his major films. McCaffery has also written *Four Great Comedians* in which he discusses the work of Chaplin as well as that of Harold Lloyd, Buster Keaton, and Harry Langdon. McCaffery believes that these four were the essence of silent comedy at its best, and this book is an analysis what they did in their films and how they did it.

Chaplin's films themselves have received almost as much attention as he has. *Charlie Chaplin* by Theodore Huff, a useful 1951 book that has now been reprinted, includes biographical information as well as a full chapter on each of Chaplin's major films, with background information, the story of the production, a plot summary, and critical interpretations. The introduction is an essay on the importance of Chaplin and his art. *Chaplin's Films* by Uno Asplund, a Swedish critic, presents a European view of Chaplin's career and could have provided insight into Chaplin's European popularity; unfortunately, Asplund's study is rather superficial. *The Films of Charlie Chaplin* is a routine reference guide to Chaplin's canon of films. Authors Gerald McDonald, Michael Conway, and Mark Ricci present cast, credits, synoposis, brief excerpts from reviews, and photographs for each film. There is little depth or critical analysis, but the information provided is important to anyone wanting to go further in a study of Chaplin's career.

Monty by Robert LaGuardia depicts Montgomery Clift as a rebel on and off the screen. This excellent study discusses Clift's roles from *Red River* to *From Here to Eternity* and *The Misfits,* as well as his relationships with other stars.

Juliet Benita Colman was only fourteen when her father, Ronald Colman, died; her book, *Ronald Colman,* is her attempt to recapture the father she hardly knew. This is, however, a full and serious biography that focuses on Colman's life rather than his films; nonetheless, several of the films—*Lost Horizon*, *A Tale of Two Cities*, and *The Light That Failed*—are discussed at length. All of Colman's films are described in *The Films of Ronald Colman* by Lawrence J. Quirk. Opening with an overview of Colman's career and a discussion of his British films, Quirk proceeds to present each of Colman's American films, citing casts and credits, providing some commentary, and concluding with a portrait gallery.

The biography of Gary Cooper has been told in George Carpozi, Jr.'s *The Gary Cooper Story.* Geared to the serious fan, this book discusses

Cooper's career, the women in his life, and includes a brief filmography. A fuller and expanded filmography is provided in *The Films of Gary Cooper* by Homer Dickens. Dickens begins with an essay depicting Cooper as "the American man," discusses his shorter films, and then gives a film by film analysis of his major films with cast, credits, a short synopsis and brief notes for each.

The autobiography of Miriam Cooper is entitled *Dark Lady of the Silents.* Cooper was one of Griffith's actresses at the peak of his career, and her story provides valuable insights into the work of both. Cooper talks about *The Birth of a Nation* and *Intolerance*, as well as her unsuccessful marriage to Raoul Walsh, an unpleasant experience with the important director who likewise began his career under Griffith.

Two very different pictures of Joan Crawford have been depicted: one by the actress herself and the other by her daughter. *A Portrait of Joan: The Autobiography of Joan Crawford* describes her movie success, beginning with a telegram that offered her a Hollywood contract at seventy-five dollars a week. Joan Crawford goes on to detail both her movie career and her marriage to the head of Pepsi-Cola, Alfred Steele. In a second book, *My Way of Life,* the successful actress and businesswoman describes working in a man's world and advises other women on how they might also succeed in business, including tips on how to look the part of a successful businesswoman. In *Mommie Dearest,* Crawford's daughter Christina depicts her mother as possessive, domineering, and generally unpleasant. The truth probably lies somewhere between these two views. A more objective approach to Crawford's life and career is *Joan Crawford* by Bob Thomas. Thomas suggests that Crawford could be difficult, but that Christina's view is extreme; he emphasizes Crawford's struggles but does not show Christina as the victim of them. *Joan Crawford* by Stephen Harvey is another of the Illustrated Histories of the Movies and presents an overview of her film career. *The Films of Joan Crawford* by Lawrence J. Quirk begins with an introduction to the woman and the artist; then discusses her films, citing cast, credits, a synposis, and review excerpts for each.

Bing by Charles Thompson is the authorized biography of Bing Crosby with emphasis on Crosby's life in films rather than on film analysis. *Bing Crosby* by Barbara Bauer is an Illustrated History of Crosby's life and career which presents Crosby on the road to Hollywood, in films as a crooner and spoofer, with Bob Hope and Dorothy Lamour on the road to almost anywhere, and in later life. Robert Bookbinder's *The Films of Bing Crosby* begins with a lengthy introduction "to the legend," lists Crosby's Academy Award songs and hit films, and presents the usual film-related information—the casts, credits, songs, and synopses.

The Crosby family has provided valuable insights into the actor's career. *Call Me Lucky* is Crosby's own story, and the title is the theme. In a manner consistent with the memory of this man, the book describes his friends and his personal life more than it analyzes his career as a film actor or singer. *Bing and Other Things* is the autobiography of his wife Kathryn, an actress who married him in 1957. The book covers her career as well as her marriage and her family. Bing's brother, Ted Crosby, wrote *The Story of Bing Crosby,* an early book in which a comment by Bing in the preface seems to capture the essence of all three of these personal studies: "This thing [the book] is hardly offered as a guide to aspirants for success in show business, but only indicates what a lucky guy I am—so far."

Marion Davies was a capable actress, but she will probably be remembered as Orson Welles' supposed model for Susan Alexander in *Citizen Kane.* Her story has been told by Fred Lawrence Guiles in *Marion Davies: A Biography,* which focuses on her life as an actress and as companion to William Randolph Hearst; Guiles' theme is that "she was a daisy but no Susan Alexander." Davies tells her own account of her life and times in *The Times We Had,* with emphasis on her films and her social life with Hearst. Interestingly enough, the foreword was written by Orson Welles.

Whitney Stine and Bette Davis have worked together to create an unusual biography/autobiography. *Mother Goddam* is a fine account of Davis' life and career which combines serious analysis with funny commentary and makes good use of film reviews and interviews; a filmography and stageography are also included. Jerry Vermilye's *Bette Davis* is another of the Pyramid Illustrated History series for the general reader with little analysis. Davis' autobiography, *The Lonely Life,* is a serious study of her life, as is clearly indicated by the title. Davis' limited discussion of her films and lack of an index and table of contents limit the book as a research tool. *Star Acting: Gish, Garbo, and Davis* by Charles Affron provides a penetrating analysis of Bette Davis' acting. Few books actually discuss acting style; this one does, primarily through the use of frame enlargements. Affron gets behind the mystique often associated with actors and actresses by examining how the face works, how the body moves, and how the director and camermen take advantage of particular talents and attributes. Gene Ringgold's *The Films of Bette Davis* is a routine expanded filmography, from reviews and photographs; Ringgold does not include the long introductory essay common to books of this type.

Doris Day: Her Own Story is another book in which the star has collaborated with an established author to produce a combination biography/autobiography. Told in the first person, the book is enhanced by A. E. Hotchner's own research and interviews with Bob Hope, James Garner, Jack Lemmon, and others. George Morris has written a Pyramid Illustrated biography of the same title, *Doris Day;* Morris's book is basically a description in words and photographs of the actress' films. *The Films of Doris Day* by Christopher Young follows the formula for books of this expanded filmography type, beginning with a long essay that summarizes the star's career, and then devotes the main part of the book to a film by film survey; a bonus is a section on Day's television work.

The myth of James Dean has been explored by Dennis Stock in *James Dean Revisited.* Stock is a photographer who knew Dean well and this book is a collection of Stock's photographs and thoughts about his former friend. A deeper analysis of Dean and his career is found in *James Dean: The Mutant King* by David Dalton. Dalton combines biography with analysis of Dean's film work and interviews with his co-stars and directors. *James Dean: A Short Life* is an intimate biography by Venable Herndon. With a limited view of Dean's films, the book does discuss Dean's problems with director George Stevens while filming *Giant.* This book is intended for a popular audience and even includes an astrological reading on the actor.

At this writing Marlene Dietrich's autobiography has not been published, but some of her thoughts about herself and her career are contained in *Marlene Dietrich's ABC*, a shallow book that covers a wide range of topics. It becomes a self study through her efforts to define and discuss an eclectic list of words and to describe a number of the people in her life (she describes Ernest Hemingway as "my personal Rock of Gibraltar"). *Marlene* is a recent biography by Charles Higham of Marlene Dietrich, light on criticism of her movies, but full of details about her life and her career both in Germany and America. *Dietrich* by Leslie Frewin is likewise of some general merit but of little value to the reader seeking analysis of the actress' career. The book is largely a social study of the actress, but it does provide background for a few films. *Marlene Dietrich* by John Kobal is a pictorial study also intended for a popular audience; it contains little biography and criticism but does include a filmography and discography. Another book with the same title by Sheridan Morley contains more commentary but it too is basically a pictorial study with stills from Dietrich's films and brief commentary on each film. *The Films of Marlene Dietrich* by Homer Dickens begins with a lengthy essay on the legend of the actress and includes a portrait gallery and expanded filmography.

Another expanded filmography, *The Films of Kirk Douglas* by Tony Thomas, follows the same pattern as Dickens' book. Thomas begins with an introduction by Vincente Minnelli, who directed Douglas in three films, and then includes his own essay on the man behind the actor. The filmography includes the usual photographs, casts, credits, and brief critical analyses.

Marie Dressler was a very popular comedienne in the early 1930s. Her autobiography, *My Own Story,* recalls the background of her life and her films, with emphasis on the films. The foreword is by Will Rogers, Sr.

In *Clint Eastwood: The Man Behind the Myth,* Patrick Agan claims to have discovered the reticent Eastwood. Agan presents a rare view of Eastwood's life (usually hidden from reports and critics), and how he went from the Rowdy of "Rawhide" in television to stardom in films.

Nelson Eddy's career with Jeanette MacDonald has been well documented in two books, each one entitled *The Films of Jeanette MacDonald and Nelson Eddy*. The first, by Eleanor Knowles, John Robert Cocchi, and J. Peter Bergman, is a lengthy analytical study of their films. In addition to listing cast and credits, the authors present analysis and commentary, summaries of the reviews, and a list of music for each film. Philip Castanza, in his book by the same title, begins with an essay on the stars and their feud. Castanza includes a portrait gallery and letters from friends, as well as the usual film by film casts, credits, and related information; he also lists their radio and television appearances and their movie duets.

In the 1920s Douglas Fairbanks, Sr. was one of the best-known men in the world, and his marriage to America's sweetheart, Mary Pickford, raised the two of them to the level of movie royalty. *His Picture in the Papers: A Speculation on Celebrity in America Based on the Life of Douglas Fairbanks, Sr.* is by Richard Schickel. While this book is more analysis of the nature of stardom and the creation of movie myths than it is biography, it does cover Fairbanks' life as well. A full study of Fairbanks' career is found in *His Majesty the American* by John C. Tibbits and James M. Walsh; in addition to documenting the career, these fine critics have delved deeply into the nature of the actor's art and methods. Fairbanks' life with Mary Pickford also has been well documented in two books, *Doug and Mary* by Gary Carey and *Mary Pickford and Douglas Fairbanks* by Booton Herndon. These books were published at about the same time and are both good records of the famous couple's life and careers.

Douglas Fairbanks, Jr. followed his father into the movie business and made numerous films, but never reached his father's greatness. The story of the "ambassador of good will, unpublicized war hero, and reluctant movie star" has been told by Brian Connell in *Knight Errant*.

The life of W. C. Fields fascinates readers as much as his films pleased audiences. In *W. C. Fields: His Follies and Fortunes,* Robert Taylor relates Fields' life. Although an older study, this is still a solid biography. A critical study of Fields' life and career is *The Art of W. C. Fields* by William K. Everson. This is a good critical study arranged chronologically, but the emphasis is on interpretation and history of Fields' work. Fields told his own story in *W. C. Fields by Himself.* This was intended as an autobiography, but it was finished by his grandson Ronald Fields. The book provides some insights into Fields' life, but only mentions Carlotta Monti, who lived with Fields during the last years of his life; Ronald Fields has mentioned her only briefly in a couple of letters which cast a negative image of her. However, Monti presented her own point of view in *W. C. Fields and Me,* a funny and warm memoir of her life with Fields that does not gloss over his weaknesses. *The Films of W. C. Fields* by Donald Deschner begins with an introduction by Arthur Knight. In addition to the film by film data customary in books of this sort, this book includes a biography of Fields and two essays written by him on the nature of comedy. Richard J. Anobile has attempted to distill the wit and wisdom of Fields' films in *A Flask of Fields;* stills and dialogue from the films recreate the "verbal and visual gems." Anobile edited another book with a similar intent: *Drat! Being the Encapsulated View of Life by W. C. Fields in His Own Words*. In this book Anobile excerpted remarks by Fields from a 1942 article in *Pic Magazine* and used them to provide a running commentary for photographs.

The Life and Crimes of Errol Flynn by Lionel Godfrey is a study of the life and career of one of filmdom's great adventurers. Godfrey looks at Flynn's life, marriage, and trial, as well as his films; Godfrey claims that the man behind the legend was quiet and thoughtful. Earl Conrad's *Errol Flynn* is a memoir that seeks to unravel the enigma of the actor and highlight his individuality. *Errol Flynn* is one of the Illustrated Histories of the Movies by George Morris and provides an overview of his career. *The Films of Errol Flynn* by Tony Thomas, Rudy Behlmer, and Clifford McCarty, includes the usual filmography data, a foreword by actress Greer Garson and Thomas' own introductory essay.

The Fondas have become one of the best known families in American cinema. Henry, Jane, and Peter have all made their individual marks in American cinema. Two books have considered them as a group. *The Fondas* by John Springer is something of an expanded filmography, which gives a film by film analysis of their films, including long excerpts from reviews; it also includes an introductory essay and commentary by Joshua Logan, Robert Ryan, and John Steinbeck. Their work in the theater and television is also covered. In *The Fabulous Fondas,* James Brough presents background on their lives and films, with interesting details on the making of *Easy Rider, The Grapes of Wrath, Mr. Rogers, Klute,* and other films. *Jane: An Intimate Biography of Jane Fonda* by Thomas Kiernan is a chronological study of the life of the actress with chapters on her major films. Kiernan's discussions of her relationship with her father and of her radicalism are particularly interesting.

In the introduction to her autobiography, *No Bed of Roses,* actress Joan Fontaine maintains that she wants to set straight the public record of her life. She describes her successful career but highlights the problems of her life that had to be overcome: a broken home in childhood and four difficult marriages.

During the 1930s and 1940s The King of Hollywood was Clark Gable. Lyn Tornabene has told the story of his reign in *Long Live the King,* an excellent biography arranged chronologically by the major periods of his life: kid, protégé, he-guy, king, hero, gentleman. Tornabene presents a favorable view of the man and an honest view of the actor; she is especially sympathetic when dealing with his relationship with Carole Lombard. The relation between the two is treated in more detail in *Gable and Lombard* by Warren G. Harris. Harris begins with Lombard's death in an airplane crash early in World War II and then flashes back to the beginning of their relationship. Harris describes their love and the positive impact that love had on each of them; he also includes a chapter on the lonely Gable in the years after Lombard's death. Gabe Essoe's *The Films of Clark Gable* is another expanded filmography. Beginning with a foreword by Charles Champlin, the book includes essays by stars who knew Gable and describes each of the sound films with prominent photographs.

Dear Mr. G—: The Biography of Clark Gable is an early study by Jean Garceau and Inez Cocke. This book is a rather routine biography covering his life and career. *Gable* by Chester Williams is a brief biography that provides a short view of Gable's important films and a filmography. *Clark Gable* by Dave Jordan is another of the Illustrated Histories of the Movies and provides an overview of Gable's films and their critical reception.

The mystery of Greta Garbo is explored by Raymond Durgnat and John Kobal in *Greta Garbo.* The authors present a biography, but their most valuable material deals with Garbo as an actress and with the Garbo films. While they make an attempt to analyze the myth that has developed around Garbo they are no more successful at explaining it than anyone else, a failing that results from the complexity of Garbo's image, rather than from a lack of insight on their part. *Garbo* by Norman Zierold is another attempt to explain her personality and film success. The reader especially interested in her acting should consult a book mentioned above, Charles Affron's *Star Acting: Gish, Garbo, and Davis,* which presents an analysis of Garbo's acting through selected frame enlargements. *Greta Garbo* by Richard Corliss is another of the Illustrated Histories of the Movies, giving an overview of Garbo's films. *The Films of Greta Garbo* is an expanded filmography by Michael Conway, Dion McGregor, and Mark Ricci that contains an important introduction by Parker Tyler and useful reviews of her films.

Ava Gardner is primarily remembered for her looks rather than her acting ability, but in her later films she did develop into an actress of some merit. Her career has been told by Judith Kass in *Ava Gardner,* another in the series of Illustrated Histories of the Movies. *Ava: A Life Story* is another of Charles Higham's biographies of the stars. As usual, Higham's book is solid, reasonably reliable, and popular, but not scholarly; a filmography is included.

John Garfield was one of the leading men at Warner Brothers during the late 1930s and 1940s; but his career was brought to an end when he was blacklisted after his testimony before the House Un-American Activities Committee. *Body and Soul: The Story of John Garfield* (the title taken from one of his best films) by Larry Swindell claims to be less biography than history; Swindell has used Garfield's life and career to provide the framework in which to study the Warner studio during that period. In *John*

Garfield, George Morris presents a briefer view of Garfield, but his analysis of Garfield's films is more extensive; this is an overview of Garfield's career with brief critical remarks. *The Films of John Garfield* by Howard Gelman begins with a biographical essay, a portrait gallery, and a brief general analysis of Garfield's films. Following the usual film-related information, Gelman focuses on Garfield's problems with the HUAC and the blacklist; excerpts from Garfield's testimony are included. James N. Beaver's *John Garfield* is another detailed filmography. Beaver begins with a long essay entitled "Saga of a Golden Boy" (another title taken from one of his films) and then moves on to the usual film by film information. A list of Garfield's stage and radio appearances is included in appendix 1.

Little Girl Lost: The Life and Hard Times of Judy Garland by Al DiOrio, Jr. is a study for a popular audience. DiOrio focuses on Garland's films and the men in her life, and he includes a discography and filmography. *Judy* by Gerold Frank is a lengthy study of her life and career, with intimate details of both her private and professional lives, her joys and her problems. Christopher Finch's *Rainbow: The Stormy Life of Judy Garland* is both a popular biography and a photographic study of her career. *Judy Garland* by James Juneau is another of the Illustrated Histories of the Movies and concentrates more on Garland's films than on her life.

The career of Lillian Gish has spanned almost the entire length of movie history. As a young girl she began making movies with D. W. Griffith at Biograph and at this writing she is still making personal appearances. The story of her early career under Griffith is told in a charming manner in *The Movies, Mr. Griffith, and Me,* one of the best autobiographies about the movie industry. In addition to documenting her own career, Gish has written one of the best firsthand accounts of the work of Griffith. In a later book, *Dorothy and Lillian Gish,* she shares some of her favorite photographs of the films and plays in which she and her sister worked. Another book mentioned above, *Star Acting: Gish, Garbo, and Davis* by Charles Affron offers an excellent analysis of Gish's acting technique. His major device is hundreds of frame enlargements which show the exact moves and expressions of the actresses. This is one of the truly important books on film.

Cary Grant with the subtitle *An Unauthorized Biography* is by Albert Govoni. Govoni follows Grant's career on Broadway and in the movies, but has more to say about Grant's relationships with his wives and with other women than about his career. Jerry Vermilye's *Cary Grant* is part of the series entitled "The Pictorial Treasury of Film Stars." In addition to presenting pictures, the book recognizes the importance of directors George Cukor and Alfred Hitchcock to Grant's career. In *The Films of Cary Grant,* Donald Deschner includes a fine introduction to Grant's films by Charles Champlin, a biography, the usual film by film analysis, and excerpts from the film reviews which are longer than usual.

Jean Harlow, the blond bombshell, was one of the most popular comediennes of the 1930s, and her story has been told by Curtis Brown in *Jean Harlow.* This book is one of the Illustrated Histories of the Movies which depicts the life and films of the woman perhaps best remembered for her sexy, comedic roles opposite Clark Gable. Her films have been preserved in book form in *The Films of Jean Harlow* by Michael Conway and Mark Ricci. The authors have included a biographical essay, commentary, a portrait gallery, and a film by film analysis.

The first of the cowboy stars was W. S. Hart, the man who created the role of the "good badman." He has told his own story in *My Life East and West,* a 1929 book that has now been reprinted. After describing his career before the movies, he discusses his films and his friendships with other stars, especially Mary Pickford, Douglas Fairbanks, Sr. and Charles Chaplin. The book is overly sentimental, characteristic of its author, but is informative.

Doug McClelland's *The Complete Life Story of Susan Hayward* covers the life and career of the actress remembered for her Oscar-winning role in *I Want to Live,* and also discusses the critical reception to her films.

Another actress remembered for her sexy roles was Rita Hayworth. John Kobal's *Rita Hayworth* is an account of Hayworth's life and career, with special attention to her early work with Fred Astaire and Gene Kelly, to her direction by George Cukor and Howard Hawks, and to her acting with Spencer Tracy and Cary Grant. *Rita Hayworth* by Gerald Peary, another in the Illustrated Histories series, briefly describes her career. *The Films of Rita Hayworth* by Gene Ringgold gives a full and complete filmography. The book opens with a lengthy essay, "The Legend of a Love Goddess," followed by the standard filmography.

A solid popular study of the life of Katharine Hepburn is *Kate* by Charles Higham. Hepburn has always been a very private person, and writing about her therefore involves special problems. Higham has given the reader an adequate account of Hepburn's life, but pays little attention to her films from a critical point of view. Alvin Marill's *Katharine Hepburn,* also one of the Illustrated Histories of the Movies, provides a brief view of Hepburn's major films. The story of her relationship with Spencer Tracy is told with love by a friend of theirs, Garson Kanin. *Tracy and Hepburn* is more of a personal memoir than a full biography, but its intimate account of their love and their support for each other is matchless.

The best source of information on the life and career of Charlton Heston is his own autobiography, *The Actor's Life: Journals, 1956-1976.* For two decades Heston kept a record of his filmmaking, and this book records the pleasures and struggles of the actor's life. His films are discussed in *The Films of Charlton Heston* by Jeff Rovin. Rovin gives the usual film by film information but includes more of the story lines and much more analysis than most books of this sort. In fact, this is one of the best of the expanded filmographies.

William Holden by Will Holtzman is another of the Illustrated Histories series of the movies. Holden's career and films are presented through commentary and photographs. *The Films of William Holden* by Lawrence J. Quirk begins with a long essay on the life and work of the actor and then follows the standard format of film by film analysis.

The long and productive career of Bob Hope is well documented by Joe Morella, Edward Z. Epstein, and Eleanor Clark in *The Amazing Careers of Bob Hope: From Gags to Riches*. The book contains Hope's biography and follows his work in vaudeville, on Broadway, on radio and television, and in the movies. Material on the USO tours and on Hope's own books is included. One of these books is *The Road to Hollywood,* an autobiography that concentrates on Hope's movie career. Written with Bob Thomas, the book claims to document Hope's "40 year love affair with the movies." After an introductory essay by Hope and an essay by Thomas, the book becomes a fairly standard expanded filmography. Hope's autobiographies also provide background on his movie career. *Have Tux, Will Travel: Bob Hope's Own Story*, written with the assistance of Peter Martin, is a self-portrait created through one-line gags. *I Owe Russia $1200* is an autobiography of his many travels, including a trip to the Soviet Union; the book does discuss several of his films.

The master of horror, Boris Karloff, has been thoroughly studied by Paul M. Jensen in *Boris Karloff and His Films*. This book is a critical study arranged chronologically: the early years, Frankenstein, the beginning, The Reign of Terror, and Monster into Father Figure. One of Karloff's self-professed close friends, Cynthia Lindsay, has recorded her memories in *Dear Boris*. This book deals mostly with his life since Lindsay is not a movie critic; in fact, the chapter on his films consists entirely of photographs with no commentary. The films, however, are examined at length in *The Films of Boris Karloff* by Richard Bojarski and Kenneth Beale. A standard expanded filmography, this book includes a biographical essay, the film by film information, and a final chapter on Karloff on television. The biography of Karloff is told by Peter Underwood in *Karloff: The Life of Boris Karloff*. This book emphasizes Karloff's work in movies, and provides a close look at the production of his films and a filmography.

Many books on Buster Keaton have been written, and the most solid and reliable of these is *Buster Keaton* by David Robinson. Robinson proceeds chronologically through Keaton's life and films, devoting a chapter to each of the major films, and others to Keaton's studio and the actor's technique and importance. Rudi Blesh's *Keaton* presents a picture of Keaton through his many professional roles; writer, producer, director, and star; Blesh combines biography with criticism and the history of Keaton's important films. The early Keaton films are reviewed in *Keaton* by Daniel Moews. This book claims to study "the silent features close up," but it also presents an overview of the shorts. *Buster Keaton and the Dynamics of Visual Art* is a dissertation by George Wead that has now been reprinted. Wead establishes the tradition in which Keaton worked with an essay on visual wit, discusses comedy before Keaton in both Europe and America, and then tries to identify Keaton's comedy by type: word-play, genre-play, stylized space and sequence, and unity of play. European critic J.-P. Lebel's *Buster Keaton* is a brief book with a useful filmography and chapters on Keaton as director, his stone face, and his gags.

A rather unusual book about Keaton is *The Best of Buster* by Richard J. Anobile. Its subtitle claims to have *The Classic Comic Scenes direct from the Films of Buster Keaton.* Following a brief introduction by Raymond Rohauer, the book reproduces frame enlargements from *The Goat, The Navigator, Seven Chances, Go West, The General,* and *Sherlock, Jr.* Finally, George Wead, along with George Lellis, has written the best reference guide to the work of Buster Keaton. *The Film Career of Buster Keaton* provides biographical background, a critical survey of Keaton's work, a synopsis—with credits and notes—of the films, a survey of the writings about Keaton, and lists of archival sources and film distributors for those interested in serious study of the actor/director.

The dances and career of Gene Kelly are covered in *Gene Kelly: A Biography* by Clive Hirschhorn, a solid biography with analysis of Kelly's films. *The Films of Gene Kelly* by Tony Thomas gives the usual expanded filmography. Like the others of this type, this book is intended for a popular audience, but has value for the student through its lists of casts, credits, plots, analyses, and surveys of the critical reception of each film.

Princess Grace by Gwen Robyns is a biography of Grace Kelly, with emphasis on the popular figure rather than on the actress. The book includes many personal photographs.

The Life, the Legend, the Legacy of Alan Ladd is the subtitle of *Ladd* by Beverly Linet. Linet was a writer for one of the Hollywood screen magazines important in the 1930s and 1940s to the career of any actor. This book reads much like the articles featured in those magazines, and as such is a good view of what the life of a star is like. It does not, however, answer the questions concerning the private tortures that led Ladd to alcohol and suicide.

The Films of Hedy Lamarr is an expanded filmography of the movies of the actress remembered primarily for her exotic and romantic appeal. Christopher Young's book follows the standard format for books of this sort, with an introduction on her career and life that consists mostly of photographs.

Burt Lancaster became best known as the tender tough guy, and his films have been the subject of *Burt Lancaster* by Tony Thomas, another of the Illustrated Histories of the Movies.

Charles Laughton was an English actor very popular in America. His biography is told by Charles Higham in *Charles Laughton.* With the authorization of Laughton's wife, actress Elsa Lanchester, Higham has explored the nature of Laughton's homosexuality while at the same time trying to examine the genius of his acting.

Perhaps no pair is associated more with comedy in film than Stan Laurel and Oliver Hardy, and several studies of their comedic art have been written. Among them is *Laurel & Hardy* by Charles Barr, a well-illustrated book that contains chapters on their technique and gags as well as others on specific genres of their comedy, such as the comic opera. *Mr. Laurel and Mr. Hardy* by John McCabe is a lightly older book consisting of biographical material on each man and a study of their career together in both the silent and the sound films. McCabe was a long time friend of Stan Laurel's, and this book is the authorized biography of the famous pair. McCabe went on to put together two more books on the comedians. *The Comedy World of Stan Laurel* is a miscellany that records Laurel's humor and makes a tentative attempt to analyze it. *Laurel and Hardy* by John McCabe, Al Kilgore, and Richard W. Bann begins with comments on the pair by Marcel Marceau, Jack Benny, Lenny Bruce, and others who loved them and follows with a biographical essay and analysis, and a film by film analysis based on photographs from their films. The authors also include their own rating of the films and the by-laws for Sons of the Desert, a fan club. Jack Scagnetti's *The Laurel and Hardy Scrapbook,* intended for a general audience, has chapters on each man with highlights of their careers before they joined forces. Scagnetti then discusses them as a team, taking them through their heyday, their decline, and finally into their period as cult figures. Scagnetti's expanded filmography is worthy of special note.

British actress Vivien Leigh is as American as Blanche DuBois and Scarlett O'Hara, her two most famous roles. Her biography has been ably written by Ann Edwards in *Vivien Leigh,* a study that depicts her screen successes, her marriage to Sir Laurence Olivier, and her insanity. In *The Oliviers: A Biography,* an early book on the couple, Felix Barker describes their lives before they met, the early years together during which Leigh made *Gone with the Wind,* and their marriage; but the book does not pass 1953 and therefore makes no mention of the final tragedy of her life. *Love Scene: The Story of Laurence Olivier and Vivien Leigh* is more up to date. Jesse Lasky, Jr. and Pat Silver focus on the love affair and breakup, but the book does include information about their stage and screen careers.

For many, the quintessence of American comedy and pathos in the 1950s and 1960s was Jack Lemmon. Don Widener in *Lemmon* has tried to capture the essence of the man and his films. This is a readable biography that achieves its richness through its detailed treatment of Lemmon's films. Joe Baltake has covered Lemmon's films in *The Films of Jack Lemmon,* a book which begins with a tribute in verse from Walter Matthau and a foreword by Judith Crist. Baltake's lengthy biography is followed by a filmography with longer than usual excerpts from reviews, and an afterword by Billy Wilder, who directed Lemmon in some of his most successful films.

An earlier comic, Harold Lloyd, told his own story in 1928 in *An American Comedy,* which has since been reprinted. This autobiography is an interesting firsthand account of making movies in the 1920s, but Richard Schickel's *Harold Lloyd* is more valuable as a critical appraisal of Lloyd's films. Schickel begins with a long essay entitled "The Shape of Laughter," in which he analyzes Lloyd's ability and techniques. He then devotes several pages to each of the feature films through frame enlargements and brief commentary and concludes with a filmography by Eileen Bowser. Another useful book is *Harold Lloyd's World of Comedy,* a distillation of Lloyd's conversations with William Cahn on comedy and the movies. Lloyd's most important films are the focus of Donald W. McCaffrey's *Three Classic Silent Screen Comedies Starring Harold Lloyd,* a discussion of Lloyd's technique through analysis of *Grandma's Boy, Safety Last,* and *The Freshman.* In *Harold Lloyd: The King of Daredevil Comedy* Adam Reilly offers a biography that includes an expanded filmography with critical essays of several pages and lengthy excerpts from Lloyd's reviews. Reilly's conclusion is a reappraisal of Lloyd by contemporary critics, among them Andrew Sarris and William K. Everson.

Larry Swindell has paid tribute to one of America's favorite comediennes in *Screwball: The Life of Carole Lombard.* This is an in-depth biography with limited analysis of Lombard's films. The films are covered in *The Films of Carole Lombard* by Frederick W. Ott, a study which includes a biography and bibliography as well as an expanded filmography.

In recent years Ida Lupino has received renewed attention as one of the first women to work in Hollywood as a director. Jerry Vermilye, in another of Pyramid's Illustrated Histories, has given a brief overview of her career—as actress, director, producer, and writer—in *Ida Lupino.*

The story of Jeanette MacDonald has been told by James Robert Parish in *The Jeanette MacDonald Story,* a biography made up primarily of anecdotes and stories told by those who knew her. Lee Edward Stern's *Jeanette MacDonald* is basically a pictorial study of MacDonald's career on Broadway and in films. *Jeanette MacDonald: A Pictorial Treasury* is largely a photograph book with a smattering of commentary by the author, Sharon Rich.

Patricia Erens has recorded the career of Shirley MacLaine in *The Films of Shirley MacLaine.* Ehrens' introduction deals with the MacLaine image, and the rest of the book covers her films. MacLaine has written her own autobiographical volumes: *Don't Fall Off the Mountain* and *You Can Get There from Here.* These personable books describe her life from her childhood in Virginia to stardom in Hollywood and Las Vegas and cover both her movie career and her social activism.

Steve McQueen is another private person, and therefore writing about his life has its problems. Malachy McCoy has written *Steve McQueen: The Unauthorized Biography.* McCoy's book is primarily the story of the man as a star and includes little analysis of his movies and a filmography.

The Films of Fredric March by Lawrence J. Quirk is a standard expanded filmography. After an introductory essay on March's life and career, Quirk moves to a film by film reference guide enhanced by pictures.

The story of Dean Martin and Jerry Lewis is told by Arthur Marx in *Everybody Loves Somebody Sometime (Especially Himself).* This book traces Martin and Lewis from their beginning as a team through their successes and eventual breakup, with emphasis on their films and shows.

The man most likely to write about Groucho Marx is Groucho himself. *Groucho and Me* is Groucho's autobiography, and in it he treats the movies with his characteristic flippancy. Groucho was also responsible for *The Grouchophile*, basically a pictorial biography of his life from childhood, through the movies and television, and into his final years of decline. Groucho collaborated with Richard J. Anobile to produce *The Marx Bros. Scrapbook*, a book of memorabilia including photographs, playbills, letters and interviews with people such as Jack Benny, Morrie Ryskind, Groucho, and Zeppo. In *The Marx Brothers*, Allen Eyles devotes a chapter to each of the films. Most of Eyles' commentary is in the form of plot summary, but he does include a chapter on the men before they began making movies.

Like Joan Crawford, Groucho has had his innermost life revealed by his child, Arthur Marx. Arthur Marx's unflattering and biased account is *Son of Groucho.* This book is balanced somewhat by Hector Arce's *Groucho.* Arce worked with Groucho and knew him well and in this authorized biography, he describes Groucho, as Arce says, "warts and all." Although he offers little close analysis of Groucho's movies, he does take pains to explain Groucho's behavior and his relationships with women, especially with his last companion, Erin Fleming. Harpo, the brother who never talked in the movies, finally speaks out in *Harpo Speaks,* a book he wrote with Rowland Barber. The book recalls his practical jokes and his humorous scenes in the movies; it is richly detailed and funny.

The Films of James Mason by Clive Hirschhorn records the career of this British actor who made many films in Hollywood and remains popular with American audiences. Hirshhorn's book is basically an expanded filmography.

Raymond Massey is a Canadian whose autobiography, *When I Was Young,* tells the story of his career in American films and on the British stage.

Ann Miller started in Hollywood at thirteen and went on to become a dancer and singer in the movies and on stage. Her autobiography, *Miller's High Life,* written with the assistance of Norma Lee Browning, is a survey of her life and career.

As an actor Robert Mitchum is probably best remembered for his masculine roles and his sleepy-eyed look. *Robert Mitchum on the Screen* by Alvin Marill is an expanded filmography. It includes a long introduction, a film by film analysis of Mitchum's career, and photographs.

The story of Tom Mix, one of the first Hollywood cowboys, has been written by a relative, Paul E. Mix, and is an effort to build up a man who does not need the help. In *The Life and Legend of Tom Mix* the author covers the Mix family and the years when Tom Mix worked on the Miller Brothers 101 Real Wild West Ranch as a cowboy; it also follows him into movies and stardom. The chapter on the legend of Tom Mix reveals the author's bias: "No finer example of clean living than Tom Mix walks the face of the earth. His life itself, as well as his pictures, has been a powerful influence for good in the lives of youth wherever the sun shines on civilization."

Few lives or careers are more difficult to analyze than that of Marilyn Monroe. To date, the best book on her is *Norma Jean* by Fred Lawrence Guiles, a solid study that attempts to get behind the myth rather than embellish it. *Marilyn Monroe* by Joan Mellen is also a serious study but is intended for a more popular audience. Mellen analyzes the actress' image and presents a biography with emphasis on the men in her life. The bulk of the book is devoted to Marilyn's films, most in the form of plot summary. Mellen also discusses what is known about Marilyn's death. *Marilyn Monroe,* edited by Edward Wagenknecht, is a collection of interviews, reminiscences, and reflections on Marilyn's life and death by those who knew her or were influenced by her films: Hollis Alpert, Edith Sitwell, Lee Strasberg, Alexander Walker, and Wagenknecht himself. *Marilyn* by Norman Mailer probably contributes to the myth more than it explains it. Some of Mailer's commentary is highly questionable; in fact, the book may be as much creative journalism as biography—but the photographs are wonderful.

Marilyn also tried to tell her own story. In *Conversations with Marilyn,* W. J. Weatherby recorded the conversations he had with Marilyn during the last two years of her life; her thoughtful comments about acting and the profession show her to be far from the dumb blonde of her early image. Another book, *My Story,* was supposedly written by Marilyn and published by a friend after her death; it is sketchy and incomplete, but interesting. Another view of the woman comes from one of her lovers. Hans Jøgen Lembourn, a Dane who had a brief affair with Marilyn, writes in his book, *Diary of a Lover of Marilyn Monroe,* a day by day description of the forty days and nights they spent together.

Actor: The Life and Times of Paul Muni by Jerome Lawrence is a biography by a longtime friend of the actor. Lawrence's book however, is far more than a personal memoir: it is the result of diligent research and scores of interviews with others who knew Muni. It provides useful background on

Muni's films and plays. *Paul Muni* by Michael Druxman is essentially an expanded filmography with essays on the man, the star, the actor, and the career.

The career of Paul Newman has been documented by Charles Hamblett in *Paul Newman.* This is a friendly biography that says more about the man and his relationship with his wife, Joanne Woodward, than about his acting and his films. While Hamblett lists the credits for Newman's films, the lack of an index makes it difficult to locate material in the text. *Paul Newman* by Michael Kerbel is another of the Illustrated Histories of the Movies providing a general study of his movies. Newman's films are also treated in *The Films of Paul Newman* by Lawrence J. Quirk. Quirk presents an introductory essay on the actor and the man and a filmography of the films in which he has acted and one (*Rachel, Rachel*) he directed.

Jack Nicholson: Face to Face by Robert David Crane and Christopher Fryer contains both interviews and commentary about Nicholson by Karen Black, Bruce Dern, Sally Struthers, Dennis Hopper, Ann-Margaret, and Nicholson himself. The book also contains a filmography.

David Niven, the versatile British actor, has written his remembrances of the people he has known and worked with in *Bring on the Empty Horses.* This lively commentary covers a range of movie people including Samuel Goldwyn, Greta Garbo, Charles Chaplin, Douglas Fairbanks, Sr., and Humphrey Bogart.

The history of Our Gang, that delightful group of neighborhood children that has survived several generations, has been told by Leonard Maltin and Richard W. Bann in *Our Gang: The Life and Times of the Little Rascals.* The authors discuss Hal Roach's studio and give an overview of the Our Gang series; after comparing Our Gang to other kids' series, the authors consider the many films made by the groups known as The Little Rascals, from the silent films into sound and television.

In another of the Illustrated Histories of the Movies, Tony Thomas has told the story of Gregory Peck in words and photographs. *Gregory Peck* is basically a biography with critical commentary, a brief bibliography, and filmography.

Many of the recent books on Mary Pickford concern her relationship with Douglas Fairbanks, Sr. and are mentioned in this chapter under his name, but *Sweetheart: The Story of Mary Pickford* by Robert Windeler is her story. Windeler presents her biography, brief film criticism, a filmography, and photographs. Kemp Niver has captured her early career in *Mary Pickford, Comedienne.* This book is devoid of commentary but tells its story through frame enlargements from the period when she worked at Biograph, from handbills, and from other memorabilia. Pickford told her own story in *Sunshine and Shadow.* This autobiography, with a foreword by Cecil B.

DeMille, gives her version of her relationship with Douglas Fairbanks, Sr., but it is not a very intimate account. The book does, however, provide background for her films and gives her assessment of them. These films are the subject of *The Films of Mary Pickford* by Raymond Lee. Lee opens with an essay on "the queen of the screen," and his portrait gallery includes photographs taken both on and off the screen. The filmography itself is too brief to be of value; its limited value is in its list of Pickford's silent films.

Sidney Poitier was one of the first black movie actors to become successful with white audiences on his own terms. *Sidney* by William Hoffman details his struggles to become successful in what had been a white man's medium and provides an inside account of the productions of Poitier's films. A fine filmography can be found in *The Films of Sidney Poitier* by Alvin Marill. Marill's commentary on Poitier's films is lengthy, and he includes a section on the actor's work on stage and television.

Vincent Price Unmasked by James Robert Parish and Steven Whitney is another expanded filmography. The authors have included a long biography and the credits for Price's Broadway plays and movies, along with brief commentary.

Alvin Marill has also written *The Films of Anthony Quinn*. The book includes an essay of appreciation by actor Arthur Kennedy, an introductory essay by Marill and the usual filmography. The conclusion deals with Quinn's work on stage and television.

One of the movies' immortal tough guys, George Raft, is fondly remembered in Lewis Yablonsky's book, *George Raft*. This is basically a biography with a filmography, bibliography and brief analysis of Raft's films.

Basil Rathbone made his reputation as the suave villain, a career that he describes in his autobiography, *In and Out of Character*. Even though he covers his entire professional life, he concentrates on his happy years in Hollywood and New York. Michael B. Druxman's *Basil Rathbone* is an expanded filmography which follows the usual format for such books except that its critical comments are short and of little value.

Robert Redford is one of the most popular actors of the 1970s, and *The Films of Robert Redford* by James Spada covers his career in film. Spada's introductory biography treats Redford's work on Broadway and television, as well as in the movies. In addition to the customary filmography Spada includes both candid shots and portraits.

Edward G. Robinson's autobiography *All My Yesterdays* covers all of Robinson's important films and his life in the movies. Also included are Robinson's personal views of his co-workers, views which seem to have become sugarcoated with the passage of time. Robinson's films are given their due in *The Cinema of Edward G. Robinson* by James Robert Parish and Alvin Marill. In addition to providing the expanded filmography, the authors comment on Robinson's stage career, his roles in short films, and his work on radio and television. Foster Hirsch gives an overview of Robinson's film career in *Edward G. Robinson,* another of the Illustrated Histories of the Movies.

The Films of Ginger Rogers by Homer Dickens follows the standard expanded filmography format, beginning with an introductory essay entitled "The American Girl." The highlights of the book are the notes on the production of Rogers' films and the photograph album of her dance routines with Fred Astaire.

Another Rogers—Will Rogers—remains the subject of considerable critical attention, none of which can seem to recreate the affection he found in the hearts of the American people. While he is not best remembered for his films, no book on him can ignore his work in film. *Will Rogers: His Life and Times* by Richard M. Ketchum is an illustrated biography, and part of the book is devoted to Rogers' career in films. *The Autobiography of Will Rogers,* first written in 1926 and since reprinted, is another commentary on the times as well as on the man and his career.

Mickey Rooney's many marriages and his friendship with Judy Garland have always interested the public; and, therefore, his autobiography, *I. E.: An Autobiography,* will delight his fans. This chatty and personal book describes his relationships with the many women in his life and the productions of his films.

Rosalind Russell enjoyed life and her autobiography, *Life is a Banquet,* is full of the warmth and joy she exhibited in so many of her movies, most notably *His Girl Friday.* The book also includes her remembrances of her work on Broadway. *Rosalind Russell* is yet another of the Illustrated Histories of the Movies written by Nicholas Yanni; it provides a critic's view of her films naturally missing in her autobiography.

Few actors are more protective of their private life than George C. Scott, but W. A. Harbinson has succeeded, as much as possible, in penetrating the inner man in *George Scott.* This biography presents the man both as a rebel and as a great actor; it describes his struggles and his successes, and includes a filmography and list of his plays.

The Films of Norma Shearer by Jack Jacobs and Myron Braum is a standard expanded filmography. Shearer's long career from the silents of the 1920s until her retirement in 1942 is covered.

An early study of the work of Frank Sinatra appeared in 1947: *The Voice: The Story of an American Phenomenon,* reprint of a *New Yorker* article by E. J. Kahn. Part biography and part analysis, the book is an interesting period piece covering the first part of Sinatra's career. That career later underwent many changes and became more complex as Sinatra got older. Arnold Shaw tried to find the key to the complexity in *Sinatra: Twentieth-Century Romantic.* Shaw explores the contradiction between Sinatra the tough guy in both private and public and Sinatra the romantic; Shaw concludes that there is no resolution of the two sides of the star. The book contains a list of Sinatra's records and films up to 1968. Columnist Earl Wilson was for a long time an intimate of Sinatra's, but after a public falling out was no longer close to Sinatra. His book, *Sinatra: An Unauthorized Biography,* is a controversial study of the actor and singer; Wilson explains his goals in his preface: "From the standpoint of a biographer, perhaps I am lucky to have been both in and out of Sinatra's favor, for I have known both Sinatras. The book is eminently fair to him, I hope, but in painting the portrait, I have not left out the warts." *The Films of Frank Sinatra* by Gene Ringgold and Clifford McCarthy is a standard expanded filmography of the crooner/actor which includes an introduction, a film by film description, and brief reviews of Sinatra's films.

Starring Miss Barbara Stanwyck by Ella Smith is another expanded filmography, but since it includes a good analysis of Stanwyck's film and information on their critical reception it is useful to the student of those films. Like other expanded filmographies, this book is enhanced by photographs, but the added information makes it a cut above most of the others. *Barbara Stanwyck* by Jerry Vermilye is another Illustrated History.

Jimmy Stewart has been one of America's most popular actors. *The Films of James Stewart* is a standard filmography. This book, by Ken D. Jones, Arthur McClure, and Alfred E. Twomey, cites the credits and gives a synopsis and excerpts from the reviews of Stewart's films. Again, the text is enhanced with photographs. In *James Stewart* Howard Thompson has provided an overview of Stewart's career in another of the Illustrated Histories.

Gloria Swanson by Richard M. Hudson and Raymond Lee is another basic filmography covering her career from bathing beauty to acclaimed actress in *Sunset Boulevard.* The authors begin with a brief introduction on the star's image and include many photographs, especially of her face, as well as information on her films.

In *Elizabeth: The Life and Career of Elizabeth Taylor*, Dick Sheppard fights his way through the gossip to try to find a woman: mother, wife, lover, actress. He follows her career from girl actress to superstar; the theme of the book is suggested by a quotation from Taylor who sees herself as Mother Courage, "I'll be dragging my sable coat behind me into old age." *Who's Afraid of Elizabeth Taylor?* is a biography that deals with the star and the myth surrounding her. The book by Brenda Maddox focuses on Taylor's life and films, but there is little background on the films or discussion of her acting. That void is filled by *The Films of Elizabeth Taylor* by Jerry Vermilye and Mark Ricci. Their introductory essay is titled "The Star."

The Films of Shirley Temple by Robert Windeler begins with an introductory essay that includes a discussion of Shirley Temple's adult career in politics. The book is well illustrated and follows the form of the standard filmography.

Mo Howard and the Three Stooges was written by Mo Howard himself. This biography recalls their madcap world in pictures and remembrances.

Spencer Tracy by Larry Swindell is a rather routine biography with good background material on the making of Tracy's films. Swindell discusses Tracy's early work in the theater, the beginning of his career in movies, his stardom in the 1930s, and his superstar status in the 1940s and 1950s. The last chapter, "The Actor for History," focuses on the legend. *Spencer Tracy* by Romano Tozzi is another of the Illustrated Histories of the Movies and provides an overview of Tracy's film career. Of all the expanded filmographies, *The Films of Spencer Tracy* must rank among the most valuable. Donald Deschner has included essays on Tracy by Stanley Kramer, Dore Schary, Bosley Crowther, and Ed Sullivan, as well as an interview with Tracy and an essay by Tracy on his craft.

Liv Ullmann is a Swedish actress of international acclaim whose autobiography, *Changing,* describes the joys and pains of her work in the United States. The sensitivity she reveals in her films can be found in this book, especially in her thoughts on her daughter. David E. Outerbridge's *Without Makeup: Liv Ullmann, a Photo-Biography* includes a long interview with the actress on acting and many photographs from her films.

In *Valentino: The Love God*, Noel Botham and Peter Donnelly present Valentino's life and career in graphic detail and use critical understanding to get behind the legend. This book has good company in Alexander Walker's *Rudolph Valentino,* which offers considerable insight in its few pages. Walker is the critic who perhaps best understands the importance of sexuality in acting, and he has no better subject than Valentino. He sees Valentino as a man who presents a strong sexual image and is at the same time a complex individual. Walker analyzes Valentino's impact on the screen and his successes; he also discusses Valentino's relationship with women and his death. *The Intimate Life of Rudolph Valentino* by Jack Scagnetti is a biography told through brief commentary and photographs; the book concludes with tributes and critiques from those who knew the actor.

In the mind of many, John Wayne has come to symbolize Hollywood's fascination with the American frontier, and Mike Tomkies has made an attempt to understand Wayne's importance to American myth and dreams in *Duke: The Story of John Wayne.* This brief biography and critical study tries to explain Wayne's legendary image: "If today [1971] he is a living legend, it is not only because of his work as an actor, but through his life as a man. In John Wayne's life—as in few others—the legend has become reality." The book concludes with a list of Wayne's films. *Shooting Star* is a biography of Wayne by Maurice Zolotow. This detailed study also tries to explain why Wayne became a cultural icon, although Wayne himself did not have a high opinion of the book. *John Wayne* by Alan G. Barbour is one of the Illustrated Histories of the Movies and describes Wayne's film career through photographs and brief commentary. *The Films of John Wayne* by Mark Ricci and Boris Zmijewsky is an expanded filmography in the usual format.

The Films of Mae West by Jon Tuska opens with an introduction by Parker Tyler, who along with Alexander Walker is one of the leading authorities on sex in the cinema. Tuska includes a biography, a portrait gallery and many other photographs, and extensive commentary on each of the films. Appropriately, he concludes with a discussion of the legend of Mae West. Michael Bayer's *May West* follows the usual format for books in this series, The Illustrated Histories of the Movies; it focuses on her films.

BOOKS ON MORE THAN ONE ACTOR

Books dealing with groups of actors are useful although difficult to categorize. The reader will note that these books are arranged chronologically, beginning with actors of the silent screen and moving on to actors of the modern period.

An interesting period piece is *Film Folk* by Rob Wagner. Wagner's book came out in 1918 and describes the people Wagner knew in the movie business, from D. W. Griffith to Charles Chaplin, Mary Pickford, and Douglas Fairbanks, Sr., as well as many less famous.

The women who worked for Griffith are the subject of a scholarly book by Anthony Slide. Slide begins *The Griffith Actresses* with an essay on "what made a Griffith girl" and includes chapters on Blanche Sweet, Mary Pickford, Dorothy Gish, Lillian Gish, Mae Marsh, Miriam Cooper, Clarine Seymour, and Carol Dempster. In *The Idols of Silence,* Slide addresses the careers of many of the lesser-known actors from the silent period. His essays on Mignon Anderson, Hobart Bosworth, and others contain brief commentary on their roles and their films. Slide also discusses the role of the fan magazines during the silent period. The book includes photographs and checklists of the films for the actors included.

Dewitt Bodeen has written two books on stars from the silent and early sound periods. *From Hollywood* describes the career of seventeen American stars who began working in films during the silent era: Theda Bara, Geraldine Farrar, Wallace Reid, John Barrymore, Lon Chaney, Douglas Fairbanks, Sr., and others. Bodeen has written a chapter for each which presents basic biographical information and the story of the production of the actor's major films. Filmographies for each are also included. In *More From Hollywood,* Bodeen continues with the same format; here his list of actors is eclectic and includes Greta Garbo, Dorothy Gish, Blanche Sweet, Clint Eastwood, and Jeanette MacDonald.

In 1932 Elinor Hughes wrote a book about the movie stars of her day, *Famous Stars of Filmdom (Men).* Now reprinted, the book offers interesting period essays on George Arliss, John Barrymore, Richard Barthelmess, Warner Baxter, Charles Chaplin, Maurice Chevalier, Ronald Colman, Douglas Fairbanks (both Sr. and Jr.), Walter Huston, Emil Jannings, Tom Mix, William Powell, and Will Rogers. Hughes' complementary study, *Famous Stars of Filmdom (Women),* includes Claudette Colbert, Joan Crawford, Marlene Dietrich, Marie Dressler, Greta Garbo, Janet Gaylor, Mary Pickford, Norma Shearer, and Gloria Swanson. While essays are not very informative, they are interesting period pieces on the myths of the stars.

David Shipman has written two books on the stars. *The Great Movie Stars: The Golden Years* begins with an introduction on the stars and the system, the box office, and the role of the fan magazines. Shipman moves on to essays on each of the stars, with brief evaluaton, a biography, comments on major films, and photographs. In *The Great Movie Stars: The International Years,* Shipman continues with the same format of biography and criticism, but there is little depth to his essays.

A number of books discuss film actresses. James Robert Parish recorded the history of the women who played comedy roles in *The Slapstick Queens.* He provides an essay on each, a full filmography, and photographs; included are Marjorie Main, Martha Raye, Joan Davis, Judy Canova, and Phyllis Diller. Parish also collaborated with Don E. Stanke on *The Glamour Girls.* For each of these actresses the authors have included a long essay of biography which includes critical reception, background, and a filmography; included here are Joan Bennett, Rita Hayworth, Audrey Hepburn, Jennifer Jones, and Kim Novak. Kalton C. Lahue has written *Ladies in Distress,* in which he presents an essay and pictures of some forty heroines from the silent period. Lahue claims that he "selected those included on the premise that they best represent the many and divergent talents which made the silent days such a pleasant memory. . . ." He has included the famous such as Mary Pickford, Greta Garbo, and Lillian Gish; but perhaps the greatest value of the book is his inclusion of actors for whom there is very little other material available: Bessie Love, Dolores del Rio, Louise Brooks, and others.

Ginger, Loretta and Irene Who? consists of a series of biographies by George Eells on women who were important in movies but never made it to superstar status. He includes Ginger Rogers, Miriam Hopkins, Ruth Etting, Kay Francis, Loretta Young, and Irene Bentley.

Two books compiled by Larry Carr study the actors through photographs: *Four Fabulous Faces: The Evolution and Metamorphosis of Garbo, Swanson, Crawford, and Dietrich* and *More Fabulous Faces: The Evolution and Metamorphosis of Dolores Del Rio, Myrna Loy, Carole Lombard, Bette Davis, and Katharine Hepburn.* The books contain essays on each star's impact and photographs of her face, hair styles, fashions, hands, screen lovers, and husbands.

Books about male actors abound. James Robert Parish has again collaborated with Don E. Stanke to produce several such books. *The Swashbuckelers* is, of course, about the men who rescued those damsels in distress: Douglas Fairbanks, Sr., Ronald Colman, Tyrone Power, Errol Flynn, Stewart Granger, Victor Mature, Cornel Wilde, and Tony Curtis; the authors have included an essay, filmography, and photographs for each. *The Debonairs* contains essays and filmographies for the suave heroes who wooed their women with talk: George Brent, Melvyn Douglas, Cary Grant, Rex Harrison, Ray Milland, Robert Montgomery, David Niven, and William Powell.

In *Gentlemen to the Rescue: The Heroes of the Silent Screen*, Kalton Lahue has written about the exploits of some thirty men, including Rudolph Valentino, Will Rogers, John Gilbert, Douglas Fairbanks, Sr., Ronald Colman, and John Barrymore. *Cads and Cavaliers: The Gentlemen Adventurers of the Movies* by Tony Thomas has chapters on Douglas Fairbanks (both Sr. and Jr.), John Barrymore, George Sanders, Vincent Price, David Niven, Basil Rathbone, and Errol Flynn; he then covers a number of lesser actors in a single chapter. There are many photographs.

Men whose image is the opposite of the gentlemanly hero have also been covered. In *Rebels: The Rebel Hero in Films,* Joe Morella and Edward Z. Epstein include chapters on Montgomery Clift, Marlon Brando and James Dean, as well as topical chapters such as "the heel as hero" and "the British rebel hero." The book is enhanced by a brief introduction by Judith Crist and extensive photographs. *The Bad Guys* by William K. Everson is a pictorial history of the villain in film, heavier on photographs than on commentary. Ian and Elisabeth Cameron have written *The Heavies,* a study of actors who have played the mean guys in films. The book lists the actors alphabetically and gives a brief biography and filmography for each. The entries are brief and without much depth, but many are included, among them Raymond Burr, Lee J. Cobb, George Kennedy, Warren Oates, Richard Widmark, and Lee Marvin. *The Tough Guys* by James Robert Parish deals with the men who get their way through force: James Cagney, Kirk Douglas, Burt Lancaster, Robert Mitchum, Paul Muni, Edward G. Robinson, and Robert Ryan. Parish has written extensive essays on each man which include comments on their major films and provide some idea of the critical reception each enjoyed.

Those erstwhile supporting characters also get their due. *The Versatiles: A Study of Supporting Character Actors and Actresses in American Motion Pictures, 1930-1955* is by Alfred E. Twomey and Arthur F. McClure. The authors provide a brief paragraph and photographs of each person, a listing of the major films, dates, and a capsule summary of the reviews. The same authors collaborated with Ken D. Jones on *Character People.* This book contains a long list of character actors, a brief statement about the career of each, a list of his or her major films, and a photograph. There is not much depth in books of this sort, but they do include actors not discussed in other books. Those actors and actresses who achieved star status as children are covered in *The Child Stars* by Norman J. Zierold. This solid book for a popular audience includes Jackie Coogan, Shirley Temple, Jane Withers, Baby Leroy, Judy Garland, Mickey Rooney, Edna Mae Durbin, Freddie Bartholomew, Jackie Cooper, and others.

Close-ups: The Intimate Profiles of Movie Stars by Their Co-stars, Directors, Screenwriters, and Friends, edited by Danny Peary, is a collection of brief essays on recent stars with an excellent overview of those covered.

No movie actor would be a star without the services of a photographer. John Engstead has been a Hollywood photographer, for many years and *Star Shots* is a record of his life with the stars. In this book he tells about the shooting and includes many of his best shots of the stars. James Abbe was a photographer in the early years, and his *Stars of the Twenties* captures the stars of the decade that saw the rise of the star system. Following an introduction by Lillian Gish and an explanatory essay by Mary Dawn Early, the book presents Abbe's excellent photographs.

No study of actors would be complete without *Stardom* by Alexander Walker. Walker has taken a historical approach to the stars in order to explain the phenomenon of stardom. He begins with the emergence of the star system with Florence Lawrence, D. W. Griffith, Lillian Gish, and Richard Barthelmess; documents the maturity of the system under Mack Sennett, Charles Chaplin, and Douglas Fairbanks, Sr.; and shows the extravagance of the system with Gloria Swanson, Pola Negri, Greta Garbo, Rudolph Valentino, and John Gilbert. He then concludes with the almost mythical stars: Bette Davis, Joan Crawford, Clark Gable, and John Wayne. In addition, Walker includes essays on such topics as ethnic stars, the role of scandal in making or breaking a star, the importance of the coming of sound, and the significance of the studios.

BIBLIOGRAPHY

Abbe, James. *Stars of the Twenties: Observed by James Abbe.* London: Thames and Hudson, 1975.

Affron, Charles. *Star Acting: Gish, Garbo, and Davis.* New York: E. P. Dutton, 1977.

Agan, Patrick. *Clint Eastwood: The Man Behind the Myth.* New York: Pyramid, 1975.

Alpert, Hollis. *The Barrymores.* New York: Dial Press, 1964.

Anobile, Richard J., ed. *The Best of Buster: The Classic Comic Scenes Direct from the Films of Buster Keaton.* New York: Crown, 1976.

______. *Drat! Being the Encapsulated View of Life by W. C. Fields in His Own Words.* New York: World, 1968.

______. *A Flask of Fields.* New York: Darien House, 1972.
Arce, Hector. *Groucho.* New York: G. P. Putnam's Sons, 1979.
Arliss, George. *My Ten Years in the Studios.* Boston: Little, Brown, 1940.
______. *Up the Years from Bloomsbury: An Autobiography.* Boston: Little, Brown, 1929.
Arvidson, Linda. *When the Movies Were Young.* New York: Benjamin Blom, 1968.
Ashley, Elizabeth. *Actress.* New York: M. Evans, 1978.
Asplund, Uno. *Chaplin's Films: A Filmography.* New York: A. S. Barnes, 1973.
Astaire, Fred. *Steps in Time.* New York: Harper, 1959.
Astor, Mary. *A Life on Film.* New York: Delacorte, 1971.
Autry, Gene. *Back in the Saddle Again.* Garden City, N.Y.: Doubleday, 1978.
Bacall, Lauren. *By Myself.* New York: Alfred A. Knopf, 1978.
Baltake, Joe. *The Films of Jack Lemmon.* Secaucus, N.J.: Citadel, 1977.
Bankhead, Tallulah. *Tallulah: My Autobiography.* New York: Harper, 1952.
Barbour, Alan, G. *Humphrey Bogart.* New York: Pyramid, 1973.
______. *John Wayne.* New York: Pyramid, 1974.
Barker, Felix. *The Oliviers: A Biography.* Philadelphia: J. B. Lippincott, 1953.
Barr, Charles. *Laurel & Hardy.* Berkeley: University of California Press, 1967.
Barrymore, Diana and Gerold Frank. *Too Much, Too Soon.* New York: Henry Holt, 1957.
Barrymore, Ethel. *Memories: An Autobiography.* New York: Harper, 1955.
Barrymore, John. *Confessions of an Actor.* New York: Benjamin Blom, 1971.
Bauer, Barbara. *Bing Crosby.* New York: Pyramid, 1977.
Bayar, Michael. *Mae West.* New York: Pyramid, 1975.
Beaver, James N., Jr. *John Garfield.* New York: A. S. Barnes, 1978.
Benchley, Nathaniel. *Humphrey Bogart.* Boston: Little, Brown, 1975.
Bennett, Joan and Lois Kibbee. *The Bennett Playbill.* New York: Holt, Rinehart and Winston, 1970.
Bergman, Andrew. *James Cagney.* New York: Pyramid, 1973.
Blesh, Rudi. *Keaton.* New York: Macmillan, 1966.
Bodeen, Dewitt. *Bogart's Face.* New York: Stanyan, 1970.
______. *From Hollywood.* New York: A. S. Barnes, 1976.
______. *More from Hollywood.* New York: A. S. Barnes, 1977.
Bojarski, Richard and Kenneth Beale. *The Films of Boris Karloff.* Secaucus, N.J.: Citadel, 1974.
Bookbinder, Robert. *The Films of Bing Crosby.* Secaucus, N.J.: Citadel, 1977.
Botham, Noel and Peter Donnelly. *Valentino.* New York: Ace Books, 1976.
Bowman, William Dodgson. *Charlie Chaplin: His Life and Art.* New York: Haskell House, 1974.
Brough, James. *The Fabulous Fondas.* New York: David McKay, 1973.
Brown, Curtis F. *Ingrid Bergman.* New York: Pyramid, 1973.
Cagney, James. *Cagney by Cagney.* Garden City, N.Y.: Doubleday, 1976.
Cahn, William. *Harold Lloyd's World of Comedy.* New York: Duell, Sloan and Pearce, 1964.
Cameron, Ian and Elisabeth Cameron. *The Heavies.* New York: Praeger, 1967.
Carey, Gary. *Doug and Mary.* New York: E. P. Dutton, 1977.
Carpozi, George, Jr. *The Gary Cooper Story.* New Rochelle, N.Y.: Arlington House, 1970.

Carr, Larry. *Four Fabulous Faces: The Evolution and Metamorphosis of Garbo, Swanson, Crawford, and Dietrich.* New Rochelle, N.Y.: Arlington, 1970.
______. *More Fabulous Faces: The Evolution and Metamorphosis of Dolores Del Rio, Myrna Loy, Carole Lombard, Bette Davis, and Katharine Hepburn.* Garden City, N.Y.: Doubleday, 1970.
Castanza, Philip. *The Films of Jeanette MacDonald and Nelson Eddy.* Secaucus, N.J.: Citadel, 1978.
Chaplin, Charles. *My Autobiography.* New York: Simon and Schuster, 1964.
______. *My Life in Pictures.* New York: Grosset and Dunlap, 1974.
Chaplin, Charles, Jr. *My Father: Charlie Chaplin.* New York: Random House, 1960.
Chaplin, Lita Grey and Morton Cooper. *My Life with Chaplin: An Intimate Memoir.* New York: Bernard Geis, 1966.
Colman, Juliet Benita. *Ronald Colman, a Very Private Person: A Biography.* New York: William Morrow, 1975.
Connell, Brian. *Knight Errant: A Biography of Douglas Fairbanks, Jr.* Garden City, N.Y.: Doubleday, 1955.
Conrad, Earl. *Errol Flynn.* New York: Dodd, Mead, 1978.
Conway, Michael, Dion McGregor and Mark Ricci. *The Films of Greta Garbo.* Secaucus, N.J.: Citadel, 1968.
Conway, Michael and Mark Ricci. *The Films of Jean Harlow.* New York: Bonanza, 1965.
Cooper, Miriam. *Dark Lady of the Silents: My Life in Early Hollywood.* Indianapolis: Bobbs-Merrill, 1973.
Corliss, Richard. *Greta Garbo.* New York: Pyramid, 1974.
Cotes, Peter and Thelma Niklaus. *The Little Fellow: The Life and Work of Charlie Spencer Chaplin.* New York: Citadel, 1965.
Crane, Robert David and Christopher Fryer. *Jack Nicholson: Face to Face.* New York: M. Evans, 1975.
Crawford, Christina. *Mommie Dearest.* New York: William Morrow, 1979.
Crawford, Joan. *My Way of Life.* New York: Simon and Schuster, 1971.
______. *A Portrait of Joan: The Autobiography of Joan Crawford.* Garden City, N.Y.: Doubleday, 1962.
Croce, Arlene. *The Fred Astaire and Ginger Rogers Book.* New York: Galahad Books, 1972.
Crosby, Bing and Pete Martin. *Call Me Lucky.* New York: Simon and Schuster, 1953.
Crosby, Kathryn. *Bing and Other Things.* New York: Meredith Press, 1967.
Crosby, Ted. *The Story of Bing Crosby.* New York: World, 1946.
Dalton, David. *James Dean: The Mutant King.* San Francisco: Straight Arrow Press, 1974.
Davies, Marion. *The Times We Had: Life with William Randolph Hearst.* Indianapolis: Bobbs-Merrill, 1975.
Davis, Bette. *The Lonely Life.* New York: G. P. Putnam's Sons, 1962.
Deschner, Donald. *The Films of Cary Grant.* Secaucus, N.J.: Citadel, 1973.
______. *The Films of Spencer Tracy.* New York: Citadel, 1968.
______. *The Films of W. C. Fields.* Secaucus, N.J.: Citadel, 1973.
Dickens, Homer. *The Films of Gary Cooper.* New York: Citadel, 1971.
______. *The Films of Ginger Rogers.* Secaucus, N.J.: Citadel, 1975.

______. *The Films of James Cagney.* Secaucus, N.J.: Citadel, 1972.

______. *The Films of Marlene Dietrich.* New York: Citadel, 1968.

Dietrich, Marlene. *Marlene Dietrich's ABC.* Garden City, N.Y.: Doubleday, 1962.

DiOrio, Al, Jr. *Little Girl Lost: The Life and Hard Times of Judy Garland.* New Rochelle, N.Y.: Arlington House, 1973.

Dressler, Marie. *My Own Story.* Boston: Little, Brown, 1934.

Druxman, Michael B. *Basil Rathbone: His Life and His Films.* New York: A. S. Barnes, 1975.

______. *Paul Muni: His Life and His Films.* New York: A. S. Barnes, 1974.

Durgnat, Raymond and John Kobal. *Greta Garbo.* New York: E. P. Dutton, 1965.

Edwards, Anne. *Vivien Leigh.* New York: Pocket Books, 1977.

Eells, George. *Ginger, Loretta and Irene Who?* New York: G. P. Putnam's Sons, 1976.

Engstead, John. *Star Shots.* New York: E. P. Dutton, 1978.

Erens, Patricia. *The Films of Shirley MacLaine.* New York: A. S. Barnes, 1978.

Essoe, Gabe. *The Films of Clark Gable.* New York: Citadel, 1970.

Everson, William K. *The Art of W. C. Fields.* Indianapolis: Bobbs-Merrill, 1967.

______. *The Bad Guys: A Pictorial History of the Movie Villain.* New York: Citadel, 1964.

Eyles, Allen. *Bogart.* Garden City, N.Y.: Doubleday, 1975.

Fields, W. C. *W. C. Fields by Himself: His Intended Autobiography.* Englewood Cliffs, N.J.: Prentice-Hall, 1973.

Finch, Christopher. *Rainbow: The Stormy Life of Judy Garland.* New York: Grosset and Dunlap, 1975.

Fontaine, Joan. *No Bed of Roses.* New York: William Morrow, 1978.

Fowler, Gene. *Good Night, Sweet Prince: The Life and Times of John Barrymore.* New York: Viking, 1944.

Frank, Gerold. *Judy.* New York: Harper and Row, 1975.

Freedland, Michael. *Fred Astaire.* London: W. H. Allen, 1976.

Frewin, Leslie. *Dietrich: The Story of a Star.* New York: Stein and Day, 1967. Originally published as *Blonde Venus.*

Garceau, Jean and Inez Cocke. *Dear Mr. G—: The Biography of Clark Gable.* Boston: Little, Brown, 1961.

Gelman, Howard. *The Films of John Garfield.* Secaucus, N.J.: Citadel, 1975.

Gifford, Denis. *Chaplin.* Garden City, N.Y.: Doubleday, 1974.

Gill, Brendan. *Tallulah.* New York: Holt, Rinehart and Winston, 1972.

Gish, Lillian. *Dorothy and Lillian Gish.* New York: Charles Scribner's Sons, 1973.

______. *The Movies, Mr. Griffith, and Me.* Englewood Cliffs, N.J.: Prentice-Hall, 1969.

Godfrey, Lionel. *The Life and Crimes of Errol Flynn.* New York: St. Martin's Press, 1977.

Govoni, Albert. *Cary Grant: An Unauthorized Biography.* Chicago: Henry Regnery, 1971.

Green, Stanley and Burt Goldblatt. *Starring Fred Astaire.* New York: Dodd, Mead, 1973.

Greenberger, Howard. *Bogey's Baby.* New York: St. Martin's Press, 1976.

Guiles, Fred Lawrence. *Marion Davies: A Biography.* New York: McGraw-Hill, 1972.

———. *Norma Jean: The Life of Marilyn Monroe.* New York: Bantam, 1969.
Hamblett, Charles. *Paul Newman.* Chicago: Henry Regnery, 1975.
Harbinson, W. A. *George Scott.* New York: Pinnacle, 1977.
Harris, Warren G. *Gable and Lombard.* New York: Simon and Schuster, 1974.
Hart, William S. *My Life East and West.* New York: Benjamin Blom, 1968.
Harvey, Stephen. *Fred Astaire.* New York: Pyramid, 1975.
———. *Joan Crawford.* New York: Pyramid, 1974.
Herndon, Booton. *Mary Pickford and Douglas Fairbanks.* New York: W. W. Norton, 1977.
Herndon, Venable. *James Dean: A Short Life.* Garden City, N.Y.: Doubleday, 1974.
Heston, Charlton. *The Actor's Life: Journals, 1956-1976.* New York: E. P. Dutton, 1978.
Higham, Charles. *Ava: A Life Story.* New York: Delacorte, 1974.
———. *Charles Laughton: An Intimate Biography.* Garden City, N.Y.: Doubleday, 1976.
———. *Kate: The Life of Katharine Hepburn.* New York: W. W. Norton, 1975.
———. *Marlene.* New York: W. W. Norton, 1975.
Hirsch, Foster. *Edward G. Robinson.* New York: Pyramid, 1975.
Hirschhorn, Clive. *The Films of James Mason.* Secaucus, N.J.: Citadel, 1977.
———. *Gene Kelly: A Biography.* Chicago: Henry Regnery, 1974.
Hoffman, William. *Sidney.* New York: Lyle Stuart, 1971.
Holtzman, Will. *William Holden.* New York: Pyramid, 1976.
Hope, Bob and Pete Martin. *Have Tux, Will Travel: Bob Hope's Own Story.* New York: Simon and Schuster, 1954.
———. *I Owe Russia $1200.* Garden City, N.Y.: Doubleday, 1963.
———. *The Road to Hollywood.* Garden City, N.Y.: Doubleday, 1977.
Hotchner, A. E. *Doris Day: Her Own Story.* New York: William Morrow, 1976.
Howard, Mo. *Mo Howard and the Three Stooges.* Secaucus, N.J.: Citadel, 1977.
Hudson, Richard M. and Raymond Lee. *Gloria Swanson.* New York: A. S. Barnes, 1970.
Huff, Theodore. *Charlie Chaplin.* New York: Arno, 1972.
Hughes, Elinor. *Famous Stars of Filmdom (Men).* Freeport, N.Y.: Books for Libraries Press, 1970.
———. *Famous Stars of Filmdom (Women).* Freeport, N.Y.: Books for Libraries Press, 1970.
Israel, Lee. *Miss Tallulah Bankhead.* New York: Dell, 1972.
Jacobs, David. *Chaplin, the Movies, and Charlie.* New York: Harper and Row, 1975.
Jacobs, Jack and Myron Braum. *The Films of Norma Shearer.* New York: A. S. Barnes, 1976.
Jensen, Paul M. *Boris Karloff and His Films.* New York: A. S. Barnes, 1974.
Jones, Ken D., Arthur F. McClure, and Alfred E. Twomey. *Character People.* New York: A. S. Barnes, 1976.
———. *The Films of James Stewart.* New York: A. S. Barnes, 1970.
Jordan, Rene. *Clark Gable.* New York: Pyramid, 1973.
Juneau, James. *Judy Garland.* New York: Pyramid, 1974.

Kahn, E. J. *The Voice: The Story of an American Phenomenon.* New York: Harper, 1947.

Kanin, Garson. *Tracy and Hepburn: An Intimate Memoir.* New York: Bantam, 1971.

Kass, Judith. *Ava Gardner.* New York: Jove Publications, 1977.

Kerbel, Michael. *Paul Newman.* New York: Pyramid, 1974.

Ketchum, Richard M. *Will Rogers: His Life and Times.* New York: Simon and Schuster, 1973.

Kiernan, Thomas. *Jane: An Intimate Biography of Jane Fonda.* New York: G. P. Putnam's Sons, 1973.

Knowles, Eleanor, John Robert Cocchi, and J. Peter Bergman. *The Films of Jeanette MacDonald and Nelson Eddy.* New York: A. S. Barnes, 1975.

Kobal, John. *Marlene Dietrich.* New York: E. P. Dutton, 1968.

______. *Rita Hayworth.* New York: W. W. Norton, 1977.

LaGuardia, Robert. *Monty.* New York: Arbor House, 1977.

Lahue, Kalton. *Gentlemen to the Rescue: The Heroes of the Silent Screen.* New York: Castle, 1972.

______. *Ladies in Distress.* New York: A. S. Barnes, 1971.

Lasky, Jesse, Jr. and Pat Silver. *Love Scene: The Story of Laurence Olivier and Vivien Leigh.* New York: Thomas Y. Crowell, 1978.

Lawrence, Jerome. *Actor: The Life and Times of Paul Muni.* New York: G. P. Putnam's Sons, 1974.

Lebel, J.-P. *Buster Keaton.* Translated by P. D. Stovin. New York: A. S. Barnes, 1967.

Lee, Raymond. *The Films of Mary Pickford.* New York: A. S. Barnes, 1970.

Lembourn, Hans Jorgen. *Diary of a Lover of Marilyn Monroe.* Translated by Hallberg Hallmundsson. New York: Arbor House, 1979.

Lindsay, Cynthia. *Dear Boris: The Life of William Henry Pratt, A. K. A. Boris Karloff.* New York: Alfred A. Knopf, 1975.

Linet, Beverly. *Ladd: The Life, the Legend, the Legacy of Alan Ladd.* New York: Arbor House, 1979.

Lloyd, Harold. *An American Comedy.* New York: Benjamin Blom, 1971.

McCabe, John. *Charlie Chaplin.* Garden City, N.Y.: Doubleday, 1978.

______. *The Comedy World of Stan Laurel.* Garden City, N.Y.: Doubleday, 1974.

______. *Mr. Laurel and Mr. Hardy.* Garden City, N.Y.: Doubleday, 1961.

______, Al Kilgore and Richard W. Bann. *Laurel & Hardy.* New York: E. P. Dutton, 1975.

McCaffrey, Donald W., ed. *Focus on Chaplin.* Englewood Cliffs, N.J.: Prentice-Hall, 1971.

______. *Four Great Comedians: Chaplin, Lloyd, Keaton, Langdon.* New York: A. S. Barnes, 1968.

______. *Three Classic Silent Screen Comedies Starring Harold Lloyd.* Rutherford, N.J.: Fairleigh Dickinson University Press, 1976.

McClelland, Doug. *The Complete Life Story of Susan Hayward.* New York: Pinnacle, 1975.

McCoy, Malachy. *Steve McQueen: The Unauthorized Biography.* Chicago: Henry Regnery, 1974.

McDonald, Gerald, Michael Conway, and Mark Ricci. *The Films of Charlie Chaplin.* New York: Citadel, 1965.
McGillian, Patrick. *Cagney: The Actor as Auteur.* New York: A. S. Barnes, 1975.
MacLaine, Shirley. *Don't Fall Off the Mountain.* New York: W. W. Norton, 1970.
______. *You Can Get There from Here.* New York: W. W. Norton, 1975.
Maddox, Brenda. *Who's Afraid of Elizabeth Taylor?* New York: M. Evans, 1977.
Mailer, Norman. *Marilyn: A Biography.* New York: Grosset and Dunlap, 1973.
Maltin, Leonard. *The Disney Films.* New York: Crown, 1973.
______ and Richard W. Bann. *Our Gang: The Life and Times of the Little Rascals.* New York: Crown, 1977.
Manvell, Roger. *Chaplin.* Boston: Little, Brown, 1974.
Marill, Alvin H. *The Films of Anthony Quinn.* Secaucus, N.J.: Citadel, 1975.
______. *The Films of Sidney Poitier.* Secaucus, N.J.: Citadel, 1978.
______. *Katharine Hepburn.* New York: Pyramid, 1973.
______. *Robert Mitchum on the Screen.* New York: A. S. Barnes, 1978.
Marx, Arthur. *Everybody Loves Somebody Sometime (Especially Himself): The Story of Dean Martin and Jerry Lewis.* New York: Hawthorne, 1974.
______. *Son of Groucho.* New York: David McKay, 1972.
Marx, Groucho. *Groucho and Me.* New York: Random House, 1959.
______. *The Grouchophile.* Indianapolis: Bobbs-Merrill, 1976.
______ and Richard J. Anobile. *The Marx Bros. Scrapbook.* New York: Crown, 1973.
Marx, Harpo and Rowland Barber. *Harpo Speaks.* New York: Bernard Geis, 1961.
Massey, Raymond. *When I Was Young.* Boston: Little, Brown, 1976.
Miller, Ann and Norma Lee Browning. *Miller's High Life.* Garden City, N.Y.: Doubleday, 1972.
Mix, Paul E. *The Life and Legend of Tom Mix.* New York: A. S. Barnes, 1972.
Moews, Daniel. *Keaton.* Berkeley: University of California Press, 1977.
Monroe, Marilyn. *My Story.* New York: Stein and Day, 1974.
Monti, Carlotta. *W. C. Fields and Me.* Englewood Cliffs, N.J.: Prentice-Hall, 1971.
Morella, Joe and Edward Z. Epstein. *The "It" Girl.* New York: Delacorte, 1976.
______. *Rebels: The Rebel Hero in Films.* New York: Citadel, 1971.
______ and Eleanor Clark. *The Amazing Careers of Bob Hope: From Gags to Riches.* New Rochelle, N.Y.: Arlington House, 1973.
Morley, Sheridan. *Marlene Dietrich.* New York: McGraw-Hill, 1977.
Morris, George. *Doris Day.* New York: Pyramid, 1976.
______. *Errol Flynn.* New York: Pyramid, 1975.
______. *John Garfield.* New York: Harcourt Brace Jovanovich, 1977.
Niven, David. *Bring on the Empty Horses.* New York: G. P. Putnam's Sons, 1975.
Niver, Kemp R. *Mary Pickford, Comedienne.* Los Angeles: Locare Research Group, 1969.
Offen, Ron. *Brando.* Chicago: Henry Regnery, 1973.
______. *Cagney.* Chicago: Henry Regnery, 1972.
Ott, Frederick W. *The Films of Carole Lombard.* Secaucus, N.J.: Citadel, 1972.
Outerbridge, David E. *Without Makeup: Liv Ullmann, a Photo-Biography.* New York: William Morrow, 1979.
Parish, James Robert. *The Jeanette MacDonald Story.* New York: Mason/Charter, 1976.

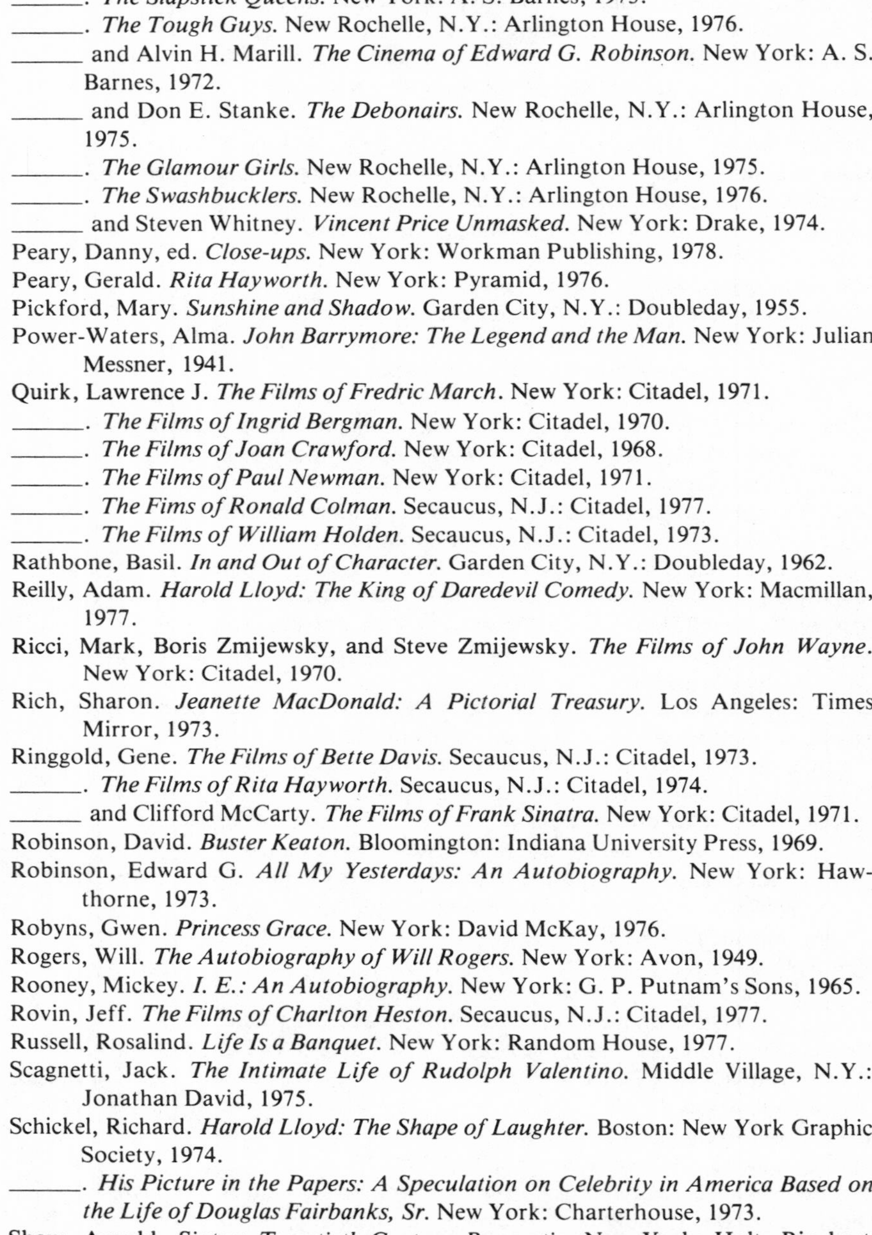

______. *The Slapstick Queens.* New York: A. S. Barnes, 1973.
______. *The Tough Guys.* New Rochelle, N.Y.: Arlington House, 1976.
______ and Alvin H. Marill. *The Cinema of Edward G. Robinson.* New York: A. S. Barnes, 1972.
______ and Don E. Stanke. *The Debonairs.* New Rochelle, N.Y.: Arlington House, 1975.
______. *The Glamour Girls.* New Rochelle, N.Y.: Arlington House, 1975.
______. *The Swashbucklers.* New Rochelle, N.Y.: Arlington House, 1976.
______ and Steven Whitney. *Vincent Price Unmasked.* New York: Drake, 1974.
Peary, Danny, ed. *Close-ups.* New York: Workman Publishing, 1978.
Peary, Gerald. *Rita Hayworth.* New York: Pyramid, 1976.
Pickford, Mary. *Sunshine and Shadow.* Garden City, N.Y.: Doubleday, 1955.
Power-Waters, Alma. *John Barrymore: The Legend and the Man.* New York: Julian Messner, 1941.
Quirk, Lawrence J. *The Films of Fredric March.* New York: Citadel, 1971.
______. *The Films of Ingrid Bergman.* New York: Citadel, 1970.
______. *The Films of Joan Crawford.* New York: Citadel, 1968.
______. *The Films of Paul Newman.* New York: Citadel, 1971.
______. *The Fims of Ronald Colman.* Secaucus, N.J.: Citadel, 1977.
______. *The Films of William Holden.* Secaucus, N.J.: Citadel, 1973.
Rathbone, Basil. *In and Out of Character.* Garden City, N.Y.: Doubleday, 1962.
Reilly, Adam. *Harold Lloyd: The King of Daredevil Comedy.* New York: Macmillan, 1977.
Ricci, Mark, Boris Zmijewsky, and Steve Zmijewsky. *The Films of John Wayne.* New York: Citadel, 1970.
Rich, Sharon. *Jeanette MacDonald: A Pictorial Treasury.* Los Angeles: Times Mirror, 1973.
Ringgold, Gene. *The Films of Bette Davis.* Secaucus, N.J.: Citadel, 1973.
______. *The Films of Rita Hayworth.* Secaucus, N.J.: Citadel, 1974.
______ and Clifford McCarty. *The Films of Frank Sinatra.* New York: Citadel, 1971.
Robinson, David. *Buster Keaton.* Bloomington: Indiana University Press, 1969.
Robinson, Edward G. *All My Yesterdays: An Autobiography.* New York: Hawthorne, 1973.
Robyns, Gwen. *Princess Grace.* New York: David McKay, 1976.
Rogers, Will. *The Autobiography of Will Rogers.* New York: Avon, 1949.
Rooney, Mickey. *I. E.: An Autobiography.* New York: G. P. Putnam's Sons, 1965.
Rovin, Jeff. *The Films of Charlton Heston.* Secaucus, N.J.: Citadel, 1977.
Russell, Rosalind. *Life Is a Banquet.* New York: Random House, 1977.
Scagnetti, Jack. *The Intimate Life of Rudolph Valentino.* Middle Village, N.Y.: Jonathan David, 1975.
Schickel, Richard. *Harold Lloyd: The Shape of Laughter.* Boston: New York Graphic Society, 1974.
______. *His Picture in the Papers: A Speculation on Celebrity in America Based on the Life of Douglas Fairbanks, Sr.* New York: Charterhouse, 1973.
Shaw, Arnold. *Sintra: Twentieth-Century Romantic.* New York: Holt, Rinehart and Winston, 1968.

Sheppard, Dick. *Elizabeth: The Life and Career of Elizabeth Taylor.* Garden City, N.Y.: Doubleday, 1974.
Shipman, David. *Brando.* Garden City, N.Y.: Doubleday, 1974.
______. *The Great Movie Stars: The Golden Years,* New York: Bonanza, 1970.
______. *The Great Movie Stars: The International Years.* New York: St. Martin's Press, 1972.
Slide, Anthony. *The Griffith Actresses.* New York: A. S. Barnes, 1973.
______. *The Idols of Silence.* New York: A. S. Barnes, 1976.
Smith, Ella. *Starring Miss Barbara Stanwyck.* New York: Crown, 1974.
Sobel, Raoul and David Francis. *Chaplin: Genesis of a Clown.* New York: Quartet Books, 1977.
Spada, James. *The Films of Robert Redford.* Secaucus, N.J.: Citadel, 1977.
Springer, John. *The Fondas.* New York: Citadel, 1970.
Stern, Lee Edward. *Jeanette MacDonald.* New York: Harcourt Brace Jovanovich, 1977.
Stine, Whitney. *Mother Goddam: The Story of the Career of Bette Davis.* New York: Hawthorne, 1974.
Stock, Dennis. *James Dean Revisited.* New York: Penguin, 1978.
Swindell, Larry. *Body and Soul: The Story of John Garfield.* New York: William Morrow, 1975.
______. *Screwball: The Life of Carole Lombard.* New York: William Morrow, 1975.
______. *Spencer Tracy: A Biography.* New York: World, 1969.
Taylor, Robert. *W. C. Fields: His Follies and Fortunes.* Garden City, N.Y.: Doubleday, 1949.
Thomas, Bob. *Joan Crawford.* New York: Simon and Schuster, 1978.
______. *Marlon: Portrait of the Rebel as an Artist.* New York: Random House, 1973.
Thomas, Tony. *Burt Lancaster.* New York: Pyramid, 1975.
______. *Cads and Cavaliers: The Gentlemen Adventurers of the Movies.* New York: A. S. Barnes, 1973.
______. *The Films of Gene Kelly, Song and Dance Man.* Secaucus, N.J.: Citadel, 1974.
______. *The Films of Kirk Douglas.* Secaucus, N.J.: Citadel, 1972.
______. *The Films of Marlon Brando.* Secaucus, N.J.: Citadel, 1973.
______. *Gregory Peck.* New York: Pyramid, 1977.
______, Rudy Behlmer, and Clifford McCarty. *The Films of Errol Flynn.* New York: Citadel, 1969.
Thompson, Charles. *Bing: The Authorized Biography.* New York: David McKay, 1975.
Thompson, Howard. *James Stewart.* New York: Pyramid, 1974.
Tibbetts, John C. and James M. Welsh. *His Majesty the American.* New York: A. S. Barnes, 1977.
Tomkies, Mike. *Duke: The Story of John Wayne.* Chicago: Henry Regnery, 1971.
Tornabene, Lyn. *Long Live the King.* New York: G. P. Putnam's Sons, 1976.
Tozzi, Romano. *Spencer Tracy.* New York: Pyramid, 1973.
Tunney, Kieran. *Tallulah: Darling of the Gods.* New York: E. P. Dutton, 1973.
Tuska, Jon. *The Films of Mae West.* Secaucus, N.J.: Citadel, 1973.

Twomey, Alfred E. and Arthur F. McClure. *The Versatiles: A Study of Supporting Character Actors and Actresses in the American Motion Picture, 1930-1955.* New York: Castle Books, 1969.
Tyler, Parker. *Chaplin: Last of the Clowns.* New York: Horizon, 1972.
Ullmann, Liv. *Changing.* New York: Alfred A. Knopf, 1977.
Underwood, Peter. *Karloff: The Life of Boris Karloff.* New York: Drake, 1972.
Vermilye, Jerry. *Barbara Stanwyck. New York. Pyramid, 1975.*
______. *Betty Davis.* New York: Pyramid, 1973.
______. *Cary Grant.* New York: Pyramid, 1973.
______. *Ida Lupino.* New York: Pyramid, 1977.
______ and Mark Ricci. *The Films of Elizabeth Taylor.* Secaucus, N.J.: Citadel, 1976.
Wagenknecht, Edward, ed. *Marilyn Monroe: A Composite View.* Philadelphia: Chilton Book Co., 1969.
Wagner, Rob. *Film Folk.* New York: Century, 1918.
Walker, Alexander. *Rudolph Valentino.* New York: Stein and Day, 1976.
______. *Stardom: The Hollywood Phenomenon.* New York: Stein and Day, 1970.
Wead, George. *Buster Keaton and the Dynamics of Visual Art.* New York: Arno, 1976.
______ and George Lellis. *The Film Career of Buster Keaton.* Boston: G. K. Hall, 1977.
Weatherby, W. J. *Conversations with Marilyn.* New York: Mason/Charter, 1976.
Widener, Don. *Lemmon: A Biography.* New York: Macmillan, 1975.
Williams, Chester. *Gable.* New York: Fleet Press, 1968.
Wilson, Earl. *Sinatra: An Unauthorized Biography.* New York: Macmillan, 1976.
Windeler, Robert. *The Films of Shirley Temple.* Secaucus, N.J.: Citadel, 1978.
______. *Sweetheart: The Story of Mary Pickford.* New York: Praeger, 1973.
Yablonsky, Lewis. *George Raft.* New York: McGraw-Hill, 1974.
Yallop, David A. *The Day the Laughter Stopped.* New York: St. Martin's Press, 1976.
Yanni, Nicholas. *Rosalind Russell.* New York: Pyramid, 1975.
Young, Christopher. *The Films of Doris Day.* Secaucus, N.J.: Citadel, 1977.
______. *The Films of Hedy Lamarr.* Secaucus, N.J.: Citadel, 1978.
Zierold, Norman J. *The Child Stars.* New York: Coward-McCann, 1965.
______. *Garbo.* New York: Stein and Day, 1969.
Zolotow, Maurice. *Shooting Star: A Biography of John Wayne.* New York: Simon and Schuster, 1974.

CHAPTER 8

Major Directors and Other Production Personnel

While chapter 7 concentrated on actors and actresses, this chapter will cover books dealing with the members of the production team: directors, producers, screenwriters, and a few others. Books on individual directors will be described first, arranged alphabetically by last name of the director, and followed by books on more than one director. Books on the other members of the production team follow, also arranged alphabetically by last name.

Arguments over the role of the director in the production of a movie go back to the first decade of this century when the studios would not put the names of either director or actors on the film for fear they would take credit for a film that actually was the product of the studio. Even today critics are not in agreement over the director's creative responsibility, but it is clear that in order to analyze a movie a critic must pay careful attention to the director's contribution.

BOOKS ON INDIVIDUAL DIRECTORS

Judith Kass' book on Robert Altman is a study of Altman's films geared to a popular audience. *Robert Altman: American Innovator* begins with a long introductory essay on Altman's career and goes on to a film by film presentation of his works consisting mainly of plot summary with little analysis. A more scholarly book is Neil Feineman's reprint of his dissertation, *Persistence of Vision: The Films of Robert Altman;* Feineman's chapters on each of Altman's films are more complete and are followed by a concluding chapter that summarizes Altman's work.

Busby Berkeley began his career as a choreographer for dance routines, and he became a director of films built around dance numbers. *The Genius of Busby Berkeley* by Bob Pike and Dave Martin is an overview of Berkeley's career in a book aimed at the popular audience but of interest to the serious student as well. The authors present a long interview with Berkeley, his biography, pictures of the Berkeley girls, and an expanded filmography including long excerpts from the reviews of Berkeley's films.

Tod Browning is best remembered as the director of horror films such as *Dracula* and *Freaks. Tod Browning* by Stuart Rosenthal is a study of Browning's work combined, it should be noted, in volume with Judith Kass' study of Don Siegel. This tribute to Browning contains a short description of his work and a filmography, consisting mainly of analysis and discussion of his films.

By far the best book on the career of Frank Capra is Frank Capra's own, *The Name Above the Title*. This book clearly and humorously describes the business of making movies and is one of the finest books ever written on the business; as an autobiography, it is rich with insights into the people around Capra and his rise in Hollywood. *Frank Capra: The Man and His Films*, edited by Richard Glatzer and John Raeburn, is an excellent anthology of essays on this Oscar-winning director. The book brings together essays by and about the man, with additional essays on his career and on his important films; a good filmography and bibliography are included. In *The Films of Frank Capra,* Don Willis has created a substantial expanded filmography which treats Capra's films by type rather than in strict chronological order. One part deals with Capra's American hero: Mr. Deeds, Mr. Smith, and John Doe; a second deals with his adaptations of the East/West theme: *The Bitter Tea of General Yen* and *Lost Horizon;* a third deals with his early films with Harry Langdon. Another book of the same title, by Victor Scherle and William Turner Levy, is a more traditional expanded filmography. The authors begin with comments on Capra by other directors, writers, and actors, but unfortunately, the comments contribute little to the reader's understanding of the director or his work. The authors go on to give a film by film presentation of Capra's work, including comments about the production by members of the cast and crew. *The Cinema of Frank Capra* is a more substantial work. Leland A. Poague has dealt with Capra's important films, and comments in depth on some major aspects of Capra's work (his comic vision, his romantic sense) and on his style and characters.

Francis Ford Coppola by Robert K. Johnson is a brief but thorough survey of Coppola's career, with considerable commentary on *The Godfather.* Johnson's thesis is that none of Coppola's films is totally satisfying but that all demonstrate his sensibility.

George Cukor is perhaps best remembered for his ability to draw fine performances from his actors. A good place to begin a study of his career is *On Cukor* by Gavin Lambert, a book of interviews with Cukor and analysis of his films. *George Cukor* by Carlos Clarens discusses Cukor's work on Broadway before he came to Hollywood, as well as his transition to film; other topics covered include Cukor's image of the new woman, his use of melodrama, and his sense of comedy. *Cukor & Co.: The Films of George Cukor and his Collaborators* is a guide to Cukor's films by Gary Carey prepared for a retrospective of his work at The Museum of Modern Art.

Carey presents an overview of Cukor's career and covers each film with casts, credits, and intelligent commentary. The book is topically arranged: "Miss Hepburn and Mr. Barry," "The Crawford Years," and so on.

Kingsley Canham combined his analysis of Michael Curtiz with analysis of Raoul Walsh and Henry Hathaway into a single volume with the directors' names as its title. Curtiz was a director who worked in Hungary, Great Britain, and Hollywood, and his most memorable film was *Casablanca.* This book contains a lengthy critical and biographical essay on him and a filmography.

Who but Cecil B. DeMille could tell his own epic? *The Autobiography of Cecil B. DeMille* is a rather routine retelling of a rather extravagant life, but is a good place to begin the study of DeMille's life and films. More substantial from a scholarly perspective is *DeMille: The Man and His Pictures* by Gabe Essoe and Raymond Lee. This book contains commentary and photographs on DeMille's movies as well as essays on the man by actors Charlton Heston and Charles Bickford, composer Elmer Bernstein, and others. *Cecil B. DeMille* by Charles Higham is a solid biography with an emphasis on DeMille's film career; the book contains commentary on the films but no analysis of them. *Yes, Mr. DeMille* is a memoir by Phil A. Koury, a man who worked for DeMille. The films themselves are treated in *The Films of Cecil B. DeMille* by Gene Ringgold and Dewitt Bodeen. The authors' biographical introduction contains notes on DeMille's films and stars. The filmography, however, is brief and sketchy.

Before he became a filmmaker himself, Peter Bogdanovich was a film critic who conducted penetrating interviews with directors. In *Allan Dawn: The Last Pioneer.* Bogdanovich surveys Dawn's directing career and records his extended interview with Dawn, in which he draws out Dawn's views on his major films, such as *Heidi* and *Rebecca of Sunnybrook Farm.* A reliable filmography is included.

Sergei Eisenstein was, of course, an important Russian director whose innovations in his craft and writings about the theory of film have made him one of the few critical figures in the development of the medium. While Eisenstein's projects in the United States in the early 1930s came to little, he remains a man who has had considerable influence in this country. Ivor Montagu is an Englishman who worked with Eisenstein and his book, *With Eisenstein in Hollywood,* is his personal memoir of the period. Included in the book are the scenarios for *Sutter's Gold* and *An American Tragedy,* which Montagu and Eisenstein wrote together at Paramount but which were never produced. A good overview of Eisenstein's career is *Eisenstein* by Yon Barna, a book covering Eisenstein's career and all of his important films. A comprehensive critical study, *Eisenstein* includes chapters on the director's visit to the United States and Mexico. Additional analysis of Eisenstein's work during this trip can be found in *Eisenstein: A Docu-*

mentary Portrait by Norman Swallow, which also includes interviews with Eisenstein's friends and colleagues. The standard biography is *Sergei M. Eisenstein: A Biography* by Marie Seton.

Robert Flaherty is considered by many to be the father of documentary filmmaking, and to study his career and films is to study the history of the genre. A fine early study of the man and his work is Richard Griffith's *The World of Robert Flaherty*. Griffith analyzes the films one by one, includes detailed information on their production and concludes with an overview. *The Innocent Eye* by Arthur Calder-Marshall focuses on the man as well as the films; this author, also, devoted a chapter to each film in an effort to get at the artist behind the films. Additionally, he includes the credits and a synopsis for each film. Perhaps no one has done more to preserve the memory and to foster the study of Flaherty than has his wife, Frances Hubbard Flaherty. In addition to encouraging the Flaherty International Film Seminars, she has written an essay on Flaherty's work, *The Odyssey of a Film-Maker,* which provides background for appreciation of Flaherty's films. An interesting perspective on one of Flaherty's films, *The Man of Aran*—the documentary of life on the Aran Isles—has been written by one of the men who lived on the island and played a key role in the making of the film. Pat Mullen's *Man of Aran* is the story of the production and an autobiography of this resident chosen to play in the film. The book first came out in 1935 and has now been reprinted. Finally, the basic reference book on Flaherty is *Robert Flaherty: A Guide to References and Resources* by William T. Murphy. The book contains biographical background, a survey of Flaherty's work, film by film credits and casts, a bibliography, and archival sources for further study.

Few directors have had more of an impact on American movies than John Ford. A good introduction to his work is *John Ford* by Joseph McBride and Michael Wilmington. The authors follow general criticism and biography with chapters on Ford's major themes: the noble outlaw (*Stagecoach*), men at war (*My Darling Clementine*), Ireland (*The Quiet Man*), rebels (*The Searchers*), what really happened (*The Man Who Shot Liberty Valance*), and the last place on earth (*Seven Women*). Andrew Sarris has attempted to get behind the myth of John Ford in *The John Ford Movie Mystery.* This book is not simply a review of Ford's career in movies but an analysis of Ford's image. Sarris is a critic who works closely with the films themselves, and this book will reward the reader with insights not found elsewhere. Peter Bogdanovich's *John Ford* is another of Bogdanovich's books which centers on an interview with the director. This one begins with an introductory essay on Ford's career, but the main part of the book consists of interviews with the director. Unfortunately, Bogdanovich tries to cover so many of Ford's films that he is able to include only a couple of sentences of Ford's thoughts on many of them. J. A. Place has concentrated on one type of Ford film in *The Western Films of John Ford.* Place includes chapters on all the great Ford Westerns, from the silents to *Cheyenne Autumn*, and includes many photographs. Place has also edited *The Non-Western Films of John Ford,* an expanded filmography covering his non-Western America, war, Irish, action, and foreign country films. *John Ford* by Andrew Sinclair is a biography and survey of Ford's career from his first film to his work for the United States government; a filmography is included. *The Cinema of John Ford* by John Baxter is a chronological study of the films from the silents to *Liberty Valance* with some good analysis and a useful filmography.

Milos Forman is a Czech director who came to America and stayed to work here. *The Milos Forman Stories* by Antonín Liehm is a study of Forman's career with lengthy review of his major films.

John Frankenheimer specializes in adventure films with a point, often starring Burt Lancaster or Angela Lansbury. In *The Cinema of John Frankenheimer* Gerald Pratley studies the films one by one. Writing in the late 1960s, Prately declared Frankenheimer to be "the most important director at work in the American cinema today." Prately has included many direct quotations from Frankenheimer, as well as chapters on his major films, such as *Seconds*, *The Fixer*, and *Grand Prix*.

Samuel Fuller is a director drawn to action and to characters who stand outside society, and his work has probably been received more favorably in France than it has in America. The major books on Fuller deal with his themes. In *Samuel Fuller,* Nicholas Garnham identifies four major themes in Fuller's films: the individual, love, society and the national identity, and energy and madness. Phil Hardy, in another book by the same title, identifies Fuller's themes as the American dream, journalism and style, American reality, Asia, and the violence of love. Hardy includes a useful filmography.

In *Light Your Torches and Pull Up Your Tights,* Tay Garnett, the director of *The Postman Always Rings Twice* and *China Seas,* tells his own story. While Garnett is considered by some to be a master of *film noir,* this book, introduced by Frank Capra, is about the people with whom he worked rather than about the making of his films.

No director has been more important than D. W. Griffith, and his work has received close scrutiny. The best overview of his career is provided by Robert M. Henderson in *D. W. Griffith.* This is the standard book on Griffith's life and work; it covers his entire career and devotes separate chapters to his major films. In *D. W. Griffith: The Years at Biograph,* Henderson focuses on the years from 1908 to 1913 when Griffith was working in New York and Los Angeles for the American Mutoscope and Biograph Company and developing his art. The book consists basically of history and analysis, but Henderson's list of over four hundred films made at Biograph is invaluable, as is his bibliography. *Focus on D. W. Griffith,* edited by Harry Geduld, is an anthology of essays by and about Griffith which is valuable as an introduction to him. Part of the book consists of essays by Griffith on his life and his films; another part essays on his art by Nicholas Vardac, Lewis Jacobs, Lillian Gish, Jay Leyda, and others. Most of these essays are on his career in general, except for three on *Birth of a Nation* and one on *Intolerance.* In *Griffith and the Rise of Hollywood,* Paul O'Dell discusses the development of the star system under Griffith and the creation of a movie colony just outside Los Angeles. O'Dell includes chapters on *Birth of a Nation, Intolerance,* as well as on Thomas Ince, a contemporary director whose methods are considered the antithesis of Griffith's. *D. W. Griffith* by Iris Barry was prepared at the Museum of Modern Art for a retrospective of Griffith's films. Barry's introductory essay discusses Griffith's early career and technical innovations, as well as his major films (*Birth of a Nation*, *Intolerance*, *Broken Blossoms*, *Way Down East*, and *Orphans of the Storm*). Also included are an interview by Beaumont Newhall with Billy Bitzer, the cameraman responsible for most of Griffith's films, and an annotated checklist of the films by Eileen Bowser.

One excellent way to study Griffith is to read the firsthand accounts of his work written by the people who worked with him. In chapter 7 are books by Lillian Gish, Miriam Cooper, and later in this chapter, one by Billy Bitzer—key people in Griffith's group. Karl Brown was a boy at the time Griffith was doing his major work, began as a second cameraman under Bitzer, and later became a director himself. *Adventures with D. W. Griffith* is Brown's story of those years and of the men and women who worked with Griffith. Griffith told his own story as well. *The Man Who Invented Hollywood: The Autobiography of D. W. Griffith* is a short memoir, edited and annotated by James Hurt, that provides some background to his career. Finally, *The Films of D. W. Griffith* by Edward Wagenknecht and Anthony Slide is an expanded filmography of Griffith's feature films (there are too many shorts to cover completely). While the book has the standard format for books of this type, an added attraction is criticism by these two fine critics and scholars.

Henry Hathaway is an American director with a flair for action films, especially Westerns, sea tales, and mysteries. His career is analyzed in the book by Kingsley Canham mentioned above, *Michael Curtiz, Raoul Walsh and Henry Hathaway.* Canham has included a lengthy essay that emphasizes Hathaway's films from critical and historical points of view.

Few directors have the versatility of Howard Hawks, a fact which challenges anyone writing about his films. In *Howard Hawks,* Robin Wood sees him as an auteur and approaches his work from a thematic perspective. Wood has grouped Hawks' films by theme: self respect and responsbility (*To Have and Have Not*), the lure of irresponsibility (*His Girl Friday*, *I Was A Male War Bride*), male relationships (*Red River*), and other themes. Peter

Bogdanovich was asked by the Museum of Modern Art to write a guide to their exhibition of Hawks' films. The result—*The Cinema of Howard Hawks*—is a brief study that provides penetrating insights, especially in the interviews that Bogdanovich conducted with Hawks. *Focus on Howard Hawks,* edited by Joseph McBride, is an anthology of interviews and essays on Hawks by Andrew Sarris, Robin Wood, Peter Bogdanovich, William Wellman and others, and also includes a useful filmography and bibliography. Even though the book does not cover all of Hawks' films with separate essays, it is a valuable introduction to Hawks' work. *The Films of Howard Hawks* by Donald Willis does cover all the important Hawks films and is arranged generically rather than chronologically. Willis groups the films under comedies, Westerns, action drama, war drama, and a special miscellaneous category that includes *The Big Sleep* and *Gentlemen Prefer Blondes.* Willis includes a scholarly analysis of several pages on each film.

The most highly regarded study of the work of that master of suspense, Alfred Hitchcock, is by another respected director, François Truffaut. Truffaut's book, *Hitchcock*, consists mainly of an interview with Hitchcock, but there is a long introduction by Truffaut that provides some of the most important insights into Hitchcock's films available. A fine book of critical analysis is *Hitchcock's Films* by Robin Wood. The book is basically a study of Hitchcock's major later films: *Strangers on a Train, Rear Window, Vertigo, North by Northwest*, *Psycho*, *The Birds*, *Marnie*, and *Torn Curtain*. Donald Spoto has written *The Art of Alfred Hitchcock,* which has become a standard and important study of the director. This book includes a long chapter on each of the major films, a discussion of the critical reaction to each, and a thorough analysis of Hitchcock's contribution to each. A full filmography with credits and casts is also included. Hitchcock for a different audience is the goal of Raymond Durgnat in *The Strange Case of Alfred Hitchcock: The Plain Man's Hitchcock.* This book traces the stages of Hitchcock's film career, discusses his moral code, and covers Hitchcock's major films briefly. *Hitchcock* by George Perry is a brief chronological study of the films; Perry includes little analysis of Hitchcock's films, but the many stills he has collected provide another means of studying Hitchcock's art. Finally, Albert J. LaValley has edited *Focus on Hitchcock,* which presents interviews with Hitchcock himself, several essays on his art by Lindsay Anderson, André Bazin, Robin Wood, Andrew Sarris, and Raymond Durgnat, and other essays on and reviews of the major films by James Agee, Pauline Kael, Raymond Chandler, Leo Braudy and others. LaValley departs form the ususal "Focus" series format to include an interesting analysis of the cornfield chase sequence in *North by Northwest.*

The life and career of director John Huston have been documented in several books, including *John Huston* by Stuart Kaminsky. This book is a critical biography of Huston, whom Kaminsky calls "the maker of magic," as both actor and director. While Kaminsky's study includes details of the filming of Huston's films, choppy writing makes it difficult reading. Another book with the same title by Axel Madsen is basically a biography focusing on the man rather than his films; however, Madsen does provide good background on the making of Huston's films. In *The Cinema of John Huston* Gerald Pratley deals with the various periods of Huston's career, goes on to analyze the important Huston films, such as *The African Queen* and *The Misfits*. He also considers Huston as an actor and makes a final appraisal of his entire career. *John Huston* by Romano Tozzi is "a pictorial treasury of his films" which is short on analysis but does list the casts and credits.

Elia Kazan has been an important director on both stage and screen, and the best introduction to his work is a series of interviews with him by Michael Ciment entitled *Kazan on Kazan.* Ciment solicits Kazan's views on his various films including *A Streetcar Named Desire*, *On the Waterfront*, *East of Eden,* and *Splendor in the Grass.* Ciment's questions are pointed, and Kazan's answers informative.

Stanley Kramer directed many films that entertain and make a point at the same time. *Stanley Kramer* by Donald Spoto is a biographical and critical study that tries to demonstrate the manner in which Kramer's personal life and political views have affected his movies. Spoto's study is complete and scholarly, yet remains readable.

Stanley Kubrick Directs is a fine beginning for the study of the director whose few films have had a marked impact on the movie industry. Alexander Walker's book includes close analysis of Kubrick's major work, including *A Clockwork Orange*, *Dr. Strangelove*, and *2001*. *The Films of Stanley Kubrick* by David Devries is a slim volume of essays on Kubrick's major films, including *The Killing*, *Paths of Glory*, *Spartacus*, *Lolita*, *Dr. Strangelove*, *2001*, and *A Clockwork Orange*. Norman Kagan in *The Cinema of Stanley Kubrick* follows a similar pattern. Kagan's book contains good analysis, descriptions of the films, and criticism. He also includes a discussion entitled "problems and prospects," which suggests ways of looking at the films that have not yet been fully explored. In *Stanley Kubrick: A Film Odyssey,* Gene D. Phillips analyzes each of Kubrick's films in detail by combining his own ideas with Kubrick's thoughts as revealed in interviews with Phillips. The result is an insightful study focusing on Kubrick's themes.

The most comprehensive and valuable study of the films of Fritz Lang is by his friend, Lotte Eisner, herself an eminent film critic. Her lengthy study, *Fritz Lang,* covers all of his films and includes essays on topics such as his technique and his work in America. *Fritz Lang* by Robert A. Armour is a shorter study of Lang's major theme, the dark struggles of his character. Armour devotes several pages to each of Lang's major films and demonstrates that Lang's plots and techniques emphasize his characters' struggles both internally and externally. *The Cinema of Fritz Lang* by Paul M. Jensen is a thorough study of Lang's films, but the scholarship and perceptions are uneven. The greatest value of Jensen's work is the background on Lang's productions which he provides. *Fritz Lang in America* by Peter Bogdanovich is perhaps the best of Bogdanovich's books on other directors. His long introductory essay concentrates on the theme of hate and revenge in Lang's films, and his interview with Lang produces penetrating insights into the mind of the older director. The interview covers only the films Lang made in the United States, and for each Lang provides some understanding of the nature of that film.

Mervyn Leroy has been a prolific filmmaker and producer, perhaps best known for his direction of *Little Caesar* and *Golddiggers of 1933.* His autobiography, *Mervyn Leroy: Take One* focuses on the stars and others with whom he worked. While it is the only substantial work available on him and is of some interest, it hardly has the value of Frank Capra's autobiography.

Richard Lester's claim to fame is his direction of two films starring the Beatles. A first-rate guide to his work is Diane Rosenfeldt's *Richard Lester,* a book which provides biographical background, a survey of Lester's career, synopses and credits for his films, a bibliography, and archival sources.

Val Lewton made his living as the producer of low budget horror films for RKO in the 1940s. *Val Lewton: The Reality of Terror* by Joel Siegel is a study of his life and films that includes both biography and criticism, and a chapter on each of the films.

Josh Logan has made his reputation with large-scale expensive films often adapted from Broadway plays. He also writes well, and in *Josh* he describes the plays and films with which he has been involved and the people who helped him, from composers to actors and producers.

Pare Lorentz and the Documentary Film is a study by Robert L. Snyder of the work of the well known documentary filmmaker. The book is largely criticism with chapters on his best-known films: *The Plow That Broke the Plains, The River, Ecce Homo!,* and *The Fight for Life.*

Joseph Losey is a director who has made his mark in films that focus on moral dilemmas. In *Losey on Losey* he comments in interviews with Tom Milne on his films, Hollywood, the relationship between theater and film (he had his start in the theater), and other topics.

Ernst Lubitsch's films were characterized by their wit, polish, and slightly irreverent sense of morality. "The Lubitsch Touch," as it came to be known, is also the name of the book by Herman Weinberg that is the standard introduction to Lubitsch's films. Weinberg begins by defining the touch and then reprints excerpts from the screenplay for *Ninotchka.* He includes interviews with many who knew and worked with Lubitsch, evaluations by eminent critics such as Paul Rotha, Dwight Macdonald, Jay Leyda, and Lotte Eisner, and tributes from Charles Chaplin, Greta Garbo, and others. An overview of the films themselves is provided in *The Cinema of Ernst Lubitsch* by

Leland A. Poague; Poague provides an analysis of the films and a critical overview which makes it clear that he is familiar with what the various critics have written on Lubitsch. *Ernst Lubitsch* by Robert Carringer and Barry Sabath is a thorough study providing biographical background, a survey of Lubitsch's career, factual data on his films, and a survey of writings about the director. Finally, the authors indicate where the archival materials on Lubitsch can be found and where the films can be rented.

Rouben Mamoulian by Tom Milne is a study of the films of the Russian-born director who made his mark through a wide range of movies made in the United States. Milne sees Mamoulian as the maker of "witty, elegant, supremely stylish" films that explore "the sensuous pleasures of movement" and analyzes them from *Applause* to *Silk Stockings.*

In *I Remember It Well,* Vincente Minnelli recalls his life, including the times with his wife Judy Garland and his daughter Liza, and his movies, especially *An American in Paris, Lust for Life,* and *Gigi.* The book provides excellent details on the making of these films. Joseph Casper focuses on Minnelli's musical films in *Vincente Minnelli and the Film Musical;* he discusses Minnelli and the musical tradition and then considers the characteristics of the musicals: the drama, the enactment, the spectacle, the music, and the dance.

F. W. Murnau was another German who came to Hollywood after establishing a European reputation. In *Murnau,* Lotte Eisner presents an intelligent analysis of Murnau's career in both Germany and the United States and even discusses his lost films (nine of the twenty-one he made). She highlights *Nosferatu*, *Sunrise*, his work in America, and the camera and lighting aspects of his technique.

Mike Nichols is a German who came to the United States long after Murnau and Lang. *Mike Nichols* by H. Wayne Schuth is a concise yet complete study of Nichols' career. Schuth's focus is on Nichols' films, which seem to be commentary on our contemporary life: *Who's Afraid of Virginia Woolf?, The Graduate*, *Catch 22*, and *Carnal Knowledge*.

Perhaps no major director is better known for his violent films than is Sam Peckinpah; that is the major theme of *Sam Peckinpah: Master of Violence* by Max Evans. Evans is a friend and co-worker of the director and this short book is his personal view of Peckinpah's work, an overview with concentration on the making of *The Ballad of Cable Hogue.*

Robin Wood's *Arthur Penn* is a critical study of another director who has used violence creatively. Wood includes chapters on Penn's major films: *The Left-Handed Gun, The Miracle Worker, Mickey One, The Chase, Bonnie and Clyde, Alice's Restaurant,* and *Little Big Man* (filmed, but not yet released at the time the book was published). In addition, Wood has included a chapter on the problems of editing Penn's films and a filmography.

Roman Polanski is a Polish-born director with French citizenship who has directed several highly successful films in the United States. *The Cinema of Roman Polanski* is a study by Ivan Butler of Polanski and his most important films, including *Rosemary's Baby* and *Repulsion.*

Otto Preminger is another European who has made successful films in a wide variety of genres in the United States. In *Preminger,* he presents a rather folksy view of the profession, with background on the making of his films, and chapters on the Blacklist, Marilyn Monroe, *Exodus, The Cardinal,* and other topics. *Behind the Scenes with Otto Preminger* is an unauthorized biography by Willi Frischauer which presents an overview of Preminger's life and career. In *The Cinema of Otto Preminger,* Gerald Pratley gives a standard expanded filmography with casts, credits, and story line for each of the major films, as well as commentary on the films.

Although Nicholas Ray may have done his best work in the late 1940s and 1950s, his films still attract a following. *Nicholas Ray* by John Francis Kreidl is a solid treatment of Ray's entire career, including a biography and a filmography, but its main value lies in its criticism of Ray's films. Kreidl has devoted most of his book to analysis of *Rebel Without a Cause,* clearly Ray's most popular film; he treats most of Ray's other films much more briefly, with the exception of Ray's unusual Western, *Johnny Guitar,* to which he devotes a full chapter.

The man who has come to represent the best of French filmmaking, Jean Renoir, fled the Nazis and immigrated to the United States; he made a number of fine films in America, although these are not the films for which he is best known. Perhaps the most important study of his films is by the master French critic André Bazin. His *Jean Renoir,* now translated into English, is the standard book on the director and includes a chapter on Renoir's experience in Hollywood. While Bazin's book is the best known study of Renoir, another book by the same title, this one by the American Leo Braudy, is also highly regarded. Braudy too deals in part with the films made in this country, and his careful analysis of all the Renoir films brings insights rarely found in film criticism.

Hal Roach was a producer and director of comedies that rivaled those of Mack Sennett. In *The Films of Hal Roach,* William K. Everson has examined Roach's style and compared him to both Charles Chaplin and Mack Sennett. His study, although brief, includes an interview with Roach and a bibliography.

Robert Rossen began as a screenwriter (three of his screenplays have been published) and later became a director of such important films as *All the King's Men* and *The Hustler.* In *The Films of Robert Rossen,* Alan Casty presents a long critical essay on Rossen's work and an extended filmography. Both the Roach book and Casty's study have been published by the Museum of Modern Art.

John Schlesinger is a British director whose films made in the United States, *Midnight Cowboy* and *The Day of the Locusts,* have been important ones. *John Schlesinger* by Nancy J. Brooker contains a biography of Schlesinger and a survey of his career; Brooker also includes factual data on the films and a survey of bibliographical material on the director.

No director is better known for his work in silent comedies than Mack Sennett, and his story is told by Kalton C. Lahue in *Mack Sennett's Keystone: The Man, the Myth, and the Comedies.* Lahue includes chapters on the Keystone legend, the early players (Charles Chaplin and others), and the Keystone Kops. He has also reprinted some Keystone scripts, a rarity that makes this book particularly valuable. Sennett has told his own story in *King of Comedy.* He discusses the production of his films and topics from the Keystone Kops to Mabel Normand, Sennett's favorite actress. This book becomes more than Sennett's life; it is also the history of the world of silent comedy.

Don Siegel has made a reputation for his direction of Clint Eastwood in some of his most successful films. *Don Siegel: Director* by Stuart Kaminsky describes Siegel's work first with Warner Brothers, then with Howard Hughes, then on to a certain amount of independence. Kaminsky covers Siegel's relationships with his stars, among them John Cassavetes, Eli Wallach, Elvis Presley, Steve McQueen, Lee Marvin, and Clint Eastwood. *Don Siegel* by Judith Kass is a short study with a filmography which includes both analysis and description of Siegel's films; it is published with Stuart Rosenthal's study of Tod Browning mentioned above in one volume.

Another Austrian who achieved success as a Hollywood director is Josef von Sternberg, who directed Marlene Dietrich in some of her finest films. *Josef von Sternberg* by Herman G. Weinberg is the standard study of the man and his career. Beginning with an interview with Sternberg and excerpts from his correspondence, it includes extracts from scenarios for *Shanghai Express* and *Anatahan.* Weinberg has also summarized critical reviews that give an excellent idea of the reception of the films and has included a filmography and bibliography. Sternberg wrote an autobiography, *Fun in a Chinese Laundry,* that is curious and interesting, although not entirely reliable. He describes the people with whom he worked, with a concentration on Dietrich. For the most part he is frank in his opinions of these people, but his memories may have faded with time. *The Cinema of Josef von Sternberg* by John Baxter is an introduction to "the Sternberg style" and survey of his career from the early German films, especially *The Blue Angel,* to the other major films including *Shanghai Express, Blonde Venus, The Scarlet Empress,* and *The Devil Is a Woman.* Again, the focus is on Marlene Dietrich. Finally, *The Films of Josef von Sternberg* by Andrew Sarris gives a general introduction to the career of Sternberg and a brief commentary on each film. Sarris' study was a catalogue for a Museum of Modern Art exhibit.

Donald Richie characterizes George Stevens as "an American romantic."

Richie's book, *George Stevens,* is a monograph from the Museum of Modern Art which contains a short introductory essay and a filmography.

Hollywood Scapegoat: The Biography of Erich von Stroheim is an early biography of another Austrian who achieved success in America as a director. First published in 1950 and now reprinted, the study by Peter Noble begins with a biographical sketch, presents essays by critics such as Paul Rotha, Herman Weinberg, and Lewis Jacobs, and includes a bibliography. *Stroheim* by Joel W. Finler depicts Stroheim as both director and actor, and presents criticism and analysis as well as a history of his work. Finler includes chapters on Stroheim's work in bringing Frank Norris' novel *McTeague* to the screen as *Greed*; he also discusses Stroheim's direction of *The Merry Widow*, *The Wedding March*, and *Queen Kelly*, and, as a postscript, his acting in *Sunset Boulevard*. *Von Stroheim* by Thomas Quinn Curtiss begins with a description of Stroheim's early acting career in the silents as the heavy, "the man you love to hate," as he was billed then. Curtiss goes on to discuss Stroheim's career as a director, with special emphasis on *Greed*, and follows him after his directing career peaked.

King Vidor, whose best films are *The Big Parade* and *Our Daily Bread,* is another director who came to Hollywood from central Europe. *King Vidor* by John Baxter is a slim volume of useful information on Vidor's major films, with brief evaluations of the important films, but few details. *King Vidor on Film Making* is Vidor's book on his craft rather than on himself. In the first part he discusses the role of the director on the set, with an emphasis on artistic freedom and the studio system; here he brings in some of his films, notably *War and Peace* and *Street Scenes.* In the second part he explains his theory of cinema, with comments on editing, music, lighting, special effects, and color. In the third part he discusses social and technological changes that have led us to a new cinema, and in the last section he deals with the relationship between film and reality. Vidor's autobiography, *A Tree Is a Tree,* covers his work from his early days with D. W. Griffith to his later successes such as *The Big Parade* and *Our Daily Bread.* The book includes frequent mention of the people Vidor worked with—especially Lillian Gish and Charles Chaplin.

During his long career Raoul Walsh has developed a reputation for he-man action films. In his autobiography, *Each Man in His Time,* he describes his career from the early days when he played John Wilkes Booth in *Birth of a Nation* to his later career when he directed Humphrey Bogart and Clark Gable. Walsh's career is also discussed in Kingsley Canham's book *Michael Curtiz, Raoul Walsh and Henry Hathaway,* mentioned above; this book provides both criticism and history of Walsh's films.

Few filmmakers have been more controversial than Andy Warhol; his films have challenged many conventional notions about the nature of cinema. *Stargazer* is Stephen Koch's tribute to "Andy Warhol's world and his films,'' a book that is slightly spoiled by Koch's awe of Warhol during his peak in the 1960s. The book's strength lies in its close analysis of many of Warhol's films. Warhol's own book, *The Philosophy of Andy Warhol (From A to B and Back Again)* is part philosophy and part autobiography. The book has its own intrinsic interest, but reading the philosophy that undergirds the films will make them no less strange to the viewer. *Andy Warhol* by Rainer Crone is an overview of Warhol's art with a major unit on Warhol's films, a discussion of both the early experimental films and the later features, and a brief commentary. It is extensively illustrated.

There is perhaps no one outstanding book with which to begin the study of Orson Welles and his films, so the reader might choose any as an introduction to that most versatile director. *Orson Welles* by Maurice Bessy opens with a long introduction by Bessy on Welles' life, his style and other aspects of his work. Bessy then presents interviews with Welles and essays by him on his view of the cinema. The rest of the book, except for the concluding filmography and bibliography, is comprised of critical essays on Welles and his films. *The Films of Orson Welles* by Charles Higham is a good history of the director's work which devotes a chapter to each film, giving the story of the production and an analysis of the art of the film. *A Ribbon of Dreams* is Peter Cowie's thematic study of Welles' films, which includes script extracts and consideration of Welles as an actor.

Orson Welles by Joseph McBride is a film by film analysis of Welles' work, including a filmography and a list of Welles' writing. A few years after publishing this book, McBride wrote another by the same title, this one an illustrated history of the actor and director. Containing both biographical material and a filmography, the second book is a consideration of Welles' contribution to film and a description of his films.

Focus on Orson Welles, edited by Ronald Gottesman, contains essays on the man, his technique, and his films. Gottesman has selected scholarly articles by screen personalities and by some of Welles' leading critics: Peter Bogdanovich, Charlton Heston, Joseph McBride, and others.

The French have also had their say about Welles. *Orson Welles* consists of criticism by André Bazin, perhaps the best known of the French critics. After a long foreword by François Truffaut and a profile of Welles by Jean Cocteau, Bazin discusses Welles' early career in theatre and radio and his transition to Hollywood in the late 1930s. The most interesting part of the book is Bazin's analysis of Welles' technique. *The Magic World of Orson Welles* by James Naremore is another fine introduction to the art of this director, with special attention to Welles' political and social persuasions that appear in his films. Finally, *Renaissance of the Film,* edited by Julius Bellone, is an anthology of essays and reviews on the work of five directors, four of them European, the fifth Welles. Bellone has chosen directors he feels have raised the art of film in the past several decades.

William Wellman made his reputation directing Westerns and war films. *A Short Time for Insanity* is his autobiography, a readable book providing some background for the study of his films but not much detail.

Billy Wilder is another Austrian who became a Hollywood director. While he began his film career as a writer, he was soon given directing responsibilities. *The Bright Side of Billy Wilder, Primarily,* by Tom Wood, is "a profile of Hollywood's greatest wit at work and play." Wood discusses Wilder's methods, techniques, and philosophy rather superficially in a book intended for a popular audience. Of more value to the student of Wilder is *Billy Wilder in Hollywood* by Maurice Zolotow. This book contains background on Wilder's American career in writing and direction and discusses *Ninotchka,* whose script Wilder worked on, and *Sunset Boulevard,* which he directed. *Billy Wilder* by Axel Madsen is a scholarly study of Wilder's films with an extended overview and a detailed film analysis. *The Film Career of Billy Wilder* by Steve Seidman contains biographical background, a critical survey of Wilder's career, synopses of Wilder's films with casts and credits, and a survey of writings about Wilder including reviews of his films.

Along with Robert Flaherty, Frederick Wiseman is the leading maker of documentary films in this country. *Frederick Wiseman,* edited by Thomas R. Atkins, is an anthology of essays which for the most part deal with general criticism of Wiseman's films rather than with single films. The essays cover Wiseman's methods and problems, and his early films from *Titicut Follies* to *Primate.* Atkins has also included reviews of Wiseman's films by Richard Schickel, Pauline Kael, and others.

William Wyler has become one of the most proficient directors at adapting novels and plays to the screen. *William Wyler* by Axel Madsen is a scholarly book which provides good background for *The Little Foxes, The Collector*, the remake of *Ben Hur*, and other Wyler films. Madsen also discusses Wyler's relations with his stars, among them Bette Davis, Gary Cooper, Clark Gable, and David Niven, and his problems with the House Un-American Activities Committee.

BOOKS ON MORE THAN ONE DIRECTOR

As was the case with books on actors, many books on directors cover more than one person and are difficult to classify. The reader should note that almost any of the books listed may have material on a particular director.

The Movie Makers: Artists in an Industry by Gene D. Phillips is a description of the workings of the movie industry and the efforts of the artists—primarily directors—to work within that complex industry. Americans considered includes James Wong Howe (a cameraman), Charles Chaplin, Howard Hawks, George Cukor, George Stevens, Fred Zinnerman, and Stanley Kubrick; British directors are also considered.

The American Cinema is Andrew Sarris' controversial book in which he ranks directors in order of importance. Few people will agree with Sarris' rankings, but all readers will find stimulating commentary here. Sarris begins with what he calls the fourteen Pantheon directors, including Charles Chaplin, John Ford, Fritz Lang, and Orson Welles, and works his way down to a category of "strained seriousness," which includes Stanley Kubrick.

In *American Film Directors* Ronald Lloyd claims to present "the world as they see it." His well-illustrated essays cover John Ford, Orson Welles, Howard Hawks, Alfred Hitchcock, Arthur Penn, Stanley Kubrick, and the new directors Peter Bogdanovich, Francis Ford Coppola, and Robert Altman.

Directors of the 1970s have received considerable attention. In *Hollywood Renaissance* Diane Jacobs talks about the movie makers of this decade: John Cassavetes, Robert Altman, Francis Ford Coppola, Martin Scorsese, and Paul Mazursky. In *Directors and Directions* John Russell Taylor writes about "cinema for the 1970s." He presents a thorough discussion of the films of eight directors, including Stanley Kubrick, Andy Warhol, and Paul Morrissey, and offers some insight into their major films.

Jon Tuska has written two books on directors. *Close-up: The Contract Director* includes "career studies" of many of the directors who worked for the studios under contract: Walter Lang, H. Bruce Humberstone, William Dieterle, Joseph Kane, William Witney, Lesley Selander, Yakina Canutt, Lewis Milestone, Ed Dmytry, and Howard Hawks. *Close-up: The Hollywood Director* has essays on better-known directors: Billy Wilder, Henry King, Frank Capra, Spencer Gordon Bennett, William Wyler, William Wellman, John Huston, Douglas Sirk, and Alfred Hitchcock. The book contains filmographies and brief comments on these directors' important films.

Great Film Directors is an important anthology of criticism and reviews of the work of twenty-three directors. Edited by Leo Braudy and Morris Dickstein, the book includes material on Frank Capra, Charles Chaplin, Robert Flaherty, John Ford, D. W. Griffith, Howard Hawks, Alfred Hitchcock, Buster Keaton, Josef von Sternberg, and Orson Welles.

Independent filmmaker Stan Brakhage had published two books on other directors. *The Brakhage Lectures* presents his views on Georges Méliès, D. W. Griffith, Carly Dreyer, and Sergei Eisenstein. *Film Biographies* includes all the essays from *The Brakhage Lectures* plus additional chapters on comedy and tragicomedy (Charles Chaplin, Laurel and Hardy, Buster Keaton, and Jean Vigo) and the narrative as religion (*The Cabinet of Dr. Caligari,* Fritz Lang, F. W. Murnau, and Alexander Dovzhenko).

Stanley Hockman has edited a valuable collection of reviews of the major works of important American directors. *American Film Directors* contains edited reviews assembled in such a way as to provide an overview of the directors' critical receptions.

The Film Director as Superstar by Joseph Gelmis is a study of the role directors came to play in the 1960s. Gelmis classifies these directors as the outsiders (Andy Warhol, John Cassavetes, and others), "the European experience" (Roman Polanski and others), and the free agents who work within the system (Francis Ford Coppola, Arthur Penn, Richard Lester, Mike Nichols, Stanley Kubrick, and Roger Corman).

Richard Koszarski has edited two valuable books of essays by directors. The essays are period pieces, written when the directors were at their prime. In each, the director discusses what he does and comments on the role of the director. *Hollywood Directors, 1914-1940* and *Hollywood Directors, 1941-1976* complement one another.

One of the best-known books of interviews with directors is Andrew Sarris' *Interviews with Film Directors.* Sarris has brought together interviews with some forty directors, interviews which have, for the most part, been conducted by others and published elsewhere; however, Sarris has enhanced these interviews with his own introductions. A companion volume is *Hollywood Voices,* which Sarris also edited. The format is similar, but the focus is on fewer directors, all of whom have worked in the United States: George Cukor, Rouben Mamoulian, Otto Preminger, Preston Sturges, John Huston, Joseph Losey, Nicholas Ray, Abraham Polansky, and Orson Welles.

Encountering Directors consists of a series of interviews conducted by Charles Thomas Samuels; no American directors are included, but one interview with Alfred Hitchcock does appear. *Directors at Work* is a series of lengthy interviews by Bernard Kantor, Irwin R. Blackner, and Anne Kramer with directors Richard Brooks, George Cukor, Norman Jewison, Elia Kazan, Stanley Kramer, Richard Lester, Jerry Lewis, Elliot Silverstein, Robert Wise, and William Wyler. Finally, critic Richard Schickel videotaped interviews with several important directors for broadcast on the Public Broadcasting System (PBS). The transcripts of those interviews have been published as *The Men Who Made the Movies*. Included are Alfred Hitchcock, Raoul Walsh, Frank Capra, Vincente Minnelli, George Cukor, Howard Hawks, William Wellman, and King Vidor.

The West Coast branch of the American Film Institute has conducted interviews with movie people for a number of years. The AFI has catalogued the tapes of these interviews, made them available for consultation, and attempted to publish the better interviews. For several years the interviews came out in a separate publication, *Dialogue on Film,* issued several times a year; now the interviews are published as part of *American Film,* the journal of the AFI (see the listings of periodicals in chapter 9). Since the issues of *Dialogue on Film* were not indexed as the editions of *American Film* are, the directors and other film people interviewed in the first series may be found in a checklist following the bibliography for this chapter.

Nineteen of the important directors who worked for Warner Brothers have been studied by William R. Meyer in *Warner Brothers Directors.* Meyer includes lengthy essays on Busby Berkeley, Michael Curtiz, Howard

Hawks, John Huston, William Wellman and other fine directors; each essay contains photographs and a filmography.

In *The American Film Directors* Maureen Lambray, a Hollywood photographer, has selected her finest portraits of eighty-two American directors from the the silent period to the 1970s.

Horizons West/Anthony Mann, Budd Boetticher, Sam Peckinpah: Studies of Authorship within the Western is by Jim Kitses. After an introductory chapter on "authorship and genre," Kitses discusses the personal visions of each of the three directors he has chosen as representatives of highly individualistic Western films.

In *The Director's Event: Interviews with Five American Film-makers,* Eric Sherman and Martin Rubin converse with Budd Boetticher, Peter Bogdanovich, Samuel Fuller, Arthur Penn, and Roman Polanski. This book is an exploration of the feelings these directors incorporate into their films.

Finally, James Robert Parish and Michael R. Pitts have produced a reference work to films of most American directors. *Film Directors: A Guide to Their American Films* lists the filmmakers, titles and dates of their films, and the names of the companies which produced these films.

BOOKS ON PRODUCERS

Stories of actors are stories of glamour, excitement, and hard work; stories of directors are stories of artistic struggles and creation. Stories of producers are stories of power. In fact, rarely has so much power been concentrated in the hands of so few as during the 1930s when the studios were run by a few men who dominated the industry the way Babe Ruth dominated baseball at the time.

The Moguls is Norman Zierold's story of the men who ran Hollywood: David Selznick, Jesse Lasky, Louis B. Mayer, Carl Laemmle, Harry Cohn, the Warner brothers, and William Fox. Zierold discusses the stars they controlled and the movies they made.

William Castle was not one of the moguls, but he did produce many of the popular horror films, including *Rosemary's Baby.* His autobiography, *Step Right Up! I'm Gonna Scare the Pants Off America* is the story behind the production of these horror films.

Walt Disney was far more than a producer and his empire extended far beyond film, but for the purposes of this discussion, the category of producer seems the most suitable. The most popular general study of Disney and his empire is *The Disney Version* by Richard Schickel, a solid book covering Disney's work in movies and other areas. Bob Thomas' book, *Walt Disney: An American Original,* now one of the standard works on Disney, details both Disney's life and his career. The lengthiest of the general studies of Disney is *The Art of Walt Disney* by Christopher Finch. Finch claims to have covered Disney "from Mickey Mouse to the Magic Kingdom" and his book does indeed cover the animated features, the live-action films and much more. When Mickey Mouse celebrated his fiftieth birthday in 1977, David Bain and Bruce Harris toasted him with a birthday salute in pictures, *Mickey Mouse.* Their photographs and frame enlargements cover Mickey's fifty years in films, television, and comics. The book is of slight scholarly value, but it is nostalgic. *The Disney Films* by Leonard Maltin gives the credits, history, photographs, and criticism of each of the features; additionally, Maltin has included chapters on Disney's short films, his television work, and the work of the Disney Studio after his death.

Thomas Edison was one of the pioneers in the movie industry and must be given major credit for developing movie technology. The production of films for his movie company was largely left to others, but any history of the early days of the industry must consider his contributions. Edison's entire career is the topic of *Edison: A Biography* by Matthew Josephson. This full-length study has a chapter devoted to Edison's work with motion pictures. Lawrence A. Frost's *The Edison Album: A Pictorial Biography of Thomas A. Edison* makes only brief mention of motion pictures, but the photographs are valuable. The most thorough study of Edison's involvement with film is found in *Origins of the American Film* by Gordon Hendricks, a scholarly book known for its exhaustive attention to details. One of the major units discusses "the Edison motion picture myth," a unit that originally had been published separately.

There are two sides to any story, and the two sides of William Fox's story are told by Glendon Allvine and Upton Sinclair. As a member of Fox's empire with first-hand knowledge of his activities, Allvine became an admirer of the producer. *The Greatest Fox of Them All* is his version of how Fox ran his studio. *Upton Sinclair Presents William Fox* is Sinclair's exposé of Fox's methods. Sinclair wrote: "no melodrama that I have been able to invent in my thirty years of inventing has been more packed with crimes and betrayals, perils and escapes, than the story of William Fox."

Samuel Goldwyn, too, has had his admirers and detractors. *The Great Goldwyn* was a favorable early study (1937) by Alva Johnson who attempted to capture the flavor of Goldwyn's language and witticisms in personal memoirs. In the mid-1970s three more objective books have been published. In *Goldwyn: A Biography of the Man Behind the Myth* Arthur Marx presents the life of the man who was a major force at MGM and later one of the most respected and feared of the independent producers. Carol Easton's *The Search for Sam Goldwyn* is likewise a biography. Goldwyn, according to Easton, was the toughest of the Hollywood producers, and she tells his story from the making of his first film, *The Squaw Man,* in 1913 through the years when his productions dominated the movie business. *Samuel Goldwyn Presents* is an expanded filmography of Goldwyn's films by

Alvin H. Marill. Marill begins with an essay on Goldwyn which considers both the man and his legend, then discusses each of the Goldwyn films.

Will Hays was the czar of the industry's own production code during the 1930s and was, therefore, the man with whom movie censorship is most often connected. He joined the industry after a successful career as lawyer and politician, and his *The Memoirs of Will H. Hays* is an autobiography that covers his entire career with heavy emphasis on his work in Hollywood.

In the past decade Howard Hughes has attracted attention because of his billions and his eccentricity; during the 1930s and 1940s he was one of Hollywood's most successful and outgoing producers. Many books deal with his later life, but *Empire: The Life, Legend, and Madness of Howard Hughes* by Donald Barlett and James B. Steele is a comprehensive biography that covers the beginning of his career in Hollywood, the movies he made, and the actresses who entertained him.

While Goldwyn left MGM and went on to independent production, another man stayed behind and ran the studio with "more stars than there were in heaven"; that man was Louis B. Mayer. *Hollywood Rajah: The Life and Times of Louis B. Mayer* is, as the title indicates, a biography and a view of Hollywood during the years of Mayer's reign. The author, Bosley Crowther, was for many years the film critic for *The New York Times* and in this book he provides the backdrop for the MGM productions. *Mayer and Thalberg: The Make-Believe Saints* is a broad study by Samuel Marx of the personalities and films that made MGM great. Mayer, the studio boss, and Irving Thalberg, the production chief, had time for a father-son relationship which eventually was threatened by their respective power and pressures; but the two men combined to lead the studio into its most important period. Samuel Marx, a story editor under Thalberg and Mayer, gives an eye-witness account of their private lives and their control of the studio.

After Mayer left MGM, the studio head became Dore Schary, who headed the company during troubled times before moving on to independent productions. *For Special Occasions* is his personal autobiography on the joys of his Jewish family life with little discussion of his work in films, but his movie industry position makes the book important to a film bibliography.

Mayer's son-in-law, David O. Selznick, worked at MGM but he, too, went on to independent production; his career became synonymous with some of the most important films of the 1930s, notably *Gone With the Wind.* He paid careful attention to every detail of film production; in fact, he actually planned the shots for *Gone With the Wind.* It is that attention to detail that makes *Memo from David O. Selznick* such fascinating reading. The book is a collection of the memoranda written by Selznick to the people associated with his productions, and it reveals the production story from the choice of actresses to the design of the sets. A solid biography of the producer is Bob Thomas' *Selznick*; this is the standard work on the man, the people with whom he worked, and his films. A useful reference book for Selznick's career is *The Selznick Players* by Ronald Bowers. In this story of Selznick and his work, the emphasis is on the actors that worked for him, including Ingrid Bergman, Vivien Leigh, Joseph Cotton, Gregory Peck, and Shirley Temple. Bowers devotes a chapter to the production of *Gone With the Wind.*

Bob Thomas has documented the life of the producer Irving Thalberg in *Thalberg: Life and Legend.* Thomas concentrates on Thalberg's work first at MGM and later as an independent producer and on his major films such as *The Big Parade*, *Ben Hur*, *Anna Christie*, and *Grand Hotel*. An interesting aspect of the book is Thomas' speculation about the influence of F. Scott Fitzgerald's novel, *The Last Tycoon,* on the legend of Irving Thalberg.

In 1927, with their company about to be run out of the business by larger companies, the Warner Brothers used available technology to produce the first commercially successful sound films, a story that is retold by Jack Warner in *My First Hundred Years in Hollywood.* This autobiography describes his life and career from the coming of sound to the production of his last film, *My Fair Lady*.

Don't Say Yes Until I Finish Talking is the biography of Darryl F. Zanuck, the power behind Twentieth Century-Fox for decades. In this book Mel Gussow provides background on the films Zanuck produced and insights into the industry. The book includes a brief but useful filmography. *Tunis Expedition* is an autobiographical book by Zanuck. In it he describes his efforts to photograph the North African campaign during World War II to document the war for the War Department and to provide public news pictures.

OTHER PRODUCTION PERSONNEL

Screenwriters, Cameramen, Gossip Columnists, and Talent Agents

Recently movie writers have been demanding more recognition for the movies whose screenplays they have written. Since their work forms the basis for the productions, the stories of their lives provide insight into the movie business itself.

James Agee was a novelist and essayist who made a valuable contribution to film through his commentary, reviews, and screenplays. His writing for and about film has been analyzed in two dissertations that have now been published. In *James Agee: A Study of His Film Criticism* John J. Snyder views Agee's film criticism as a poetic realist; Snyder is especially interested in the work of the artist as critic. Mark Wilson Flanders in *Film Theory of James Agee* discusses Agee's film aesthetics and demonstrates the practical application of Agee's theory to films. Both books include valuable bibliographies. The reader interested in Agee's entire career might consult a number of books that discuss Agee's film criticism and screenplays and survey all his writing: *The Restless Journey of James Agee* by Genevieve Moreau, *Agee* by Peter Ohlin, *James Agee: Promise and Fulfillment* by Kenneth Seib, and *A Way of Seeing: A Critical Study of James Agee* by Alfred T. Barson. Of special value to the student is *James Agee* by Victor Kramer, who presents an overview of Agee's entire career, a chapter on his film criticism, and another chapter on his screenplays as literature. In addition, David Madden has edited a volume of essays on Agee by people who worked with him or who were influenced by him. *Remembering James Agee* includes comments by John Huston and Dwight Macdonald, among others.

Raymond Chandler's novels have been made into some of the best known detective movies. *Raymond Chandler on Screen: His Novels into Films* by Stephen Pendo is a scholarly study of the films and the novels from which they came. Pendo compares each film's screenplay with its source to reveal the creative processes that led to the film; he summarizes the critical reception to the novels and films, and includes a valuable bibliography. *The World of Raymond Chandler* is an anthology of essays on Chandler's literature and films edited by Miriam Gross. An interview with Billy Wilder, and articles on the films by John Houseman and Philip French are included. Readers who wish to study Chandler's entire career might consult two books that make passing references to his cinematic work while analyzing his life and literary career: *Down These Mean Streets a Man Must Go: Raymond Chandler's Knight* by Philip Durham and *The Life of Raymond Chandler* by Frank MacShane.

Few well-known novelists have had as much success in Hollywood as William Faulkner. His cinematic career is the subject of *Faulkner and Film* by Bruce Kawin, who writes on Faulkner's relationship with director Howard Hawks, on the production of the film based on *The Sound and the Fury,* and on Hollywood's attempt to film "Jefferson" on location. Kawin's last chapter is on Faulkner's place in film history; he includes a filmography and bibliography. The books on Faulkner's literary career are too numerous to list here, but *Faulkner: A Biography* by Joseph Blotner is the standard study of Faulkner's life and career.

A number of major American writers were lured to Hollywood by the financial rewards, but none was more affected by the experience than F. Scott Fitzgerald. *Crazy Sundays: F. Scott Fitzgerald in Hollywood* is by Aaron Latham, who discusses Fitzgerald's Hollywood experience: the parties, the drinking, the scrapes, the illnesses, and the work. Latham also provides close analysis of the scripts Fitzgerald wrote. The standard biography on Fitzgerald is *The Far Side of Paradise: A Biography of Scott Fitzgerald* by Arthur Mizener. This comprehensive survey covers much of Fitzgerald's work in Hollywood. In *Zelda: A Biography* Nancy Milford has recalled the life of Fitzgerald's wife, Zelda, the Fitzgeralds' marriage, and his life and work in Hollywood. While he lived in California, however, Fitzgerald spent much of his time with columnist Sheilah Graham; and she has described their life together and his move work in *Beloved Infidel: The Education of a Woman*, a frank and intimate memoir. Fitzgerald did not write an autobiography, but much of his fiction is set in Hollywood and depicts the life there. The *Pat Hobby Stories*, a collection of his short stories that originally ran in *Esquire*, are about a Hollywood writer. Fitzgerald was writing *The Last Tycoon* before his death and this unfinished novel about the life of a studio boss has been published and made into a movie.

My Side by Ruth Gordon is the autobiography of a woman renowned both for her writing and her acting. The stories she tells about her experiences as a screenwriter and about the people she has known in the movie and theatrical business make for interesting reading.

Off With Their Heads: A Serio-Comic Tale of Hollywood is by a woman who was there. Frances Marion was the screenwriter for *Anna Christie*, *Dinner at Eight*, *Camille*, and others. This is her diary, an insider's view of screenwriting.

"The wit, world, and life of Herman Mankiewicz" is the subject of *Mank* by Richard Meryman. Meryman's study of the primary author of *Citizen Kane,* and of the people he knew and worked with, demonstrates both the highs and lows of the screenwriter's life.

Dalton Trumbo was one of the most widely respected screenwriters, but the blacklisting that resulted from his testimony before the House Un-American Activities Committee (more accurately, from his lack of testimony) took years to overcome. The story of his writing and his struggles is told in a fine biography, *Dalton Trumbo* by Bruce Cook. Some of the story is told in Trumbo's own words in *Additional Dialogue: Letters of Dalton Trumbo, 1942-1962;* these letters cover Trumbo's trial, his period in jail, the blacklist, and his work.

Hollywood would never have achieved its place in American culture had it not been for the gossip columnists who fed the public a diet of information about the stars and their films. Many of the columnists have written their own books about Hollywood which are discussed elsewhere (see especially chapter 3). Two columnists have had a book written about them. George Eells' *Hedda and Louella* is a dual biography of Hedda Hopper and Louella Parsons, the queens of the Hollywood gossip columnists. The book's contents are slightly sensational, but Eells' presentation is professional.

Edith Head is Hollywood's most famous clothes designer, and her books describe the life and work that have brought her numerous Oscars. *The Dress Doctor,* her autobiography, emphasizes the stars she has dressed. She concentrates on the women from Mae West to Kim Novak, but does include a chapter on the men, such as Bing Crosby and Tony Perkins. In *How to Dress for Success,* Head uses her experience to advise women on how to dress for social and professional occasions.

Few cameramen become important enough to have their own stories told, but Billy Bitzer was one. He became famous as the man who ran the camera for D. W. Griffith, and his ability to innovate with the camera and lighting contributed heavily to Griffith's success. In his autobiography, *Billy Bitzer: His Story,* he starts with his beginning in the movie business in 1894 and goes through the years with Griffith at Biograph and on to feature productions. The book contains separate chaptgers on *Birth of a Nation, Intolerance, Hearts of the World,* and *Broken Blossoms.*

Last but not least, there is the talent agent who brings together the people who make the film. *The Irish Peacock* is the autobiography of one, Billy Grady. In what Grady calls "the confessions of a legendary talent agent," the man who discovered Van Johnson, Donna Reed, Dan Dailey, and others discusses his work in Hollywood.

BIBLIOGRAPHY

Allvine, Glendon. *The Greatest Fox of Them All.* New York: Lyle Stuart, 1969.

Armour, Robert A. *Fritz Lang.* Boston: Twayne, 1978.

Atkins, Thomas R., ed. *Frederick Wiseman.* New York: Simon and Schuster, 1976.

Bain, David and Bruce Harris, eds. *Mickey Mouse.* New York: Harmony Books, 1977.

Barlett, Donald and James B. Steele. *Empire: The Life, Legend, and Madness of Howard Hughes.* New York: W. W. Norton, 1979.

Barna, Yon. *Eisenstein.* Bloomington: Indiana University Press, 1973.

Barry, Iris. *D. W. Griffith, American Film Master.* Garden City, N.Y.: The Museum of Modern Art, 1965.

Barson, Alfred T. *A Way of Seeing: A Critical Study of James Agee.* Amherst: University of Massachusetts Press, 1972.

Baxter, John. *The Cinema of John Ford.* New York: A. S. Barnes, 1971.

______. *The Cinema of Josef von Sternberg.* New York: A. S. Barnes, 1971.

______. *King Vidor.* New York: Simon and Schuster, 1976.

Bazin, André. *Jean Renoir.* Translated by W. W. Halsey, II and William H. Simon. New York: Dell, 1973.

______. *Orson Welles.* Translated by Jonathan Rosenbaum. New York: Harper and Row, 1978.

Bellone, Julius, ed. *Renaissance of the Film.* New York: Macmillan, 1970.

Bessy, Maurice. *Orson Welles: An Investigation Into His Films and Philosophy.* Translated by Ciba Vaughan. New York: Crown, 1971.

Bitzer, G. W. *Billy Bitzer: His Story.* New York: Farrar, Straus and Giroux, 1973.

Blotner, Joseph. *Faulkner: A Biography.* New York: Random House, 1974.

Bogdanovich, Peter. *Allan Dwan: The Last Pioneer.* New York: Praeger, 1971.

______. *The Cinema of Howard Hawks.* New York: The Film Library of the Museum of Modern Art, 1962.

______. *Fritz Lang in America.* New York: Praeger, 1967.

______. *John Ford*. Berkeley: University of California Press, 1978.

Bowers, Ronald. *The Selznick Players*. New York: A. S. Barnes, 1976.

Brakhage, Stan. *The Brakhage Lectures*. Chicago: The Goodlion Press, 1972.

______. *Film Biographies*. Berkeley: Turtle Island, 1977.

Braudy, Leo. *Jean Renoir: The World of His Films*. Garden City, N.Y.: Doubleday, 1972.

______ and Morris Dickstein, eds. *Great Film Directors: A Critical Anthology*. New York: Oxford University Press, 1978.

Brooker, Nancy J. *John Schlesinger*. Boston: G. K. Hall, 1978.

Brown, Karl. *Adventures with D. W. Griffith*. New York: Da Capo Press, 1973.

Butler, Ivan. *The Cinema of Roman Polanski*. New York: A. S. Barnes, 1970.

Calder-Marshall, Arthur. *The Innocent Eye: The Life of Robert J. Flaherty*. New York: Harcourt, Brace and World, 1963.

Canham, Kingsley. *Michael Curtiz, Raoul Walsh and Henry Hathaway*. New York: A. S. Barnes, 1973.

Capra, Frank. *The Name Above the Title: An Autobiography*. New York: Macmillan, 1971.

Carey, Gary. *Cukor & Co.: The Films of George Cukor and His Collaborators*. New York: The Museum of Modern Art, 1971.

Carringer, Robert and Barry Sabath. *Ernst Lubitsch*. Boston: G. K. Hall, 1978.

Casper, Joseph Andrew. *Vincente Minnelli and the Film Musical*. New York: A. S. Barnes, 1977.

Castle, William. *Step Right Up! I'm Gonna Scare the Pants Off America*. New York: G. P. Putnam's Sons, 1976.

Casty, Alan. *The Films of Robert Rossen*. New York: Museum of Modern Art, 1969.

Ciment, Michel. *Kazan on Kazan*. New York: Viking, 1974.

Clarens, Carlos. *George Cukor*. London: Secker and Warburg, 1976.

Cook, Bruce. *Dalton Trumbo*. New York: Charles Scribner's Sons, 1977.

Cowie, Peter. *A Ribbon of Dreams: The Cinema of Orson Welles*. New York: A. S. Barnes, 1973.

Crone, Rainer. *Andy Warhol*. New York: Praeger, 1970.

Crowther, Bosley. *Hollywood Rajah: The Life and Times of Louis B. Mayer*. New York: Holt, Rinehart and Winston, 1960.

Curtiss, Thomas Quinn. *Von Stroheim*. New York: Farrar, Straus and Giroux, 1971.

DeMille, Cecil B. *The Autobiography of Cecil B. DeMille*. Englewood Cliffs, N.J.: Prentice-Hall, 1959.

Devries, Daniel. *The Films of Stanley Kubrick*. Grand Rapids, Mich.: William B. Eerdmans Publishing Co., 1973.

Durgnat, Raymond. *The Strange Case of Alfred Hitchcock: or, the Plain Man's Hitchcock:* London: Faber and Faber, 1974.

Durham, Philip. *Down These Mean Streets A Man Must Go: Raymond Chandler's Knight*. Chapel Hill: The University of North Carolina Press, 1963.

Easton, Carol. *The Search for Sam Goldwyn*. New York: William Morrow, 1976.

Eells, George. *Hedda & Louella*. New York: G. P. Putnam, 1972.

Eisner, Lotte H. *Fritz Lang*. New York: Oxford University Press, 1977.

______. *Murnau*. Berkeley: University of California Press, 1964.

Essoe, Gabe and Raymond Lee. *DeMille: The Man and His Pictures.* New York: A. S. Barnes, 1970.

Evans, Max. *Sam Peckinpah: Master of Violence.* Vermillion, S.D.: Dakota Press, 1972.

Everson, William K. *The Films of Hal Roach.* New York: Museum of Modern Art, 1971.

Feineman, Neil. *Persistence of Vision: The Films of Robert Altman.* New York: Arno, 1978.

Finch, Christopher. *The Art of Walt Disney: From Mickey Mouse to the Magic Kingdoms.* New York: Harry N. Abrams, 1973.

Finler, Joel W. *Stroheim.* Berkeley: University of California Press, 1968.

Fitzgerald, F. Scott. *The Last Tycoon, An Unfinished Novel.* New York: Charles Scribner's Sons, 1969.

______. *The Pat Hobby Stories.* New York: Charles Scribner, 1962.

Flaherty, Frances Hubbard. *The Odyssey of a Film-Maker: Robert Flaherty's Story.* Urbana, Ill.: Beta Phi Mu, 1960.

Flanders, Mark Wilson. *Film Theory of James Agee.* New York: Arno, 1977.

Frischauer, Willi. *Behind the Scenes with Otto Preminger.* New York: William Morrow, 1974.

Frost, Lawrence A. *The Edison Album: A Pictorial Biography of Thomas A. Edison.,* Seattle: Superior, 1969.

Garnett, Tay. *Light Your Torches and Pull Up Your Tights.* New Rochelle, N.Y.: Arlington House, 1973.

Garnham, Nicholas. *Samuel Fuller.* New York: Viking, 1971.

Geduld, Harry M., ed. *Focus on D. W. Griffith.* Englewood Cliffs, N.J.: Prentice-Hall, 1971.

Gelmis, Joseph. *The Film Director as Superstar.* Garden City, N.Y.: Doubleday, 1970.

Glatzer, Richard and John Raeburn, eds. *Frank Capra: The Man and His Films.* Ann Arbor: The University of Michigan Press, 1975.

Gordon, Ruth. *My Side.* New York: Harper and Row, 1976.

Gottesman, Ronald, ed. *Focus on Orson Welles.* Englewood Cliffs, N.J.: Prentice-Hall, 1976.

Grady, Billy. *The Irish Peacock: The Confessions of a Legendary Talent Agent.* New Rochelle, N.Y. Arlington House, 1972.

Graham, Sheilah and Gerold Frank. *Beloved Infidel: The Education of a Woman.* New York: Bantam, 1958.

Griffith, D. W. *The Man Who Invented Hollywood: The Autobiography of D. W. Griffith.* Louisville, Ky.: Touchstone, 1972.

Griffith, Richard. *The World of Robert Flaherty.* Boston: Little, Brown, 1953.

Gross, Miriam, ed. *The World of Raymond Chandler.* London: Weidenfeld and Nicolson, 1977.

Gussow, Mel. *Don't Say Yes Until I Finish Talking: A Biography of Darryl F. Zanuck.* Garden City, N.Y.: Doubleday, 1971.

Hardy, Phil. *Samuel Fuller.* New York: Praeger, 1970.

Hays, Will H. *The Memoirs of Will H. Hays.* Garden City, N.Y.: Doubleday, 1955.

Head, Edith and Jane Kesner Ardmore. *The Dress Doctor.* Boston: Little, Brown, 1959.

______ and Joe Hyams. *How to Dress for Success.* New York: Random House, 1967.

Henderson, Robert M. *D. W. Griffith: His Life and Work.* New York: Oxford University Press, 1972.

______. *D. W. Griffith: The Years at Biograph.* New York: Farrar, Straus and Giroux, 1970.

Hendricks, Gordon. *Origins of the American Film.* New York: Arno, 1972.

Higham, Charles. *Cecil B. DeMille.* New York: Charles Scribner's Sons, 1973.

______. *The Films of Orson Welles.* Berkeley: University of California Press, 1971.

Hochman, Stanley, ed. *American Film Directors.* New York: Frederick Ungar, 1974.

Jacobs, Diane. *Hollywood Renaissance.* New York: A. S. Barnes, 1977.

Jensen, Paul M. *The Cinema of Fritz Lang.* New York: A. S. Barnes, 1969.

Johnson, Alva. *The Great Goldwyn.* New York: Random House, 1937.

Johnson, Robert K. *Francis Ford Coppola.* Boston: Twayne, 1977.

Josephson, Matthew. *Edison: A Biography.* New York: McGraw-Hill, 1959.

Kagan, Norman. *The Cinema of Stanley Kubrick.* New York: Holt, Rinehart and Winston, 1972.

Kaminsky, Stuart M. *Don Siegel: Director.* New York: Curtis Books, 1974.

______. *John Huston.* Boston: Houghton Mifflin, 1978.

Kantor, Bernard, Erwin R. Blackner, and Anne Kramer. *Directors at Work: Interviews with American Film-Makers.* New York: Funk and Wgnalls, 1970.

Kass, Judith. *Don Siegel.* New York: A. S. Barnes, 1975. In the same volume with Rosenthal, Stuart. *Tod Browning.*

______. *Robert Altman: American Innovator.* New York: Popular Library, 1978.

Kawin, Bruce F. *Faulkner & Film.* New York: Ungar, 1977.

Kitses, Jim. *Horizons West/Anthony Mann, Budd Boetticher, Sam Peckinpah: Studies of Authorship within the Western.* Bloomington: Indiana University Press, 1969.

Koch, Stephen. *Stargazer: Andy Warhol's World and His Films.* New York: Praeger, 1973.

Koszarski, Richard, ed. *Hollywood Directors, 1914-1940.* New York: Oxford University Press, 1976.

______. *Hollywood Directors, 1941-1976.* New York: Oxford University Press, 1977.

Koury, Phil A. *Yes, Mr. DeMille.* New York: G. P. Putnam's Sons, 1959.

Kreidl, John Francis. *Nicholas Ray.* Boston: Twayne, 1977.

Kramer, Victor. *James Agee.* Boston: Twayne, 1975.

Lahue, Kalton. *Mack Sennett's Keystone: The Man, the Myth, and the Comedies.* New York: A. S. Barnes, 1971.

Lambert, Gavin. *On Cukor.* New York: G. P. Putnam's Sons, 1972.

Lambray, Maureen. *The American Film Directors.* New York: Rapoport, 1976.

Latham, Aaron. *Crazy Sundays: F. Scott Fitzgerald in Hollywood.* New York: Viking, 1971.

LaValley, Albert J., ed. *Focus on Hitchcock.* Englewood Cliffs, N.J.: Prentice-Hall, 1972.

LeRoy, Mervyn. *Mervyn LeRoy: Take One.* New York: Hawthorne, 1974.

Liehm, Antonín J. *The Milos Forman Stories.* White Plains, N.Y.: International Arts and Sciences Press, 1975.

Lloyd, Ronald. *American Film Directors.* New York: Franklin Watts, 1976.

Logan, Joshua. *Josh: My Up and Down, In and Out Life.* New York: Delacorte, 1976.

[Losey, Joseph]. *Losey on Losey.* Garden City, N.Y.: Doubleday, 1968.

McBride, Joseph, ed. *Focus on Howard Hawks.* Englewood Cliffs, N.J.: Prentice-Hall, 1972.

______. *Orson Welles.* New York: Viking, 1972.

______. *Orson Welles.* New York: Harcourt Brace Jovanovich, 1977.

______ and Michael Wilmington. *John Ford.* New York: Da Capo Press, 1975.

MacShane, Frank. *The Life of Raymond Chandler.* New York: E. P. Dutton, 1976.

Madden, David, ed. *Remembering James Agee.* Baton Rouge: Louisiana State University Press, 1974.

Madsen, Axel. *Billy Wilder.* Bloomington: Indiana University Press, 1969.

______. *John Huston.* Garden City, N.Y.: Doubleday, 1978.

______. *William Wyler: The Authorized Biography.* New York: Thomas Y. Crowell, 1973.

Maltin, Leonard. *The Disney Films.* New York: Crown, 1973.

Marill, Alvin H. *Samuel Goldwyn Presents.* New York: A. S. Barnes, 1976.

Marion, Frances. *Off with Their Heads!: A Serio-Comic Tale of Hollywood.* New York: Macmillan, 1972.

Marx, Arthur. *Goldwyn: A Biography of the Man Behind the Myth.* New York: W. W. Norton, 1976.

Marx, Samuel. *Mayer & Thalberg: The Make-Believe Saints.* New York: Random House, 1975.

Meryman, Richard. *Mank.* New York: William Morrow, 1978.

Meyer, William R. *Warner Brothers Directors.* New Rochelle, N.Y.: Arlington House, 1978.

Milford, Nancy. *Zelda: A Biography.* New York: Harper and Row, 1970.

Milne, Tom. *Rouben Mamoulian.* Bloomington: Indiana University Press, 1969.

Minnelli, Vincente. *I Remember It Well.* Garden City, N.Y.: Doubleday, 1974.

Mizener, Arthur. *The Far Side of Paradise: A Biography of F. Scott Fitzgerald.* Boston: Houghton Mifflin, 1951.

Montague, Ivor. *With Eisenstein in Hollywood: A Chapter of Autobiography.* New York: International Publishers, 1969.

Moreau, Genevieve. *The Restless Journey of James Agee.* Translated by Miriam Kleiger and Morty Schiff. New York: William Morrow, 1977.

Mullen, Pat. *Man of Aran.* Cambridge: The MIT Press, 1970.

Murphy, William T. *Robert Flaherty: A Guide to References and Resources.* Boston: G. K. Hall, 1978.

Naremore, James. *The Magic World of Orson Welles.* New York: Oxford, 1978.

Noble, Peter. *Hollywood Scapegoat: The Biography of Erich von Stroheim.* New York: Arno, 1972.

O'Dell, Paul. *Griffith and the Rise of Hollywood.* New York: A. S. Barnes, 1970.

Ohlin, Peter. *Agee.* New York: Ivan Obolensky, 1966.

Parish, James Robert and Pitts, Michael R. *Film Directors: A Guide to Their American Films.* Metuchen, N.J.: Scarecrow, 1974.

Pendo, Stephen. *Raymond Chandler on Screen: His Novels into Film.* Metuchen, N.J.: Scarecrow, 1976.

Perry, George. *Hitchcock*. Garden City, N.Y.: Doubleday, 1975.
Phillips, Gene D. *The Movie Makers: Artists in an Industry*. Chicago: Nelson-Hall, 1973.
______. *Stanley Kubrick: A Film Odyssey*. New York: Popular Library, 1975.
Pike, Bob and Martin, Dave. *The Genius of Busby Berkeley*. Reseda, Calif.: CFS Books, 1973.
Place, J. A. *The Non-Western Films of John Ford*. New York: Citadel, 1976.
______. *The Western Films of John Ford*. New York: Citadel, 1974.
Poague, Leland A. *The Cinema of Ernst Lubitsch*. New York: A. S. Barnes, 1978.
______. *The Cinema of Frank Capra: An Approach to Film Comedy*. New York: A. S. Barnes, 1975.
Pratley, Gerald. *The Cinema of John Frankenheimer*. New York: A. S. Barnes, 1969.
______. *The Cinema of John Huston*. New York: A. S. Barnes, 1977.
______. *The Cinema of Otto Preminger*. New York: Castle, 1971.
Preminger, Otto. *Preminger*. Garden City, N.Y.: Doubleday, 1977.
Richie, Donald. *George Stevens: An American Romantic*. New York: Museum of Modern Art, 1970.
Ringgold, Gene and Dewitt Bodeen. *The Films of Cecil B. DeMille*. New York: Citadel, 1969.
Rosenfeldt, Diane. *Richard Lester*. Boston: G. K. Hall, 1978.
Rosenthal, Stuart. *Tod Browning*. New York: A. S. Barnes, 1975. In the same volume with Kass, Judith. *Don Siegel*.
Samuels, Charles Thomas. *Encountering Directors*. New York: Capricorn Books, 1972.
Sarris, Andrew. *The American Cinema: Directors and Directions 1929-1968*. New York: E. P. Dutton, 1968.
______. *The Films of Josef von Sternberg*. Garden City, N.Y.: Doubleday, 1966.
______, ed. *Hollywood Voices: Interviews with Film Directors*. Indianapolis: Bobbs-Merrill, 1971.
______. *Interviews with Film Directors*. New York: Avon, 1967.
______. *The John Ford Movie Mystery*. Bloomington: Indiana University Press, 1975.
Schary, Dore. *For Special Occasions*. New York: Random House, 1962.
Scherle, Victor and William Turner Levy. *The Films of Frank Capra*. Secaucus, N.J.: Citadel, 1977.
Schickel, Richard. *The Disney Version: The Life, Times, Art, and Commerce of Walt Disney*. New York: Simon and Schuster, 1968.
______. *The Men Who Made the Movies: Interviews with Frank Capra, George Cukor, Howard Hawks, Alfred Hitchcock, Vincente Minnelli, King Vidor, Raoul Walsh, and William A. Wellman*. New York: Atheneum, 1975.
Schuth, H. Wayne. *Mike Nichols*. Boston: Twayne, 1978.
Seib, Kenneth. *James Agee: Promise and Fulfillment*. Pittsburgh: University of Pittsburgh Press, 1968.
Seidman, Steve. *The Film Career of Billy Wilder*. Boston: G. K. Hall, 1977.
Selznick, David O. *Memo from David O. Selznick*. Edited by Rudy Behlmer. New York: Viking, 1972.
Sennett, Mack. *King of Comedy*. New York: Pinnacle Books, 1954.

Seton, Marie. *Sergei M. Eisenstein: A Biography.* New York: Grove, 1960.

Sherman, Eric and Rubin, Martin. *The Director's Event: Interview with Five American Film-makers.* New York: Atheneum, 1970.

Siegel, Joel. *Val Lewton: The Reality of Terror.* New York: Viking, 1973.

Sinclair, Andrew. *John Ford.* New York: Dial Press/James Wade, 1979.

Sinclair, Upton. *Upton Sinclair Presents William Fox.* New York: Arno, 1970.

Synder, John J. *James Agee: A Story of His Film Criticism.* New York: Arno, 1971.

Snyder, Robert L. *Pare Lorentz and the Documentary Film.* Norman: University of Oklahoma Press, 1968.

Spoto, Donald. *The Art of Alfred Hitchcock.* New York: Hopkinson and Blake [1967].

______. *Stanley Kramer.* New York: G. P. Putnam's Sons, 1978.

von Sternberg, Josef. *Fun in a Chinese Laundry.* New York: Macmillan, 1965.

Swallow, Norman. *Eisenstein: A Documentary Portrait.* New York: E. P. Dutton, 1976.

Taylor, John Russell. *Directors and Directions: Cinema for the Seventies.* New York: Hill and Wang, 1975.

Thomas, Bob. *Selznick.* Garden City, N.Y.: Doubleday, 1970.

______. *Thalberg: Life and Legend.* Garden City, N.Y.: Doubleday, 1969.

______. *Walt Disney.* New York: Simon and Schuster, 1976.

Tozzi, Romano. *John Huston: A Pictorial Treasury of His Films.* New York: Falcon Enterprises, 1971.

Truffaut, François. *Hitchcock.* New York: Simon and Schuster, 1976.

Trumbo, Dalton. *Additional Dialogue: Letters of Dalton Trumbo, 1942-1962.* New York: M. Evans, 1970.

Tuska, Jon. *Close-up: The Contract Director.* Metuchen, N.J.: Scarecrow, 1976.

______. *Close-up: The Hollywood Director.* Metuchen, N.J.: Scarecrow, 1978.

Vidor, King. *King Vidor on Film Making.* New York: David McKay, 1972.

______. *A Tree Is a Tree.* New York: Harcourt, Brace, 1953.

Wagenknecht, Edward and Anthony Slide. *The Films of D. W. Griffith.* New York: Crown, 1975.

Walker, Alexander. *Stanley Kubrick Directs.* New York: Harcourt Brace Jovanovich, 1971.

Walsh, Raoul. *Each Man in His Time: The Life Story of a Director.* New York: Farrar, Straus, and Giroux, 1974.

Warhol, Andy. *The Philosophy of Andy Warhol (From A to B and Back Again).* New York: Harcourt Brace Jovanovich, 1975.

Warner, Jack. *My First Hundred Years in Hollywood.* New York: Random House, 1965.

Weinberg, Herman G. *Josef von Sternberg: A Critical Study.* New York: E. P. Dutton, 1966.

______. *The Lubitsch Touch: A Critical Study.* New York: E. P. Dutton, 1971.

Wellman, William. *A Short Time for Insanity: An Autobiography.* New York: Hawthorn, 1974.

Willis, Donald C. *The Films of Frank Capra.* Metuchen, N.J.: Scarecrow, 1974.

______. *The Films of Howard Hawks.* Metuchen, N.J.: Scarecrow, 1975.

Wood, Robin. *Arthur Penn.* New York: Praeger, 1969.

______. *Hitchcock's Films.* New York: Castle, 1965.
______. *Howard Hawks.* Garden City, N.Y.: Doubleday, 1968.
Wood, Tom. *The Bright Side of Billy Wilder, Primarily.* Garden City, N.Y.: Doubleday, 1970.
Zanuck, Darryl F. *Tunis Expedition.* New York: Random House, 1943.
Zierold, Norman J. *The Moguls.* New York: Coward-McCann, 1969.
Zolotow, Maurice. *Billy Wilder in Hollywood.* New York: G. P. Putnam's Sons, 1977.

A CHECKLIST OF FILMMAKERS INTERVIEWED IN THE AMERICAN FILM INSTITUTE'S DIALOGUE ON FILM (AS A SEPARATE PUBLICATION—1972–1975)

Federico Fellini
Rouben Mamoulian
Frank Capra
Charlton Heston/Jack Nicholson (Vol. 1, No. 1)
Robert Aldrich (Vol. 1, No. 2)
Milos Forman/Ingrid Thulin (Vol. 1, No. 3)
John Cassavetes/Peter Falk (Vol. 1, No. 4)
Alfred Hitchcock (Vol. 1, No. 5)
Paul Williams (Vol. 1, No. 6)
Cable Television (Vol. 1, No. 7)
University Advisory Committee Seminar (Vol. 2, No. 1)
David Wolper and Company (Vol. 2, No. 2)
Ed Enshwiller/Stan Brakhage (Vol. 2, No. 3)
Richard Attenborough (Vol. 2, No. 4)
Liv Ullmann (Vol. 2, No. 5)
NBC Executives (Vol. 2, No. 6)
Ronald Neame/Lonne Elder III (Vol. 2, No. 7)
Jon Voight (Vol. 2, No. 8)
Stanley Kramer (Vol. 2, No. 9)
Rick Rosenberg/Robert Christiansen (Vol. 2, No. 10)
Conrad Hall (Vol. 3, No. 1)
Henry Fonda (Vol. 3, No. 2)
Henry Mancini (Vol. 3, No. 3)
William Friedkin (Vol. 3, No. 4)
Bernardo Bertolucci/Fritz Lang (Vol. 3, No. 5)
Lucille Ball (Vol. 3, No. 6)
Steven Spielberg/Hal Barwood/Matthew Robbins/Vilmos Zsigmond (Vol. 3, No. 7)
Roman Polanski (Vol. 3, No. 8)
Laszlo Kovacs/Vilmos Zsigmond (Vol. 4, No. 1)
Paul Mazursky/Paul Morrissey (Vol. 4, No. 2)
Olivia de Havilland (Vol. 4, No. 3)
George C. Scott/Trish Van Defere (Vol. 4, No. 4)
Robert Altman (Vol. 4, No. 5)
Hal B. Wallis (Vol. 4, No. 6)
Martin Scorsese (Vol. 4, No. 7)
George Stevens (Vol. 4, No. 8)

CHAPTER 9

Major Films

The heart of any study of film is the film itself. The purpose of this chapter is to direct the reader to available books on the major films, although most of the writing on individual films is in books on the artists themselves or in journal articles. Almost all of the books in chapters 7 and 8 refer to films and several of the reference books in chapter 11 will direct the reader toward articles on the films. This chapter will suggest a few of the books on specific films which are now readily available.

SCREENPLAYS

Some of the books on films give the history of the production of an especially popular film, such as *Gone With the Wind,* or the critical reception of a film that must be studied, such as *Birth of a Nation.* But a large proportion of the books on films are reprints of the screenplays themselves. For the person serious about studying a film, there is, perhaps, no more important tool than the screenplay—except, of course, for the finished film. Unlike the student of almost any other art form, the student of film cannot always have the subject of his attention immediately before him. He may have seen the film months ago and may have a hard time remembering the name of the brother-in-law's cousin who appeared during the second scene or the exact wording of that important dialogue. This is where the screenplay helps. It cannot recreate the visuals, but it can provide factual information about the plot, characters, and setting.

The reader should be aware that there are several types of screenplays, each with its own strengths and weaknesses. The shooting script is the version written by the screenwriter and refined by the producer and director; it is the guide from which the director works. From the writer's point of view this is the original creative material on which the film is based, but often little of what he has written is incorporated into the final film. The director feels free to make whatever changes he feels are necessary, and often has a rewrite man present to doctor the script as the shooting progresses. This means that the reader of the shooting script should not assume that what he is reading is exactly the same as the film. Major changes may have been made.

The next type of screenplay is the shooting continuity, or shot analysis. This is written after the film is finished and taken directly from the film itself; it is a verbal reproduction of what is in the film. Naturally, this is the most accurate source of information about the film in its finished form, but it is dry reading and lacks the creative energy of the shooting script.

Finally, there is what might be called a photo-screenplay. For this, the editor has taken a frame enlargement (a photograph made from one frame of the film) from each shot in the film and strung these enlargements together in book form. Of course, the sense of movement is missing, but the reader can come close to reading the film. Each shot is represented and the dialogue printed under the photographs; the reader will be able to determine what types of shots were used, what the content of each shot is, and how the shots relate to one another. Such a book is very useful to the student of the film, but it is expensive and tells the reader little about the intentions of the screenwriter.

Richard J. Anobile has published a series of photo-screenplays on important American movies. Each contains a brief essay by Anobile on the film and the reproduction of the shots in still photographs. Included in the series are *Alfred Hitchcock's Psycho*, *Casablanca* (including an interview with Ingrid Bergman), *Ernst Lubitsch's Ninotchka*, *Frankenstein*, *The General*, *John Ford's Stagecoach* (including a brief essay by Ford), *The Maltese Falcon*, *Rouben Mamoulian's Dr. Jekyll and Mr. Hyde*, and *Woody Allen's Play It Again, Sam* (including an interview with the director Herbert Ross).

Screenplays have been published since 1917 when William Addison Lathrop came out with *Little Stories from the Screen,* a book that has now been reproduced. The book claimed to include "synopses of produced photoplays in exactly the same form in which they were submitted to the studios." Although the best-known films from the period are not included, the book does contain interesting examples of early screenplays.

Two important reference guides provide access to more recent screenplays: *Published Screenplays: A Checklist* by Clifford McCarty came out in 1971 and is now slightly dated. McCarty lists 388 scripts that have been published; for each title he names the production company, director, author of the screenplay, source of the screenplay, and location of the screenplay. He has included the screenplays for some shorts and experimental films, as well as for the features. *Published Radio, Television, and Film Scripts: A Bibliography* by Howard G. Poteet is a more recent reference. Poteet lists 668 published scripts. He provides less information for each film than does

McCarty, but he of course lists more films. The student should consult both books as neither is all-inclusive. Using the two books, the reader can obtain a good idea of the screenplays published through 1975.

Since 1975, the number of published screenplays has continued to grow. A few of the screenplays published since Poteet's book are *The Blue Dahlia* by Raymond Chandler, including a foreword by John Houseman; *Faulkner's Intruder in the Dust,* by Regina Fadimon, including a lengthy introduction and Ben Maddow's screenplay; Marx Brothers' *Monkey Business and Duck Soup; More About All about Eve* by Joseph Mankiewicz, including a long colloquy by Gary Carey; *Morocco and Shanghai Express,* two screenplays by Jules Furthman for Josef von Sternberg and Marlene Dietrich, in the same volume; *San Francisco* by Anita Loos, with her afterword; *Viva Zapata!* by John Steinbeck; and *Nashville* by Joan Tewkesburg.

The trend toward publishing screenplays is continuing. The University of Wisconsin Press is soon to publish a new series of Warner Brothers' screenplays which is expected to be extensive. The general editor is Tino Balio.

COLLECTIONS OF SCREENPLAYS

Several collections of screenplays have been published. *The Best Pictures, 1939-1940,* edited by Jerry Wald and Richard Macauley, contains the screenplays for *Bachelor Mother, Ninotchka, Rebecca, Mr. Smith Goes to Washington, Dr. Ehrlich's Magic Bullet, Destry Rides Again,* and *Goodbye, Mr. Chips.* The editors have included an essay on the year 1939-1940 in film and credits for the films. John Gassner and Dudley Nichols have edited two volumes of screenplays. The first, *Twenty Best Film Plays,* contains an essay by Gassner on the screenplay as literature and one by Nichols on the writer's role in film production, as well as the screenplays for such movies as *It Happened One Night, My Man Godfrey, Here Comes Mr. Jordan, Fury,* and *Stagecoach.* The second, *Best Film Plays—1945* includes the screenplays for *The Lost Weekend, Spellbound, The Southerner, Double Indemnity,* and six others.

Four more books of screenplays have been edited by George Garrett, O. B. Hardison, Jr., and Jane R. Gelfman. Each volume contains an introduction on the importance of each script included, a discussion of the nature of film production, a glossary, and a full bibliography. Their *Film Scripts One* contains the scripts for *Henry V, The Big Sleep,* and *A Streetcar Named Desire; Film Scripts Two* contains *High Noon, Twelve Angry Men,* and *The Defiant Ones*; *Film Scripts Three* contains *The Apartment, The Misfits*, and *Charade*; and *Film Scripts Four* contains *A Hard Day's Night*, *The Best Man,* and *Darling.*

Richard Maynard, film editor for *Scholastic Magazine,* has edited a series of books containing screenplays of a number of movies suitable for high school students. The movies are grouped according to themes. *Identity* includes screenplays for *That's Me, The Loneliness of the Long Distance Runner*, *Cool Hand Luke*, and *Up the Down Staircase*; *Men and Women* includes *Splendor in the Grass*, *The Family Man*, and *Nothing But a Man*; *Power* includes *Mr. Smith Goes to Washington, A Face in the Crowd,* and *The Candidate*; *Values in Conflict* includes *High Noon*, *The Hustler*, and *The Savage Innocents*. Each of these films is introduced with a brief note, and a helpful teacher's guide is included in each volume.

Viking Press has brought out a few gems from the MGM collection of film scripts. Each of these is a separate volume, but the format is the same for each: each book opens with credits and cast, then prints the script with indications of the additions and deletions in the final film version. Included in the series are *Adam's Rib,* by Ruth Gordon and Garson Kanin; *A Day at the Races,* by Robert Pirosh, George Seaton, and George Oppenheimer; *A Night at the Opera,* by George S. Kaufman, Morrie Ryskind, and James Kevin McGuinness; *Ninotchka,* by Charles Brackett, Billy Wilder, and Walter T. Reisch; *North by Northwest,* by Ernest Lehman; and *Singin' in the Rain,* by Betty Comden and Adolph Green.

GENERAL BOOKS ON FILMS

Some books are sources for the study of more than one film. Each year the editors of *Film Review Digest*, David M. Brownstone and Irene M. Franck, publish reviews for the most important films released during that year; they do not cover all periodicals reviewing films, but they do excerpt reviews from some twenty-eight periodicals.

Several sources cover films over a long period of time. Stanley Kauffmann has edited *American Film Criticism,* which gives "reviews of significant films at the time they first appeared." He cites one or two reviews of approximately one hundred seventy films from the early films through *Citizen Kane*. Another general source is the *Dictionary of 1,000 Best Films* by R. A. E. Picard. For his selection of films, Picard gives brief plot outlines and credits. Along the same lines is *Favorite Movies,* edited by Philip Nobile. For this book, Nobile asked twenty-seven critics to name their favorite movies and defend their choices. Some name only one; others name several; others explain why they cannot name any. Critics Dwight Macdonald, Peter Bogdanovich, Andrew Sarris, Judith Crist and many others select such films as *2001, Psycho, Casablanca,* and *Rules of the Game.*

A variation in books of this sort is *The Fifty Worst Films of All Time* by Harry Medved, a writer so young he had to be driven to the movie theater while working on this book. Medved's comments on *Airport 1975* will suffice to indicate the tone of his book: "It's a bird! It's a plane! It's an enormous flying turkey—with Charlton Heston (who else)? as an airborne Messiah."

All those movies that have become the favorites of the Academy of Motion

Pictures are honored in *The Oscar Movies* by Roy Picard. Picard covers all the movies that have won Oscars, giving brief mention of each winner.

Included in the category of general books on movies are two on "B" movies, those made on low budgets with tight shooting schedules. While most of these were second-rate films, many young actors got the chance through them to polish their craft, and they filled Saturday afternoon double features for many of us. *"B" Movies: An Informal Survey of the American Low-Budget Film, 1933-45* is by Don Miller. *Kings of the Bs* by Todd McCarthy and Charles Flynn includes invaluable filmographies of 325 American directors. There is a dearth of material on many of these directors, so this book becomes the single source for some. In addition to the filmographies, the authors have included history and criticism.

The Classic Cinema, edited by Stanley J. Solomon, is a collection of essays on some of the most important films of the past, among them *Intolerance, The Gold Rush, Citizen Kane,* and *Vertigo.* Solomon includes casts, credits, and three essays by recognized scholars on each film. Another book on important films of the past is *Ten Film Classics: A Re-Viewing.* In this book, Edward Murray takes a new look at films most film scholars have studied well, among them *Citizen Kane, On the Waterfront,* and *Bonnie and Clyde.* His refreshing new views may stimulate some rethinking among his readers.

BOOKS ON SPECIFIC FILMS

Last, but certainly not least, are the books written on specific films. These books often provide close analysis of an individual film, as well as the history of its production and critical reception.

The Magic Factory is the story by Donald Knox of the MGM production of *An American in Paris.* Knox includes chapters on the people and the studio, on preparation for making the book into a film, and on the ballet. He also provides brief excerpts from reviews.

One of Griffith's early attempts at photographing battle—a process that became central in *Birth of a Nation*—was in a short film entitled *The Battle at Elderbush Gulch.* Kemp R. Niver has written a book which introduces this little-known film. Niver includes reviews, reproductions of the publicity on the film, and a photo-script which reproduces the film shot by shot.

Birth of a Nation itself has received much critical attention. *Focus on Birth of a Nation,* edited by Fred Silva, is an excellent introduction to the film. Silva's book opens with an essay by James Agee on Griffith and then reprints several contemporary reviews of the film and commentary by Lillian Gish. Many of Silva's essays deal with the controversy surrounding the film and the charges of racism levelled against it. Silva also includes essays by Andrew Sarris, Thomas Cripps, and Lewis Jacobs.

Bonnie and Clyde is another film that has received much critical attention.

Focus on Bonnie and Clyde by John G. Cawelti is a collection including introductory essays by Cawelti himself and Jim Hillier and an interview with director Arthur Penn, reviews by Bosley Crowther and Richard Schickel, and other essays by Cawelti, Charles Thomas Samuels, and others. *The Bonnie and Clyde Book* by Sandra Wake and Nicola Hayden contains the screenplay, an essay by Arthur Penn, and criticism by Hollis Alpert, Judith Crist, and others.

Casablanca by Howard Koch, the screenwriter for the movie, contains the script and the story of the production. Criticism of the film is provided by Richard Corliss, Howard Barnes, and Bosley Crowther.

The Citizen Kane Book by Pauline Kael, Herman J. Mankiewicz, and Orson Welles contains an essay entitled "Raising Kane" by Kael, the script by Mankiewicz and Welles, and a shot analysis. *Focus on Citizen Kane* by Ronald Gottesman is another anthology of material on the film. In addition to an interview with Welles and reviews, the book includes essays on the production by Welles, by Bernard Herrmann the composer, and by Gregg Toland the cameraman. Analysis and commentary is given by Andrew Sarris, Arthur Knight, André Bazin, François Truffaut, and others.

Jack Brodsky and Nathan Weiss were responsible for the publicity on *Cleopatra,* and their correspondence on the film, *The Cleopatra Papers,* reveals the fascinating history of the production, including the romance between Richard Burton and Elizabeth Taylor.

Copperfield '70 by George Curry is the story of the making of the latest version of David Copperfield. Curry includes the screenplay and stills as well as technical data.

The Story Behind The Exorcist, by Peter Travers and Stephanie Reiff, contains the story of the production, the cast, and critical reaction to the film. The ritual of the Catholic church in connection with exorcism is given in an appendix.

Filmguide to "The General" by E. Rubenstein is a useful study of the Buster Keaton classic. This book contains an outline of the plot, a sketch of Buster Keaton, the story of the production, analysis and criticism, and factual data about the film and Keaton.

GWTW: The Making of Gone With the Wind by Gavin Lambert tells the story of the production of the film classic, including the monumental problems involved, with an emphasis on the contribution of producer David O. Selznick. It also contains careful criticism of the film by Lambert himself. *Scarlett, Rhett, and a Cast of Thousands* by Roland Flamini is another excellent study of the film with details on the production and information on the stars and directors. However, Flamini's book is not as strong on analysis as is Lambert's *GWTW.*

Filmguide to The Grapes of Wrath by Warren French is an excellent introduction to serious study of the classic film based on John Steinbeck's novel. French includes an essay on John Ford, and analysis and criticism of the film, as well as the story of the production and other factual data. Of special interest is French's comparison of the novel, the screenplay, and the finished film.

The original ten-hour shooting script for *Greed,* Erich von Stroheim's film based on Frank Norris' novel *McTeague,* has been published in a volume entitled *Greed.* It includes an essay by the author/director on "the dreams of realism," critical essays by Joel Finler and Herman Weinberg, essays on the production by those who were there, and two contemporary reviews. *The Complete Greed* is a photo-screenplay reconstructed by Herman G. Weinberg; because *Greed* was drastically cut in its final form, this is an invaluable contribution to the study of this important film. Weinberg is also responsible for *Stroheim,* a photo-reproduction of the most important scenes from Stroheim's nine films. While this book is by no means a complete photo-screenplay, it does show the crucial scenes and gives the cast and synoposis for each film as well.

A Special Kind of Magic consists of a series of interviews by Roy Newquist with the stars of *Guess Who's Coming to Dinner*—Spencer Tracy, Katharine Hepburn, Sidney Poitier, and Katherine Houghton—and with the director Stanley Kramer. Tracy did not interview often or well, so a special value of this book is the record of Tracy's thoughts on what was to be his last film.

The Making of King Kong by Orville Goldner and George E. Turner is the history of the production of the original monster classic. The authors relate this production to the other films by the producer and other films made at that time. *The Girl in the Hairy Paw: King Kong as Myth, Movie, and Monster* is edited by Ronald Gottesman and Harry Geduld and comments on the production itself and the importance of the film. The remake of the movie also has been documented in *The Creation of Dino Laurentis' King Kong* by Bruce Bahremburg.

The Story of the Misfits is the journal kept by James Goode of the last film of both Marilyn Monroe and Clark Gable. Goode includes interviews with Marilyn Monroe and John Huston.

Gerald R. Barrett and Thomas L. Erskine have published three books following the same format which deal with movies made from short stories, *An Occurrence at Owl Creek Bridge, The Rocking Horse Winner,* and *Silent Snow, Secret Snow.* Each book consists of a lengthy introduction on the task of converting fiction into film, the short story itself and criticism of it, and finally, a shot analysis and criticism of the film.

The filming of Orson Welles' *Othello* is the subject of *Put Money in Thy Purse* by Michael MacLiammoir. This diary of the actor who played Iago in Welles' 1952 film contains behind-the-scenes drama and comedy.

Psycho by James Naremore contains an analysis and criticism of the Alfred Hitchcock thriller, as well as an outline of the plot and the story of the production. Naremore's essay on Hitchcock and a Hitchcock filmography complete the book.

In 1954 a film was made about a strike by the workers in a New Mexico zinc mine. *Salt of the Earth* depicts the lives of these workers and their strife with the company, and it has been repressed ever since its production. *Salt of the Earth* by Herbert Biberman is the story of its production and the law suits that resulted and includes the screenplay. Another book by the same title by Michael Wilson and Deborah Silverton Rosenfelt also includes the screenplay, as well as an analysis of the background and significance of the strike and the film.

Paul Sylbert's book *Final Cut* is the story of the production of *The Struggle.* This film was a fiasco but the book contains interesting information on film production itself.

The Trial is a book by Orson Welles on his movie based on Franz Kafka's novel of the same title. The book contains a translation of the French script of the film as well as an interview with Welles.

Jerome Agel has edited a book called *The Making of Kubrick's 2001* which contains interviews, recreations of scenes cut from the movie, the history of the production, and other material. *Filmguide to "2001: A Space Odyssey"* by Carolyn Geduld focuses on analysis and criticism of the film and also contains an outline of the plot, an essay on Kubrick, and a Kubrick filmography.

The Wedding March was to be another of Stroheim's film extravaganzas the film and it was edited by another director; the two films that resulted were not to Stroheim's liking. Herman G. Weinberg has put together a book which attempts to recreate the film as Stroheim intended it in *The Complete Wedding March of Eric von Stroheim*, a reconstruction of the film in photographs.

The Making of the Wizard of Oz is Aljean Harmetz's story of the production of the film classic. Harmetz includes information on the studio, the script, the music, the casting, the directors, the stars, the Munchkins, the costumes, the special effects, and even the auction of the magical red shoes.

BIBLIOGRAPHY

Agel, Jerome, ed. *The Making of Kubrick's 2001.* New York: New American Library, 1968.

Anobile, Richard J., ed. *Alfred Hitchcock's Psycho.* New York: Macmillan, 1974.

______, ed. *Casablanca.* New York: Macmillan, 1974.

______, ed. *Ernst Lubitsch's Ninotchka.* New York: Universe Books, 1975.

______, ed. *Frankenstein.* New York: Universe Books, 1974.

______, ed. *The General.* New York: Universe Books, 1975.

______, ed. *John Ford's Stagecoach.* New York: Universe Books, 1975.

______, ed. *The Maltese Falcon.* New York: Macmillan, 1974.

______, ed. *Rouben Mamoulian's Dr. Jekyll and Mr. Hyde.* New York: Universe Books, 1975.

______, *Woody Allen's Play It Again, Sam.* New York: Grosset and Dunlap, 1972.

Bahremburg, Bruce. *The Creation of Dino de Laurentis' King Kong.* New York: Pocket Books, 1976.

Barrett, Jerald R., and Thomas L. Erskine, eds. *From Fiction to Film: Ambrose Bierce's An Occurrence at Owl Creek Bridge.* Encino, Calif.: Dickenson, 1973.

______, eds. *From Fiction to Film: Conrad Aiken's Silent Snow, Secret Snow.* Encino, Calif.: Dickenson, 1972.

______. eds. *From Fiction to Film: D. H. Lawrence's The Rocking Horse Winner.* Encino, Calif.: Dickenson, 1974.

Biberman, Herbert. *Salt of the Earth: The Story of a Film.* Boston: Beacon, 1965.

Brackett, Charles, Billy Wilder, and Walter Reisch. *Ninotchka.* New York: Viking, 1966.

Brodsky, Jack, and Nathan Weiss. *The Cleopatra Papers: A Private Correspondence.* New York: Simon and Schuster, 1963.

Brownstone, David M., and Irene M. Franck. *Film Review Digest Annual, 1976.* Millwood, N.Y.: KTO Press, 1976.

Cawelti, John G. *Focus on Bonnie and Clyde.* Englewood Cliffs, N.J.: Prentice-Hall, 1973.

Chandler, Raymond. *The Blue Dahlia.* Carbondale: Southern Illinois University Press, 1976.

Comden, Betty, and Adolph Green. *Singin' in the Rain.* New York: Viking, 1972.

Curry, George. *Copperfield '70: The Story of the Making of the Omnibus 20th Century Fox Film of Charles Dickens' David Copperfield.* New York: Ballantine Books, 1970.

Fadimon, Regina K. *Faulkner's Intruder in the Dust.* Knoxville: University of Tennessee Press, 1978.

Flamini, Roland. *Scarlett, Rhett, and a Cast of Thousands: The Filming of Gone With the Wind.* New York: Macmillan, 1975.

French, Warren. *Filmguide to The Grapes of Wrath.* Bloomington: Indiana University Press, 1973.

Furthman, Jules. *Morocco and Shanghai Express.* New York: Simon and Schuster, 1973.

Garrett, George P., O. B. Hardison, Jr., and Jane R. Gelfman, eds. *Film Scripts Four.* New York: Appleton:Century-Crofts, 1972.

______. *Film Scripts One.* New York: Appleton-Century-Crofts, 1971.

______. *Film Scripts Three.* New York: Appleton-Century-Crofts, 1972.

______. *Film Scripts Two.* New York: Appleton-Century-Crofts, 1971.

Gassner, John and Dudley Nichols, eds. *Best Film Plays—1945.* New York: Crown, 1946.

______, eds. *Twenty Best Film Plays.* New York: Crown, 1943.

Geduld, Carolyn. *Filmguide to 2001: A Space Odyssey.* Bloomington: Indiana University Press, 1973.

Goldner, Orville and George E. Turner. *The Making of King Kong.* New York: A. S. Barnes, 1975.

Goode, James. *The Story of the Misfits.* Indianapolis: Bobbs-Merrill, 1963.

Gordon, Ruth and Garson Kanin. *Adam's Rib,* New York: Viking, 1949.
Gottesman, Ronald, ed. *Focus on Citizen Kane*. Englewood Cliffs, N.J.: Prentice-Hall, 1971.
______ and Harry Geduld, eds. *The Girl in the Hairy Paw: King Kong as Movie, Myth, and Monster.* New York: Avon, 1976.
Harmetz, Aljean. *The Making of the Wizard of Oz.* New York: Knopf, 1977.
Kael, Pauline, Herman J. Mankiewicz, and Orson Welles. *The Citizen Kane Book.* Boston: Little, Brown, 1971.
Kaufman, George S., Morrie Ryskind, and James Kevin McGuinness. *A Night at the Opera*. New York: Viking, 1962.
Kauffmann, Stanley, ed. *American Film Criticism: From the Beginnings to Citizen Kane; Reviews of Significant Films at the Time They First Appeared.* New York: Liveright, 1972.
Knox, Donald. *The Magic Factory: How MGM Made An American in Paris.* New York: Praeger, 1973.
Koch, Howard, ed. *Casablanca.* Woodstock, N.Y.: The Overlook Press, 1973.
Lambert, Gavin. *GWTW: The Making of Gone With the Wind*. Boston: Little, Brown, 1973.
Lathrop, William Addison. *Little Stories from the Screen.* New York: Garland, 1978.
Lehman, Ernest. *North By Northwest.* New York: Viking, 1959.
Loos, Anita. *San Francisco.* Carbondale: Southern Illinois University Press, 1979.
McCarthy, Todd and Charles Flynn. *Kings of the Bs: Working within the Hollywood System: An Anthology of Film History and Criticism*. New York: E. P. Dutton, 1975.
McCarty, Clifford. *Published Screenplays: A Checklist*. Kent, Ohio: The Kent State University Press, 1971.
MacLiammoir, Michael. *Put Money in Thy Purse: The Diary of the Film of Othello.* London: Eyre Methuen, 1952.
Mankiewicz, Joseph L. *More About All About Eve.* New York: Random House, 1972.
Marx Brothers. *Monkey Business and Duck Soup*. New York: Simon and Schuster, 1972.
Maynard, Richard A., ed. *Values in Conflict*. New York: Scholastic Book Services, 1974.
______, ed. *Identity.* New York: Scholastic Book Services, 1974.
______, ed. *Men and Women.* New York: Scholastic Book Services, 1974.
______, ed. *Power.* New York: Scholastic Book Services, 1974.
Medved, Harry. *The Fifty Worst Films of All Time.* New York: Popular Library, 1978.
Miller, Don. *"B" Movies: An Informal Survey of the American Low-Budget Film, 1933-1945*. New York: Curtis, 1973.
Murray, Edward. *Ten Film Classics: A Re-Viewing.* New York: Frederick Ungar, 1978.
Naremore, James. *Psycho.* Bloomington: Indiana University Press, 1973.
Newquist, Roy. *A Special Kind of Magic.* New York: Rand McNally, 1967.
Niver, Kemp R. *D. W. Griffith's The Battle at Elderbush Gulch.* Los Angeles: Locare Research Group, 1972.
Nobile, Philip, ed. *Favorite Movies: Critics' Choice.* New York: Macmillan, 1973.

Pirosh, Robert, George Seaton, and George Oppenheimer. *A Day at the Races.* New York: Viking, 1964.
Picard, R. A. E. *Dictionary of 1,000 Best Films.* New York: Association Press, 1971.
Pickard, Roy. *The Oscar Movies.* New York: Taplinger, 1978.
Poteet, Howard G. *Published Radio, Television, and Film Scripts: A Bibliography.* Troy, N.Y.: The Whitston Publishing Co., 1975.
Rubenstein, E. *Filmguide to The General.* Bloomington: Indiana University Press, 1973.
Silva, Fred. *Focus on Birth of a Nation.* Englewood Cliffs, N.J.: Prentice-Hall, 1971.
Solomon, Stanley J., ed. *The Classic Cinema: Essays in Criticism.* New York: Harcourt Brace Jovanovich, 1973.
Steinbeck, John. *Viva Zapata!: The Original Screenplay.* New York: Viking, 1975.
Von Stroheim, Erich. *Greed.* New York: Simon and Schuster, 1972.
Sylbert, Paul. *Final Cut: The Making and Breaking of a Film.* New York: Seabury Press, 1969.
Tewkesburg, Joan. *Nashville.* New York: Bantam, 1976.
Travers, Peter, and Stephanie Reiff. *The Story Behind The Exorcist.* New York: Crown, 1974.
Wake, Sandra and Nicola Hayden. *The Bonnie and Clyde Book.* New York: Simon and Schuster, 1972.
Wald, Jerry and Richard Macauley, eds. *The Best Pictures—1939-1940.* New York: Dodd, Mead, 1940.
Welles, Orson. *The Trial.* New York: Simon and Schuster, 1970.
Weinberg, Herman G. *The Complete Greed of Erich von Stroheim.* New York: Arno, 1972.
______. *The Complete Wedding March of Erich von Stroheim.* Boston: Little, Brown, 1974.
______. *Stroheim: A Pictorial Record of His Nine Films.* New York: Dover, 1975.
Wilson, Michael and Deborah Silverton Rosenfelt. *Salt of the Earth.* Old Westbury, N.Y.: The Feminist Press, 1978.

CHAPTER 10

International Influence on American Film

While the film industry got its start in America and Hollywood's productions have been the standard by which other national film industries have been measured, American films have been tremendously enriched by international influences. Because of the money, other resources, and artistic freedom offered in this country, there has been an influx of European talent to America. As the previous chapters have shown, many important Hollywood actors and directors were Europeans who immigrated to this country.

Moreover, the international contribution has not been limited to this alone. Many of the films made abroad were recognized for their innovating techniques, and American filmmakers learned much from them. It is beyond the scope of books in this series to deal with the popular culture in countries other than the United States; indeed, the research materials on foreign films would swell this book beyond manageable size and deserve to be studied in their own right. However, since no study of American films would be complete without understanding the international influences upon them, this chapter is devoted to books on foreign films and will simply suggest to the reader a few places to begin a study of foreign films. The focus is on books that present an overview of the film industry abroad rather than on specific filmmakers.

INTERNATIONAL OVERVIEWS

A good starting point is a general history of international films. *The History of World Cinema* by David Robinson provides such an overview. Robinson's book is useful but so broad in scope that it has little depth, detail, or analysis. Robinson does, however, include some selected filmographies.

Peter Cowie has been a leading historian of the international cinema, and his books have contributed to an understanding of the international film scene. His *World Filmography, 1968* was the first of a series that evolved into *International Filmguide,* an annual volume that documents the film activity for the past year. Cowie honors and profiles directors of each year and discusses his choices for the outstanding films of the year. He lists filmographies and awards, and surveys international activity by country. This wealth of information makes *International Filmguide* one of the most useful reference books available.

The International Film Industry by Thomas H. Guback discusses the relationship between the American film industry and the European. Guback is especially interested in the reception to American films in Europe and vice-versa. He also highlights American investment in European productions.

Books on European directors deserve mention here. *Three European Directors* by James M. Wall contains essays on François Truffaut, Federico Fellini, and Luis Buñuel. *Six European Directors* by Peter Harcourt contains "essays on the meaning of film style" in the work of Sergei Eisenstein, Jean Renoir, Ingmar Bergman, Jean-Luc Godard, Luis Buñuel, and Federico Fellini. *Cinema Eye, Cinema Ear* by John Russell Taylor is the history of the men who shaped the art form in the 1960s, the *auteurs* of a complex medium. His key European filmmakers are Fellini, Buñuel, Bergman, Truffaut, Godard, Michelangelo Antonioni, Alfred Hitchcock, Alain Resnais, and Robert Bresson. *The Ambiguous Image* is Roy Armes' study of "narrative style in modern European cinema"; in this regard, he cites the work of Buñuel, Antonioni, Bergman, Jacques Tati, and others.

SPECIFIC NATIONAL FILM INDUSTRIES

One need not go far to find influential foreign film industries. Both Canada and Mexico have distinguished themselves in recent years with their movies.

Supported by the National Film Board of Canada, the Canadian industry has been especially rich. A good introduction to the industry is *Canadian Film Reader,* an anthology edited by Seth Feldman and Joyce Nelson. This solid resource begins with essays on the National Film Board, and discusses the production of feature films, experimental films, and new directions in film. A readable history of Canadian film from 1895 to 1939, the year the National Film Board was established, is *Embattled Shadows* by Peter Morris. Morris has interviewed the early filmmakers still alive and viewed the films of the period in order to assemble a comprehensive history of the early days of Canadian cinema. He places the films into their historical, social, and artistic contexts. *Inner Views* by John Hofsess presents in-depth analysis of the work of ten Canadian filmmakers. In *A Handbook of Canadian Film,* Eleanor Beattie has written a fact book on Canadian film. Beattie includes information on filmmakers, actors, music, film study in Canada, free films, and children's films. A book associated with the journal *Take One* is *Marshall Delaney and the Movies.* Marshall Delaney is the pen name of

Robert Fulford, a major Canadian film reviewer, and this book is a collection of his reviews, with the addition of two essays on Canadian film and Hollywood. Pierre Berton's *Hollywood's Canada* is a study of "the Americanization of our national image" in which Berton examines what Hollywood has done to the image of his country and does not like what he sees.

The impact of the film industries on South America is the subject of *Latin American Cinema: Film and History,* edited by E. Bradford Burns. In this study of film in Latin America Burns has included essays on the relationship between film and history in Latin America. Burns is a historian who has used film to study Latin American customs and history. *The Mexican Cinema* by Beatriz Reyes Nevares is a collection of interviews with thirteen Mexican directors. Nevares' book opens with an introduction by Burns that gives an overview of the Mexican film industry.

No country has devoted more energy to its film industry than Britain. The early history of silent film in Britain is told by Rachel Low in *The History of the British Film,* a multi-volume set based on work done at the British Film Institute. Low's scholarly book treats British silent film in depth and is an important work on the industry in early days. A full history of filmmaking in Britain is *The Film Business* by Ernest Betts. In his history of British cinema from 1896 to 1972, Betts provides a brief coverage of the early days and a more complete coverage of the 1930s, with an emphasis on Alfred Hitchcock, Anthony Asquith, Victor Saville, and Herbert Wilcox. He then discusses the war years, the documentary, and John Grierson, the decline of British films during the early days of television, and finally, the new directors of the 1970s, such as Lindsay Anderson and Tony Richardson. *The Great British Picture Show* by George Perry covers the British industry from the 1890s to the 1970s with emphasis on the documentary, World War II, and the hope for the future after World War II. *Hollywood UK* by Alexander Walker is "an attempt to illustrate the diversity of talents and motives, economic changes, historical accidents and occasional artistic achievement making up what is called the British film industry during a brief, turbulent part of its existence—the sixties." Roger Manvell's *New Cinema in Britain* deals with British films since World War II in a popular book emphasizing the experimental features produced in Britain. *A Mirror for England* by Raymond Durgnat is a "survey of some major recurring themes in British movies between 1945 . . . and 1958"—among them English history in films, the age of acquiescence, and romantics and moralists. *British Cinema* by Denis Gifford is an alphabetical guide to British cinema with brief entries on hundreds of British films and filmmakers. Ivan Butler's *Cinema in Britain: An Illustrated Survey* is a year by year survey of the best of British movies, again with brief entries. Butler emphasizes the importance of the British contribution to early filmmaking.

The Swedish film industry has long been active, and its superstar, Ingmar

Bergman, is internationally known. *Sweden 1* by Peter Cowie is an alphabetical list of Swedish films and filmmakers, with brief comments on each. *Sweden 2* contains essays on the great Swedish directors: Victor Sjostrom, Mauritz Stiller, Bergman, and others, including some directors not yet well known in the United States. *Film in Sweden: The New Directors,* written by Stig Björkman in conjunction with the Swedish Film Institute, discusses Bo Widerberg, Vilgot Sjoman, Mai Zetterling, and other new directors.

Finnish films are less known in the United States than Swedish films, but Peter Cowie's *Finnish Cinema* is a fine introduction to them. Cowie presents a history and survey of movies in Finland, including chapters on Nyrki Tapiovaara, films of World War I and World War II, the pastoral tradition in Finnish cinema, the signs of change, and the new directors.

Germany has been important in international cinema since the 1910s. *The German Cinema* by Roger Manvell and Heinrich Fraenkel is a chronological history of film in Germany through the 1960s and modern Germany. *Germany* by Felix Bucher is an alphabetical listing of stars, directors, and others in German filmmaking, with brief entries on each person.

One of the outstanding books in film criticism is Siegfried Kracauer's *From Caligari to Hitler.* Kracauer theorizes that German films from the silent period into the early 1930s reflected the climate that allowed for the Nazi takeover and now help explain this mental climate. Whether readers agree with Kracauer or not, his thesis is a challenging one. *The Weimar Chronicle: Prelude to Hitler* is a general study of the same period covered by Kracauer; this excellent book by Alex de Jonge is an analysis of the German culture between the wars and includes a chapter on film, theatre, and the cabaret.

Three books deal with German filmmaking from 1933 on. *Film in the Third Reich* by David Stewart Hull is a year by year study of German films from 1933 to 1945, with an emphasis on propaganda and the influence of Joseph Goebbels. Hull's book underscores the power of the movies. *Nazi Cinema* by Erwin Leiser is a study of Goebbels' use of film as a propaganda tool to reinforce the value of dying for the fatherland. Leiser includes histories and analyses of *Triumph of the Will, Olympia, I Accuse,* and *Jud Suss.* A related book is *Swastika* by Baxter Philips, a study of the "cinema of oppression." Using many photographs and sparse commentary, Philips has covered the cinema of Lenin and Stalin, Mussolini, Hitler, Franco, and Hirohito.

The French film industry is another that has been active in its own right and influential on the American industry. An overview of the French industry is given by Marcel Martin in *France,* an alphabetical listing of French directors, actors, and films. France's most important films have been made since World War II and there are several books that document the modern period. *French Cinema Since 1946* by Roy Armes is a two-volume study of French filmmaking; volume one deals with the great tradition of French films and volume two with the personal styles of the various directors. *The New Wave* by Peter Graham discusses the important directors in French filmmaking since World War II, directors who have had a profound influence on international filmmaking. Graham presents essays by Alexander Astrus, André Bazin, Claude Chabrol, and Jean-Luc Godard; he also includes an interview with François Truffaut and essays on film theory. Another book by the same title by James Monaco presents close analytical study of the films of Truffaut, Godard, Chabrol, Eric Rohmer, and Jacques Rivette.

The history of the Italian cinema through World War II is told in Vernon Jarratt's *The Italian Cinema*. A more recent general history is Pierre Leprohon's book by the same title. Leprohon covers Italian movies from 1895 to the late 1960s and discusses films under the Fascists, Neo-realism, and other subjects.

Film has been an important medium behind the Iron Curtain since the Russian Revolution. *Eastern Europe* by Nina Hibbin is an illustrated guide to the postwar cinema of directors, actors, and technicians in Albania, Bulgaria, Czechoslovakia, East Germany, Hungary, Poland, Romania, Russia, and Yugoslavia. *The Most Important Art* by Mira and Antonín Liehm is a historical overview of "Eastern film after 1945" in the countries covered in Hibbin's book.

The importance of Russian film has been documented in *Kino: A History of the Russian and Soviet Film* by Jay Leyda. Leyda begins with the rudimentary beginnings of the industry before the Revolution and then presents detailed analysis of the period from the Revoution through the mid-1950s. This is a scholarly and important book. *The Motion Picture in the Soviet Union: 1918-1952: A Sociological Analysis* is a reprint of John David Rimberg's dissertation. Rimberg begins with a review of the various studies of Russian film and goes on to discuss the political definitions and functions of that film. Central to the book is a discussion of the content of the films and the role of censorship in Russian film. Another dissertation is *The Cultural-Political Traditions and Developments of the Soviet Cinema, 1917-1972* by Louis Harris Cohen; this book also surveys the literature on the subject and then the Russian film industry itself, with an analysis of its administration and economy. *Soviet Cinema* by Alexander S. Birkos is a reference book on Russian film which lists and briefly discusses directors, films, and studios.

A book devoted to the history of Hungarian films from 1896 through the 1970s is *Word and Image* by Istvan Nemeskürty. In addition to the history, Nemeskürty includes stills and a filmography.

Closely Watched Films: The Czechoslovak Experience is by Antonin Liehm, who includes chapters on thirty-two Czech filmmakers. Czechoslovak films have been well received in the United States, and this record of their production is especially interesting.

Georges Sadoul has edited a volume on *The Cinema in the Arab Countries.*

His collection covers Arab culture and cinema, the history of Arab films, a geography of Arab cinema, and a survey of problems and recommendations for the future.

Indian Film by Eric Barnouw and S. Kirshnaswamy covers fifty years of Indian films beginning with the colonial period. The authors discuss the development and dissolution of the studio system, and the rise of Indian films to international fame under the leadership of Satyajit Ray. *75 Years of Indian Cinema* by Firoze Rangoonwalla is a historical survey of Indian cinema from 1895; Rangoonwalla covers that history through 1975. Kobita Sarkar has written a comprehensive survey of modern Indian cinema in *Indian Cinema Today.* Sarkar covers the historical background, directors, the star system, censorship, violence and humor, sex and romance, song and dance, and the experimental film.

The Japanese have developed an internationally important film industry. In *The Japanese Film: Art and Industry,* Joseph L. Anderson and Donald Richie follow the usual format of a national film industry history, but they also include essays on different aspects of Japanese films: their content, technique, directors, audience, and actors. Richie's own book, *Japanese Cinema,* discusses the relationship between film and other arts in Japan. *Japan* by Arne Svensson gives a brief alphabetical overview of directors, actors, and films. Joan Mellen has written two more books on the Japanese cinema. *The Waves at Genji's Door* presents "Japan through its cinema" and is designed to make Japanese films familiar and accessible to American audiences. Her arrangement is thematic: for example, women in Japanese films, the family in the cinema, and World War II. In *Voices from the Japanese Cinema,* Mellen interviews directors and actors to recreate the insider's view of the Japanese cinema.

The Talkies Era: A Pictorial History of Australian Sound Film Making, 1930-1960 by Eric Reade is a brief study of the small but flourishing film industry in Australia. Unfortunately, the most important Australian films have been made since 1960 and are not included in this volume.

Finally, Jay Leyda has recorded the history of film in China in *Dianying: Electric Shadows, An Account of Films and the Film Audience in China.* Leyda begins in 1896 and continues through the late 1960s.

BIBLIOGRAPHY

Anderson, Joseph L., and Donald Richie. *The Japanese Film: Art and Industry.* New York: Grove, 1960.

Armes, Roy. *The Ambiguous Image.* London: Secker and Warburg, 1976.

______. *French Cinema Since 1946.* 2 vols. New York: A. S. Barnes, 1970.

Barnouw, Eric and S. Krishnaswamy. *Indian Film.* New York: Columbia University Press, 1963.

Beattie, Eleanor. *A Handbook of Canadian Film.* Toronto: Peter Martin Association, 1973.

Berton, Pierre. *Hollywood's Canada.* Toronto: McClelland and Stewart, 1975.
Betts, Ernest. *The Film Business: A History of British Cinema, 1896-1972.* London: George Allen and Unwin, 1973.
Birkos, Alexander S. *Soviet Cinema.* Hamden, Conn.: Archon, 1976.
Björkman, Stig. *Film in Sweden: The New Directors.* New York: A. S. Barnes, 1977.
Bucher, Felix. *Germany.* New York: A. S. Barnes, 1970.
Burns, E. Bradford, ed. *Latin American Cinema: Film and History.* Los Angeles: University of California Press, 1975.
Butler, Ivan. *Cinema in Britain: An Illustrated Survey.* London: Tantivy, 1973.
Cohen, Louis Harris. *The Cultural-Political Traditions and Developments of the Soviet Cinema, 1917-1972.* New York: Arno, 1974.
Cowie, Peter. *Finnish Cinema.* New York: A. S. Barnes, 1976.
______, ed. *International Filmguide, 1978.* New York: A. S. Barnes, 1977.
______. *Sweden 1.* New York: A. S. Barnes, 1970.
______. *Sweden 2.* New York: A. S. Barnes, 1970.
______. *World Filmography, 1968.* New York: A. S. Barnes, 1977.
Durgnat, Raymond. *A Mirror for England: British Movies From Austerity to Affluence.* London: Faber and Faber, 1970.
Feldman, Seth and Joyce Nelson, eds. *Canadian Film Reader.* Toronto: Peter Martin, 1977.
Fulford, Robert. *Marshall Delaney and The Movies: The Contemporary World as Seen on Film.* Toronto: Peter Martin, 1974.
Gifford, Denis. *British Cinema: An Illustrated Guide.* New York: A. S. Barnes, 1968.
Graham, Peter. *The New Wave: Critical Landmarks.* Garden City, N.Y.: Doubleday, 1968.
Guback, Thomas H. *The International Film Industry: Western Europe and America Since 1945.* Bloomington: Indiana University Press, 1969.
Harcourt, Peter. *Six European Directors. Essays on the Meaning of Film Style.* Baltimore: Penguin, 1974.
Hibbin, Nina. *Eastern Europe: An Illustrated Guide.* New York: A. S. Barnes, 1969.
Hofsess, John. *Inner Views: Ten Canadian Film-Makers.* New York: McGraw-Hill, 1975.
Hull, David Stewart. *Film in the Third Reich: A Study of the German Cinema from 1933-1945.* Berkeley: University of California Press, 1969.
Jarratt, Vernon. *The Italian Cinema.* London: The Falcon Press, 1951.
de Jonge, Alex. *The Weimar Chronicle: Prelude to Hitler.* New York: New American Library, 1978.
Kracauer, Siegfried. *From Caligari to Hitler: A Psychological History of the German Film.* Princeton: Princeton University Press, 1947.
Leiser, Erwin. *Nazi Cinema.* Translated by Gertrude Mander and David Wilson. New York: Macmillan, 1974.
Leprohon, Pierre. *The Italian Cinema.* Translated by Roger Greaves and Oliver Stallybrass. New York: Praeger, 1972.
Leyda, Jay. *Dianying: Electric Shadows, An Account of Films and the Film Audience in China.* Cambridge: MIT Press, 1972.
______. *Kino: A History of the Russian and Soviet Film.* New York: Macmillan, 1960.

Liehm, Antonín J. *Closely Watched Films: The Czechoslovak Experience.* White Plains, N.Y.: International Arts and Sciences Press, 1974.

Liehm, Mira and Antonín J. Liehm. *The Most Important Art.* Berkeley: University of California Press, 1977.

Low, Rachael. *The History of the British Film, 1906-1914.* New York: R. R. Bowker, 1973.

Manvell, Roger. *New Cinema in Britain.* London: Studio Vista/Dutton Picturebook, 1969.

______ and Heinrich Fraenkel. *The German Cinema.* New York: Praeger, 1971.

Martin, Marcel. *France.* New York: A. S. Barnes, 1971.

Mellen, Joan. *Voices from the Japanese Cinema.* New York: Liveright, 1975.

______. *The Waves at Genji's Door.* New York: Pantheon, 1976.

Monaco, James. *The New Wave.* New York: Oxford University Press, 1976.

Morris, Peter. *Embattled Shadows.* Montreal: McGill-Queen's University Press, 1978.

Nemeskürty, Istvan. *Word and Image: History of the Hungarian Cinema.* Translated by Z. Horn and F. Macnid. Budapest: Corvina, 1974.

Nevares, Beatriz Reyes. *The Mexican Cinema.* Albuquerque: University of New Mexico Press, 1976.

Perry, George. *The Great British Picture Show from the Nineties to the Seventies.* New York: Hill and Wang, 1974.

Philips, Baxter. *Swastika.* New York: Warner Books, 1976.

Rangoonwalla, Firoze. *75 Years of Indian Cinema.* New Delhi: Indian Book Company, 1975.

Reade, Eric. *The Talkies Era: A Pictorial History of Australian Sound Film Making, 1930-1960.* Melbourne, Australia: Lensdowne, 1972.

Richie, Donald. *Japanese Cinema: Film Style and National Character.* Garden City, N.Y.: Doubleday, 1971.

Rimberg, John David. *The Motion Picture in the Soviet Union: 1918-1952: A Sociological Analysis.* New York: Arno, 1973.

Robinson, David. *The History of World Cinema.* New York: Stein and Day, 1973.

Sadoul, Georges, ed. *The Cinema in the Arab Countries.* Beirut: Interarab Centre of Cinema and Television, 1966.

Sarkar, Kobita. *Indian Cinema Today: An Analysis.* New Delhi: Sterling, 1975.

Svensson, Arne. *Japan.* New York: A. S. Barnes, 1971.

Taylor, John Russell. *Cinema Eye, Cinema Ear: Some Key Film-Makers of the Sixties.* New York: Hill and Wang, 1964.

Walker, Alexander. *Hollywood UK: The British Film Industry in the Sixties.* New York: Stein and Day, 1974.

Wall, James M., ed. *Three European Directors.* Grand Rapids, Mich.: William B. Eerdmans Publishing Company, 1973.

CHAPTER II

Reference Works and Periodicals

Reference books that clearly apply to specific subjects covered elsewhere in this book have been discussed in their appropriate sections, but reference works which are more general in focus are discussed in this chapter. For convenience, they will be divided into four units: general references, bibliographic references, reference books on films, and reference books for and about screen personalities. The last part of this chapter will discuss film periodicals.

GENERAL REFERENCES

Reel Facts by Cobbett Steinberg contains a fascinating array of information about the movies. Steinberg lists the winners of all the important awards, several "ten best" lists, top moneymakers, top box office stars and their earnings, profits of the studios, the film festivals, and rules and regulations of the codes.

Guidebook to Film by Ronald Gottesman and Harry M. Geduld is also a useful grab bag of facts about film. The authors list film schools, museums and archives, books, journals, awards, and so on. This sort of book dates almost as fast as a bibliography of film books, but it is an important work.

The *International Motion Picture Almanac, 1977* is part of an annual series of useful information about the films of the previous year. The editor, Richard Gertner, includes brief biographies of people active in the business, credits for the feature films released during the year, and an index for technical data on the films.

Elsevier's Dictionary of Cinema, Sound, and Music by W. E. Clason is a useful tool for scholars of international film. Clason cites the technical terms relating to film, gives a brief definition, and then translates it into French, Spanish, Italian, Dutch, and German.

Roger Manvell's *The International Encyclopedia of Film* discusses major films, stars, and movements in a reference intended for the popular audience.

His entries are rather brief but his coverage is extensive. Most important films, their stars, and directors are covered at some point.

The Focal Encyclopedia of Film and Television Techniques is a more scholarly guide to technical information about film production and will be most useful to the serious filmmaker.

The Oxford Companion to Film by Liz-Anne Bawden is a useful resource for both the popular audience and the scholar. Its brief entries on film personalities, films, and movements provide comprehensive information in its most affordable form. Although it contains some errors, Bowden's book is a convenient reference tool.

The Filmgoer's Companion by Leslie Halliwell is now in its sixth edition. Halliwell concentrates on the films and the stars, but his catalogue covers a wide range of subjects.

A Companion to the Movies by Roy Pickard is another reference geared to a popular audience. Pickard's lists are of some value, even though they are limited and selective. He covers comedy, fantasy, thrillers, Westerns, musicals, romance, epics, war films, swashbucklers, adventure films, novels made into films, and plays made into films. For each genre he comments on the important films and gives a who's who.

BIBLIOGRAPHIC WORKS

One of the most frustrating aspects of film research is trying to find bibliographical materials. The problem was first addressed in 1916 with the publication by S. Gershank of the first movie bibliography, *Motography*. This list of books in various languages is surprisingly long for so early a date and contains some excellent film criticism. A study of it reveals the early reception to motion pictures and the early attempts to understand their aesthetics. It has been reprinted as part of *Aspects of American Film History Prior to 1920* by Anthony Slide.

More recent film books and periodicals abound, but locating them and knowing which one has the needed article or chapter is difficult. Fortunately, a number of bibliographic references direct the reader to both articles and books.

To locate recent articles on films, two places to begin are *The Reader's Guide to Periodical Literature* and the *Humanities Index*. Both periodicals list articles on specific films annually (monthly in supplements) and are especially useful in locating reviews of recent films. For the most part these bibliographies cover only general magazines, rather than the film journals. Reviews are usually listed under "moving pictures."

The first important general guide to articles on film used to be *The Film Index* by Harold Leonard. This work is now considered the standard source for articles appearing before 1940. Recently Richard Dyer McCann and Edward S. Perry have edited a volume which complements Leonard's book.

The New Film Index covers the period from the late 1930s until the early 1970s. While the reader might have to spend some time searching for his information under several possible categories, he will usually be rewarded.

Linda Batty has also written a guide to articles from the same period. *Retrospective Index to Film Periodicals, 1930-1971* is especially useful as an index to articles on particular films. Batty's lists are not complete and contain no annotations, but she does cover reviews of individual films, film subjects, and reviews of major film books.

The Critical Index by John and Lana Gerlach is a "bibliography of articles on film in English, 1946-1973." The authors have included articles on a wide range of subjects (from acting to American Indians) and include brief annotations, but their lists are by no means complete.

The *Index to Critical Film Reviews in British and American Film Periodicals* is a useful guide in three volumes but is not as complete as its title suggests. Nonetheless, Stephen E. Bowles' book indexes thirty-one periodicals, more than most indexes attempt to cover.

Mel Schuster has published two bibliographies. *Motion Picture Directors: A Bibliography of Magazine and Periodical Articles, 1900-1972* lists articles on directors' lives and artistic contributions. The book contains a wide range of articles without annotatons. *Motion Picture Performers: A Bibliography of Magazine and Periodical Articles, 1900-1969* catalogues articles from such diverse magazines and journals as *The Saturday Evening Post, The Atlantic, Film Fan Monthly,* and *Film Quarterly.*

The Literature of the Film: A Bibliographical Guide to Film as Art and Entertainment, 1936-1970 by Alan R. Dyment includes chapters on film history, aesthetics and criticism, personalities, screenplays and film studios, technique, genre, film and society, and the film industry.

Two major annual indexes to periodical articles are now being published. Vincent Aceto, Jane Graves, and Fred Silva have begun an annual bibliography, *Film Literature Index,* which covers 126 film journals in full and another 150 general journals selectively. Unfortunately, there is no annotation of the entries. Karen Jones is the general editor of the *International Index to Film Periodicals,* which covers fewer journals than the *Film Literature Index* but does include helpful brief annotations and a few journals not indexed by the latter. The researcher would do well to consult both indexes.

Several books are devoted to surveying other film books, as is this volume. The other books are basically annotated lists of film books, with little comparison, grouping or judgments; but they are important tools in film research. Peter J. Bukalski's *Film Research: A Critical Bibliography* is basically a selected bibliography, but Bukalski also discusses the concept and practice of film research, annotates the essential books and periodicals, and covers film rentals and purchase. A recent addition to bibliographies of film books is *The Film Book Bibliography, 1940-1975,* by Jack C. Ellis, Charles Derry, and Sharon Kern. This fine book lists over five thousand film books in a wide range of categories, including reference, technique, history, biography, individual films, and education. Most of the entries are not annotated, but the size of the bibliography makes this an important book.

Cinema Booklist by George Rehrauer is an annotated bibliography which lists books in alphabetical order. This order means that the books are not grouped as logically as those in some of the other bibliographies, but the excellent index helps overcome this problem. The *Chicorel Index to Film Literature,* edited by Marietta Chicorel, contains extensive categories or groups of books, but no index and no annotations. Sometimes titles are listed under questionable groupings, but a large number of books are covered.

REFERENCE BOOKS ON FILMS

Many of the films made in America have been lost, but the researcher can obtain some idea of what has been made by studying the copyright records. The Library of Congress has published its *Catalogue of Copyright Entries: Motion Pictures,* now in four volumes. This book gives the dates, length, and producers for the films that have received copyrights, including features, shorts, and television commercials. This work is complemented by Howard Lamarr Walls' *Motion Pictures, 1894-1912*. Walls has identified these early films from the records at the Copyright Office. During these years, movies were copyrighted by depositing paper prints of the films with the Library of Congress. While paper prints are fragile, they are far more stable than the nitrate films from which they were taken. Kemp R. Niver has studied these films in another reference on that period, *Motion Pictures from the Library of Congress Paper Print Collection, 1894-1912,* a basic catalogue for the films held in this valuable collection.

The American Film Institute has begun a series that should become a standard reference book for all films made in this country. Each volume will cover a decade and provide the release date, credits, casts, and plot summary for each movie made. Eventually the series will include volumes on short films and newsreels, as well as on features. The first volume is *The American Film Institute Catalogue of Motion Pictures Produced in the United States, Feature Films, 1921-1930,* edited by Kenneth W. Munden. The volume for the 1960s, edited by Richard Krafsur, is also out now.

Another reference on recent films, to be sponsored annually by the Academy of Motion Picture Arts and Sciences, is now being published (as of 1978). The first edition of the *Annual Index to Motion Picture Credits,* edited by Verna Ramsey, is an annual of data for all films eligible for the Academy Awards and for many not eligible. Information for each film will include the names of the production and distribution companies, approximate completion date, the names of the major production personnel, and the cast. Such data on very recent films is often difficult to obtain, and having it available within months of the end of the year will be a boon to the researcher.

A recent book by Richard Shale, *Academy Awards,* should become the standard guide to the Academy Awards. Shale lists the nominees and winners by category from 1927 through 1977, and his bibliography and index are important research tools. In *The Academy Awards: A Pictorial History,* Paul Michael gives a year by year history from 1927 to 1971. He includes a brief statement about the outstanding aspects of the year's films, a list of the awards, and photographs of the important winners.

Several books provide basic reference data on films: credits, production information, and other facts needed by both the general and the scholarly audiences.

Leslie Halliwell has written another useful aid to film study. *Halliwell's Film Guide* is a survey of 8,000 movies made in English. Halliwell provides the country of origin, date, a two-sentence plot summary, cast and credits, and a one-sentence review excerpt. He also gives his personal rating of the films.

Screen World, 1977 is one of a series of annual books (the 1977 edition is the twenty-eighth volume in the series) that provide information on the films released during the previous year. John Willis gives brief credits and cast lists as well as pictures from hundreds of the year's movies. He also lists the top box office stars, the important new actors, the Academy Award winners, foreign film released in the U.S., and obituaries.

The scope of *American Film-Index, 1908-1915* is enormous. Einar Lauritzen and Gunnar Lundquist have provided the production credits for over 23,000 films of the period, from the first film directed by D. W. Griffith. They present the dates, brief credits, and brief histories of the productions of all the films.

Georges Sadoul's *Dictionary of Films* provides technical information on over 1,200 feature films and includes credits and a brief plot summary.

A Title Guide to the Talkies, 1927-1963 by Richard Betrand Dimmitt lists basic information (title, date, distributor, and story source) for 16,000 feature films. This book is complemented by Andrew Aros' *A Title Guide to the Talkies, 1964-1974,* which provides the same information for films of the next decade.

The American Movies Reference Book: The Sound Era by Paul Michael is another index to the players, films, directors, producers, and awards of American movies.

The Film Buff's Bible, edited by D. Richard Baer, discusses 13,000 films in a concise format. Baer lists the films, their dates, running times, distributors, and rates each according to his own rating guide.

Two additional reference books will guide readers to rather specialized knowledge of the cinema. Both books are aimed at limited audiences.

Silent Movies is not strictly speaking a reference book, but it is a quiz book on silent films that will force most readers to seek out other reference books. The reader is invited by the author, Stanley Applebaum, to test his memory against pictures from the movies.

The Filmgoer's Book of Quotes, edited by Leslie Halliwell, tests the fan's memory of famous lines from movies, movie people, and famous movie advertisements. Max Wilk's *Wit and Wisdom of Hollywood* is an "assortment of Hollywood jokes, toasts, anecdotes, letters, footnotes, and feuilletons."

Two books guide the reader to movies likely to be seen on television. These are *Movies on TV* by Steven Scheuer and *TV Movies* by Leonard Maltin (the last is recommended by the library staff of the American Film Institute in Washington). Both give the titles, dates, running times, casts, brief annotations, and the author's personal ratings.

Any serious student of film will at some point be interested in renting or purchasing film. *Feature Films on 8mm and 16mm* by James Limbacher is a standard guide to films and their distributors. Limbacher lists the films, running times, directors, brief cast lists, and distributors. *Film Programmer's Guide to 16mm Rentals* by Kathleen Weaver does not list casts and deals only with 16mm films, but Weaver does cite recent prices for the rentals (while these prices tend to go out of date quickly these days, having them as a guide is helpful). For films intended primarily for the classroom, especially documentaries, the reader should consult the *NICEM Index to 16mm Educational Films.* Another resource for educators is the *Educational Film Locator,* which is a "union list of titles held by member libraries of the Consortium of University Film Centers." Member universities may rent from this catalogue of 200,000 titles.

A similar resource for film librarians is *The Film User's Handbook: A Basic Manual for Managing Library Film Services* by George Rehrauer. Rehrauer covers the background for film services, developing and designing an institutional film program, and other topics of interest to film librarians. A person working outside education might wish to refer to Janet Weiner's *How To Organize and Run a Film Society.* Weiner discusses the best films that might work with a special group, distributors, financing, programming, equipment, and promotion.

The filmmaker who wishes to enter his work in the growing number of film festivals or the fan who wishes to attend may be interested in *Film and TV Festival Directory.* Shirley Zwerdling lists festivals in this country and abroad, both those for professionals and those for amateurs.

Two books serve as basic reference guides for those serious about collecting films and their memorabiliia. *Collecting Movie Memorabilia* by Sol Chaneles helps the collector locate stills, posters and lobby cards, curios, fan magazines, press books, movie books, sound tracks, archives, museums, and even novelizations. *Collecting Classic Films* by Kalton C. Lahue describes the steps in locating and buying old films and also tells the collector how to store and project the films. The reader should also consult the catalogues of companies which sell films to collectors. Many of these catalogues provide useful information on the films and on collecting them.

REFERENCE BOOKS FOR AND ABOUT SCREEN PERSONALITIES

The World Encyclopedia of the Film, edited by Tim Cawkwell and John M. Smith, contains entries on directors, actors, and others involved in film production. The editors provide brief entries and filmographies but no critical judgments or bibliographies. Some of the more general encyclopedias listed under the general reference section are more useful in this regard.

A technical book for those trying to locate actors for casting is published by the Academy of Motion Picture Arts and Sciences three times a year. The actors' pictures and their agents' telephone numbers can be found in the *Academy Players Directory.*

Voices of Film Experience—1894 to the Present is a good resource on hundreds of movie personalities. Jay Leyda's entries, arranged alphabetically, often contain both interviews and critical comments. David Ragan's *Who's Who in Hollywood, 1900-1976* is not as extensive but is still of value. In his brief entries on actors, Ragan gives a short list of their films and brief biographical information. Georges Sadoul's *Dictionary of Filmmakers* is an important guide to filmmakers. Sadoul's one thousand entries include directors and screenwriters but no actors.

Filmarama by John Stewart, when it is finished, will contain six volumes of lists of film people. Stewart's first volume lists actors and directors, their films and television work.

David Thomson's *A Biographical Dictionary of Film* is one of the more useful reference guides. Thomson covers both directors and actors, providing some biography, a few critical comments, and a brief filmography and bibliography for most.

Who Was Who on Screen by Evelyn Mack Truitt is basically a list of actors, their dates, and films.

If the reader needs personal information on an actor, the answer can probably be found in a recent publication by Kenneth S. Marx, *Star Stats: Who's Whose in Hollywood.* This book provides the stage name, real name, names of relatives, and lists of marriages for the stars. Using a computer format, Marx has also listed the Academy Award nominees and winners and the most recent places of residence for the stars.

John T. Weaver has published *Forty Years of Screen Credits—1929-1969.* The book concentrates on actors, giving their dates and the films for which they are credited. In *Twenty Years of Silents, 1908-1928* Weaver followed the same format for silent actors and their films.

A reference guide to screenwriters is *Who Wrote the Movie and What Else Did He Write?,* a joint venture of the Academy of Motion Picture Arts and Sciences and the Writers Guild of America. This guide to the work of screenwriters from 1936 to 1969 includes both a film index and a writer index.

Any list of film scholars will quickly become outdated but *Directory of American Film Scholars* by Leona and Jill Phillips, written in 1975, provides the names and addresses of the scholars, as well as their institutional affiliation, interests, and publications.

There are two important references for, rather than about, filmmakers. *The Motion Picture Market Place, 1976-1977,* edited by Tom Costner, is a handy guide to the industry. This book covers a wide range of information, from the place to rent costumes to the name of the personnel director at Warner Brothers or the name of the typist who can put your screenplay into the proper format. *Doing It Yourself* is a handy guide for filmmakers who decide to distribute their own films. The author, Julia Reichert, assisted by Amelia Rothschild and other independent filmmakers associated with New Day Films, tells filmmakers how to promote and rent out their own films.

PERIODICALS

The leading guide to film periodicals is *Film and Television Periodicals in English,* published by the American Film Institute. This factfile, compiled by the librarians of the AFI, is an up-to-date list of all journals and newspapers devoted to the electronic media. It is especially valuable for anyone seeking a reasonably complete list of these periodicals or for anyone trying to locate the name and address of a particular journal. Copies may be purchased by writing to the AFI, Kennedy Center, Washington, D.C. 20566.

Several journals that have ceased publication have been reprinted and are generally available in book format. *The Penguin Film Review, 1946-1949* has been reissued under the editorship of Roger Manvell; and the 1939-1940 issues of *Film: A Quarterly of Discussion and Analysis* have been reissued by Arno Press. *Hound and Horn* is a reprint of selected articles from this now classic journal. Many of the articles are on directors (Sergei Eisenstein, V. I. Pudovkin, George Pabst, F. W. Murnau, and Ernst Lubitsch), some are on actors (James Cagney, Greta Garbo, and Marlene Dietrich), and some on other topics (animation).

All of the reviews from *The New York Times* have been reprinted in book form. *The New York Times Film Reviews, 1913-1968* is a six-volume collection of the reviews of every film that opened in New York and was covered by the newspaper. The reviews vary in quality, but they do provide important factual information and some idea of the ways the films were received when first released.

The following is a list of periodicals which are currently being published and which are available to researchers. Periodicals tend to cease publication rather suddenly, but at the time this chapter is being written, the following periodicals are being published:

Action! is published by the Directors' Guild of America six times a year and features articles on filmmakers and their products. It provides a behind-the-scenes look at the industry and is intended for a more popular audience than its title and sponsor suggest.

Adam Film World is a pornographic magazine based on pornographic films. This bi-monthly contains articles, interviews, and explicit photographs on and from erotic movies.

After Dark is a monthly arts magazine that frequently covers film with feature articles, interviews, and reviews. It also contains many pictures.

Afterimage is published nine times a year in newspaper format. Sponsored by the Visual Studio Workshop, it is a voice for independent film, video, and photography and includes articles, interviews, reviews, and a calendar of events, primarily for the New York area.

American Cinematographer has been a serious and important magazine for the professional or advanced amateur since 1919. Published monthly, it focuses on movie production and photography, providing behind-the-scenes looks into film production and information on new equipment and books.

American Cinemeditor is published quarterly by American Cinema Editors. Intended for the professional, it provides information on editing and new equipment.

American Classic Screen, the bi-monthly journal of the National Film Society, concentrates on America's film heritage. Some of its articles are serious criticism, but for the most part the journal is geared to the interests of film buffs and collectors. It includes many photographs.

American Film, sponsored by the American Film Institute, is published ten times a year. This magazine has become the standard publication on films and television for a popular audience. Its articles are based on scholarly research, but they have a lighter touch than articles in scholarly journals. Most issues feature articles on current productions, a bit of film or television history, a glance at independent filmmakers, columns on both media, and book reviews. This important magazine should be in every library.

Art and Cinema is an expensive magazine that comes out three times a year. The quality of the paper and printing justifies the cost, and the content meets the same high standards. The magazine focuses on contemporary filmmakers and their work with in-depth interviews, articles, and reviews.

Audio-Visual Communications is a publication intended for the educator which contains surveys and reviews of the latest movie equipment designed for the classroom and media centers. This monthly also features articles on film production for the classroom and discussion of topics such as animation or sound.

The Big Reel is a monthly periodical in the newspaper format intended for film collectors. It serves as a guide and market place for collectors, but it also contains articles and illustrations of interest.

Bright Lights, which has an irregular publication schedule, is a journal that focuses on American film directors, with an emphasis on auteur criticism. It contains articles on directors and their films and many photographs, as well as reviews of films and film books.

Camera Obscura: A Journal of Feminism and Film Theory is published three times a year by the Camera Obscura Collective of Women Filmmakers. The emphasis is on feminism in film and the articles for the most part consist of essays on the films themselves and interviews with filmmakers. The magazine also includes information on current activity in the industry that is of interest to women.

Center for Southern Folklore Newsletter concentrates on folklore from the Southeast. This periodical includes a great deal of information on material in media other than film, but the center has sponsored and distributed a number of important ethnographic films, and this newsletter is an excellent way of keeping up with their cinematic work. Presently it is published semi-annually, but it may become a quarterly soon.

Cine-Tracts—A Journal of Film and Cultural Studies, a Canadian quarterly that deals largely with Canadian filmmaking, is not limited to articles on Canada. It contains articles on films and film theory as well as interviews.

Cineaste is a quarterly "magazine on the art and politics of cinema." This somewhat leftist journal deals with film in its "social, political, and economic context." Its articles and interviews often emphasize classic or overlooked films.

Cinefantastique deals with science fiction, horror, and fantasy films. This quarterly publishes reviews, interviews, and articles such as "*The Fury*: A Locational Journal" and "The Ghost of Hans J. Salter."

Cinegram Magazine is sponsored by the Ann Arbor Film Cooperative and might best be described as a serious movie magazine. "Geared to popular, non-technical know-how and news of film and video," it is published quarterly.

Cinema Journal is a publication of the Society of Cinema Studies and is one of the important film journals. This journal is published semi-annually and is scholarly and serious and focuses on articles on the history of film.

Cinemagic, a quarterly with an emphasis on movie special effects, contains information for both the professional and the amateur on how to create special effects. Recent issues have described how to make a giant spider and a miniature flying saucer.

Classic Film Collector provides articles on classic films and collecting them. This quarterly in a newspaper format publishes longer articles than do most magazines for collectors.

Daily Variety is the trade newspaper for the people in the movie and television industry. It contains production information, industry news, and film reviews.

Fantastic Film Magazine Magazine of Fantasy and Science Fiction in the Cinema is a bi-monthly with richly illustrated articles and interviews that cover the magic and special effects of the two genres.

Film and Broadcasting Review, sponsored by the U.S. Catholic Conference, is a semi-monthly newsletter. Basically it provides ratings on recently released movies and television shows for parents, parishes, organizations, libraries, and educators. The reviews and articles are written from a clearly Catholic point of view.

Film and History is a quarterly sponsored by the Historians' Film Commission. It contains articles on film as an aid in studying history and culture and also publishes reviews of films and film books.

Film Collector's World, a newspaper for collectors, is issued bi-weekly. It contains some articles, interviews, and information on festivals, but the emphasis is on the sale and purchase of film collectibles. It is largely made up of advertisements.

Film Comment, one of the important film periodicals, is published bi-monthly by the Film Society of Lincoln Center. It contains scholarly articles and reviews, articles by filmmakers that tell how they made their important films, and columns on both the industry and the independents. This magazine is a slick production of good quality, and it publishes book reviews, interviews, and reviews of the international festivals.

Film Criticism comes out three times a year and is a scholarly journal that publishes lengthy articles of film criticism and theory. It also includes book reviews and interviews.

Film Culture is published quarterly ("approximately," according to its publisher) by and for independent filmmakers. The editor is Jonas Makas, the guiding light of independent filmmakers and one of them himself. The lengthy journal prints theoretical articles, interviews with independent filmmakers, notes by the filmmakers, and analysis of independent films.

Film Library Quarterly is sponsored by the Film Library Information Council. This quarterly claims that its emphasis is on "social documentary, avant-garde, and independent film articles." Its articles, interviews, and reviews feature video as well as film.

Film News is a magazine published five times a year for librarians and other educators who want to know which recently released films are suitable for their use. Its articles cover films on topics such as death or the writer in America, and its columns review recent films.

Film Quarterly, in publication since 1945, is another of the important film journals. It includes interviews, scholarly articles on recent films (narrative, experimental, documentary, and animated), general criticism, and lengthy reviews of recent films.

The Film Reader is an annual for serious readers that includes articles and interviews on two different general subjects in each issue. It also includes biofilmographies of the people important in each subject area.

Filmmakers Film and Video Monthly was known until recently as the *Filmmakers Newsletter,* but has changed to this more accurate name. It is a magazine for the professional working in the studios, independent production houses, universities, television studios, and corporations. It features articles on what is going on in the industry, and its articles on current productions are especially valuable. Each issue features an article on a recent production and usually contains another about shooting on location.

Filmmusic Notebook concentrates on music in films. This scholarly journal sponsored quarterly by the Film Music Collective is well done and contains articles, interviews, biographies, and filmographies.

Film Review Digest, modeled after *Book Review Digest,* provides reviews of films. Published quarterly, it excerpts reviews of approximately one hundred feature films in each issue and also lists full credits for the films. This is a basic tool for librarians.

Films in Review, a readable and useful magazine, is issued ten times a year. It contains articles with filmographies on movie people, and often has the only useable, scholarly article on many important but lesser-known actors and directors. It also includes interviews, and book and film reviews.

The Films of Yesteryear, a product of the recent fad for nostalgia, is a quarterly that covers movies from 1930 to 1948. It claims to be "an archival project basically" and contains illustrations and questions and answers about the films of yesterday.

Funnyworld Magazine is a quarterly publication which covers "the world of film animation and comic art." It goal is to promote serious attention to both animation and comic art. It contains articles, interviews, and reviews.

The Hollywood Reporter, a daily (except for the weekends), is another newspaper for the entertainment industry. It does contain some film reviews, but consists mostly of newsbriefs of action in the film industry.

Hollywood Studio Magazine claims to emphasize "nostalgia with an update." It is published ten times a year for collectors and movie fans. Its articles feature the stars and Hollywood itself. It also contains a large classified section and items of interest to fan clubs.

Humanities Index has in the past several years become a standard guide found in most reference libraries. It indexes recent articles on the humanities found in a wide array of magazines and journals. It is important to those interested in film because it lists reviews for films released recently.

Image, a quarterly magazine sponsored by the International Museum of Photography at the George Eastman House in Rochester, New York, is a quality periodical which publishes scholarly articles on photography and film. It often includes technical information on the preservation of film materials. Naturally, it includes numerous photographs.

Independent Film Journal is a monthly for theater owners, producers, and distributors of motion pictures. Information in each issue contain editorial comment, up-to-date trade news, and reviews of films with casts, credits, ratings, running times, and synopses.

International Film Collector is a quarterly magazine for collectors who want to buy, sell, or trade.

Journal of Popular Film and Television is a quarterly containing articles on the roles of television and film in our culture. It also contains book reviews, bibliographies, and filmographies.

Journal of the University Film Association is a quarterly that publishes scholarly articles on film history and criticism, as well as film education. It is an important journal for college-level teachers and students.

Jump Cut: A Review of Contemporary Cinema is issued four to six times a year in newspaper format and features articles written from a political and critical perspective. Its goal is to develop a radical film criticism based on a "vigorous Marxist cultural and aesthetic theory."

Landers Film Reviews provides a bi-monthly service for librarians and calls itself *The Information Guide to 16mm Films and Multi-Media Materials.* It contains short but valuable reviews of films for the classroom, and it ranks the films by age/grade level and rates them.

Literature/Film Quarterly contains articles on the relationship between film and literature. Its scholarly articles explore films made from works of literature, usually novels and plays, but sometimes the articles deal with literary motifs or images as they are used in film. It has become one of the important film journals.

Media and Methods provides information for secondary school teachers. Published nine times a year, it features articles on the use of media by teachers, reviews of recent films, surveys of equipment, and course suggestions.

Millimeter: Magazine of the Motion Picture and Television Production Industries is a monthly publication that publishes interviews and articles on films, television, and equipment. One interesting feature is a column on location productions.

Millennium Film Journal, published by the Millennium Film Workshop, is "dedicated to avant-garde film." This important journal comes out three times a year and features the independent and avant-garde filmmaker. The articles are written by both filmmakers and critics.

Mindrot: The Animated Film Quarterly wins the prize for the catchiest journal title. It contains information and articles on animators, and often includes interviews and filmographies. *Mindrot* is especially fun to read.

Newsreel Magazine is the official organ of the Motion Picture Collectibles Association. For the serious collector, this magazine contains researched articles on the authenticity and value of collectibles such as autographs, letters, and photographs.

On Location claims to be "the film and videotape production magazine" for professionals. Issued monthly, it contains articles and interviews on production.

Photon is a journal of fantasy films with an irregular publication schedule. It contains articles, retrospectives, book and film reviews, even some satire. It is a fan magazine with some class.

Popular Photography contains information for both still photographs and movie makers. This monthly provides "how-to" articles, as well as surveys of newly released movie equipment, especially cameras and projectors. There is a monthly column on "movie method," which covers topics such as better editing.

Pratfall has an irregular publication record, but it is a tribute to Laurel and Hardy. It contains reviews, articles, and interviews about the world of the famous comedy team.

Quarterly Review of Film Studies is a scholarly journal. It identifies a single general theme for each issue, themes such as semiology, structuralism as practical film criticism, feminism, and ideological criticism. In addition to articles, it also contains book and film reviews.

Reader's Guide to Periodical Literature, like the *Humanities Index* cited earlier, lists movie reviews under the heading "moving picture plays—single works."

Screen Actor is a quarterly sponsored by the Screen Actors Guild for its members. It contains articles on the profession of acting, and interviews with casting directors and others in fields of interest to actors.

Screen Thrills is a bi-monthly publication of information for movie buffs and collectors. It contains articles on the stars, advertisements for collectibles, and reviews. Its articles appear to be of a higher quality than those published in the various newspapers for collectors.

Shakespeare on Film Newsletter, issued twice a year, is aimed at educators. It provides information on films dealing with Shakespeare and suggests ways of using these films in the curriculum.

Show Business is a weekly in newspaper format. It publishes casting news for films and the theater as well as general production information. Its brief articles are supplemented by book and film reviews.

Shooting is "a publication designed to provide a broad scope of information regarding cinema and television production." This monthly, begun in 1978, includes articles for the professional on cameras, lists of producers, agents, and other topics relating to production.

Sight and Sound has been published quarterly by the British Film Institute since 1932, but is widely circulated and highly regarded in this country. It includes interviews and lengthy articles on British films and others on film history and theory.

Sightlines, a quarterly publication, is sponsored by the Educational Film

Library Association. It contains articles on film production and classroom use, as well as useful filmographies for teachers.

Super-8 Filmmaker concentrates on the growing number of people working with the super 8mm format. Issued eight times a year, it contains articles on filmmaking and regular columns on special effects and animation. In one sense it is a buyer's guide to 8mm equipment, and many of its articles report on tests of new equipment.

Take One is the leading Canadian journal widely distributed in the United States. A monthly publication, it contains interviews, filmographies, general articles, reviews of books and films, and columns on the festivals. It is of special use to the teacher of film studies.

Under Western Skies, another magazine for those who like their nostalgia in large doses, seeks to recreate "the Old West that we fondly remember from the Silver Screen and the smaller screen of the TV and that magical box the Radio." Published four times a year, it consists mainly of filmographies and articles of nostalgia. Its articles frequently cover little-known actors or films.

Variety is the weekly newspaper for the entertainment industry. It contains statistics and data on current and recently released productions, as well as film reviews.

Velvet Light Trap, Journal of Film History and Criticism, is published quarterly by the Wisconsin Centre of Film and Theatre Research, one of the important research centers on film in the United States. Each issue is built around a topic relating to the history, criticism, or theory of film.

Wide Angle, A Film Quarterly of Theory, Criticism, and Practice, is a scholarly journal that also publishes theme issues.

The World of Yesterday is published five times a year by the same group that publishes *Under Western Skies* and *The Films of Yesteryear*. It deals with nostalgia films other than Westerns. All of these magazines are cheaply printed and difficult to read (in part because they lack tables of contents). The main articles are usually based on well-known information, but the photographs they include and the reprints of forgotten articles by important film people are of interest to film buffs, and often to scholars.

BIBLIOGRAPHY

Academy of Motion Picture Arts and Sciences. *Academy Players Directory.* Los Angeles: Academy of Motion Picture Arts and Sciences, 1977.

Aceto, Vincent, Jane Graves, and Fred Silva. *Film Literature Index.* Albany, N.Y.: Filmdex, 1975.

Applebaum, Stanley. *Silent Movies.* New York: Dover, 1974.

Aros, Andrew. *A Title Guide to the Talkies, 1964-1974.* Metuchen, N.J.: Scarecrow, 1977.

Baer, D. Richard, ed. *The Film Buff's Bible of Motion Pictures.* Hollywood, Calif.: Hollywood Film Archive, 1972.

Batty, Linda. *Retrospective Index to Film Periodicals, 1930-1971.* New York: R. R. Bowker, 1975.

Bawden, Liz-Anne. *The Oxford Companion to Film.* New York: Oxford University Press, 1976.

Bowles, Stephen E. *Index to Critical Film Reviews in British and American Film Periodicals.* New York: Burt Franklin, 1974.

Bukalski, Peter J. *Film Research: A Critical Bibliography.* Boston: G. K. Hall, 1972.

Catalogue of Copyright Entries: Motion Pictures. Washington: The Library of Congress, 1951, 1953, 1960, 1971.

Cawkwell, Tim and John M. Smith, eds. *The World Encyclopedia of the Film.* New York: Thomas Y. Crowell, 1972.

Chaneles, Sol. *Collecting Movie Memorabilia.* New York: Arco Publishing, 1977.

Chicorel, Marietta, ed. *Chicorel Index to Film Literature.* New York: Chicorel Library Publishing, 1975.

Clason, W. E. *Elsevier's Dictionary of Cinema, Sound and Music.* New York: Elsevier, 1956.

Costner, Tom, ed. *Motion Picture Market Place, 1976-1977.* Boston: Little, Brown, 1976.

Dimmitt, Richard Betrand. *A Title Guide to the Talkies: A Comprehensive Listing . . . , 1927-1963.* 2 vols. Metuchen, N.J.: Scarecrow, 1965.

Dyment, Alan R. *The Literature of the Film: A Bibliographic Guide to Film as Art and Entertainment, 1936-1970.* New York: White Lion Publishers, 1975.

Educational Film Locator. New York: R. R. Bowker, 1978.

Ellis, Jack C., Charles Derry, and Sharon Kern. *The Film Book Bibliography, 1940-1975.* Metuchen, N.J.: Scarecrow, 1979.

Film and Television Periodicals in English. Washington: The American Film Institute, 1979.

Film: A Quarterly of Discussion and Analysis. New York: Arno, 1968.

The Focal Encyclopedia of Film and Television Techniques. New York: Hastings House, 1969.

Gerlach, John C., and Lana Gerlach. *The Critical Index: A Bibliography of Articles on Film in English, 1946-1973. . . .* New York: Teachers College Press, 1974.

Gershank, S. *Motography.* Reprinted in Anthony Slide. *Aspects of American Film History Prior to 1920.* Metuchen, N.J.: Scarecrow, 1978.

Gertner, Richard, ed. *International Motion Picture Almanac, 1977.* New York: Quigley, 1977.

Gottesman, Ronald, and Harry M. Geduld. *Guidebook to Film: An Eleven-in-One Reference.* New York: Holt, Rinehart and Winston, 1972.

Halliwell, Leslie. *The Filmgoer's Companion.* New York: Hill and Wang, 1977.

______. *The Filmgoer's Book of Quotes.* New Rochelle, N.Y.: Arlington House, 1973.

______. *Halliwell's Film Guide.* New York: Charles Scribner's Sons, 1978.

Hound and Horn. New York: Arno, 1972.

Jones, Karen. *International Index to Film Periodials, 1974.* New York: St. Martin's Press, 1975.

Krafsur, Richard, ed. *The American Film Institute Catalogue of Motion Pictures Produced in the United States, Feature Films, 1961-1970.* New York: R. R. Bowker, 1976.

Lahue, Kalton C. *Collecting Classic Films.* New York: American Photographic Book Publishing Co., 1970.

Lauritzen, Einar, and Gunnar Lundquist. *American Film-Index, 1908-1915.* Stockholm: Akademibokhandeln, 1976.

Leonard, Harold, ed. *The Film Index: A Bibliography.* New York: Museum of Modern Art and the H. W. Wilson Co., 1941.

Leyda, Jay, ed. *Voices of Film Experience—1894 to the Present.* New York: Macmillan, 1977.

Limbacher, James. *Feature Films on 8mm and 16mm: A Directory of Feature Films Available for Rental, Sales, and Lease in the United States.* New York: R. R. Bowker, 1977.

MacCann, Richard Dyer and Edward S. Perry. *The New Film Index: A Bibliography of Magazine Articles in English, 1930-70.* New York: E. P. Dutton, 1975.

Maltin, Leonard, ed. *TV Movies.* New York: New American Library, 1974.

Manvell, Roger, ed. *The International Encyclopedia of Film.* New York: Crown, 1972.

______, ed. *The Penguin Film Review, 1946-1949.* Totowa, N.J.: Rowman and Littlefield, 1978.

Marx, Kenneth S. *Star Stats: Who's Whose in Hollywood.* Los Angeles: Price, Stern and Sloan, 1979.

Michael, Paul. *The Academy Awards: A Pictorial History.* New York: Crown, 1972.

______. *The American Movies Reference Book: The Sound Era.* Englewood Cliffs, N.J.: Prentice-Hall, 1969.

Munden, Kenneth W., ed. *The American Film Institute Catalogue of Motion Pictures Produced in the United States, Feature Films, 1921-1930.* New York: R. R. Bowker, 1971.

The New York Times Film Reviews, 1913-1968. New York: The New York Times and Arno, 1970.

NICEM Index to 16mm Educational Films. Los Angeles: NICEM, 1973.

Niver, Kemp R. *Motion Pictures from the Library of Congress Paper Print Collection, 1894-1912.* Berkeley: University of California Press, 1967.

Phillips, Leona and Jill Phillips. *Directory of American Film Scholars.* New York: Gordon, 1975.

Picard, Roy. *A Companion to the Movies, from 1903 to the Present Day: A Guide. . . .* New York: Hippocrene Books, 1972.

Ragan, David. *Who's Who in Hollywood, 1900-1976.* New Rochelle, N.Y.: Arlington House, 1976.

Ramsey, Verna, ed. *Annual Index to Motion Picture Credits, 1978.* Westport, Conn.: Greenwood, 1979.

Rehrauer, George. *Cinema Booklist.* Metuchen, N.J.: Scarecrow, 1972.

______. *The Film User's Handbook: A Basic Manual for Managing Library Film Services.* New York: R. R. Bowker, 1975.

Reichert, Julia. *Doing It Yourself.* New York: Association of Independent Video and Filmmakers and New Day Films, 1977.

Sadoul, Georges. *Dictionary of Filmmakers.* Translated by Peter Morris. Berkeley: University of California Press, 1972.

______. *Dictionary of Films.* Translated by Peter Morris. Berkeley: University of California Press, 1972.

Scheuer, Steven, ed. *Movies on TV.* New York: Bantam, 1974.
Schuster, Mel. *Motion Picture Directors: A Bibliography of Magazine and Periodical Articles, 1900-1972.* Metuchen, N.J.: Scarecrow, 1973.
______. *Motion Picture Performers: A Bibliography of Magazine and Periodical Articles, 1900-1969.* Metuchen, N.J.: Scarecrow, 1971.
Shale, Richard. *Academy Awards.* New York: Frederick Ungar, 1978.
Slide, Anthony. *Aspects of American Film History Prior to 1920.* Metuchen, N.J.: Scarecrow, 1978.
Steinberg, Cobbett. *Reel Facts.* New York: Vintage, 1978.
Stewart, John. *Filmarama.* Metuchen, N.J.: Scarecrow, 1975.
Thomson, David. *A Biographical Dictionary of Film.* New York: William Morrow, 1976.
Truitt, Evelyn Mack. *Who Was Who on Screen.* New York: R. R. Bowker, 1974.
Walls, Howard Lamarr. *Motion Pictures, 1894-1912. Identified from the Records of the U.S. Copyright Office.* Washington: Library of Congress, 1953.
Weaver, Kathleen, ed. *Film Programmer's Guide to 16mm Rentals.* Albany, Calif.: Reel Research, 1975.
Weaver, John T. *Forty Years of Screen Credits—1929-1969.* Metuchen, N.J.: Scarecrow, 1970.
______. *Twenty Years of Silents, 1908-1928.* Metuchen, N.J.: Scarecrow, 1971.
Weiner, Janet. *How to Organize and Run a Film Society.* New York: Macmillan, 1973.
Who Wrote the Movie and What Else Did He Write? An Index of Screenwriters and Their Film Works, 1936-1969. Los Angeles: The Academy of Motion Picture Arts and Sciences and the Writers Guild of America, 1970.
Wilk, Max. *The Wit and Wisdom of Hollywood: From The Squaw Man to The Hatchet Man.* New York: Warner, 1971.
Willis, John. *Screen World, 1977.* New York: Crown, 1977.
Zwerdling, Shirley, ed. *Film and TV Festival Directory.* New York: Back Stage Publications, 1970.

CHECKLIST OF PERIODICALS

Action! Los Angeles, 1966-
Adam Film World. Los Angeles, 1966-
After Dark. New York, 1968-
Afterimage. Rochester, N.Y., 1972-
American Cinematographer. Hollywood, 1919-
American Cinemeditor. Los Angeles, 1950-
American Classic Screen. Lawrence, Kans., no date
American Film. New York, 1974-
Art and Cinema. New York, 1973-
Audio-Visual Communications. New York, 1967-
The Big Reel. Summerfield, N.C., 1974-
Bright Lights. Los Angeles, 1974-
Camera Obscura. Berkeley, 1977-
Center for Southern Folklore Newsletter. Memphis, Tenn., 1978-
Cine-Tracts—A Journal of Film and Cultural Studies. Montreal, 1977-

Cineaste. New York, 1967-
Cinefantastique. Oak Park, Ill., 1970-
Cinegram Magazine. Ann Arbor, 1978-
Cinema Journal. Iowa City, 1962-
Cinemagic. Warren, Mich., 1972-
Classic Film Collector. Davenport, Iowa, 1962-
Daily Variety. Hollywood, 1933-
Fantastic Films Magazine. Chicago, no date
Film and Broadcasting Review. New York, 1976-
Film and History. Newark, N.J., 1971-
Film Collector's World. Rapid City, Ill., 1976-
Film Comment. New York, 1972-
Film Criticism. Edinboro, Pa., 1979-
Film Culture. New York, 1955-
Film Library Quarterly. New York, 1967/68-
Film News. New York, 1939-
Film Quarterly. Berkeley, 1945-
The Film Reader. Evanston, Ill., 1976-
Film Review Digest. Millwood, N.Y., 1975-
Filmmakers Film and Video Monthly. Ward Hill, Mass., 1968-
Filmmusic Notebook. Los Angeles, 1974-
Films in Review. New York, 1950-
The Films of Yesteryear. Clearwater, Fla., 1977-
Funnyworld Magazine. New York, 1966-
The Hollywood Reporter. Hollywood, 1930-
Hollywood Studio Magazine. Sherman Oaks, Calif., 1959-
Humanities Index. New York, 1974-
Image. Rochester, N.Y., 1952-
Independent Film Journal. New York, 1933-
International Film Collector. Lawrence, Mass., 1972-
Journal of Popular Film and Television. Bowling Green, Ohio, 1971-
Journal of the University Film Association. Philadelphia, 1943-
Jump Cut. Berkeley, 1974-
Landers Film Reviews. Los Angeles, 1956-
Literature/Film Quarterly. Salisbury, Md., 1973-
Media and Methods. Philadelphia, 1964-
Millimeter. New York, 1973-
Millennium Film Journal. New York 1978-
Mindrot. Minneapolis, no date
Newsreel Magazine. Indian Rocks Beach, Fla., 1978-
On Location. Hollywood, no date
Photon. Brooklyn, 1963-
Popular Photography. New York, 1956-
Pratfall. Universal City, Calif., 1968-
Quarterly Review of Film Studies. Pleasantville, N.Y., 1976-
Reader's Guide to Periodical Literature. New York, 1900-
Screen Actor. Los Angeles, 1959-

Screen Thrills. Raleigh, N.C., 1977-
Shakespeare on Film Newsletter. Glen Head, N.Y., 1976-
Show Business. New York, 1947-
Shooting. Passaic, N.J., 1978.
Sight and Sound. London, 1932-
Sightlines. New York, 1967-
Super-8 Filmmaker. Palo Alto, Calif., 1972-
Take One. Montreal, 1966-
Under Western Skies. Clearwater, Fla., 1978-
Variety. New York, 1905-
Velvet Light Trap. Madison, Wis., 1971-
Wide Angle. Athens, Ohio, 1976-
The World of Yesterday. Clearwater, Fla., 1976-

APPENDIX I

Selected Chronology of American Films and Events

An explanation: The films and events listed in this chronology were selected because they began or represented a trend or were considered milestones or landmarks for the motion picture industry. In addition, certain films are included because they were generally regarded as outstanding, because they were among the best American efforts of a given year, or because they are personal favorites. Space does not permit a complete roster of important films, but the "Reference Books on the Films" noted in chapter 11 will lead the reader to this information. The "General References" cited in that chapter and the works noted in chapter 1, "History of Film," will amplify the chronology of industry events.

1877 Eadweard Muybridge photographs a horse running and using sequential photographs makes the horse appear to move.

1891 Edison patents the Kinetograph and Kinetoscope.

1893 *Fred Ott's Sneeze* is filmed at Edison Studios by William Dickson.

1895 Lumière brothers show first films to a paying audience. American Mutoscope (which eventually became the Biograph Studio) is formed.

1896 First official showing for a paying audience in America takes place at Koster and Bial's Music Hall, New York City; *John Rice—May Irvin Kiss,* filmed by Edison, causes first public outcry against movies.

1899 Vitagraph (which eventually became Warner Brothers) is formed.

1902 Thomas L. Talley's Electric Theatre opens in Los Angeles as the first permanent building for showing movies in the United States; *A Trip to the Moon* is filmed by Georges Méliès.

1903 Edwin S. Porter films *The Life of an American Fireman* and *The Great Train Robbery* for Edison.

1905 America's first nickelodeon opens in Pittsburgh.

1907 D. W. Griffith becomes an actor for Edison.

1908 D. W. Griffith directs his first film for Biograph.

1909 Windsor McCay draws *Gertie the Dinosaur,* one of the first popular animated films; Mary Pickford becomes a movie actress; Independent Motion Picture Company (soon shortened to IMP) founded to produce films.

1910 Florence Lawrence leaves Biograph for IMP and becomes the first star to be given publicity.
1912 Mack Sennett directs his first film about cops at Keystone; Lillian and Dorothy Gish act in their first film for D. W. Griffith.
1913 D. W. Griffith directs *Judith of Bethulia.*
1914 *The Perils of Pauline* begins the craze for serials.
1915 Charlie Chaplin makes *The Tramp;* D. W. Griffith releases *Birth of a Nation.*
1916 Thomas Ince produces *Civilization;* D. W. Griffith directs *Intolerance.*
1917 Marshall Neilman directs Mary Pickford in *Rebecca of Sunnybrook Farm.* John Ford directs his first movie, *The Tornado.*
1918 D. W. Griffith directs *Hearts of the World.*
1919 Cecil B. DeMille directs *Male and Female;* D. W. Griffith, Charles Chaplin, Mary Pickford, and Douglas Fairbanks form United Artists.
1920 D. W. Griffith directs *Way Down East* with Lillian Gish and Richard Barthelmess. Pickford and Fairbanks marry.
1921 Henry King directs *Tol'able David;* Valentino stars in *The Sheik.*
1922 Will H. Hays becomes president of the Motion Picture Producers and Distributors of America. Robert Flaherty makes *Nanook of the North.*
1923 C. B. DeMille directs *The Ten Commandments.*
1924 Metro-Goldwyn-Mayer formed. Erich von Stroheim directs *Greed;* Fairbanks stars in *The Thief of Baghdad.*
1925 Charles Chaplin makes *The Gold Rush;* W. S. Hart stars in *Tumbleweeds;* Harold Lloyd stars in *The Freshman.*
1926 Buster Keaton makes *The General;* Frank Capra makes *The Strong Man* with Harry Langdon.
1927 Warner Brothers releases *The Jazz Singer,* the first major sound film; William Wellman directs *Wings,* which wins the first Academy Award.
1928 Walt Disney produces *Steamboat Willie* with Mickey Mouse; *Our Dancing Daughters* is the typical flapper film; *Lights of New York* is the first all-talking film.
1929 King Vidor directs *Hallelujah!* with an all-black cast.
1930 Greta Garbo talks in *Anna Christie;* Mervyn LeRoy directs *Little Caesar;* Lewis Milestone directs *All Quiet on the Western Front.*
1931 Tod Browning directs *Dracula* with Bela Lugosi; James Whale directs *Frankenstein* with Boris Karloff.
1932 Josef von Sternberg directs *Shanghai Express* with Marlene Dietrich.
1933 George Cukor directs *Dinner at Eight;* Technicolor perfects the three-color process; Mae West stars in *She Done Him Wrong.*
1934 Capra directs *It Happened One Night* with Clark Gable and Claudette Colbert; The Hays Office issues the Motion Picture Code.
1935 The Marx Brothers make *A Night at the Opera:* Fred Astaire and Ginger Rogers dance in *Top Hat.*
1936 Fritz Lang directs *Fury,* his first American film; Cukor directs *Camille* with Garbo; Chaplin makes *Modern Times.*
1937 Capra directs *Lost Horizon* with Ronald Colman; Disney produces *Snow White and the Seven Dwarfs.*
1938 William Wyler directs *Jezebel* with Bette Davis.

1939 John Ford directs *Stagecoach* starring John Wayne; *The Wizard of Oz* and *Gone With the Wind* are produced; Ernst Lubitsch directs *Ninotchka* with Garbo.

1940 Cukor directs *The Philadelphia Story.*

1941 Orson Welles makes *Citizen Kane;* Hawks directs *His Girl Friday* with Cary Grant and Rosalind Russell.

1942 Michael Curtiz directs *Casablanca* with Humphrey Bogart and Ingrid Bergman; Capra begins the *Why We Fight* series.

1943 Wellman directs *The Ox-Bow Incident.*

1944 Vincente Minnelli directs *Meet Me in St. Louis* with Judy Garland.

1945 Curtiz directs *Mildred Pierce* with Joan Crawford; Billy Wilder directs *The Lost Weekend.*

1946 Howard Hawks directs *The Big Sleep* with Bogart and Lauren Bacall; Ford directs *My Darling Clementine* with Henry Fonda.

1947 The House Un-American Activities Committee begins hearings which eventually lead to conviction of the Hollywood Ten and the establishment of the blacklist; David O. Selznick and King Vidor make *Duel in the Sun.*

1948 John Huston directs *The Treasure of the Sierra Madre;* Ford directs *Red River* with Wayne.

1949 Ford and Wayne make *She Wore a Yellow Ribbon;* Cukor directs *Adam's Rib* with Katharine Hepburn and Spencer Tracy; Robert Rossen makes *All the King's Men.*

1950 Billy Wilder directs *Sunset Boulevard.*

1951 Minnelli makes *An American in Paris* with Gene Kelly; the movie studios begin to cooperate with television; *A Streetcar Named Desire* opens the way for more permissive films. Safety film replaces nitrate film as the standard movie stock.

1952 Fred Zinneman directs *High Noon* with Gary Cooper; Gene Kelly makes *Singin' in the Rain; Bwana Devil* is made in 3-D.

1953 Lang directs *The Big Heat; The Robe* is made in Cinema-Scope; George Stevens directs *Shane.*

1954 Elia Kazan directs *On the Waterfront* with Eva Marie Saint and Marlon Brando.

1955 Nicholas Ray directs *Rebel Without a Cause* with James Dean.

1956 Don Siegel directs *Invasion of the Body Snatchers;* Josh Logan directs *Picnic;* Stevens directs *Giant.*

1957 Mark Robson directs *Peyton Place.*

1958 Stanley Kramer directs *The Defiant Ones* with Sidney Poitier and Tony Curtis; Minnelli directs *Gigi.*

1959 Alfred Hitchcock directs *North by Northwest;* Wilder directs *Some Like It Hot* with Marilyn Monroe.

1960 Hitchcock directs *Psycho.*

1961 Huston directs *The Misfits,* the last film for Marilyn Monroe, Clark Gable, and Montgomery Clift.

1962 John Frankenheimer directs *The Manchurian Candidate;* Robert Mulligan directs *To Kill a Mockingbird.*

1963 Richard Burton and Elizabeth Taylor star in *Cleopatra;* Martin Ritt directs *Hud* with Paul Newman.

1964 007, James Bond appears in *Goldfinger*; Stanley Kubrick directs *Dr. Strangelove*.

1965 Robert Wise directs *The Sound of Music.*

1966 Mike Nichols directs *Who's Afraid of Virginia Woolf?* with Elizabeth Taylor and Richard Burton.

1967 Arthur Penn directs *Bonnie and Clyde;* Nichols directs *The Graduate* with Dustin Hoffman.

1968 Kubrick directs *2001;* Andy Warhol and Paul Morrissey make *Trash.*

1969 Peter Fonda and Dennis Hopper make *Easy Rider;* John Wayne wins an Academy Award for *True Grit;* John Schlesinger directs *Midnight Cowboy.*

1970 Franklin J. Schaffner directs *Patton*; Robert Altman directs *M*A*S*H.*

1971 Peter Bogdanovich directs *The Last Picture Show;* Sam Peckinpah directs *Straw Dogs.*

1972 Francis Ford Coppola makes *The Godfather;* Bob Fosse makes *Cabaret.*

1973 George Roy Hill directs *The Sting;* George Lucas directs *American Graffiti.*

1974 Roman Polanski directs *Chinatown.*

1975 Milos Forman directs *One Flew Over the Cuckoo's Nest;* Altman directs *Nashville.*

1976 John G. Avildsen and Sylvester Stallone make *Rocky;* Alan J. Pakula directs *All the President's Men.*

1977 Woody Allen makes *Annie Hall* with Diane Keaton; Lucas directs *Star Wars.*

1978 Paul Mazursky directs *An Unmarried Woman* with Jill Clayburgh; Michael Cimini directs *The Deer Hunter;* Warren Beatty and Buck Henry make *Heaven Can Wait;* Richard Donner directs *Superman.*

1979 Martin Ritt directs *Norma Rae* with Sally Fields; James Bridges directs *China Syndrome;* Coppola finally releases *Apocalypse Now,* which had been years in production.

APPENDIX 2

Research Collections

In dealing with archives that house film materials, the researcher may find some libraries that collect films and others that collect film-related materials. Locating the film itself may be one of the most difficult problems for the researcher. Most of the early nitrate films have been destroyed for one reason or another, often because the film stock itself is unstable. The researcher can depend on only five centers in the United States for major—and expensive—efforts to preserve films: The Library of Congress and the American Film Institute in Washington, the Museum of Modern Art in New York, Eastman House in Rochester, and the Film and Television Archives at the University of California, Los Angeles.

Each of these archives is collecting, preserving, and holding films and does a first-rate job of maintaining our film heritage, but there are problems. The work is costly and time-consuming. Not all films are held in viewable prints, and the archives have not yet been able to publish an index of their holdings. Readers interested in the problems of preserving film for archives should consult Ralph N. Sargent's *Preserving the Moving Image,* a book sponsored by both the Corporation for Public Broadcasting and the National Endowment for the Arts. This is a technical book for archivists and would-be archivists. Sargent's first section deals with the techniques for handling valuable and old film, and its treatment and storage; his second section deals with new approaches and techniques; the third deals with videotape.

Aside from the films themselves, film-related material may include film scripts, stills, journals, books, costumes, and fugitive materials, such as letters and posters. All of the archives mentioned with film collections also have some film-related material, but the best additional collections of related material are at the Library and Museum of the Performing Arts (a branch of the New York Public LIbrary at Lincoln Center) and the Theater Arts Library at the University of California at Los Angeles.

There is as yet no single catalogue of film research centers, but a start has been made. *Motion Pictures, Television, and Radio: A Union Catalogue of Manuscript and Special Collections in the Western United States* is the result of a mammoth project edited by Linda Harris Mehr. This important book describes the film holdings of most of the libraries and museums in the Western United States. Such a project is badly needed for the rest of the country.

Whether the researcher is looking for films or film-related materials, he should write to the archives to inquire whether they have the necessary material before making the effort to visit the centers themselves. Security is understandably tight at these centers, and the researcher should take proper identification and should be prepared to demonstrate the seriousness of his research.

The best general survey of libraries that house film collections and service film scholars is *Film Study Collections* by Nancy Allen. This book is a guide to the development of the collections by librarians and their use by researchers. For the librarian, Allen describes collection development—both retrospective and current, selecting periodicals, and evaluating both published materials and nonprint materials. For the scholar and film fan, Allen describes the use and location of filmscripts, bookstores and film memorabilia dealers, major U.S. archives, reference services, and the holdings in film study of many important libraries. She even provides a chapter of basic library instruction for those who do not know how to use a library. This important book should be in every private and public collection.

A general guide to the archives can be found in the *North American Film and Video Directory,* by Olga S. Weber. This guide lists the archives and their locations and approximate sizes, but its value is limited. It lists only archives with film collections and does not describe the holdings or distinguish between significant holdings and minor ones.

Finally, it might be noted that while the distributors of films do not maintain research collections, they are usually most helpful to the researcher. Most are happy to work with researchers. Some of their better catalogues (such as those from Macmillan/Audio-Brandon and Films, Inc.) are useful sources of information, and the people in charge of collections for the companies are often knowledgeable and helpful.

MAJOR RESEARCH CENTERS AND ARCHIVES

The major research centers and archives are in three places: Washington, New York, and California. In Washington the place to begin is the American Film Institute (AFI) at the John F. Kennedy Center for the Performing Arts (Washington, D.C. 20566). The AFI maintains a working collection of 20,000 film stills. The collection spans the history of film and is filed by film title with cross-referencing to actor/actress. Members of the AFI may call or write for copies of nearly all of the stills at a reasonable price (currently $8 a still for members and $10 for non-members). Recent television programming is also represented. The AFI Kennedy Center offices also house a small reference library of approximately 800 books, back and current issues of over 100 film/television periodicals, and vertical files on films, television, and personalities. These facilities are available to members and nonmembers by appointment. These materials are noncirculating, but this is a pleasant place to work. As for film materials, there are about 14,000 films in the AFI Collection, which is maintained at the Library of Congress. There are a number of genre groups that the AFI has been building up over the years. These include approximately 90 all-black cast films, almost 200 silent Paramount features, a wealth of pre-1915 shorts plus a scattering of "famous players in famous plays" material which has a bearing upon theatrical research as well as film. The AFI has published a catalogue of their holdings at the Library of Congress, focusing on those that have been donated by United Artists. This guide will provide the researcher with the year, producer, director, major actor, and condition of the print for each of the films in this collection. The key problem at this point is the availability of reference prints for scholarly viewing. Since this is continually in a state of flux, it is necessary to consult directly with the Library of Congress staff for the availability of specific titles.

The AFI also has a branch in southern California. The Charles K. Feldman Library at the Center for Advanced Film Studies is at the AFI West Coast Office (501 Doheny Road, Beverly Hills, Calif. 90210). In addition to several special collections, this library holds some two thousand film books and many bound periodicals and shooting scripts. It also has a catalogued collection of oral history transcripts and seminar transcripts, and a collection of about 150 periodicals.

Back in Washington, the researcher may wish to consult the Motion Picture Section of the Library of Congress (Washington, D.C. 20540). Since 1894 when Edison's film of Fred Ott's sneeze was deposited for copyright reasons, the library has been a depository of American film. The collection is by no means complete because the laws have been changed several times; but it is the most extensive available and now contains over 50,000 titles and 300,000 stills. Many of these films may be viewed by serious researchers at the library, but the viewing facilities are not open to high school students, and college undergraduates must present a letter from their professor endorsing the project. Viewing times must be scheduled in advance. The motion picture section also provides reference files and books for researchers, but the library's general collection houses the majority of the large holdings in film.

In New York City the researcher has at his disposal the facilities of the Museum of Modern Art (11 West 53d Street, New York, N.Y. 10019). The library at MOMA holds some 20,000 books and subscribes to over fifty journals in modern art, photography and motion pictures. MOMA is also collecting and preserving films; but unlike most of the other film archives, this collection does permit rental of some of the films. Anyone interested should write to the museum for a catalogue.

The library at MOMA contains a few special collections of interest to the film scholar. It houses manuscript material dealing with D. W. Griffith, including some of his notebooks and correspondence. Also the researcher will find papers associated with Robert Flaherty, Thomas Ince, Georges Méliès, and Douglas Fairbanks, Sr. The library also contains an extensive collection of *Photoplay Magazine* and a still collection of over one million prints.

The Library and Museum of the Performing Arts, a branch of the New York Public Library at Lincoln Center (111 Amsterdam Avenue, New York, N.Y. 10023) is another major resource for film materials. The library has not collected the films, but its collection of print materials and photographs is unsurpassed. From as early as 1907 the library has been collecting film books and periodicals, and now the collection includes fan magazines, important journals, and countless pieces of film information in the Robinson Locke Collection of Dramatic Scrapbooks. The researcher will find material on Mary Pickford, Douglas Fairbanks, Sr., Charles Chaplin, and many others. Many film companies, such as MGM and Universal, have deposited company materials and records at the library; and in addition the library holds over one million stills. Since 1930 the librarians have preserved the movie reviews for every movie released in New York.

In upper New York state, the research center at the International Museum of Photography at George Eastman House, (900 East Avenue, Rochester, N.Y. 14607) is another major source. Eastman House specializes in the history and aesthetics of photography and motion pictures and is one of the centers preserving movie film. The library holds over 20,000 books and 10,000 bound periodical volumes on both media, and subscribes to about sixty-four current periodicals. The museum houses objects important to the early history of moving pictures, including Edison's Kinetoscope.

On the West Coast, in addition to the AFI library described above, the researcher may find assistance at the Margaret Herrick Library at the Academy of Motion Picture Arts and Sciences (9038 Melrose Avenue, Hollywood, Calif. 90069). This library has concentrated on motion picture history, biography, and production. It contains almost nine thousand books and bound periodicals, and it subscribes to seventy-five periodicals. Its most important holding, however, is its special collections. Among the movie people for whom there are significant materials in these collections are Richard Barthelmess, Thomas Ince, Jean Hersholt, Louella Parsons, and Hedda Hopper. This library is also known for its still collection.

Nearby at the University of California at Los Angeles, the Theater Arts Library (Los Angeles, Calif. 90024) contains important film holdings. In addition to large numbers of books, screenplays, and stills, the library subscribes to 138 periodicals dealing with film and television. The screenplay, television, and radio script collections comprise 2,800 unpublished scripts dating from the early 1900s to the present. The library also maintains an extensive collection of some 30,000 articles, pamphlets, clippings, reviews, and other ephemera dealing with personalities, productions, institutions, and various topics relating to all aspects of film, radio, and television. There is also a large and diverse collection of rare and early film posters and programs dating from 1915 to the present. Collections in the Rare Book Room deal with such movie people as Tony Curtis, John Houseman, Thomas Ince, Stanley Kramer, Jeanette MacDonald, Dudley Nichols, and King Vidor. A guide to the materials at UCLA has been published as *Motion Pictures: A Catalogue of Books, Periodicals, and Production Stills.*

The Performing Arts Division of the Library at the University of Southern California (University Park, Los Angeles, Calif. 90007) also houses a large film research center. This film collection contains approximately 15,000 books and serials, including current subscriptions to over two hundred serials. In the film-related materials, the library owns 110,000 stills, 1,000 posters, and 1,400 pressbooks. The collection of scripts is large—6,000 titles, including special collectons from MGM and Twentieth Century-Fox studios. These studios have also deposited a large assortment of synopses, treatments, dialogue continuities, and story conference notes in this library. In addition, Universal Studios has deposited 2,700 scripts, production records, and office files, primarily from the period 1940-1960, and Warner Brothers has given the library approximately 3,500 boxes of the Burbank studio files to 1967. A computer printout index has been made of this collection. One hundred fifty collections from private individuals round out the holdings. All of the material up to about 1974 has been indexed in *Primary Cinema Resources: An Index to Screenplays, Interviews and Special Collections at the University of Southern California* by Christopher D. Wheaton and Richard B. Jewell.

COLLEGE AND UNIVERSITY COLLECTIONS

Several colleges and universities have very important collections though not of the general nature or size of the film holdings at UCLA or USC. Dartmouth College Library (Hanover, N.H. 03755) contains a valuable collection of movie scripts established in memory of Irving Thalberg by Walter Wanger and various studios. As this collection of about 2,700 scripts was developed for classroom and study purposes, the coverage is selective rather than comprehensive.

The Wisconsin Center for Theatre Research at the University of Wisconsin—Madison (Vilas Communication Hall, Madison, Wis. 53706) contains numerous collections dealing with the performing arts. The largest single one is The United Artists Corporation Collection, which contains the records of the company for over three decades. For research purposes, the Wisconsin Center also houses 1,970 films from the Warner Film Library, the RKO Film Library, and the Monogram Film Library.

The recently founded American Archives of the Factual Film (Iowa State University Library, Ames, Iowa 50011) represents the first serious effort by a major library to gather together materials that document the development of the factual film in the United States and abroad. The center—using the collection of Ott Coellin, one of its primary benefactors, as the nucleus—intends to collect and archive factual films and the film-related materials that document their history and development. The AAFF will also conduct oral interviews and collect files and records of film-oriented organizations and institutions. This collection, still rather small, numbers approximately 1,600 films. Since the field is large and the need for such a collection great, it should grow rapidly.

The Lilly Library at Indiana University (Bloomington, Ind. 47401) has a small script collection of about five hundred scripts, ranging from *Wings* to several films produced in the 1970s. It is basically a collection of scripts of well-known or historically interesting films. The original scripts for such classics as *Gone With the Wind* and *Citizen Kane* are included along with others with interesting annotations which belonged to directors or principal actors, selections from such genres as Saturday matinée serials, Westerns, comedy series (Marx Brothers, Bowery Boys, and so on), war films and others. The collection of scripts is supported by about 350 pressbooks. The library holds the correspondence between Sergei Eisenstein and Upton Sinclair concerning the making of *Que Viva Mexico!* The correspondence is discussed and published in part in Harry Geduld and Ronald Gottesman's *Sergei Eisenstein and Upton Sinclair: The Making & Unmaking of Que Viva Mexico!*

The manuscript department at the Columbia University Library (New York, N.Y. 10027) contains archives that relate to film. These include the papers of Eric Barnouw, David Flaherty, Robert Flaherty, Leah Salisbury, and Annie Laurie Williams. The Minneapolis College of Art and Design (200 East 25th Street. Minneapolis, Minn. 55404) has a concentration on films and filmmaking and contains a special collection of the Arno Reprints on History of Film and Filmmaking. The library at Arizona State University (Tempe, Ariz. 85281) holds the Jimmy Star historical collection of the American film.

The special collections section of the Mugar Memorial Library at Boston University (771 Commonwealth Avenue, Boston, Mass. 02215) holds papers of Mary Astor, Nathaniel Benchley, Bette Davis, Gene Kelly, Frank Nugent, and others. The library at Brigham Young University (Provo, Utah 84602) contains 500 unpublished scripts. Included are 275 scripts relating to Cecil B. DeMille productions and another sizable group relating to Howard Hawks productions. The library also holds material from the National Association of Theatre Owners and from Republic Pictures.

The University of Iowa library (Iowa City, Iowa 52240) has special collections dealing with screenwriter Robert Blees, The Victor Animatograph Company, and Twentieth-Century Fox, as well as an assortment of scripts. The Hoblitzelle Theatre Arts Library at the University of Texas—Austin (P.O. Box 7219, Austin, Tex. 78712) has extensive special collections on American and British film. The holdings include scripts, interviews, descriptions of costume and scene design, and many stills.

Naturally, many more university libraries contain useful collections of film study material, but is is impossible to list them all. The books by Allen and Mehr discussed at the beginning of this appendix describe holdings in many other university libraries, and the reader should consult those books for further information.

PUBLIC LIBRARIES

Most public libraries in good-sized cities have some sort of film collection that is available for loan, but a few libraries have significant research collections in film as well. The Free Library of Philadelphia (Logan Square, Philadelphia, Penn. 19103) owns almost two thousand films for distribution, but its chief value lies in its collection of film materials. It owns 1,500 books on film subjects, including biographies; and it holds thirty-five current and retrospective periodicals, including *Motion Picture Classic, 1915-1931* and *Moving Picture World, 1912-*. Its collection also contains 25,000 stills dating from the early silent period and selections of heralds from the early motion picture companies such as Lubin, Essanay, and Selig, most of them dating from 1912 to 1916. In addition to these holdings, the theatre collection maintains files of newspaper clippings, mainly from local and New York sources, as well as photographs of motion picture personalities.

Several other public libraries have important but less substantial film research collections than those mentioned above. The Natural History Museum of Los Angeles County (900 Exposition Blvd., Los Angeles, Calif. 90007) owns a few valuable prints of aviation films, but they are difficult to use. The Cleveland Public Library (325 Superior Avenue, Cleveland, Ohio 44114) features the W. Ward Marsh cinema archives. The visual materials center at the Chicago Public Library (78 East Washington Street, Chicago, Ill. 60602) has a large film loan system and a clippings file for reviews.

STUDIO AND CORPORATE COLLECTIONS

Several studios have research collections that are, for the most part, intended for the use of their own researchers, but are open to the public on a limited basis. Disney Productions (500 S. Buena Vista, Burbank, Calif. 91505) holds 20,000 books and large files of clippings, photographs, pamphlets, cartoons, and jokes for background research in motion pictures. The research department of Metro-Goldwyn-Mayer (10202 West Washington Blvd., Culver City, Calif. 90232) has holdings of about the same size and content. They serve as researchers for motion picture companies on a fee basis. For over thirty years they have maintained an index to illustrations and articles in current journals and newspapers that might be useful in movie production. The research library at Twentieth Century-Fox Corporation (10201 West Pico Blvd., P.O. Box 900, Los Angeles, Calif. 90213) is somewhat larger. It holds 35,000 books, 5,000 bound periodicals, 10,000 bound newspapers, pamphlets, and plays. Of special interest is the library's collection of World War II photographs. The library at the research department at Universal City Studios (100 Universal City Plaza, Universal City, Calif. 91608) contains the usual studio background materials but also has materials on film history. This library is not normally open to the public.

Other organizations have some holdings of importance. The Motion Picture Association of America (522 Fifth Avenue, New York, N.Y. 10036) has a small library which specializes in the history, financing, and censorship of movies. The library at Dell Publishing Company (1 Dag Hammarskjold Plaza, New York, N.Y. 10017) has a large file collection of photographs and biographies on movie personalities and a sizable collection of stills.

MISCELLANEOUS HOLDINGS

The National Audio Visual Center (General Services Administration Reference Section, Washington, D.C. 20409) describes the services of this governmental agency:

> The National Audio-Visual Center was created in 1969 to serve the public by (1) making Federally produced audiovisual materials available for use through distribution services and (2) serving as the central clearinghouse for all U.S. Government audiovisual materials.

Basically the center serves as an archives and distribution center for the thousands of films produced by the government. For the most part the films are documentaries on subjects such as medicine, dentistry, education, aviation and space technology, and environmental sciences. Some are designed for a general audience, while others are rather technical. This center also distributes important documentaries made for the government by such directors as Pare Lorentz, Robert Flaherty, William Wyler, Willard Van Dyke, Josef von Sternberg, and Frank Capra.

The Air Force also distributes films from its Central Audio Visual Depository (HQ AAVA/DOSD, Norton AFB, Calif. 92409). Access is limited, but the collection is an important source for the study of military documentaries.

The Anthology Film Archives (80 Wooster Street, New York, N.Y. 10012) is a library and archives that concentrates on independent experimental film. The Archives holds a Repertory Film Collection which demonstrates the art of cinema through a regular cycle of screenings. Their Film History Collection is based on historical criteria and includes many films important to the history of independent film. They also have memorial collections of deceased independent filmmakers and a sizable reference library.

CANADA

In Canada the researcher should contact the film study center at the Canadian Film Institute (1762 Carling Avenue, Ottawa, Ont. K2A 2H7). This library has a small collection of books and a sizable holding of stills and other film materials.

A FINAL NOTE

It should be re-emphasized that many of the research centers dealing with film offer limited access to the general public. A scholar normally should have no trouble gaining admittance if he or she writes in advance and explains the project, but anyone interested in using a center described in this section should contact the center before visiting it. In general, the public libraries and the universities are open to the public, but even their special collections may have limited access.

BIBLIOGRAPHY

Allen, Nancy. *Film Study Collections.* New York: Frederic Ungar, 1979.

The American Film Institute. *Catalog of Holdings of the American Film Institute Collection and the United Artists Collection at the Library of Congress.* Washington, D.C.: The American Film Institute, 1978.

Geduld, Harry and Ronald Gottesman. *Sergei Eisenstein and Upton Sinclair: The Making and Unmaking of Que Viva Mexico!* Bloomington: Indiana University Press, 1970.

Mehr, Linda Harris, ed. *Motion Pictures, Television and Radio: A Union Catalogue of Manuscript and Special Collections in the Western United States.* Boston: G. K. Hall, 1977.

Motion Pictures: A Catalogue of Books, Periodicals, Screenplays, and Production Stills. Boston: G. K. Hall, 1972.

Sargent, Ralph N. *Preserving the Moving Image.* n.p.: Corporation for Public Broadcasting and The National Endowment for the Arts, 1974.

Weber, Olga S. *North American Film and Video Directing.* New York: R. R. Bowker, 1976.

Wheaton, Christopher D. and Richard B. Jewell. *Primary Cinema Resources: An Index to Screenplays, Interviews and Special Collections at the University of Southern California.* Boston: G. K. Hall, 1975.

Subject Index

Academy Awards, 7, 197, 199
Academy of Motion Picture Arts and Sciences, 196, 199
Accident, 42
Acting, 12, 37, 38, 41, 46, 48
Adam's Rib, 177
Adventure films, 55–56, 194
Advertising, 30
Aesthetics, of film, 42, 43, 49, 50, 63, 91
Africa, 93, 98
African Queen, The, 44, 150
Agee, James, 41, 163
Air Force Central Audio Visual Depository, 223
Airport 1975, 177
Aitken, Harry, 14
Alice's Restaurant, 152
Allen, Rex, 66
Allen, Woody, 17, 175
All the King's Men, 7, 153
"Almos' a Man," 80
Altman, Robert, xxii, 143, 158
American Archives of the Factual Film, 221
American Film, 44
American Film Institute, 6, 41, 196, 218
American in Paris, An, 152, 178
American Tragedy, An, 145
Anderson, Bronco Billy, 66
Anderson, Lindsay, 187
Anderson, Mignon, 130
Anger, Kenneth, 27, 70
Animal House, xxii
Animation, 25, 30, 40, 46, 56, 82, 98
Anna Christie, 163, 165
Ann-Margret, 17
Anthology Film Archives, 223
Anthropology, and film, 92
Antonioni, Michaelangelo, 63, 186
Apartment, The, 176
Applause, 106
Arabia, 189
Arbuckle, Roscoe, 17, 105
Architecture, and film, 82
Arizona State University, 221
Arliss, George, 105, 131
Arnheim, Rudolf, 34
Arvidson, Linda, 105
Arzna, Dorothy, 95
Ashley, Elizabeth, 105
Asian-Americans, and film, 92
Asquith, Anthony, 187
Astaire, Fred, xxi, 105, 118, 127
Astor, Mary, 17, 221
Australia, 190
Auteur, 36, 39, 41, 65, 108
Authorship, 40
Autry, Gene, 66, 106
Avant-Garde film, 37, 40
Axelrod, Jonathan, 28

Bacall, Lauren, 17
Bachelor Mother, 176
Balázs, Béla, 34, 35, 36
Ball, Lucille, 15
Ballad of Cable Hogue, The, 152
Bankhead, Tallulah, 106
Bara, Theda, 15, 63, 95, 130
Bardot, Brigitte, 95

Barnouw, Eric, 221
Barron, Arthur, 69
Barrymore, Diana, 107
Barrymore, Ethel, 107
Barrymore, John, 58, 63, 107, 130, 131, 132
Barrymores, the, 15, 106
Barthelmess, Richard, 131, 133, 220
Bartholomew, Freddie, 133
"Bartleby," 80
Baseball, 7
Battle at Elderbush Gulch, The, 178
Baxter, Warner, 131
Bazin, André, 34, 35, 36
Beatty, Warren, 63
Benchley, Nathaniel, 221
Ben Hur, 157, 163
Bennett, Joan, 106, 131
Bennett, Spencer Gordon, 158
Benny, Jack, 123
Bentley, Irene, 131
Bergman, Ingmar, xxii, 36, 40, 44, 63, 95, 186, 188
Bergman, Ingrid, 17, 95, 107, 163, 175
Berkeley, Busby, 143, 159
"Bernice Bobs Her Hair," 80
Bernstein, Elmer, 83
Best Man, The, 176
Bible, 96
Big Parade, The, 155, 163
Big Sleep, The, 149, 176
Biograph, 9, 10, 13, 147
Birds, The, 42, 149
Birth of a Nation, The, xviii, 5, 7, 64, 93, 111, 148, 155, 166, 174, 178
Bitzer, Billy, xviii, 166
Black Cat, The, 59
Blacklist, 91, 153, 165
Blacks and film, 6, 65, 91, 92–94, 98
Blackton, Stuart J., 14
Blanche, Alice Guy, 95
Blees, Robert, 222
Blonde Venus, 154
Blood of Jesus, The, 92
Blow-up, 41
Blue Angel, The, 154
Blue Hotel, The, 44
"Blue Hotel, The," 80
Boetticher, Budd, 27, 66, 160
Bogart, Humphrey, 17, 44, 63, 91, 106, 107, 125, 155
Bogdanovich, Peter, xxii, 27, 158, 160
Bonnie and Clyde, 41, 42, 44, 45, 58, 64, 152, 178
Boston University, 221
Bosworth, Hobart, 130
Bow, Clara, xx, 15, 63, 108
Boyd, William, 66
Boy's Town, 68
Brackage, Stan, 70
Brando, Marlon, 12, 17, 44, 108, 132
Brent, George, 132
Bresson, Robert, 37, 186
Bride Comes to Yellow Sky, The, 44
Bride of Frankenstein, 59
Brigham Young University, 222
Britain, 187
Broadway Melody, 39
Broken Blossoms, 148, 166
Brook, Peter, 81
Brooks, Clives, 58
Brooks, Louise, 131
Brooks, Richard, 159
Brother Rat, 68
Browning, Tod, 144
Buñuel, Luis, 82, 186
Burr, Raymond, 132

Cabaret, 79
Cabinet of Dr. Caligari, The, xx, 39, 60, 71, 77, 158
Cagney, James, 44, 108, 132
Camera, 37
Cameraman, 29
Camille, 165
Canada, 186, 223
Canadian Film Institute, 223
Candidate, The, 177
Canova, Judy, 131
Canutt, Yakima, 39, 158
Capra, Frank, xxi, 14, 39, 41, 44, 56, 69, 87, 144, 158, 159, 223
Cardinal, The, 153
Carnal Knowledge, 63, 152
Cars, 30
Casablanca, 96, 145, 175, 177, 179
Cassavetes, John, 154, 158, 159
Castle, William, 160
Catch 22, 41, 78, 79, 152
Cat on a Hot Tin Roof, 79, 81
Censorship, and film, xxi, 5, 48, 63, 89–90, 91, 190
Chabrol, Claude, 189

Chandler, Raymond, 59, 164
Chaney, Lon, 130
Chaney, Lon, Jr., 60
Chase, The, 152
Cheyenne Autumn, 147
Chiang, David, 64
Chicago Public Library, 222
Chimes at Midnight, 81
Chaplin, Charles, xix, 3, 6, 7, 9, 15, 17, 27, 37, 40, 41, 56, 57, 77, 82, 96, 105, 109, 118, 125, 130, 131, 133, 153, 154, 155, 157, 158, 219
Charade, 176
Che!, 88
Cher, 13
Chevalier, Maurice, 131
China, 190
China Seas, 147
Chinatown, 64
Christ, 96
Cinema, 37
Cinema-Scope, xxii
Cinéma vérité, 36, 68. *See also* Documentary
Cisco Kid, The, 66
Citizen Kane, xxi, 40, 42, 79, 91, 98, 112, 165, 177, 178, 179, 221, 46
City, in film, 91
Civilization, xix
Civil War, 64
Clair, René, 40, 82
Cleopatra, 44, 179
Cleveland Public Library, 222
Clift, Montgomery, 110, 132
Clockwork Orange, 41, 150
Cobb, Lee J., 132
Cocteau, Jean, 59
Cohan, George M., 108
Cohen, Mickey, 17
Cohn, Harry, 14, 160
Colbert, Claudette, 131
Collecting films, 198
Collector, The, 157
Colman, Ronald, 110, 131, 132
Color, 25, 37, 38, 39, 42, 46
Columbia, xx, 14
Columbia University, 221
Comedies, 8, 11, 18
Comedy, 5, 9, 25, 36, 37, 41, 43, 55, 56–57, 64, 109, 121, 122, 158, 194
Comics, and film, 5, 7, 48, 77
Communist, 12, 16
Composition, and film, 98
Coogan, Jackie, 133
Cool Hand Luke, 177
Cooper, Gary, 63, 110, 157
Cooper, Jackie, 133
Cooper, Miriam, 111, 130
Coppola, Francis Ford, xxii, 144, 158, 159
Corman, Roger, 159
Cort, David, 69
Cortez, Stanley, 29
Costume designing, 29
Cotton, Joseph, 163
Crane, Stephen, 80
Crawford, Joan, 111, 131, 133
Crime films, 57–58
Crosby, Bing, 57, 111, 166
Cubism, 82
Cukor, George, 27, 117, 118, 144, 157, 159
Curriculum, and film, 97, 98
Curtis, Tony, 132, 220
Curtiz, Michael, 6, 145, 159
Czechoslovakia, 189

Dada, 70
Dailey, Dan, 166
Dali, Salvador, 82
Damone, Vic, 17
Dance, and film, 82, 83
Dancing Mothers, 9
Daniels, William, 29
Darling, 176
Darnell, Linda, 15
Dartmouth College, 221
Davies, Marion, 112
Davis, Bette, 17, 112, 131, 133, 157, 221
Davis, Delmer, 12
Davis, Joan, 131
Davis, Ossie, 93
Dawn, Allan, 145
Day, Doris, 45, 95, 112
Day at the Races, A, 177
Day of the Locusts, The, 153
Dean, Eddie, 66
Dean, James, 12, 17, 63, 113, 132
Death in Venice, 95
Deep Throat, 63
Defiant Ones, The, 176
deForest, Lee, xx
Dell Publishing Company, 223
del Rio, Dolores, 131
DeMille, Cecil B., xx, 145

Dempster, Carol, 130
DeNiro, Robert, 13
Depression, xxi, 5, 11, 88, 98
Depth, 25
Deren, Maya, 70
Destiny, xx
Destry Rides Again, 176
Detective films, 55, 58-59
Detective Story, 39
Devil Is a Woman, The, 154
Dialogue on Film, 159
Diamond, I. A. L., 28
Diary of a County Priest, 97
Dickens, Charles, 37
Dickson, W. K. L., xvii, 3, 8
Dieterle, William, 158
Dietrich, Marlene, xxi, 11, 15, 63, 95, 113, 131, 154, 176
Diller, Phyllis, 131
Dinner at Eight, 165
Directing, 46
Disaster films, 55
Disney, Walt, 57, 160
Disney Productions, 222
Disney Studio, 30
Distribution, 30
Dmytry, Ed, 158
Dr. Dolittle, 15
Dr. Ehrlich's Magic Bullet, 176
Dr. Jekyll and Mr. Hyde, 40, 60, 68, 175
Dr. Moreau, 60
Doctors, 7
Dr. Stranglove, 42, 65, 150
Documentary, 4, 23, 24, 25, 35, 37, 40, 41, 46, 47, 49, 68-69, 92, 187
Dos Passos, John, 78
Double Indemnity, 176
Douglas, Kirk, 113, 132
Douglas, Melvyn, 132
Dovzhenko, Alexander, 158
Doyle, Arthur, Conan, 59
Dracula, 144
Drama, and film, 4, 22, 37, 40, 44, 47, 48, 57, 77, 78, 80-81, 82, 194
Dramatic, 37
Dreiser, Theodore, 78
Dressler, Marie, 113, 131
Drew Associates, 68
Drugs, in the movies, 44
Drums Along the Mohawk, 87
Dryer, Carl, 59-60, 96, 158
DuBois, Blanche, 121
Durango Kid, 66
Durbin, Edna Mae, 133
Durham, Philip, 164, 167

Eastern Europe, 189
Eastman, George, xvii
East of Eden, 150
Eastwood, Clint, 63, 113, 130, 154
Easy Rider, 96, 115
Ecce Homo!, 151
Eddy, Nelson, 113
Edison, Thomas, xvii, xviii, xx, 3, 8, 9, 10, 14, 82, 161
Editing, 4, 23, 30, 37, 38, 39, 41, 46, 47, 48
Education, and film, 41, 97-99
Eisenstein, Sergei, xx, 34, 35, 36, 37, 38, 40, 41, 145, 158, 186, 221
Ekberg, Anita, 17
Enoch Arden, 78
Entr'acte, 37
Epic films, 55, 56, 194
Essenay, xix, 9, 222
Ethnic groups, 94
Ethnic stars, 133
Etting, Ruth, 131
Exodus, 153
Exorcist, The, 179
Experimental films, 37, 45, 46, 49, 190
Expressionism, xxii, 4, 5, 23, 36, 39, 82, 91

Face in the Crowd, A, 177
Fail Safe, 65
Fairbanks, Douglas, Jr. 114, 131
Fairbanks, Douglas, Sr., xx, 9, 11, 15, 29, 41, 56, 63, 114, 118, 125, 130, 131, 132, 133, 219
Falstaff, 81
Family Man, The, 177
Fantasy films, 11, 44, 49, 59-62, 194
Farewell to Arms, A, 79
Farrar, Geraldine, 130
Faulkner, William, 78, 164, 176
Faye, Alice, 15
Fejos, Paul, 6
Fellini, Federico, xxii, 41, 186
Fields, W. C., xxi, 6, 57, 67, 114
Fight for Life, The, 151
Film, 37
Film, as art, 41, 42, 48, 49
Film festivals, 193
Film noir, 11, 58, 59, 64

Finland, 188
Fischer, Terrence, 64
Fitzgerald, Zelda, 164
Fixer, The, 147
Flaherty, David, 221
Flaherty, Robert, 7, 9, 36, 68, 146, 219, 221, 223
Fleming, Erin, 123
Flynn, Errol, 17, 115, 132
Fonda, Henry, 16
Fondas, the, 115
Forbidden Planet, 59
Ford, Glenn, 16
Ford, John, xxi, 9, 16, 40, 44, 55, 87, 146, 158, 180
Forman, Milos, 6, 147
Fox, William, 13, 161
Fox, The, 95
Fox Studio, xx
Frampton, Hollis, 71
France, 12, 188
Francis, Kay, 131
Franco, 188
Frankenheimer, John, 147
Frankenstein, 60, 96, 119, 175
Freaks, 144
Freed, Arthur, 62
Free Library of Philadelphia, 222
French Connection, 68
Freshman, The, xix, 122
From Here to Eternity, 110
Frontier, on film, 65
Fuller, Samuel, 27, 39, 57, 82, 147, 160
Fury, 176

Gable, Clark, xxi, xxii, 63, 115, 133, 155, 157, 180
Gabor, Zsa Zsa, 16
Gangster films, 55, 57–58, 91
Garbo, Greta, 9, 11, 15, 63, 95, 116, 125, 130, 131, 133
Gardner, Ava, 116
Gardner, James, 112
Garfield, John, 116
Garland, Judy, 16, 17, 41, 117, 133
Garmes, Lee, 29
Garnett, Tay, 147
Gaylor, Janet, 131
General, The, xix, 120, 175, 179
Genre, 5, 8, 36, 38, 40, 46, 47, 48, 49, 50
Gentlemen Prefer Blondes, 149
German-American, and film, 92
Germany, 9, 188
Giant, 113
Gibson, Hoot, 15
Gigi, 152
Gilbert, John, 133
Gish, Dorothy, xix, 130
Gish, Lillian, xix, 9, 117, 131, 133, 155
Gishes, the, 3
Goat, The, 120
Godard, Jean-Luc, 39, 40, 88, 186, 189
Godfather, The, 39, 58, 68, 96, 144
Godzilla, 60
Goebbels, Joseph, 188
Gold, Ernest, 83
Golddiggers of 1933, 11, 151
Gold Rush, The, xix, 46, 178
Goldwyn, Samuel, 12, 13, 125, 161
Gone with the Wind, 7, 14, 64, 121, 162, 163, 174, 179, 221
Goodbye, Mr. Chips, 176
Gordon, Ruth, 17, 28, 165
Gorin, Jean-Pierre, 88
Gould, Elliott, 17
Go West, 120
Grable, Betty, 15, 95
Graduate, The, 42, 45, 91, 152
Grady, Billy, 166
Graham, Sheilah, 165
Grand Hotel, 163
Grandma's Boy, 122
Grand Prix, 147
Granger, Stewart, 132
Grant, Cary, 44, 117, 118, 132
Grapes of Wrath, The, 46, 78, 79, 98, 115, 179
Great Gatsby, The, 79
Great Train Robbery, The, xviii, 65
Greed, 40, 180
Green Berets, 88
Greene, Graham, 59, 78
Green for Danger, 58
Grierson, John, 68, 187
Griffith, David W., xviii, 3, 5, 7, 9, 10, 13, 14, 15, 27, 36, 37, 45, 48, 81, 88, 105, 111, 117, 130, 133, 147, 155, 158, 197, 219
Gruber, Frank, 12
Guess Who's Coming to Dinner, 180
Guinness, Alec, 12

Hale, Monte, 66

Hamlet, 78, 80, 81
Hard Day's Night, A, 176
Harding, Ann, 15
Hardy, Oliver, 121
Harlow, Jean, xxi, 63, 95, 118
Harrison, Rex, 132
Hart, W. S., 63, 66, 118
Hathaway, Henry, 148
Hawks, Howard, 27, 42, 118, 148, 157, 158, 159, 160, 164, 222
Hays, Will, H., 162
Hays Office, xxi, 13, 89
Hayward, Susan, 118
Hayworth, Rita, 95, 118, 131
Head, Edith, 16, 165
Hearst, William Randolph, 112
Hearts of the World, 166
Hecht, Ben, 28
Heidi, 145
Hello, Dolly!, 15
Hemingway, Ernest, 78, 113
Henry, Buck, 28
Henry V, 80, 81, 176
Hepburn, Audrey, 95, 131
Hepburn, Katharine, 15, 118, 131, 180
Here Comes Mr. Jordan, 6, 68, 176
Herman, Bernard, 83
Hersholt, Jean, 220
Heston, Charlton, 118, 177
High Noon, 42, 176, 177
High Sierra, 58
Hirohito, 188
Hiroshima, Mon Amour, 65
Hiroshima-Nagasaki, 65
His Girl Friday, 46, 127, 148
History, and film, 87–88
Hitchcock, Alfred, xxi, 6, 36, 41, 44, 59, 82, 91, 96, 117, 149, 158, 159, 180, 186, 187
Hitler, 188
Holden, William, 12, 119
Holliday, Judy, 12
Hollywood, 4, 5, 9, 12, 16–18, 40, 44, 64, 65, 91, 92, 110, 166, 187
Hollywood Ten, 90
Holmes, Helen, 66
Holt, Tim, 66
Homosexuality, 63, 94
Hope, Bob, 111, 112, 119
Hopkins, Miriam, 131
Hopper, Hedda, 165, 220
Horror films, 11, 55, 59, 91, 96
Houghton, Katherine, 180
Houseman, John, 220
House Un-American Activities Committee, 4, 11, 12, 13, 90, 116, 157, 165
Howard, Mo, 129
Howe, James Wong, 16, 29, 157
Hughes, Howard, 154, 162
Humberstone, H. Bruce, 158
Hunchback of Notre Dame, 15
Hungary, 189
Hunter, Jeff, 17
Hunter, Ross, 12
Hustler, The, 153, 177
Huston, John, 39, 44, 57, 149, 150, 158, 159, 160
Huston, Walter, 131

I Am Curious Yellow, 63
Ince, Thomas, xix, 14, 148, 219, 220
Independent filmmaking, 6, 25. *See also* Experimental films
India, and film, 190
Indiana University, 221
Indians, and film, 6, 7, 65, 92, 94
Informer, The, 40, 79
International Museum of Photography at George Eastman House, 220
In the Street, 39
Intolerance, xviii, 111, 148, 166, 178
Invasion of the Body Snatchers, 59, 61
Irish, and films, 92
Italian-Americans, and film, 92
Italy, 12, 189
It Happened One Night, 176
I Want to Live, 118
I Was a Male War Bride, 148

Jannings, Emil, 81, 131
Japan, xxii, 190
Jaws, 60
Jazz, 83
Jazz Singer, The, xx, 10, 15
Jewish Americans, and film, 92
Jewison, Norman, 159
Johnny Guitar, 153
Johnson, Nunnally, 28
Johnson, Van, 166
Jolson, Al, xx
Jones, Jennifer, 131
Joyce, James, 78
Jules and Jim, 77

Julius Caesar, 80, 81

Kael, Pauline, 35
Kafka, Franz, 181
Kalem, 9
Kandinsky, Wassily, 82
Kane, Joseph, 158
Kanin, Garson, 28
Karloff, Boris, 60, 119
Kazan, Elia, 12, 17, 57, 108, 150, 159
Keaton, Buster, xix, 9, 17, 56, 57, 67, 81, 110, 119, 158
Kelly, Gene, 91, 95, 118, 120, 221
Kennedy, George, 132
Kennel Murder Case, The, 58
Keystone (Kops), xix, 9, 56, 57, 154
Killers, The, 58
Killing, The, 150
King, Henry, xx, 158
King Kong, 59, 60, 82, 96, 180
King Lear, 81
Kiss of Death, 58
Klute, 94, 115
Kracauer, Siegfried, 34, 35
Kramer, Stanley, 150, 159, 220
Kubelka, Peter, 71
Kubrick, Stanley, xxii, 157, 158, 159, 181
Kuleshov, Lev, 38
Kung Fu, 64
Kurosawa, Akira, 64, 81

Ladd, Alan, 120
Laemmle, Carl, 15, 160
Lamarr, Hedy, 95, 120
Lamour, Dorothy, 15, 111
Lancaster, Burt, 120, 132, 147
Lanchester, Elsa, 121
Lang, Fritz, xx, xxi, 6, 40, 42, 57, 77, 150, 158
Lang, Walter, 158
Langdon, Harry, xix, 56, 57, 110
Language, of film, 36, 37, 39, 40, 46, 47, 48, 50, 84, 98
Lansbury, Angela, 147
Lardner, Ring, Jr., 28
Lasky, Jesse, 160
Last Laugh, The, 46
La Strada, 96
Last Tango in Paris, 63, 95
Last Tycoon, The, 163
Latin America, 187
Latin Americans, and film, 94
Laughlin, Tom, 13
Laughton, Charles, 120
Laurel, Stan, 121
Laurel and Hardy, 56, 57, 158
Lawrence, Florence, 133
Leacock, Richard, 68, 69, 70
Lee, Bruce, 17, 64
Left-Handed Gun, The, 152
Leigh, Janet, 12
Leigh, Vivien, xii, 95 121, 163
Lemmon, Jack, 17, 112
Lenin, 188
Leroy, Baby, 133
Leroy, Mervyn, 151
Lester, Richard, 151, 159
Lewis, Jerry, 123, 159
Kewton, Val, 39, 60, 151
Libraries, and film, 99, 198
Library and Museum of the Performing Arts, New York Public Library at Lincoln Center, 219
Library of Congress, 196, 219
Lighting, 41
Light That Failed, The, 110
Linder, Max, 7
Lindsay, Vachel, 34, 36, 40
Literature, and film, 47, 49, 50, 77, 78–82, 98
Little Big Man, 152
Little Caesar, 58, 151
Little Foxes, 157
Little Rascals, The, 125
Lloyd, Harold, xix, 41, 56, 57, 110, 122
Loew, Marcus, xix
Logan, Josh, 151
Lugosi, Bela, 60
Lolita, 150
Lombard, Carole, 15, 115, 122, 131
Loneliness of the Long Distance Runner, The, 177
Lone Ranger, 66
Lorentz, Pare, 68, 151, 223
Losey, Joseph, 42
Lost Horizons, 110
Lost Weekend, The, 176
"Lottery, The," 79
Louisiana Story, 46
Love, Bessie, 131
Love and Pain and the Whole Damn Thing, 56
Loy, Myrna, 131

Lubin, 222
Lubitsch, Ernst, xx, 6, 151
Lucas, George, 16, 62
Lumière, Louis, 27
Lumière brothers, xvii, 36, 68
Lung, Ti, 64
Lupino, Ida, 122
Lust for Life, 152

Macbeth, 80, 81
McCarey, Frank, 87
McCarthy, Joseph, 12, 90, 98
McCoy, Tim, 66
McCrea, Joel, 66
MacDonald, Jeanette, 113, 122, 130, 220
MacGraw, Ali, 13
MacLaine, Shirley, 122
McQueen, Steven, 123, 154
McTeague, 77, 155, 180
Madame Bovary, 79
Main, Marjorie, 131
Makavajev, Dusan, 88
Maltese Falcon, The, 58, 96, 106, 175
Mamoulian, Rouben, 152, 159, 175
Mankiewicz, Herman, 28, 165
Mankiewicz, Joseph, 28
Mann, Anthony, 66, 160
Man of Aran, The, 146
Mansfield, Jayne, 17
Man Who Shot Liberty Valance, The, 40, 146, 147
Mao, Angelo, 64
March, Frederic, 123
"March of Time," 62
Marion, Frances, 95, 165
Marnau, F. W., 158
Marnie, 149
Marsh, Mae, 130
Martin, Dean, 123
Marvin, Lee, 132, 154
Marx, Groucho, 123
Marx, Harpo, 123
Marx, Zeppo, 123
Marx brothers, xxi, 56
Mason, James, 123
Massey, Raymond, 58, 123
Mauerhofer, Hugo, 36
May, Elaine, 95
Mayer, Louis B., xix, 13, 160, 162
Maynard, Ken, 66
Maysles brothers, 68, 69
Mekas, Jonas, 70
Méliès, Georges, xvii, xviii, 36, 62, 81, 158, 219
Melville, Samuel, 57
Merry Widow, The, 155
Metro-Goldwyn-Mayer, xix, 11, 14, 162, 163, 178, 220, 222
Metropolis, 61, 77
Metz, Christian, 34, 35, 36
Mexico, 187
Mickey Mouse, xxii, 16, 161
Mickey One, 152
Midler, Bette, 17
Midnight Cowboy, 39, 45, 63, 97, 153
Midsummer Night's Dream, A, 77, 80, 81
Miles, Sylvia, 17
Milestone, Lewis, 16, 158
Milland, Ray, 132
Miller, Ann, 123
Miller, Arthur, 29, 78
Miller, Henry, 78
Minnelli, Vincente, 152, 159
Minorities, and film, 92
Miracle, The, 89
Miracle Worker, The, 152
Misfits, The, 110, 150, 176, 180
Miss Lulu Bett, 6
Mr. Rogers, 115
Mr. Smith Goes to Washington, 176, 177
Mitchum, Robert, 17, 124, 132
Mitry, Jean, 34
Mix, Tom, 29, 66, 124, 131
Moby Dick, 79
Modern Times, xix, 43, 109
Monogram, 221
Monroe, Marilyn, 15, 17, 44, 63, 91, 95, 124, 153, 180
Monsieur Verdoux, 77
Montage, 4, 5, 37
Montgomery, Robert, 132
Moore, Colleen, 7
Moorehead, Agnes, 16
Morality, and movies, 44
Morrissey, Paul, 158
Mother, xx, 40
Motion Picture Association of America, 223
Movie industry, 13–15
Movie memorabilia, 198
Movietone, 62
Mrs. Miniver, 7, 88
Muni, Paul, 124, 132

Munsterberg, Hugo, 34
Murnau, F. W., xx, 6, 152
Museum of Modern Art, 219
Music, and film, 37, 46, 48, 77, 82, 83
Musicals, 5, 6, 11, 18, 41, 55, 62, 83, 194
Mussolini, 188
Mutiny on the Bounty, 68
Mutual Studio, 57
Muybridge, Eadweard, xvii
My Darling Clementine, 146
My Fair Lady, 81, 163
My Man Godfrey, 176
Myth, and film, 47, 59, 65, 66, 87

Narrative, and film, 5, 23, 38, 39, 40, 46, 48, 77, 79
National Audio Visual Center, 223
Natural History Museum of Los Angeles, 222
Naturalism, 4
Navigator, The, 120
Nazimova, Alla, 64
Nazis, xxii, 6, 188
Negri, Pola, 95, 133
Negro Soldier, The, 92–93
Neilan, Marshal, 7
Neo-realism, 5, 36, 91, 189
Newman, Alfred, 83
Newman, Paul, 125
Newspapers, and film, 62
Newsreels, 62
Nichols, Dudley, 12, 28, 220
Nichols, Mike, 152, 159
Nicholson, Jack, 17, 125
Night at the Opera, A, 42, 44
Night of the Living Dead, 60
Ninotchka, 151, 157, 175, 176, 177
Niven, David, 125, 132, 157
Noa-Noa, 44
Normand, Mabel, 154
Norris, Frank, 155
North by Northwest, 149, 177
Nosferatu, 60, 152
Nothing but a Man, 93, 177
A Nous La Liberté, 37
Novak, Kim, 95, 131, 165
Novels, and film, 4, 37, 40, 48, 58, 78, 79, 82, 194
Nuclear war, 65, 88
Nugent, Frank, 28, 221
Nyrki, Tapiovaara, 188

Oates, Warren, 132
Occurrence at Owl Creek Bridge, An, 180
O'Hara, Scarlett, 121
O'Kalem, 9
Olivier, Laurence, 81, 121
O'Neill, Eugene, 78
On the Beach, 12
On the Waterfront, 12, 42, 150, 178
Orphans of the Storm, 148
Othello, 80, 81, 180
Our Daily Bread, 155
Our Gang, 125
Ox-Bow Incident, The, 79

Pabst, G. W., 40
Painting and film, 37, 82
Paralta, 9
Paramount, xix, 11, 15
Parks, Gordon, 93
Parsons, Louella, 165, 220
Pascal, Gabriel, 81
Paths of Glory, 150
Peck, Gregory, 125, 163
Peckinpah, Sam, 65, 66, 152, 160
Penn, Arthur, xxii, 27, 152, 158, 159, 160
Pennabaker, D. A., 69
Perkins, Tony, 166
Perrault, Pierre, 70
Persona, 97
Petulia, 43
Photoplay Magazine, 7, 62
Picasso, Pablo, 82
Pickford, Mary, xix, 3, 6, 9, 15, 63, 95, 114, 118, 125, 130, 131, 219
Picnic, 94
Pincecs, Ed, 69
Planet of the Apes, 43, 68
Play It Again, Sam, 175
Plow That Broke the Plains, The, 151
Poe, Edgar Allan, 80
Poetry, and film, 37, 39, 71, 78, 81, 82
Poitier, Sidney, 126, 180
Polanski, Roman, 27, 152, 159, 160
Polish-Americans, and film, 92
Politics, and film, 9, 40, 41, 47, 65, 88
Popular arts, and film, 83–84
Pornography, 12, 63, 64
Porter, Edwin S., xviii, 8, 27, 64
Porter, Katherine Anne, 9
Postman Always Rings Twice, The, 149
Potemkin, xx

Powell, William, 131, 132
Power, Tyrone, 132
Preminger, Otto, xxi, 6, 42, 153, 159
Presley, Elvis, 63, 154
Price, Vincent, 126, 132
Pride and Prejudice, 79
Primate, 157
Propaganda, and film, 88, 91
Psycho, 60, 149, 175, 177, 180
Psychology, and film, 95-96
Public Enemy, 58
Pudovkin, V. I., xx, 40
Puerto Ricans, and film, 92
Pygmalion, 78

Queen Kelly, 9, 155
Que Viva Mexico!, 221
Quiet Man, The, 146
Quinn, Anthony, 126

Rachel, Rachel, 126
Raft, George, 126
Rainer, Luise, 95
Ramona, 78
Rathbone, Basil, 58, 126, 132
Ray, Man, 82
Ray, Nicholas, 57, 153, 159
Ray, Satyajit, 190
Raye, Martha, 131
Realism, 5, 30, 36, 37, 47, 91
Reality, and film, 48, 50
Rear Window, 149
Rebecca, 176
Rebecca of Sunnybrook Farm, 145
Rebel without a Cause, 12, 153
Redford, Robert, 63, 126
Red River, 110, 148
Reed, Carol, 41
Reed, Donna, 166
Reid, Mrs. Wallace, 95
Reid, Wallace, 130
Religion, and film, 96-97, 158
Renoir, Jean, 41, 153, 186
Republic Pictures, 222
Repulsion, 153
Resnais, Alain, 186
Reviewers, 43-45
Reynolds, Burt, 17
Reynolds, Debbie, 95
Rhetoric of Film, The, 47
Richardson, Tony, 187
Richard III, 80, 81
Riefenstahl, Leni, 68
Rin Tin Tin, 67
Ritter, Tex, 66
River, The, 151
Rivette, Jacques, 189
RKO, 15, 67, 151, 221
Roach, Hal, 16, 57, 67, 125, 153
Robin Hood, 57
Robinson, Edward G., xxi, 126, 132
Rocking Horse Winner, The, 180
Rocky, 87
Rogers, Ginger, xxi, 15, 106, 127, 131
Rogers, Roy, 66
Rogers, Will, 127, 131
Rohmer, Eric, 189
Romeo and Juliet, 78, 80, 81
Rooney, Mickey, 127, 133
Rosemary's Baby, 43, 60, 153, 160
Ross, Herbert, 175
Rossellini, Roberto, 88, 107
Rossen, Robert, 153
Rouch, Jean, 70
Roundtree, Richard, 93
Rubin, Martin, 27
Rules of the Game, 177
Russell, Jane, 15, 16
Russell, Rosalind, 127
Russia, 9, 189
Ryan, Robert, 132
Ryskind, Morrie, 123

Safety Last, 122
St. Louis Blues, The, 92
Salisbury, Leah, 221
Salt of the Earth, 94, 181
Samurai films, 64
Sanders, George, 132
San Francisco, 16
Sarris, Andrew, 35
Satyricon, 60
Savage Innocents, The, 177
Saville, Victor, 187
Scarlet Empress, The, 154
Scarlet Letter, The, 79
Scar of Shame, The, 92
Scenes from a Marriage, xxii
Schary, Dore, 16, 162
Schlesinger, John, 153
Scholastic Magazine, 176
Science fiction films, 30, 41, 55, 61

Scott, George C., 17, 127
Screenplays, 174–177
Sculpture, and film, 82
Searchers, The, 40, 146
Seastrom, Victor, xx, 6
Seconds, 147
Segal, Erich, 28
Selander, Lesley, 158
Selig Polyscope Company, 14, 222
Selznick, David O., 12, 160, 162
Semiology, 38, 42
Semiotics, 37
Sennett, Mack, xix, 14, 27, 57, 105, 133, 153, 154
Sequels, 68
Serials, 67–68
Set design, 29
Seven Chances, 120
Seventh Heaven, 9
Seventh Seal, 96
Seven Women, 146
Sex, in movies, 12, 44, 63, 96, 190
Seymour, Clarine, 130
Shaft, 93
Shakespeare, and film, 77, 80–81, 108
Shamberg, Michael, 69
Shamroy, Leon, 29
Shane, 94
Shanghai Express, 154
Shaw, George Bernard, 81
Shearer, Norma, 127, 131
Sherlock Holmes, 58
Sherlock, Jr., 120
Shootist, The, 65
Short films, 48, 67–68
Short stories, and film, 4, 79–80
Sidney, Sylvia, 15
Siegel, Don, 39, 55, 57, 154
Siegfried, 40
Signoret, Simone, 95
Silk Stockings, 152
Silverstein, Elliot, 159
Simon, John, 35
Sinatra, Frank, 17, 127
Sinclair, Upton, 221
Singin' in the Rain, 177
Siodmak, Robert, 57
Sirk, Douglas, 158
Sjoman, Vilgot, 188
Sjostrom, Victor, 188
Smilin' Through, 56
Smith, Albert, 14
Society, and film, 9, 41, 48
Sociology, and film, 90–92
Solaris, 61
Some Like It Hot, 94
Sound, xxi, 4, 5, 7, 8, 15, 25, 37, 38, 39, 40, 41, 42, 46, 47, 48, 83, 133, 163
Sound and the Fury, The, 79, 164
Sound effects, 46
South, the, 88
Southern, Terry, 28
Southerner, The, 176
Soviets, 5
Space. *See* Time and Space
Spartacus, 150
Special effects, 30, 40
Spectacular films, 41
Spellbound, 176
Spiegel, Sam, 12
Splendor in the Grass, 150, 177
Sport films, 55
Squaw Man, The, 161
Stagecoach, 29, 42, 68, 175, 176
Stalin, 188
Stanley and Livingstone, 93
Stanwyck, Barbara, 128
Star Wars, xxii
Stein, Gertrude, 78
Steinbeck, John, 78
Steiner, Max, 83
Stevens, George, 12, 113, 154, 157
Stevenson, Robert Louis, 40
Stewart, James, 41, 128
Stiller, Mauritz, 188
Strangers on a Train, 149
Strauss, Karl, 29
Straw Dogs, 64
Streetcar Named Desire, A, 81, 108, 150, 176
Streisand, Barbra, 3, 16
Strong Man, The, xix
Struggle, The, 181
Studios, 13–15, 133
Stunting, 29
Sturges, Preston, 28, 39, 159
Suddenly Last Summer, 81
Sunrise, 152
Sunset Boulevard, 12, 94, 128, 157
Super 8mm, 23
Surrealism, xxii, 16, 36, 60, 70, 71, 82
Susann, Jacqueline, 17
Suspense films, 59

Sutter's Gold, 145
Swanson, Gloria, xx, 15, 128, 131, 133
Sweden, 187
Sweet, Blanche, 130

Tale of Two Cities, A, 110
Talmadge, Norma, 7, 14
Taming of the Shrew, The, 80
Tarzan, 56, 93
Tate, Sharon, 17
Tati, Jacques, 44, 186
Taylor, Elizabeth, 16, 17, 63, 95, 128
Technicolor, xxii
Television, xxii, 4, 5, 12, 24, 40, 44, 48, 60, 61, 62, 68, 69, 82, 84, 187
Temple, Shirley, 15, 128, 133, 163
Tender Trap, The, 94
Texas Chain Saw Massacre, 64
Thalberg, Irving, xix, 162, 163
Thanhouser, 9
That's Me, 177
Theology, and film, 36–38, 42
Thief of Baghdad, The, 59
Thing, The, 59
Things to Come, 61
Third Man, The, 39
Three Stooges, 129
3-D, xxii
THX 1138, 61
Time and space, in film, 23, 38, 39, 41, 42, 46
Titicut Follies, 157
Tol'able David, 9
Tom Jones, 78
Torn Curtain, 88, 149
Towering Inferno, 105
Tracy, Spencer, 118, 129, 180
Tramp, The, xix
Treasure of the Sierra Madre, The, 42, 79, 96
Trial, The, 181
Triangle Film Corporation, 14
Trip to the Moon, A, xviii, 60
Triumph of the Will, 88
Truffaut, François, xxii, 186, 189
Trumbo, Dalton, 165
Turner, Lana, 17
Turpin, Ben, xix
Twelve Angry Men, 176
Twentieth Century-Fox, 15, 163, 220, 222, 223
20,000 Leagues Under the Sea, 59
2001, 43, 61, 96, 150, 177, 181
Tyson, Cicely, 93

Uggams, Leslie, 16
Ullmann, Liv, 129
Uncle Tom's Cabin, 93
Underground films, 4. *See also* Experimental films
United Artists, xx, 221
Universal Studio, 11, 15, 60, 220, 223
University of Iowa, 222
University of Southern California, 220
University of Texas, 222
University of Wisconsin, 221
Up the Down Staircase, 177
Upturned Face, The, 80
USIA, 69

Valentino, Rudolph, xx, 9, 11, 63, 78, 129, 133
Vampires, 60, 61
Van Dyke, Willard, 69, 223
Verne, Jules, 61
Vertigo, 149, 178
Victor Animatograph Company, 222
Video, 40
Vidor, King, 27, 155, 159, 220
Vietnam, 64, 65
Vigo, Jean, 59, 158
Violence, in movies, 41, 44, 60, 63, 64, 98, 190
Visual arts, and film, 82
Vitagraph, 9, 14
Vitaphone, 10
Viva Zapata, 94
Voight, Jon, 17
von Sternberg, Josef, xxi, 9, 41, 82, 154, 158, 176, 223
von Stroheim, Erich, xx, 6, 9, 27, 41, 155, 180, 181

Wale, James, 6
Walker, Jimmy, 66
Wallach, Eli, 154
Walsh, Raoul, xix, 155, 159
Walthall, H. B., xix
War films, xxi, xxii, 11, 30, 55, 64–65, 68, 69, 88, 93, 97, 98, 157, 187, 188, 194
War Game, The, 65
Warhol, Andy, 82, 155, 158, 159
Warner Brothers, xx, 6, 11, 13, 15, 116, 154, 159, 163, 221
War of the Worlds, 60
Warren, Robert Penn, 78
Way Down East, 87, 148

Wayne, John, 16, 44, 63, 64, 65, 129, 133
Webber, Lois, 95
Wedding March, The, 155, 181
Welch, Raquel, 15
Welles, Orson, xxi, 81, 156, 158, 159, 180
Wellman, William, 16, 157, 158, 159, 160
Wells, H. G., 61
West, Mae, xxi, 15, 16, 63, 94, 130, 165
West, Nathanael, 78
West, the, 98
Westerns, 8, 18, 36, 37, 41, 45, 55, 64, 65–67, 77, 91, 160, 194
Wexler, Haskell, 16
When Worlds Collide, 61
White, Pearl, 9, 67
Who's Afraid of Virginia Woolf?, 39, 152
Widerberg, Bo, 188
Widmark, Richard, 132
Width, 25
Wiene, Robert, xx
Wilcox, Herbert, 187
Wilde, Cornel, 132
Wilder, Billy, 28, 157, 158
Williams, Annie Laurie, 221
Williams, Tennessee, 17, 78, 81
Wilson, Margery, 95
Wise, Robert, 159
Wiseman, Frederick, 68, 69, 157
Withers, Jane, 133
Witney, William, 158
Wizard of Oz, The, 96, 181
Wolf Man, The, 60
Wolheim, Louis, 64
Women, and film, 11, 65, 94–95, 190
Wood, Frank, 40
Woodward, Joanne, 12, 17, 125
Wolfe, Thomas, 78
Woolf, Virginia, 78
Wright, Richard, 86
Wuthering Heights, 79
Wyler, William, 12, 157, 158, 159, 223

Yankee Doodle Dandy, 108
York, Michael, 56
Young, Loretta, 15, 131
"Young Goodman Brown," 79
Yu, Wong, 64

Z, 41
Zanuck, Darryl F., 15, 163
Zetterling, Mai, 188
Zinnerman, Fred, 157
Zukor, Adolph, xix, 13

Index of Authors, Editors, and Interviewees

Abbe, James, 133
Aceto, Vincent, 195
Adair, John, 92
Adams, William B., 23
Adler, Renata, 43
Affron, Charles, 112, 116, 117
Agan, Patrick, 113
Agee, James, 43, 49, 149, 178
Agel, Jerome, 181
Aldrich, Robert, 173
Allen, Nancy, 99, 218
Allvine, Glendon, 161
Alpert, Hollis, 44, 124, 179
Alpert, Lewis, 91
Altman, Robert, 173
Amberg, George, 49
Amelio, Ralph J., 61
Anderson, Joseph L., 190
Anderson, Lindsay, 69, 149
Anderson, Yvonne, 26, 98
Andrew, J. Dudley, 34, 36
Anger, Kenneth, 17
Annan, David, 59
Ann-Margaret, 125
Anobile, Richard J., 115, 120, 123, 175
Applebaum, Stanley, 198
Arce, Hector, 123
Arijon, Daniel, 23
Arliss, George, 105
Armes, Roy, 36, 186, 188
Armour, Robert A., 150
Arnheim, Rudolph, 36, 82
Aros, Andrew, 197
Arvidson, Linda, 105
Ashley, Elizabeth, 105
Asplund, Uno, 110
Astaire, Fred, 106
Astor, Mary, 106
Astrus, Alexander, 189
Atkins, Thomas R., 61, 63, 64, 157
Attenborough, Richard, 173
Autry, Gene, 106
Averson, Richard, 50, 88
Aylesworth, Thomas G., 60

Bacall, Lauren, 106
Baddeley, W. Hugh, 25
Baer, D. Richard, 197
Bahremburg, Bruce, 180
Bain, David, 161
Balázs, Béla, 37
Balio, Tino, 13, 15, 176
Ball, Lucille, 173
Ball, Robert Hamilton, 81
Baltake, Joe, 121
Bankhead, Tallulah, 106
Bann, Richard W., 121, 125
Barbour, Alan G., 7, 107, 130
Bardèche, Maurice, 4
Barker, Felix, 121
Barlett, Donald, 162
Barna, Yon, 145
Barnes, Howard, 179
Barnouw, Erik, 68, 190
Barr, Charles, 121
Barrett, Jerald R., 180
Barrios, Jaime, 99
Barris, Alex, 18, 62
Barry, Iris, 36, 148
Barsacq, Léon, 29

Barrymore, Diana, 107
Barrymore, Ethel, 107
Barrymore, John, 107
Barsam, Richard Meran, 45, 68, 69
Barson, Alfred T., 164
Barwood, Hal, 173
Battcock, Gregory, 70
Battestin, Martin C., 42, 78
Batty, Linda, 195
Bauer, Barbara, 111
Bawden, Liz-Anne, 194
Baxter, John, 6, 7, 10, 13, 29, 58, 62, 147, 154, 155
Bayer, Michael, 130
Bayer, William, 24
Bazelon, Irwin, 83
Bazin, Andre, 37, 42, 149, 153, 156, 179, 189
Beale, Kenneth, 119
Beattie, Eleanor, 186
Beaver, James N., Jr., 117
Beck, Marilyn, 44
Bedford, Michael, 60
Behlmer, Rudy, 115
Beja, Morris, 79
Bellone, Julius, 156
Benchley, Nathaniel, 107
Bennett, Joan, 107
Benny, Jack, 121
Bentley, Eric, 80
Bergman, Andrew, 11, 108
Bergman, J. Peter, 114
Berk, Lynn M., 84
Bernstein, Elmer, 145
Bertolucci, Bernardo, 173
Berton, Pierre, 187
Bessy, Maurice, 156
Betancourt, Jeanne, 95
Bettetini, Gianfranco, 38
Betts, Ernest, 187
Biberman, Herbert, 181
Bickford, Charles, 145
Billings, Pat, 13
Birch, David C., 84
Birkos, Alexander S., 189
Bitzer, G. W., 148, 166
Björkman, Stig, 188
Black, Karen, 125
Blackner, Irwin R., 159
Blesh, Rudi, 119
Blotner, Joseph, 164
Bluestone, George, 79
Blum, Daniel, 9
Blumenberg, Richard, 46
Bobker, Lee R., 24, 46
Bodeen, Dewitt, 130, 145
Bogdanovich, Peter, 44, 145, 146, 148–49, 151, 156, 177
Boggs, Joseph M., 46
Bogle, Donald, 93
Bohn, Thomas W., 5
Bojarski, Richard, 119
Bone, Jan, 47
Bookbinder, Robert, 111
Bordwell, David, 46
Botham, Noel, 129
Bourgeois, Jacques, 99
Bowers, Ronald L., 14, 163
Bowles, Stephen E., 195
Bowman, William Dodgson, 109
Bowser, Eileen, 10, 122, 148
Bowskill, Derek, 25
Boyum, Joy Gould, 42
Brackett, Charles, 177
Brakhage, Stan, 72, 158
Brasillach, Robert, 4
Braudy, Leo, 38, 149, 153, 158
Braum, Myron, 127
Brenner, Marie, 13
Brewer, Terry, 57
Brodbeck, Emil E., 23
Brode, Douglas, 12, 49
Brodsky, Jack, 179
Brody, Stephen, 90
Brooker, Nancy J., 154
Brosnan, John, 30
Brough, James, 115
Brown, Curtis F., 107, 118
Brown, Karl, 148
Brownlow, Kevin, 9
Brownstone, David M., 177
Bruce, Lenny, 121
Bruno, Michael, 95
Bucher, Felix, 188
Bukalski, Peter J., 195
Buñuel, Luis, 71
Burch, Noël, 39
Burns, E. Bradford, 187
Butler, Ivan, 26, 96, 153, 187
Byron, Stuart, 56

Cagney, James, 108

Cahn, William, 122
Calder, Jenni, 65
Calder-Marshall, Arthur, 146
Cameron, Elisabeth, 132
Cameron, Ian, 55, 58, 132
Canham, Kingsley, 145, 148
Capra, Frank, 144
Carey, Gary, 114, 144, 176
Carmen, Ira H., 89
Carpozi, George, Jr., 110
Carr, Larry, 131
Carr, William H. A., 17
Carringer, Robert, 152
Cary, Diana Serra, 66
Casebier, Allan, 46
Casper, Joseph, 152
Cassavetes, John, 173
Castanza, Philip, 114
Castle, William, 160
Casty, Alan, 4, 153
Cavell, Stanley, 39
Cawelti, John G., 66, 179
Cawkwell, Tim, 199
Cecchettini, Philip Alan, 6
Ceplair, Larry, 90
Ceram, C. W., 3, 10
Chabrol, Claude, 189
Champlin, Charles, 39, 116, 117
Chandler, Raymond, 149, 176
Chaneles, Sol, 198
Chaplin, Charles, 109, 151
Chaplin, Charles, Jr., 109
Chaplin, Lita Grey, 109
Chase, Donald, 26
Chicorel, Marietta, 196
Christiansen, Robert, 173
Ciment, Michael, 150
Clair, René, 37
Clarens, Carlos, 59, 144
Clark, Eleanor, 30, 119
Clason, W. E., 193
Cocchi, John Robert, 114
Cocke, Inez, 116
Cocteau, Jean, 43, 156
Cogley, John, 90
Cohen, Louis Harris, 189
Cohen, Marshall, 50
Cohn, Lawrence, 62
Colman, Hila, 24
Colman, Juliet Benita, 110
Comden, Betty, 177
Connell, Brian, 114
Conner, Edward, 58
Conrad, Earl, 115
Conway, Michael, 110, 116, 118
Cook, Bruce, 90, 165
Cooke, Alistair, 43
Cooper, John C., 42
Cooper, Miriam, 111
Corliss, Richard, 28, 116, 179
Costa, Sylvia Allen, 27
Costello, Donald P., 81
Costner, Tom, 200
Cotes, Peter, 109
Cowie, Peter, 4, 7, 156, 185, 188
Cox, Harvey, 42
Coynik, David, 24, 46
Crane, Robert David, 125
Crawford, Christina, 111
Crawford, Joan, 111
Cripps, Thomas, 92, 178
Crist, Judith, 44, 121, 132, 177, 179
Croce, Arlene, 106
Crone, Rainer, 156
Crosby, Bing, 111
Crosby, Kathryn, 112
Crosby, Ted, 112
Crowther, Bosley, 14, 39, 129, 162, 179
Currie, Hector, 46
Curry, George, 179
Curtis, Anthony, 11
Curtis, David, 70
Curtiss, Thomas Quinn, 155

Dalton, David, 113
David, Jonathan, 8
Davies, Marion, 112
Davis, Bette, 112
Davis, Robert E., 24
Dawson, Bonnie, 95
Day, Doris, 112
Debrix, Jean R., 41
de Havilland, Olivia, 91, 173
de Jonge, Alex, 188
Delany, Marshall, 186
DeMille, Cecil B., 126, 145
Denby, David, 49
DeNitto, Dennis, 46
Deren, Myra, 49
Dern, Bruce, 125
Derry, Charles, 60, 195
Dettman, Bruce, 60

Deschner, Donald, 114, 117, 129
Devries, Daniel, 150
Dick, Bernard F., 39
Dickens, Homer, 108, 111, 113, 127
Dickinson, Thorold, 46
Dickstein, Morris, 158
Dietrich, Marlene, 113
Dillard, R. H. W., 42, 60
Dimmitt, Richard Betrand, 197
DiOrio, Al, Jr., 117
Donnelly, Peter, 129
Donner, Clive, 80
Dos Passos, John, 78
Dovzhenko, Alexander, 81
Dowdy, Andrew, 12
Dreiser, Theodore, 78
Dressler, Marie, 113
Drew, Donald J., 96
Druxman, Michael B., 68, 125, 126
Dunne, John Gregory, 15
Durgnat, Raymond, 39, 56, 116, 149, 187
Durham, Philip, 164
Dwoskin, Stephen, 6
Dyment, Alan R., 195

Eames, John Douglas, 14
Easton, Carol, 161
Eckert, Charles, 80
Edelson, Edward, 56, 60, 61
Edera, Bruno, 56
Edmonds, I. G., 15
Edmonds, Robert, 92
Edwards, Anne, 121
Eells, George, 131, 165
Eidsvik, Charles, 77
Eisenstein, Sergei, 37, 80
Eisner, Lotte H., 82, 150, 151, 152
Elder, Lonne, III, 173
Ellis, Jack C., 5, 195
Emmens, Carol A., 80
Englund, Steven, 90
Engstead, John, 133
Enser, A. G. S., 78
Enshwiller, Ed, 173
Epstein, Edward Z., 30, 65, 108, 119, 132
Erens, Patricia, 122
Ernest, Morris, 89
Erskine, Thomas L., 180
Essoe, Gabe, 56, 116, 145
Evans, Mark, 83
Evans, Max, 152
Everson, William K., 8, 58, 65, 114, 122, 132, 153
Eyles, Allen, 13, 66, 107, 123

Fadiman, William, 26
Fadimon, Regina K., 176
Falk, Peter, 173
Farber, Manny, 39
Farber, Stephen, 89
Farrell, James, 78
Faulkner, William, 78
Feineman, Neil, 143
Feldman, Seth, 186
Fell, John L, 5, 46, 79
Fellini, Federico, 173
Fenin, George N., 65
Ferguson, Otis, 44
Ferlita, Ernest, 96
Feyen, Sharon, 49
Fielding, Raymond, 62
Fields, Ronald, 114
Fields, W. C., 114
Finch, Christopher, 117, 160
Finler, Joel W., 155, 180
Fitzgerald, F. Scott, 78, 165
Fitzgerald, Michael G., 15
Flaherty, Frances Hubbard, 146
Flamini, Roland, 179
Flanders, Mark Wilson, 163
Florescu, Radu, 61
Flynn, Charles, 178
Fonda, Henry, 173
Fontaine, Joan, 115
Fordin, Hugh, 62
Forman, Milos, 173
Fowler, Gene, 107
Fraenkel, Heinrich, 188
Franck, Irene M., 177
Frank, Gerold, 117
Freedland, Michael, 105
French, Brandon, 94
French, Philip, 13, 65, 164
French, Warren, 179
Frewin, Leslie, 113
Friar, Natasha A., 94
Friar, Ralph E., 94
Friedkin, William, 173
Frischauer, Willi, 153
Frost, Lawrence A., 161
Froug, William, 28
Fryer, Christopher, 125

Fulford, Robert, 186–87
Fulton, A. R., 4
Furhammar, Leiff, 88
Furthmen, Jules, 176

Gaffney, Maureen, 99
Garbo, Greta, 151
Garceau, Jean, 116
Garnett, Tay, 147
Garnham, Nicholas, 147
Garrett, George P., 43, 176
Garson, Greer, 115
Gassner, John, 176
Geduld, Carolyn, 181
Geduld, Harry M., 10, 22, 27, 77, 148, 180, 193, 221
Gelfman, Jane R., 176
Gelman, Barbara, 7
Gelman, Howard, 117
Gelmis, Joseph, 158
Gerlach, John C., 195
Gerlach, Lana, 195
Gershank, S., 194
Gertner, Richard, 193
Gessner, Robert, 47
Giannetti, Louis D., 39, 47
Gidal, Peter, 71
Gifford, Denis, 60, 61, 109, 187
Gill, Brendan, 106
Gilliatt, Penelope, 44
Gilman, Richard, 80
Gish, Lillian, 117, 133, 148, 178
Glaessner, Verina, 64
Glatzer, Richard, 144
Glut, Donald F., 60, 67
Godard, Jean-Luc, 189
Godfrey, Lionel, 115
Goldblatt, Burt, 59, 105
Goldner, Orville, 180
Goldstein, Laurence, 47
Goode, James, 180
Goodgold, Ed, 68
Goodwin, Michael, 88
Gordon, Ruth, 165, 177
Gottesman, Ronald, 22, 156, 179, 180, 193, 221
Gould, Michael, 82
Govoni, Albert, 117
Gow, Gordon, 12, 59
Grady, Billy, 166
Graham, Peter, 189
Graham, Sheilah, 165
Grant, Barry K., 55
Grau, Robert, 8
Graves, Jane, 195
Green, Adolph, 177
Green, Stanley, 105
Greenberg, Harvey R., 96
Greenberg, Joel, 11
Greenberger, Howard, 106
Greene, Graham, 44
Grierson, John, 69
Griffith, D. W., 148
Grifith, Richard, 4, 7, 11, 146
Griggs, John, 65
Gross, Miriam, 164
Guback, Thomas H., 186
Guiles, Fred Lawrence, 12, 112, 124
Gussow, Mel, 163

Halas, John, 26
Halberstam, David, 90
Hall, Conrad, 173
Hall, James B., 82
Halliwell, Leslie, 194, 197, 198
Hamblett, Charles, 125
Hammel, William M., 84
Hampton, Benjamin B., 3
Handel, Leo A., 91
Happé, Bernard L., 24
Harbinson, W. A., 127
Harcourt, Peter, 186
Hardison, O. B., 42, 176
Hardy, Phil, 147
Harley, John Eugene, 89
Harmetz, Aljean, 181
Harmon, Jim, 67
Harrington, John, 47, 78
Harris, Bruce, 161
Harris, Radie, 17
Harris, Warren G., 116
Harrison, Helen P., 99
Hart, Douglas C., 58
Hart, William S., 118
Harvey, Stephen, 106, 111
Haskell, Molly, 94
Hayden, Nicola, 179
Haydock, Ron, 58
Hays, Will H., 8, 162
Hayward, Stan, 26
Head, Edith, 165
Heinzkill, Richard, 43

Helfman, Harry, 98
Henderson, Robert M., 13, 147
Hendricks, Gordon, 14, 161
Hermon, William, 46
Herndon, Booton, 114
Herndon, Venable, 113
Herrmann, Bernard, 179
Heston, Charlton, 118, 145, 156
Hibbin, Nina, 189
Higham, Charles, 11, 12, 15, 29, 39, 113, 116, 118, 120, 145, 156
Hillier, Jim, 69, 179
Hirsch, Foster, 56, 127
Hirschhorn, Clive, 120
Hitchcock, Alfred, 173
Hobson, Andrew, 25
Hobson, Mark, 25
Hockman, Stanley, 158
Hofer, Lynne, 99
Hoffman, William, 126
Hofsess, John, 186
Holloway, Ronald, 96
Holtzman, Will, 119
Hope, Bob, 119
Hopper, Dennis, 125
Hopper, Hedda, 16
Horvath, Joan, 24
Horwitz, James, 66
Hotchner, A. E., 112
Houseman, John, 164, 175
Houston, Beverley, 47
Houston, Penelope, 12
Howard, Mo, 129
Huaco, George A., 91
Hudson, Richard M., 128
Huff, Theodore, 110
Hughes, Elinor, 131
Hull, David Stewart, 188
Hunnings, Neville March, 89
Hunter, Linda, 17
Hunter, William, 40
Hurley, Neil, 96
Hurt, James, 80, 148
Huss, Roy, 47, 60
Huston, John, 164
Hyams, Joseph, 17

Isaacs, Neil, 79
Isaksson, Folke, 88
Israel, Lee, 106
Issari, M. Ali, 68

Jackson, Arthur, 83
Jackson, Martin A., 87
Jacobs, David, 109
Jacobs, Diane, 158
Jacobs, Jack, 127
Jacaobs, Lewis, 4, 42, 43, 49, 69, 91, 148, 155, 178
Jacobus, Lee A., 82
Jarratt, Vernon, 189
Jarvie, I. C., 90
Jensen, Paul M., 119, 150
Jewell, Richard B., 220
Jinks, William, 47
Jobes, Gertrude, 13
Johnson, Alva, 161
Johnson, Lincoln, 47
Johnson, Robert K., 144
Johnson, Ron, 47
Johnson, William, 61
Jones, G. William, 96
Jones, Karen, 195
Jones, Ken D., 65, 128, 133
Jordan, Dave, 116
Jordan, Rene, 116
Jorgens, Jack J., 81
Josephson, Matthew, 161
Jowett, Garth, 5
Juneau, James, 117

Kael, Pauline, 43, 44, 108, 149, 157, 179
Kagan, Norman, 64, 150
Kahn, E. J., 127
Kahn, Gordon, 90
Kaminsky, Stuart M., 55, 149, 150, 154
Kanin, Garson, 118, 177
Kantor, Bernard, 159
Kardish, Laurence, 4
Karimi, Amir Massoud, 59
Kass, Judith, 116, 143, 154
Katz, John Stuart, 97
Kauffmann, Stanley, 44, 80, 177
Kaufman, George S., 177
Kaufman, Jay, 47
Kawin, Bruce F., 40, 164
Kay, Karyn, 94
Kazan, Elia, 80
Kerbel, Michael, 125
Kern, Sharon, 196
Kerr, Walter, 57
Ketchum, Richard M., 129
Kiernan, Thomas, 115

Kilgore, Al, 121
Kinder, Marsha, 47
Kinsey, Anthony, 25
Kirby, Jack Temple, 88
Kirschner, Allen, 49
Kirschner, Linda, 49
Kirshnaswamy, S., 190
Kitses, Jim, 66, 160
Klumph, Helen, 28
Klumph, Inez, 28
Knight, Arthur, 4, 179
Knight, Derrick, 67
Knowles, Eleanor, 114
Knox, Donald, 178
Kobal, John, 62, 113, 116, 118
Koch, Howard, 179
Koch, Stephen, 155
Konzelman, Robert G., 97
Korte, Walter, 42
Koszarski, Richard, 159
Koury, Phil A., 145
Kovacs, Laszlo, 173
Kowalski, Rosemary Ribich, 95
Kracauer, Siegfried, 37, 199
Krafsur, Richard, 196
Kramer, Anne, 159
Kramer, Stanley, 173
Kramer, Victor, 164
Kreidl, John Francis, 153
Kreuger, Miles, 62
Kuhns, William, 47, 67, 97
Kuleshov, Lev, 37

La Bare, Tom, 23
LaGuardia, Robert, 110
Lahue, Kalton C., 14, 57, 66, 67, 131, 132, 154, 198
Lambert, Gavin, 59, 144, 179
Lambray, Maureen, 160
Landay, Eileen, 93
Lang, Edith, 83
Lang, Fritz, 173
Larkin, Rochelle, 14
Larson, Rodger, 98, 99
Lasky, Jesse, Jr., 121
Latham, Aaron, 164
Lathrop, William Addison, 175
Lauritzen, Einar, 197
LaValley, Albert J., 149
Lawder, Standish D., 82
Lawrence, Jerome, 124
Lawson, John Howard, 48
Lawton, Richard, 7
Laybourne, Kit, 98
Leab, Daniel J., 93
Leach, Michael, 63
Lebel, J. P., 120
Lee, Raymond, 30, 58, 126, 128, 145
Lee, Walt, 59
Leese, Elizabeth, 29
Le Grice, Malcolm, 70
Lehman, Ernest, 177
Lehman, Peter, 40
Leiser, Erwin, 188
Leish, Kenneth W., 7
Leites, Nathan, 96
Lellis, George, 120
Lembourn, Hans Jogen, 124
Lennig, Arthur, 9
Leonard, Harold, 194
Leprohon, Pierre, 189
Leroy, Mervyn, 151
Lethe, Robert I., 63
Levin, G. Roy, 69
Levy, William Turner, 144
Lewis, Arthur, 16
Lewis, Jerry, 25
Leyda, Jay, 69, 148, 151, 189, 190, 199
Liehm, Antonín J., 147, 189
Liehm, Mira, 189
Limbacher, James L., 25, 198
Linden, George W., 48
Linder, Carl, 23
Lindgren, Ernest, 48
Lindsay, Cynthia, 119
Lindsay, Vachel, 35, 49, 80
Linet, Beverly, 120
Lipton, Lenny, 23, 25
Livingston, Don, 27
Lloyd, Harold, 122
Lloyd, Ronald, 158
Logan, Joshua, 115, 151
Löker, Altan, 59
London, Mel, 25
London, Rose, 80
Loos, Anita, 16, 176
Lorentz, Pare, 44, 89
Losey, Joseph, 151
Lotman, Jurij, 37
Lounsbury, Myron Osborn, 40
Lovell, Alan, 69
Low, Rachel, 187

Lowndes, Douglas, 98
Luhr, William, 40
Lundquist, Gunnar, 197
Lynch, F. Dennis, 91

McArthur, Colin, 57
Macauley, Richard, 176
MacBean, James Roy, 88
McBride, Joseph, 149, 156
McCabe, John, 109, 121
McCaffrey, Donald W., 57, 110, 122
MacCann, Richard Dyer, 12, 36, 68, 91, 194
McCarthy, Todd, 178
McCarty, Clifford, 115, 128, 175
McClain, Bebe Ferrell, 23
McClelland, Doug, 89, 118
McClure, Arthur F., 65, 91, 128, 132
McConathy, Dale, 29
McConnell, Frank D., 40
McCoy, Malachy, 123
McCreadie, Marsha, 95
Macdonald, Dwight, 45, 151, 164, 177
McDonald, Gerald D., 110
McGillian, Patrick, 108
Macgowan, Kenneth, 48
McGregor, Don, 116
McGuinness, James Kevin, 177
MacLaine, Shirley, 122
MacLiammoir, Michael, 180
McMurty, Larry, 42
McNally, Raymond, 61
MacShane, Frank, 164
Madden, David, 164
Maddow, Ben, 176
Maddox, Brenda, 128
Maddux, Rachel, 79
Madsen, Axel, 157
Madsen, Roy Paul, 40
Mailer, Norman, 124
Malone, Michael, 63
Maltin, Leonard, 67, 125, 161, 198
Mamber, Stephen, 68
Mamoulian, Rouben, 173
Manchel, Frank, 60, 97
Mancini, Henry, 173
Mankiewicz, Joseph L., 176
Mankiewicz, Herman J., 179
Manvell, Roger, 40, 48, 70, 81, 95, 109, 187, 188, 193
Mapp, Edward, 93
Marceau, Marcel, 121
Marchak, Alice, 17
Marcoreles, Louis, 70
Marcus, Fred, 78, 79
Marens, Greil, 88
Marill, Alvin H., 118, 124, 126, 162
Marinis, Louise, 24
Marion, Frances, 165
Marner, Terence St. John, 27, 30
Martin, Dave, 143
Martin, Marcel, 188
Martin, Peter, 119
Marx, Arthur, 123, 161
Marx, Groucho, 123
Marx, Harpo, 123
Marx, Kenneth S., 199
Marx Brothers, 176
Massey, Raymond, 123
Mast, Gerald, 5, 40, 50, 56
Matthau, Walter, 121
Matthews, J. H., 82
Mauerhofer, Hugo, 49
Maugham, W. Somerset, 109
May, John R., 96
Mayer, Arthur, 7, 11
Maynard, Richard A., 66, 88, 93, 98, 176
Mazursky, Paul, 173
Medved, Harry, 177
Meeker, David, 83
Mehr, Linda Harris, 217
Mekas, Jonas, 45
Mellen, Joan, 63, 94, 124, 190
Mencken, H. L., 78
Menville, Douglas, 62
Meryman, Richard, 165
Metz, Christian, 37
Meyer, William R., 159
Meyers, Richard, 18
Michael, Paul, 197
Michaels, Norman, 58
Milford, Nancy, 164
Millar, Gavin, 30
Miller, Ann, 123
Miller, Don, 178
Miller, Randall M., 92
Milne, Tom, 152
Minnelli, Vincente, 113, 152
Mintz, Marilyn D., 64
Mix, Paul E., 124
Mizener, Arthur, 164
Moews, Daniel, 119
Moley, Raymond, 89

Monaco, James, 48, 189
Monaco, Paul, 90
Monroe, Marilyn, 124
Montagu, Ivor, 38, 145
Montgomery, John, 57
Monti, Carlotta, 114
Moreau, Genevieve, 164
Morella, Joe, 30, 65, 108, 119, 132
Morley, Sheridan, 113
Morris, George, 112, 115, 117
Morris, Peter, 186
Morrissey, Paul, 173
Morrow, James, 48
Mullen, Pat, 146
Munden, Kenneth W., 196
Münsterberg, Hugo, 35
Murray, Edward, 43, 78, 178
Murray, James P., 93
Murphy, William T., 146

Nachtbar, John G., 66
Naremore, James, 156, 180
Neame, Ronald, 173
Nelson, Joyce, 186
Nemeskürty, Istvan, 189
Nevares, Beatriz Reyes, 187
Newquist, Roy, 180
Nichols, Bill, 42
Nichols, Dudley, 12, 176
Nicholson, Jack, 173
Nicoll, Allardyce, 43, 80
Niklaus, Thelma, 109
Nilsen, Vladimir, 38
Niven, David, 125
Niver, Kemp R., 10, 125, 178, 196
Nobile, Philip, 177
Noble, Peter, 92, 155
Norris, Frank, 77, 180
North, Joseph H., 8
Null, Gary, 93

O'Connor, John E., 87
O'Dell, Paul, 148
Offen, Ron, 108
Ohlgren, Thomas H., 84
Ohlin, Peter, 164
O'Leary, Liam, 9
Olivier, Laurence, 81
Oppenheimer, George, 177
Orton, Barry, 84
Otash, Fred, 17
Ott, Frederick W., 122
Outerbridge, David E., 129

Parish, James Robert, 14, 15, 58, 62, 67, 122, 126, 131, 132, 160
Parker, David, 83
Parrish, Robert, 16
Pascal, Valerie, 81
Pate, Janet, 58
Pate, Michael, 28
Patterson, Lindsay, 93
Peary, Danny, 133
Peary, Gerald, 79, 94, 118
Pechter, William S., 40
Pendleton, John, 84
Pendo, Stephen, 164
Penn, Arthur, 179
Perkins, V. F., 41
Perlman, William J., 42
Perry, Edward S., 194
Perry, George, 149, 187
Petzold, Paul, 23, 29
Phelps, William Lyon, 42
Philips, Baxter, 188
Philips, Gene D., 150, 157
Phillips, Jill, 200
Phillips, Leona, 200
Picard, R. A. E., 177
Pickard, Roy, 178, 194
Pickford, Mary, 125
Pike, Bob, 143
Pines, Jim, 93
Pinter, Harold, 80
Piper, James, 99
Pirie, David, 61
Pirosh, Robert, 177
Pitts, Michael R., 58, 62, 67, 160
Place, J. A., 147
Poague, Leland A., 144, 152
Pohle, Robert W., Jr., 58
Polanski, Roman, 173
Pommer, Eric, 71
Porter, Vincent, 67
Potamkin, Harry Alan, 41
Poteet, Howard G., 98, 175
Powdermaker, Hortense, 92
Powers, Anne, 94
Power-Waters, Alma, 107
Pratley, Gerald, 147, 150
Pratt, George C., 10
Preminger, Otto, 153

Prendergast, Roy M., 83
Pudovkin, V. I., 38

Quick, John, 23, 56
Quigley, Martin, Jr., 8
Quirk, Lawrence J., 56, 107, 110, 111, 119, 123, 125

Raeburn, John, 144
Ragan, David, 199
Ramsaye, Terry, 3, 8
Ramsey, Verna, 196
Randall, Richard S., 89
Rangoonwalla, Firoze, 190
Rathbone, Basil, 126
Ray, Man, 71
Reade, Eric, 190
Reed, Herbert, 49
Reed, Rex, 16, 45
Reginald, R., 62
Rehrauer, George, 67, 196, 198
Reichert, Julia, 200
Reiff, Stephanie, 179
Reilly, Adam, 122
Reisch, Walter, 177
Reisz, Karel, 30
Renan, Sheldon, 69
Reynertson, A. J., 27
Rhode, Eric, 5
Ricci, Mark, 110, 116, 118, 128, 130
Rice, Susan, 99
Rich, Sharon, 122
Richards, Jeffrey, 55, 87
Richardson, Robert, 78
Richie, Donald, 154, 190
Riefenstahl, Leni, 69
Rilla, Wolf, 28
Rimberg, John David, 189
Ringgold, Gene, 112, 118, 128, 145
Rissover, Frederic, 84
Robbins, Matthew, 173
Roberts, Kenneth H., 25
Robinson, David, 9, 56, 119, 185
Robinson, Edward G., 126
Robinson, E. G., 42
Robinson, W. R., 42
Robyns, Gwen, 120
Rockwood, Louis, 25
Rogers, Will, 127
Rohauer, Raymond, 120
Rooney, Mickey, 127
Rosen, Marjorie, 94
Rosenberg, Rick, 173
Rosenfeldt, Diane, 151
Rosenfelt, Deborah Silverton, 181
Rosenthal, Stuart, 144
Rosow, Eugene, 57
Ross, Lillian, 80
Ross, T. J., 60, 66, 77
Rotha, Paul, 41, 69, 151, 155
Rothel, David, 66
Rothschild, Amelia, 200
Rovin, Jeff, 59, 118
Rubenstein, E., 179
Rubin, Martin, 27, 160
Russell, Rosalind, 127
Ryan, Robert, 115
Ryskind, Morrie, 177

Sabath, Barry, 152
Sadoul, Georges, 189, 197, 199
Sampson, Henry T., 93
Samuels, Charles Thomas, 41, 159, 179
Sandburg, Carl, 77
Sargent, Ralph N., 217
Sarkar, Kobita, 190
Sarris, Andrew, 41, 42, 43, 45, 71, 88, 122, 146, 149, 154, 158, 159, 177, 178, 179
Scagnetti, Jack, 121, 129
Schary, Dore, 129, 162
Scherle, Victor, 144
Scheuer, Steven, 198
Schickel, Richard, 41, 45, 114, 122, 157, 159, 160
Schillaci, Anthony, 42
Schrank, Jeffrey, 67
Schumach, Murray, 89
Schuster, Mel, 195
Schuth, H. Wayne, 152
Scorsese, Martin, 173
Scott, Audrey, 29
Scott, George C., 173
Scott, George c., 173
Scott, James F., 41
Seaton, George, 177
Seib, Kenneth, 164
Seidman, Steve, 157
Seldes, Gilbert, 10
Selznick, David O., 162
Sennett, Mack, 154
Sennett, Ted, 57
Seton, Marie, 146

Shadoian, Jack, 57
Shaheen, Jack G., 65
Shale, Richard, 197
Shales, Tom, 6
Sharples, Win, Jr., 25
Shatzkin, Roger, 79
Shaw, Arnold, 127
Shaw, George Bernard, 80
Sheppard, Dick, 128
Sheridan, Marion, 98
Sherman, Eric, 27, 160
Shipman, David, 108, 131
Siegel, Esther, 83
Siegel, Joel, 151
Silke, James R., 15
Silliphant, Stirling, 79
Silva, Fred, 178, 195
Silver, Alain, 61, 64
Silver, Pat, 121
Silverstein, Norman, 47
Simon, John, 43, 45
Sinclair, Andrew, 147
Sinclair, Upton, 42, 161
Sitney, P. Adams, 70, 71
Sitwell, Edith, 124
Skaggs, Calvin, 80
Skolsky, Sidney, 17
Skrade, Carl, 42
Slide, Anthony, 9, 14, 95, 130, 148, 194
Smallman, Kirk, 23
Smith, Ella, 128
Smith, John M., 199
Smith, Julian, 65
Smith, Paul, 87
Smith, Sharon, 95
Snyder, John J., 163
Snyder, Robert L., 151
Sobel, Raoul, 109
Sohn, David, 48, 97, 98
Solomon, Stanley J., 48, 55, 178
Sontag, Susan, 42
Soren, David, 59
Spada, James, 126
Spears, Jack, 7, 64
Speed, F. Maurice, 43
Spehr, Paul C., 8
Spielberg, Steven, 173
Spoto, Donald, 149, 150
Spottiswood, Raymond, 22, 24
Spraos, John, 12
Springer, John, 115
Stanke, Don E., 132
Staples, Donald, 46
Starr, Cecile, 48, 50
Stauffacher, Frank, 71
Stedman, Raymond William, 67
Steele, James B., 162
Steen, Mike, 16
Steinbeck, John, 115, 176, 197
Steinberg, Cobbett, 193
Steinbrunner, Chris, 58, 59
Stephenson, Ralph, 41
Stern, Lee Edward, 122
Stevens, George, 173
Stewart, David C., 97
Stewart, John, 199
Stine, Whitney, 112
Stock, Dennis, 113
Strasberg, Lee, 124
Strick, Marv, 63
Strict, Philip, 61
Stringer, Michael, 30
Stromgren, Richard L., 5
Struthers, Sally, 125
Suid, Lawrence H., 64
Suid, Murray, 48
Sullivan, Ed, 129
Svensson, Arne, 190
Swallow, Norman, 146
Swindell, Larry, 116, 122, 129
Sylbert, Paul, 181

Talbot, Daniel, 43
Taylor, Deems, 7
Taylor, John Russell, 83, 158, 186
Taylor, Robert, 114
Tewkesburg, Joan, 176
Thomas, Bob, 108, 111, 119, 160, 162, 163
Thomas, Tony, 11, 83, 108, 113, 115, 120, 125, 132
Thompson, Charles, 111
Thompson, David, 91
Thompson, Howard, 128
Thompson, Kristin, 46
Thomson, David, 199
Thulin, Ingrid, 173
Thurman, Judith, 8
Tibbetts, John C., 114
Toeplitz, Jerzy, 16
Toland, Gregg, 179
Tomkies, Mike, 129
Tornabene, Lyn, 115

Tozzi, Romano, 129, 150
Travers, Peter, 179
Trent, Paul
Trojanski, John, 25
Truffaut, François, 42, 149, 156, 179
Truitt, Evelyn Mack, 199
Trumbo, Dalton, 165
Tudor, Andrew, 36, 91
Tunney, Kieran, 106
Turner, George E., 180
Tuska, Jon, 58, 65, 66, 130, 158
Twomey, Alfred E., 128, 132
Tyler, Parker, 16, 38, 43, 63, 70, 109, 116, 130

Ulanov, Barry, 82
Ullmann, Liv, 129, 173
Underwood, Peter, 119
Ursini, James, 61

Vale, Eugene, 28
Vallance, Tom, 83
VanDerBeck, Stan, 71
Van Devere, Trish, 173
Van Dyke, Willard, 69
Van Hecke, B. C., 58
Vardac, Nicholas, 80, 148
Vermilye, Jerry, 112, 117, 122, 128
Vesterman, William, 84
Vidor, King, 155
Vizzard, Jack, 89
Voight, Jon, 173
von Sternberg, Josef, 80, 154
von Stroheim, Erich, 180
Vreeland, Diana, 29

Wagenknecht, Edward, 9, 124, 148
Wagner, Geoffrey, 79
Wagner, Rob, 130
Wake, Sandra, 179
Wald, Jerry, 176
Walker, Alexander, 63, 124, 129, 133, 150, 187
Wall, James M., 96, 186
Wallis, Hal B., 173
Walls, Howard Lamarr, 196
Walsh, James M., 114
Walsh, Raoul, 155
Ware, Dereck, 29
Warhol, Andy, 156
Warner, Jack, 163
Warshow, Robert, 77
Wead, George, 120
Weatherby, W. J., 124
Weaver, John T., 199
Weaver, Kathleen, 198
Weber, Olga S., 218
Weinberg, Herman G., 151, 154, 155, 180, 181
Weiner, Janet, 198
Weis, Elisabeth, 56
Weiss, Ken, 68
Weiss, Nathan, 179
Weiss, Paul, 49
Welles, Orson, 81, 179, 181
Wellman, William, 149, 157
Wells, H. G., 77
Welsch, Janice R., 95
Wenden, D. J., 8
West, George, 83
Wheaton, Christopher D., 220
Whetmore, Edward Jay, 84
White, David Manning, 50, 84, 88
Whitney, James, 71
Whitney, John, 71
Whitney, Steven, 126
Whittemore, Don, 6
Widener, Don, 121
Wigal, Donald, 49
Wilbur, Richard, 42
Wilder, Billy, 122, 164, 177
Wilk, Max, 198
Williams, Chester, 116
Williams, Paul, 173
Willis, Donald C., 60, 144, 149
Willis, John, 197
Wilmington, Michael, 146
Wilson, Earl, 17, 128
Wilson, Michael, 181
Windeler, Robert, 125, 128
Winston, Douglas Garrett, 78
Wise, Arthur, 29
Wiseman, Thomas, 49
Wistrich, Enid, 89
Witcombe, Rick Trader, 64
Wolfenstein, Martha, 95
Woll, Allen L., 83, 94
Wollen, Peter, 38
Wolper, David, 173
Wood, Michael, 91
Wood, Robin, 148, 149, 152
Wood, Tom, 157
Worth, Sol, 92
Wortley, Richard, 64

Wright, Basil, 4
Wright, Will, 65

Yablonsky, Lewis, 126
Yacowar, Maurice, 81
Yallop, David A., 105
Yanni, Nicholas, 127
Young, Christopher, 112, 120
Young, Freddie, 29
Young, Vernon, 49
Youngblood, Gene, 70

Zanuck, Darryl F., 163
Zeffirelli, Franco, 81
Zierold, Norman J., 116, 133, 160
Ziplow, Steven, 64
Zmijewsky, Boris, 130
Zolotow, Maurice, 129, 157
Zsigmond, Vilmos, 173
Zwerdling, Shirley, 198

About the author

ROBERT A. ARMOUR is associate professor of English at Virginia Commonwealth University in Richmond. His recent publications include his book *Fritz Lang* and many articles for scholarly journals.

WITHDRAWN